GOPAL KRISHNA GOKHALE

Gandhi's Political Guru

GOPAL KRISHNA GOKHALE

Gandhi's Political Guru

Govind Talwalkar

PENTAGON PRESS

Gopal Krishna Gokhale: Gandhi's Political Guru

Govind Talwalkar

First Published in 2015

ISBN 978-81-8274-833-0

Published by
PENTAGON PRESS
206, Peacock Lane, Shahpur Jat,
New Delhi-110049
Phones: 011-64706243, 26491568
Telefax: 011-26490600
email: rajan@pentagonpress.in
website: www.pentagonpress.in

Branch:
Flat No.213, Athena-2,
Clover Acropolis,
Viman Nagar,
Pune-411014
Email: pentagonpresspune@gmail.com

Printed at Aegean Offset Printers, Greater Noida, U.P.

To the memory of
late Shri Srinivas Sastri, political heir of
Gopal Krishna Gokhale,
an educationist and a great liberal

CONTENTS

PREFACE

I read Srinivas Sastri's book—*My Master Gokhale*—more than fifty years ago. After a few weeks I came across a copy of the speeches of Gopal Krishna Gokhale, published by Natesan and Co. In the following years I read *My Master Gokhale* and other books by Sastri as well as speeches of Gokhale several times. I made use of them in my journalistic writings and for my books.

I decided to write a biography of Gokhale. However, it got postponed for one reason or the other. Meanwhile, several biographical books on Gokhale in Marathi and English had been published. So why this addition?

I thought one more book on Gokhale would be justified, if the story of Gokhale's life and his career as a moderate leader, whose motto was to spiritualize politics, were written in the context of those times. Therefore, in addition to books, I made use of the contemporary newspapers and periodicals in Marathi as well as English and also some unpublished material. Some of the sources had not been used before. Moreover, I have also used many of Gokhale's original articles, letters and notes. There are some biographies of Gokhale. However, in those books very few Marathi sources were used.

I felt that it was necessary to give details about the economic problems and how Gokhale dealt with them in the Central Legislative Assembly and in his deposition before the Welby Commission. Gokhale was a great parliamentarian. I have elaborated this in my book.

I have described how the life was in those times and the social, economic and political problems of the then India. I have dealt with in detail the drought and famines; and along with them, the revenue policies and tariffs. I have analysed why the East India Company succeeded in defeating the Maratha rulers.

Articles and newsletters in the old newspapers and periodicals had reflected the mood of the period, and had discussed the problems of the day in all their aspects. They would, I hope, help in dispelling some of the assumptions about various leaders and parties, both British and Indian. It is interesting to see a newspaper like 'The Times' holding the view that India was conquered by the sword and had to be governed by the sword, while at the same time vehemently opposing the Tory government for giving concessions to the Manchester mill owners at the expense of India.

While Gladstone, a liberal, had no compunction in making India pay for the military expeditions in Egypt and elsewhere, which was totally unjustified, the Viceroy, Lord Ripon opposed such imposition. Lord Morley, a liberal disciple of Gladstone, contrary to his image, acted no better than a Tory.

I was able to throw light on all this, perusing the contemporary writings in the newspapers and also the correspondence of the persons concerned.

Though Gokhale played a role in all-India politics, he had to function in Maharashtra and in the Bombay Presidency. I have described how Gokhale faced the local problems and his political rivals. The Congress then was divided into the radical and the liberal groups. Their differences came to a boiling point at the Surat session and the Congress split. There is more material about this struggle and about the partition of Bengal in my book.

Gokhale's contribution to Ferguson College as a professor and the principal was unique. The Servants of India Society was a noble dream of Gokhale; and this organization made its mark and received praise from Indians as well as foreigners. I could use the previously unused sources to discuss this.

Gokhale played a leading role in bringing about the Morley-Minto reforms. But at the same time, the Muslim League tried hard to get separate electorates for Muslims. I have analyzed this role of the Muslim League more.

Because of the Servants of India Society and its Gokhale Library in Pune, I could get Gokhale papers, Gokhale Digest and also a file of Gokhale's articles in Sudharak, the English section of which he was the editor. Gokhale's correspondence shows how the Indian National Congress was never a disciplined organization. In the first decade it became dormant, and in the second, it split. Inflated egos of some leaders also hampered the growth of the organization.

I must thank Dadabhai Naoroji Trust for giving me the Dadabhai papers.

While preparing to write this book, my wife and I were living in Houston, Texas with our daughters. I could make use of the generously endowed library of the Rice University and also the public library and the inter-library loan services. Thus, I got the old files of the British newspapers and periodicals. The library staff was very helpful.

I think the extracts from these newspapers and periodicals are a distinct feature of my book on Gokhale and they provide the contemporary background.

My book first appeared in Marathi in 2003 under the title, *Nek Namdar Gokhale*. Mouj Prakashan, Mumbai will be bringing out the second edition of the book in Marathi this year to commemorate Gokhale's death centenary. The

English edition was published in the centenary year of the Servants of India Society in 2005 under the title, *Gopal Krishna Gokhale, His Life and Times*. Some of the material from that is taken in this new book.

Gokhale was the first to call for the spiritualization of politics, which attracted Gandhiji, who used to call Gokhale a "Mahatma".

This year and the next year are important landmarks to commemorate and pay tribute to Gopal Krishna Gokhale. Mahatma Gandhi regarded Gokhale as his political guru. 9 January 2015 marked the centenary of Gandhi's return to India from South Africa for good. Gokhale's death centenary was on 19 February 2015. His 150th birth anniversary is on 9 May 2016. I revised my earlier book on Gokhale in English and made some changes. I thought it would be a timely homage to celebrate and honour his contributions. I am glad that the new edition of my book, under the title *Gopal Krishna Gokhale: Gandhi's Political Guru,* is being published in this landmark year.

I would like to thank Mr. Rajan Arya, CEO of the Pentagon Press for publishing this new edition. I also thank Mr. Virender Negi and the other staff members of the Pentagon Press, who helped with the publication of my book.

My publisher friend Mr. Ashok Kothawale of the Majestic Prakashan, Mumbai has provided some of the photographs, for which I am grateful to him. I am also thankful to Gokhale Institute, Pune and Mr. Gopalkrishnan of dutchkerala.com for some photographs.

My daughters Sushama and Dr. Nirupama helped me getting the reference material, compiling bibliography, going through the manuscript and making necessary corrections, as well as looking after all the technicalities.

My wife Shakuntala gave me constant encouragement for this book, as with my other books over the years. She deserves my heartfelt thanks. She was keen to see the new edition of my book on Gokhale. Sadly, she passed away on 2 August 2014. So she is not here to participate in the happy occasion. We miss her.

20 March 2015

Govind Talwalkar
govindtalwalkar@hotmail.com

Chapter One

EARLY STRUGGLE

Gopal Krishna Gokhale was born on May 9, 1866, in Kotluk in the Chiplun taluk, which was then in the Ratnagiri district (presently in Raigad district). All the Gokhales in Maharashtra are Chitpawan Brahmins originating from Velneshwar, which is in the Chiplun taluk. They eventually spread out from Velneshwar to different parts of Maharashtra. Gopal Krishna Gokhale's ancestor, Balaji Mahadev Gokhale, established a village, Tamhanmala, ten miles from Chiplun. As was the custom then, Balaji Gokhale secured the rights as a rent collector called *Khot*. Krishnaji Gokhale was one of the sons of Shridharpant who was Gopal's grandfather. Gopal's mother, Balutai (Satyabhama), was the daughter of Bhaskarrao Oak who was also a *Khot.*

Gopal's father, Krishnajipant, moved to Kolhapur for his studies where he was the schoolmate of Mahadev Govind Ranade, who in later years became the mentor and guru of Gopal Krishna Gokhale. Krishnajipant could not complete his studies, but with the help of his uncle succeeded in getting a job in Kagal, a *jahagir* under the Kolhapur *darbar.* He died early. As Gopal's elder brother, Govindrao was not academically inclined, he was given a clerical job by his uncle in Kagal. Govindrao paid for the education of his brother, Gopal, in Kolhapur. His education continued without interruption because of the determination and the sacrifice of his brother and his wife. Gokhale always felt obliged to them and never failed to send them a fixed sum of money after he started earning. When his popular book on mathematics was selected as a textbook for schools, Gokhale assigned all the royalty to his brother and sister-in-law.

Some people lose their sensitivity because of the hardships they suffer in their childhood and in young days; while others become revengeful. Gokhale was neither. He was always introspective and would think of improving himself. Gokhale was, nevertheless, impetuous and had a complaining nature. Because of his impetuousness, he sometimes quickly lost his temper and reprimanded people; but within no time he would recover and beg their pardon. With the passage of time he learnt to control his temper. After his matriculation, Gokhale went to Pune for his college studies. He worked very hard even to the point of neglecting his health. In his college days he used to play tennis, but gave it up because of his public duties. Honesty and truthfulness were his characteristics. In his school when his teacher complimented him, as he alone in his class was able to correctly solve a mathematical problem, Gokhale broke down, to the amazement of his teacher. He confessed that he had been able to solve that problem with someone's help. Just as he was honest, he was also differential to his elders; and when he saw greatness in somebody, he was reverential. He was devoted to Dadabhai Naoroji and Justice Ranade and accepted the leadership of Pherozeshah Mehta. Gokhale came under the spell of Tilak and Agarkar because of their sacrifices. Hence, he joined them as a teacher in the Deccan education society. Gokhale's contemporary, Ganesh Raghunath Abhyankar said that Gokhale was always grateful to those who had helped him in any way. He remembered that when Specy bank fell on bad days, Gokhale was advised by a Parsi gentleman to withdraw his deposits, but he refused to do so, telling his friend that Sir Chunilal Mehta, who was the chairman of the bank, had given him a blank cheque to be cashed anytime, when in need. Gokhale did not have any occasion to cash the cheque, but he remained ever grateful for the generosity of Sir Chunilal.

Gokhale had a sharp memory, which he cultivated diligently. He had memorised the speeches of Edmund Burke and some plays of Shakespeare. Since 1885, Gokhale set out to acquire mastery over the English language. He could recite Burke's speeches, demanding the impeachment of Warren Hastings, the French Revolution and the American war of Independence as well as John Milton's *Paradise Lost.* He used to give those books to a neighbour and ask him to test him for mistakes. For every mistake, he would pay a fine of an anna; but such occasions were rare. Gokhale's another friend said that Gokhale had with him a book—*Public Speaker*—which he studied every day in the early hours of the morning and then recited passages from it. Vasudevrao Patwardhan was Gokhale's contemporary. He remembered that some people taking advantage of Gokhale's innocence would ask him to memorise some of the passages and laugh behind his back. Writing in 'Manoranjan', a Marathi magazine, Patwardhan said that in school or in college, Gokhale was never known as a first class student. Unlike bright students who could understand the subject in no time, absorb it and never forget it, Gokhale did not possess that faculty. His memory was not exceptional or extraordinary. His name was never in the list of those who stood first in the university and he was never known for extraordinary intellect. Gokhale joined the Elphinstone College, Mumbai, for his senior BA. After graduation, he joined an engineering college, but found it unsuitable. He also thought of appearing for the ICS, but it was beyond his means. So he joined the law course. At the same time, the Deccan Education Society invited him to be a teacher in the New English School. His monthly salary was thirty-five rupees with a yearly bonus of Rs.120. Gokhale, with his colleague, taught in a class for the Public Service Commission examination, which brought in another forty rupees per month.

The New English School was started by Vishnu Krishna Chiplunkar with the assistance of Tilak and Agarkar. They also started a Marathi weekly, '*Kesari*' and an English one, Maratha. Gokhale was much impressed by this enterprise. After joining the school he became closer to Agarkar whose views about social reforms he shared. The New English School, '*Kesari*' and '*Maratha*', all had a special place in the political life of Maharashtra and also that of India. In the Maratha regime or under the Peshwa rule, education was not the responsibility of the government. Eight years before the Peshwa rule came to an end, Christian missionaries had established a printing press in Pune. But it did not occur to the last Peshwa to make use of this new invention. Under the Peshwa, Brahmins used to receive some annual grant for learning Sanskrit. After the end of the Peshwa rule, Elphinstone, who was the Resident, abolished this largesse and allotted that money to start schools. The yearly largesse depended on the whims of a ruler, but under the new rule, education was institutionalised. Initially, the curriculum and the textbooks were improvised and had no scientific basis. Very few teachers were qualified and would not continue in the profession for long. Textbooks were of a poor quality. Even the law students used to be crowded in a small room to give their examinations. They did so by consulting the textbooks and also indulging in mass copying.

However, a radical change came about very shortly and there came, in Mumbai and Pune, a resurgent generation of erudite teachers and diligent and scholarly students. Dadabhai, Bhau Daji, Ranade, Bhandarkar, Telang all belonged to this first generation, and Tilak and Agarkar followed them. Gokhale belonged to the third generation. In Pune, the government school was very renowned. Its principal, Madhavrao Kunte, was a scholar and an efficient administrator. Vishnushastri Chiplunkar was not happy in the government service. So he resigned and started a press, 'Chitrashala', and a high school, the 'New English School' on January 2, 1880 with the assistance of Tilak and Agarkar. As the school could enlist the services of well-known and dedicated teachers, its progress was fast. Chiplunkar thought that the government school would come to grief very soon. But it lasted thirty years before it closed down. Even though Tilak had passed his law examination, he did not practice law, but offered his services to the new school. Agarkar, who was a postgraduate (MA), could have secured a lucrative and cozy government job, but preferred to be a teacher.

With such a teaching staff, it was no wonder that various scholarships came easily to the New English School's students. There was a great demand for admission. Wordsworth, a grandson of the poet, was the principal of the Elphinstone College in Mumbai. He visited the New English School two years after its inception and was very impressed by its progress. He wrote that he was pleasantly surprised to see the success of the school. According to him, the school was an example of the new spirit and strength generated by the English education. There was nothing more ennobling than the educated Indians shunning government jobs to start their enterprises. Wordsworth felt this would have a lasting impact on the future course of India. Chiplunkar died in 1883, two years after the inauguration of the New English School. At the same time, Vaman Shivram Apte, who was a good teacher and a skilful manager, joined the school. The governor of Bombay had by then appointed a commission under Sir William Hunter to delve into the educational problems. Apte appeared before the Commission and pleaded powerfully for generous grants for the private schools and least interference in their administration. Hunter appreciated the deposition of Apte and had heard about the New English School. He wrote that he had not found any such great school in the whole of the country. According to him, the school had successfully competed with the government high school and surpassed it without taking any government grant. Hunter had no doubt that the New English School would compete with any first class school in any country.

On February 20, 1884, 'The Times of India', while reporting the prize distribution ceremony held on February 13, said: "This school is one of the most remarkable results of our English education. It is entirely managed by native graduates, it is self-supporting, and it gives a liberal education at a small cost to eight hundred boys. The founders of the school feel what the Jesuits have always felt and acted on...that real power lies with those who educate and mould the young. Like Jesuits the Superintendent of the school and his colleagues give their services for the love of education and only take a pittance from the revenue of school to support themselves. They are men who have taken good degrees and might be enjoying handsome salaries if they had entered government service. They, however, preach the doctrine—and they practice what they preach—that graduates of the University, if they possess self-respect and patriotism, ought not to look to a foreign government for place and pay, but it is their duty to achieve a name and place of their own in education, in literature, in commerce or at the bar. No doubt these enthusiastic men will preach love of the country to these disciples, but it is better after all to have patriotism preached by educated men than the wandering mendicants. We have given the people of India education, and now it is for us to do all we can to have the moral energy created on our side and not against us".[1]

As the school was receiving encomiums from various quarters, the idea of starting a college took a definite shape, and in a public meeting on October 24, 1884, the formation of the Deccan Education Society was announced. The meeting was presided over by Sir William Wedderburn who was a Civil Servant and played an important role next year in the formation of the Indian National Congress. The D.E. Society had on its council, persons like Wedderburn, Mandlik, Telang, Wordsworth, Narayanbhai Dandekar and Yeshwant Moreshwar Kelkar. Wordsworth and Mandlik were appointed as trustees of the Society. The then governor of Bombay, Sir James Fergusson, was sympathetic to the Society. Hence, the University readily granted permission to the college. Lee-Warner, the director of Public Instruction of the Bombay government, while writing on the subject of recommendation of the Education Commission, commended the D.E. Society and its Fergusson College in these words: "The Native Society at Poona, which is generally called the Patriotic Society, entertains an objection to the Bengal system (of assessing grants at a certain proportion of the income guaranteed from private sources). This Society has lately started the Fergusson College, and attracted by an appeal to patriotism, the very best outturn from our High Schools which the educated ranks of the Brahmin and other Hindu society in Poona can afford. It believes that it will distance all rivals in the examination-room and it has no fear of result system. It argues that the salaries paid to its teachers afford no index to their value. The College wishes to be largely independent of any European element in its lecture-rooms and to impress upon its students the patriotic sentiments of its independent founders. The experiment has no parallel in any city in India, and is interesting from other points of view than the educational aspect".[2]

Lord Sandhurst, governor of Bombay, while inaugurating the building of the college, said that in England the life members of a society were elected from the donors, but here it was quite different. This society demanded sacrifices from the life members. Lord Sandhurst appealed for generous donations to the society and gave a cheque of rupees one thousand. The goodwill shown to the society encouraged others to emulate its example, and in Pune another society, the Shikshan Prasarak, was formed which started the Nutan Marathi Vidyalaya as a memorial to Vishnushastri Chiplunkar and later, Sir Parshurambhau College. The Bombay government, desiring to reduce the expenditure, decided to hand over the Deccan College to the Deccan Education Society. As a *quid pro quo,* the government was to give some grant to the D.E. Society, which was not averse to such a deal, at least in principle. But while negotiating the details, the government put forward various conditions. The Deccan College was started with the amount of money, which the Peshwas were expending yearly on the learned Brahmins. Justice Ranade apprehended that after the transfer of the Deccan College to the D.E. Society, this amount would be permanently reverted to the Treasury. So he called a public meeting and demanded an extension of the lease to the Deccan College. As Ranade was connected with the D.E. Society from its inception, the society's executives consulted him about the government proposal. He advised them not to agree to the appointment of any European professors and government nominees on the executive committee. As this was not acceptable to the government, the proposal fell through.

Later, describing the condition under which Deccan College was functioning, Gokhale wrote in 'Sudharak,' on March 17, 1890, that the people of Pune promised a sum of fifteen thousand rupees to the college, provided the government would extend its lease of the college. However, "Promises are always more or less very inconvenient, but if they are not to be 'the mere idle wind that passes by a breath, a bubble', the inconveniences must be borne by all honourable men, if for nothing else, at least for the temporary advantage to which they show you when you make them. It is, therefore, high and solemn responsibility—one which it would be dishonour to shirk-resting on the shoulders of those, who made the promises three years ago, to come forward now with their promised contributions. And by doing so, they would entitle themselves to high praise of all, for everyone wishes that the Deccan College, which hitherto had done such noble work for the people of Maharashtra, should be maintained in a high state of efficiency, and be accessible to poor students as well as to rich ones".

As the New English School set a new trend in the field of education, 'Kesari' and 'Maratha' changed the pattern of journalism. The first issue of 'Maratha' came out on January 2, 1881 followed by 'Kesari' on January 4. Both papers initially had to incur losses, but 'Kesari' in few years began to break even, and then making a small profit. The 'Maratha' was always in financial difficulties and had to depend on 'Kesari' for sustenance. Vishnushastri, Agarkar and Namjoshi all shared a love for writing and contributed much to the weeklies. Tilak, however, was a reluctant writer. Agarkar edited 'Kesari' and Tilak was the editor of 'Maratha'. Before the advent of 'Kesari', the papers in Maharashtra were edited indifferently. The new weeklies were bold in their approach and were forthright. The immediate cause for their popularity was the case of Shivaji Maharaj, the prince of Kolhapur state. It was rumoured that he was suffering from fits of insanity. The Diwan of Kolhapur, Mr. Barve, and the English Resident were suspected to be responsible for this ailment. It was presumed that some jewellery had also been stolen. As both the 'Kesari' and 'Maratha' received oral and written complaints followed by some letters, which were supposed to be written by Barve, both papers started a campaign that caused a libel suit. As the case proceeded, those who had complained against Barve and the Resident were reluctant to come forward as witnesses and even the letters, which were purported to be written by Barve, proved to be fake. This resulted in the imprisonment of both Tilak and Agarkar. But it invoked tremendous sympathy in Maharashtra. People came forward to contribute to the fund raised to pay for the court case.

Gokhale, who was then a student in the college, acted in a play that was staged to collect money for Tilak and Agarkar. They were released after about a hundred days. Later, the Kolhapur maharaja became insane and was detained in a fort at Ahmednagar where he died of maltreatment and torture.

Tilak and Agarkar were pleased with Gokhale's work as a teacher in the New English School. They asked him to accept the post of a lecturer in the newly started Fergusson College. He was elated by this offer but was doubtful about the response of his elder brother who naturally was expecting him to earn a good and comfortable living. However, when Agarkar pleaded with Gokhale's elder brother, he gave his consent. In no time Gokhale was promoted as a professor and later as the principal of the College. As a life-member of the Deccan Education Society, Gokhale took the responsibility of collecting funds for the Society, which he discharged with zeal as his wont and established himself as one of the important members of the institution. After his death, his colleague and a pioneer in female education in Maharashtra, D.K. Karve, told an anniversary meeting that the Fergusson College owed Gokhale a debt because the magnificent building of the college was the result of Gokhale's untiring efforts in raising funds.

As a professor, Gokhale was very helpful to the students. He used to memorise almost all the prescribed books. T.K Shahani, who was Gokhale's student and later the principal of the College in Bhavnagar, Gujarat, wrote that while teaching a book on Nelson, Gokhale took great pains. He says, "The spirit of doing things in thorough fashion was now beginning to take hold of him and prompted him to take several trips to Bombay, solely with a view to study the build of a fighting vessel as an object lesson. The 'fore' and 'aft', the 'starboard' and the 'larboard', the tack etc. to be well understood had necessarily to be seen; and Gokhale soon proved to be quite equal to it." But Shahani has also said that though Gokhale tried his best to make his subject clear to the students, he could not make it as interesting as his colleague, Vasudevrao Kelkar. R.P. Paranjpe, one of Gokhale's students, made his name as a Senior Wrangler. He was then invited by Gokhale to be the principal of the Fergusson College. Gokhale had the magnanimity to not only relinquish his post but work as a professor under Paranjpe. Paranjpe tells us that Gokhale at various times taught mathematics, history, economics and English literature by turn. He was, therefore, called a 'made to order professor'. In fact, according to Paranjpe, Gokhale was not a professor in a true sense of the term and was reluctant to call himself a one. By 1891 Gokhale had lost interest in mathematics, but because of his proficiency in the subject, he was able to explain any subject to the public as a political leader. Paranjpe said, "His (Gokhale's) teaching of English suffered by a comparison with that of his colleague, Prof. Vasudevrao Kelkar. The latter was a true connoisseur of poetry and light literature and entered into the spirit of any novel or poem better than

Gokhale. He is said to have taught some very difficult books in an inimitable manner, especially those for which students have no extraneous help in the shape of copious annotations, but several times he hurried over difficult books. This was too much for the average student who did not come to the class sufficiently prepared beforehand. Gokhale, on the other hand, was very methodical. He never slurred over even the easiest passages, took great pains to explain all the allusions and especially all the historical references. But his teaching was not calculated to give one the love of literature as such, if it was not already there. Perhaps, one can say that his teaching was more useful to the average examinee than that of professor Kelkar." Though Gokhale was a teacher of mathematics, he tried to persuade Paranjpe to take up English as his subject for the degree examination and not go in for science.

Gokhale used to care about his students and guide them. Nevertheless, he could not mingle with them easily. He was reserved and even after entering public life, he generally used to meet people by appointment, in contrast to his mentor, Ranade, who had an open house. Even when Ranade was engrossed in some serious work, he was surrounded by a number of people and used to join them when free. Gokhale was particular about his clothes. When he went to England to depose before the Welby Commission, he wore a Parsi type long coat and never failed to don a typical headgear—*pugree*—of Pune. He also asked Dinshaw Wacha to wear a Parsi cap in London. Later on, Gokhale used to wear western clothes whenever he visited England. Even while at home, he would not meet a stranger without wearing a jacket. Srinivas Sastri, Gokhale's political heir, writing about his fastidiousness about his dress and appearance, narrates that once when the governor was to visit the Servants of India Society, Gokhale told him that he (Sastri) must shave, and provided a razor to him. Gokhale had travelled extensively in India and abroad. He was interested in acquainting himself with the social life of the people but being busy in his public work, he never wrote about the places of interest he visited.

What manner of man was he? Sastri's account is very graphic. He says, "Gokhale's figure is familiar—his handsome face, his fair colour, his long coat of gray, his red pugree, his scarf of white with thin lace border. Still when I tell you he wore a cap sometimes, and often tied a long narrow strip of coloured cloth round his head as a loose turban, and that for many years, like any domesticated Deccani, he changed into holy time-honoured silk at meals, and that till he made his first voyage he grew a long tuft at the back of his head and tied it into a knot...."

"Being diabetic, he was placed under (a) strict diet but didn't always observe it. He must have his brinjals daily, seasoned with chillies in as angry a style as would have pleased any Andhra of Krishna District. Ghee (clarified butter), prized above everything else by the true Brahmana, he avoided like poison; he could not endure it even on his neighbour's plate. Someone told me this was because, for a long time, he had had to swallow quantities of it along with medicines. Curds were a favourite dish, and he grew lyrical when he expatiated on the unqualified merits of a preparation of curds called *srikhand.* He found it in his heart to forgive the Peshwa who lost an empire eating it. I would like to believe his admiration was only academic, for he was not blest with the marvellous eupepsia of the ordinary Maharashtrian."

"Gokhale loved his daughters but never demonstrated it as other fathers usually do… Gokhale had a playful habit of betting on all occasions and sundry. Though he never had much money, his mode of life, ever since I knew him, was high, higher than would have been expected of him. He tipped servants like a prince. He subscribed generously for causes. He helped friends open-handedly." Sastri also narrated an incident from Gokhale's life, which showed his truthfulness and courage to admit an error. This happened at the residence of Mrs. Sarla Ray, who was a friend of Gokhale. He regularly visited her when he attended the Imperial Legislative Council, in Calcutta. Once Mrs. Ray said to Gokhale that with all his liberal views, he was still wearing the sacred thread around his neck, to denote that he was a Brahmin by birth. Gokhale saw the point and the next morning Mrs. Ray received an envelope, enclosed in which was Gokhale's sacred thread cut into pieces with a note. Mrs. Ray told this to the students of the school which she had established in the name of Gokhale.[4]

The Deccan Education Society, which was receiving plaudits all round and was poised to progress rapidly, was beset with a tragedy followed by internecine feuds and controversies. Chiplunkar died before the college started and Apte followed him without seeing the completion of the college building. This was a great blow to the society but the internal feuds and quarrels crippled it for some time. Gokhale was disgusted by the quarrels among those he held in high esteem. He even thought of quitting the society. However, Apte persuaded him to stay on and told him that senior members had some schemes of expanding the activities of the society and they were looking to Gokhale with great expectations. Apte also said that the college had not become a full-fledged one and to achieve that status the society was in need of a dedicated and hard working person like Gokhale.

Differences in the society arose out of personal attitudes, prejudices and predilections. Both Tilak and Agarkar, who were editing 'Maratha' and 'Kesari', had identical views on politics, but had fundamental differences on social subjects. These came out into the open, and that affected the College staff, which was divided; and the students were disturbed and confused. Tilak then decided to resign from his life-membership of the society. He sent his resignation with a letter, which ran into forty printed pages and was accusatory. He traced the history of the society and regretted the fact that the original idea of having an institution like that of Jesuits was botched. Various rules and regulations were breached and exceptions were made without any consideration of propriety. Some of the points of disputes could have been resolved, if both parties had an open mind and were ready to compromise in the spirit of give and take. Dr. Bhandarkar, who presided over the meeting of the Governing Council, declared that the differences were irreconcilable and Tilak's resignation should be accepted. The council then accepted the resignation on February 3, 1891. Thus ended a glorious chapter in the history of the Deccan Education Society, which was started with lofty ideals. Tilak was in a minority in the society. He would otherwise have accepted this readily, but he gave a fight. His biographer, N.C. Kelkar, says that Tilak was not a person who would accept defeat without a fight. But he adds that Tilak did not venture to start a parallel educational institution, as he thought that both the new and old institutions would come to a sorry pass by the competition. In a larger sense, this dispute in the Deccan Education Society proved to be a blessing in disguise. It would have been better if the parting of ways had come without bitterness. But it could not be avoided; and that paved the way for Tilak and Gokhale to play their historical roles in the arena of national politics. It, of course, took eighteen more years for Gokhale to resign from the society, not because of any differences, but because an opportunity had come for him to play a bigger role.

Controversy in the Deccan Education Society was preceded by that over the editorial policy of 'Kesari' and 'Maratha'. Agarkar was all for social reforms, and justified government intervention in social matters which Tilak would not tolerate. Agarkar then resigned from Kesari and started his own weekly, 'Sudharak', which for about a year or so was bilingual. Agarkar edited Marathi section while Gokhale, the English. Gokhale was Agarkar's supporter; but unlike his mentor, Ranade, he did not play a leading role in the Social Conference nor did he go headlong with Agarkar, which might be because of personal reasons. His wife suffered from white leprosy and physical intimacy was impossible. Therefore, his uncle prevailed upon him to marry again. Gokhale was apprehensive about the fact that if he publicly came out as an ardent advocate of social reforms, he would invite bitter personal criticism from his orthodox critics. He also could not go with Agarkar in challenging the religious tenets. Agarkar was agnostic and never minced words. Not only Gokhale, but also most of the social reformers, did not dare to subscribe to the radicalism of Agarkar in social as well as political matters. In politics, Agarkar was nearer to Tilak than with any moderates. Gokhale used to call himself an agnostic in the initial period of his public life; but he changed his views eventually. He started yoga and invoked the blessings of Dattatreya. Srinivas Sastri remembers that Gokhale used to eagerly await a weekly letter from an astrologer. Later, when K. Natarajan, editor of *Social Reformer* met him in Calcutta, he saw a paperweight on Gokhale's table on which were inscribed the words—'God is Love'. Dr. Bhandarkar was aware of this change in Gokhale's attitude and told Natarajan that Gokhale was going to announce this publicly. Lallubhai Samaldas was one of those who were very close to Gokhale. This industrialist friend of Gokhale laid the foundation stone of the building, 'Gokhale Hall', in Pune on September 10, 1925. Addressing the gathering, Mr. Samaldas said, "Like many of us, he (Gokhale) passed through the stage of agnosticism, but he came back to the faith in the *Bhagwad Gita* and the teachings of *Upanishads*. The last time I saw him, I remember having found him reading Moksha Dharma from the Shanti Parva of *Mahabharat;* and thereafter we had a very interesting discussion about the advisability and necessity of belief in higher power.... He had almost made it a rule at that time to read every day few English hymns or the few mantras of the *Upanishads* and shlokas from the *Gita.* He had not, of course, the faith of a Bhandarkar or a Ranade in the personal Deity....He did believe in the Parabramha of Hindu philosophy."[5]

As editor of the English section of the *Sudharak,* Gokhale wrote several editorials and notes. They cover the period between January 27 and September 1890. Gokhale generally spoke and wrote in English, but he also had a mastery over Marathi, his mother tongue. He wrote two articles on the subject of the use of Marathi in the University. Writing on April 21, 1890, Gokhale criticised both Justice Telang and the Syndicate for curtailing the study of vernacular languages. Gokhale pointed out that the founders of the educational system had given a proper place to the study of the vernacular languages. He then said, "We have always been most sensible of the importance of the languages which alone are understood by the great mass of population.... It is indispensable, therefore, that in any general system of education, the study of them should be assiduously attended to." Gokhale appealed to intensify the agitation in favour of the vernacular languages and form a committee to conduct this agitation. Gokhale's advocacy of the vernacular languages was impressive; and the 'Sudharak' received a large number of letters supporting the plea. Some letter-writers expressed their willingness to serve on the committee, if the university were prepared to appoint one.

Gokhale was modern enough to criticise Prof. Jinsivale, an erudite but an extreme orthodox orientalist and a Sanskrit scholar. Jinsiwale had criticised Western civilisation and made some derogatory remarks against English ladies. Gokhale took strong exception to such retrograde views and intemperate language. But when some social reformers asked the Missionary society, which employed Jinsivale, to proceed against him, Gokhale expressed his disapproval and said that intolerance or extremism on both sides was equally reprehensible.

Gokhale did not confine his writings in the 'Sudharak' to the issues pertaining only to Maharashtra, but chose wider subjects. Thus, we find him reproducing an article about Parnell, an Irish leader. Afterwards when the report of a committee absolved Parnell of any complicity in the revolutionary or violent activities, Gokhale gave extensive excerpts from the report. The commission had found almost all charges against Parnell and other respondents unfounded. They were charged that their denunciation of the Phoenix park murder was insincere; but the commission declared that the facsimile letter, on which this charge was based, was forged. The commission also did not accept that Parnell and his associates were conspiring against the British government, for a revolution in Ireland. Why did Gokhale give such extensive excerpts from this report? He did so to convey to the bureaucracy in India not to rush to accuse anybody of conspiracy without a proper inquiry.

Gokhale wrote an article discussing the grievances of the workers of the then Great Indian Peninsula Railway, presently Western railway, and especially of the subordinate staff. There were no definite leave-rules, which the employees in government offices enjoyed. The subordinate railway staff was getting only ten days leave. There was no fixed rule for leave for temporary illness. The leave for private business was dependent on the discretion of the officer concerned, while the working hours of these employees stretched up to twelve. Gokhale asked the company to reduce the dividend to win the satisfaction of the employees. In another article, Gokhale referred to the strike by the Anglo-Indian skilled staff of the railway company. Because of unity and perseverance, they could get their demands accepted. Gokhale asked the subordinate staff to follow the example of this skilled staff and organise as well as persevere.

Gokhale, like Ranade, was not soft towards Indian states and their chiefs. He cited with approval some extracts from an article by Lee-Warner who had asked why the Indian leaders did not pressurise the rulers of Indian states to accept so many demands, which these leaders made on the British government? Gokhale said that this was a legitimate question and the Indian leaders should exert pressure on the rulers of the states. Lee-Warner wrote, "In almost every self-governed state of India the ruler could do no wrong and is invested with absolute powers. He is not controlled by a legislative body. His laws are his executive orders. There is no code of these executive orders that have the force of law and no public discussion at their introduction. If his ministers claim as public property anything to which a subject prefers a claim, the latter has no legal redress. The Judiciary is not independent. Occasionally municipalities have been created,—but the municipal boards are under strict state control". Gokhale endorsed the criticism of Lee-Warner. Gokhale's views about the administration of the Indian states were not fashioned by Lee-Warner's article. On July 7, 1890 he had published an obituary of Rao Bahadur Srinivas Rao, the chief justice of Gwalior. Srinivas Rao served in Indore and Devas as a subordinate judge and was then promoted as a district judge, in which capacity he served for twelve years. Those were trying periods of his life, as the Raja of Indore used to make unlawful demands, and expected Rao to fulfil his wishes. Srinivas Rao stood up to his guns in all matters. Holkar expected Rao to subordinate the interests of the state in preference to his own, which Rao refused to do. Ultimately, the Resident who was impressed by Rao's integrity, arranged his transfer to Devas and then Rao was appointed as the chief justice of Gwalior. It must be remembered that Holkar was one of the benefactors of the Deccan Education Society; but Gokhale was forthright in his criticism of the irresponsible behaviour of Holkar.

Gokhale had written several articles in 'Sudharak' on financial problems, which were the precursors of his illuminating budget speeches in the Imperial Legislative Council in later years. He was an ardent advocate of the various demands of the Indian National Congress like simultaneous civil service examination in England and in India; more representation to the Indians in higher government jobs; reduction of the salt tax; expansion of the legislatures and acceptance of elective principle for the legislative bodies.

Gokhale could not continue to edit 'Sudharak' for long, as he had increased responsibilities as a secretary to the Pune Sarvajanik Sabha and the editor of its prestigious quarterly journal. It was Agarkar who recommended him to Justice Ranade. Gokhale's respect for Ranade bordered on devotion and veneration. Ranade was also impressed by Gokhale's sincerity and his willingness to work hard. Their relationship was unique. Though Gokhale was the editor of the Sabha's journal, no article appeared without the approval of Ranade, who would go through each one and make suitable changes. The journal published very thoughtful and scholarly articles and won recognition from the government as well as discerning people.

Ranade, Tilak, Agarkar and Gokhale, who were the four more prominent leaders in the social and political life of Maharashtra, held different views on political and social problems, but they also cooperated on various occasions. As a social reformer, Agarkar was a fighter and was never afraid to use harsh language. Ranade on the other hand, always acted as a teacher and was persuasive. Tilak was totally absorbed in politics and thought that social reforms could wait and political rights must get precedence. Gokhale, though a social reformer, devoted himself to politics and constitutional reforms. But the attitude of these four leaders on different problems was sometimes complex. All of them had studied the writings of Mill and Spencer as did most of their contemporaries. But Ranade thought that both Mill and Spencer were the products of the Western civilisation and should not be followed in India, which had a rich tradition of her own. Mill and Herbert Spencer, according to Ranade, reacted against the rigidity of some Christian sects in their times. But Ranade maintained that such rigidity was an anathema to Hindu philosophy as it was much more liberal. When Agarkar opposed the views of Dr. Bhandarkar and quoted Spencer, Ranade came down heavily against him and said that those who wanted to follow Spencer and Mill should better find a place in some other country. But it was Tilak who came to the rescue of Agarkar. Later when Spencer died, Tilak wrote a scholarly editorial, which could be said to be one of his best, eulogizing the contribution of Spencer to the human thought and said that scholarly persons like Spencer belong not to any nation but to the whole world. They were the sages or *rishis.* Writing an obituary of Max Muller, Tilak emphasised the need for studying the Western scholars in order to understand the Eastern religious treatises. Ranade was a prominent member of the Prarthana Samaj, which was against idol worship but he gave discourses in the Prarthana Samaj on the devotional poetry of the Marathi saints. He used to sing their devotional songs every morning when, according to both his wife and Gokhale, his face would glow.

Ranade, Tilak and Agarkar wrote and spoke extensively about religion and philosophy. They might not have agreed with each other; but they relished these philosophical discussions. Gokhale was not so inclined. He differed from Ranade and Tilak in respect of the study of Indian or Maratha, history. Ranade, in fact, wrote a book—*Rise of the Maratha Power*. Tilak wrote several articles about the Maratha history and started the Shivaji festival. Gokhale never wrote or spoke on Maratha or Indian history. He, indeed, advised his students to study European history. He had taken upon himself to have as much knowledge as possible about the economic and social problems of India and enlighten people on the subject.

Gokhale made several speeches about Ranade after the death of his mentor. He also helped in raising a memorial to him. Gokhale wanted to write a biography of Ranade but could not do so for want of time. His high regard for Ranade was evident on every occasion. Eulogising Gandhi's service to Indians in South Africa and his spiritual qualities. Gokhale said, "In all my life I have known only two men who have affected me spiritually in the manner that Mr. Gandhi does—our great patriarch, Mr. Dadabhai Naoroji and my late master Mr. Ranade—men before whom not only we are ashamed doing anything unworthy, but in whose presence our very minds are devoid of thinking anything that is unworthy." Gandhi experienced Gokhale's reverence for Ranade. When Gokhale visited Africa to study the problems of the resident Indians, Gandhi found Gokhale's scarf a little creased. He offered to iron it. But Gokhale was reluctant. Gandhi writes, "When Gokhale came to South Africa, he had with him a scarf which was a gift from Mahadev Govind Ranade. He treasured the memento with the utmost care and used it only on special occasions. One such occasion was the banquet given in his honour by the Johannesburg Indians. The scarf was creased and needed ironing. It was not possible to send it to the laundry and get it back in time. I offered to try my art. "I can trust your capacity as a lawyer, but not as a washerman," said Gokhale. "What if you should soil it? Do you know what it means to me? With this he narrated, with much joy, the story of the gift. I still insisted, guaranteed good work, got his permission to iron it, and won his certificate. After that I did not mind if the rest of the world refused me its certificate."[6] After taking charge of the editorship of the Sarvajanik Sabha journal, a letter from Gokhale to G.V. Joshi, an eminent economist, also tells us about Gokhale's high regard for Ranade. He wrote to Joshi on October 17, 1889: "The Sabha has conferred me an honour of which I am conscious I am quite unworthy....The opening offered me endeavour to cultivate relationships of acquaintance, if nothing higher, with one for whom I all along cherished the deepest regard, whose earnest and unassuming exertion for the welfare of the country...I must content myself with only admiring from respectful distance. Mr. Ranade, at whose feet I am at present and hope to always sit as a very humble pupil, was kind enough to show me your last letter to him in connection with an article on the economic situation".

Gokhale learned from Ranade that there were no rewards in public life and representations to the government might not receive any response; but leaders of the people had to persevere, as these representations were also meant to educate the people. This might be a thankless task, Ranade nevertheless told Gokhale that their generation was destined to fail. However, in their failure lay future success. Ranade was a creative genius, who was all the while, striving to bring about all round progress. He had an eye to pick talent, which he would harness in the service of the country. He thought that the Indians were bad at building institutions, and therefore, instead of relying on individuals, he built various institutions. There was the Sarvajanik Sabha to ventilate the grievances of the people; its journal discussed different problems and enlightened the government as well as the people. The Social Conference was championing the cause of social reforms; and the industrial fairs and conferences were making people aware of the economic problems and inducing them to enter the field of trade and industry. Because of his contribution to the cause of the welfare and awakening in India, Lokmanya Tilak paid the highest tribute to him after Ranade's death. He said that Maharashtra was dormant but it was Ranade who awakened it. If people had become bold, it was solely because of Ranade.

Ranade had a clear picture of the future India before him. He said: "With a liberated manhood, with a faith that never shirks duty; with a sense of justice that deals fairly to all; with unclouded intellect and powers fully cultivated; and lastly, with a love that overleaps all bound; renovated India will take her proper rank among the nations of the world, and be the master of the situation and of her own destiny. This is the goal to be reached— this is the promised land. Happy are they who see it in distant vision, happier those who are permitted to work and clear the way on to it, happiest they who live to see it with their eyes and tread upon the holy soil once more. Famine and pestilence, oppression and sorrow, will then be myths of the past, and the gods will then again descend to the earth and associate with men as they did in times which we now call mythical."[7]

Gokhale had accepted this as his goal. He struggled hard to achieve it and even if he was deterred and faced a setback at times, he never gave up. Gokhale benefited from the knowledge and experience of Ranade and he made the best of it. Ranade was a high court judge at the time of the inception of the Congress. But for some years he continued to help it, shunning the limelight. Not being a government servant, Gokhale had no such restraints. He plunged himself in the Congress politics and attracted the attention of the Congress leaders by his maiden speech. Then onwards he achieved greater success and an eminent position in the public life of India.

REFERENCES

1. P.M. Limaye, *The History of the Deccan Education Society*, Deccan education Society, Poona, 1935, pp. 17-18.
2. P.M. Limaye, *The History of the Deccan Education Society*, Deccan education Society, Poona, 1935, p. 52.
3. T.K. Shahani, *Gopal Krishna Gokhale*, R. K. Mody, Bombay, 1929, p. 54.
4. V.S. Sastri Srinivas, *My Master Gokhale*, Model Publications, Madras, 1946, pp. 263-65, 268-70, 272-73.
5. Gokhale Digest (It is a collection of Gokhale's speeches, notes and writings collected and bound by the Servants of India Society after the death of Gokhale. It is not a publication. So the date of the publication is not given. They are just bound volumes).
6. Mohandas K. Gandhi, *An Autobiography: the Story of My Experiments With Truth*, Beacon Press, Boston, 1962, p. 213.
7. M.G. Ranade, *The Miscellaneous Writings*, Sahitya Akademi, New Delhi, 1992, pp. 179-180.

Chapter Two

EAST INDIA COMPANY'S RULE

Between the end of the Maratha rule in 1818 brought by the East India Company (EIC) and the establishment of the Indian National Congress (INC) in 1885, many earth-shaking events took place in India as well as in Europe. By 1848 the whole of India came under the control of the Company. It took more than three decades for an all India political organisation—the Indian National Congress—to come into being. The opportunity to play a role in the politics of the Congress came to Gokhale four years after its inception and then there was no turning back for him. In a way, his rise in the Congress was fast. His dedication, diligence and honesty brought him increasing responsibilities, which he discharged to the satisfaction of the majority of his fellow-Congressmen, and as the Congress moulded his life, he, in turn, put a stamp of his personality on the organisation. The significance of the historical role, which the Congress played in the life of India could be well appreciated, if we go into the causes of the collapse of power of the different rulers in India, and the EIC becoming the sole arbiter of the destiny of India. There was no tradition of popular political organisations in India. A country like India, with a continental proportion, was bound to initiate political institutions on provincial or regional basis before launching a national organisation. They were the inevitable outcome of the new spirit generated by the English education introduced by the East India Company.

The sixteenth century saw the arrival of some European trading companies to India. Among them the English and the French were more successful. A quarter of a century after the death of Aurangzeb, the Moghul Empire was on the verge of collapse. Invasion by Nadir Shah gave a fatal blow; and the Marathas or Rajputs could not replace the Moghuls. As the empire became weak, provincial satraps started asserting their authority. It was, therefore, easy for the English and the French Companies to get more and more concessions for their trade. They also saw an opportunity to acquire territories and offered the services of their disciplined and well-armed battalions, which some Indian rulers readily accepted. Between the French and the English the latter showed more ingenuity in expanding their trade and getting territories under their control. The East India Company did not spare any efforts pressurising the Indian rulers to accept its military help and protection. Some of them, realising the real motives of the Company, tried to unite; but their efforts proved to be futile.

The EIC officials were keen that the Peshwa, Bajirao the second, should agree to a military arrangement; but he had been putting them off for quite some time. That was the time when Arthur Wellesley had succeeded in convincing the rulers in the Tanjore region to accept military help from the Company. Under his scheme, the local rulers' authority on their territory remained undisturbed and their security guaranteed. The rulers were assured military help against any aggression. This arrangement resulted in the loss of independence of the rulers, who became indolent. In the process, the Company's authority became pervasive and the people felt that not the Indian rulers but the Company was supreme. As Bajirao invited more and more trouble due to his greedy and suspicious nature, he had no option but to take the help of the Company. He had a long-standing grudge against Holkar who was opposed to his getting the office of the Peshwa. Bajirao, being a weak ruler, many of his jahagirdars and other high officials acted independently, avoiding payment of their dues. When he asked for help from Scindia of Gwalior, Holkar took it as an affront, and Bajirao's finance minister, Nana Phadnavis, disapproved of this alliance. Mahadji Scindia, even with a vast territory under his control, was, like other Maratha rulers, always in financial difficulties. He spent lavishly without any regard for the income. A letter written by one Sadashiv Dinkar to Nana Phadnavis, four years before Mahadji moved to Pune, is revealing. He said: 'though Mahadji had received ten lak Rs. recently, he had spent every penny. Mahadji's army in the Deccan was in a dire state. Even though the soldiers had sold their horses, they were unable to pay their debts. He had increased his infantry but those who fought for him and annexed Gwalior and Dohad are the worst sufferers. Nobody knows whether those who enlisted were actually serving in the army. Expenditure is very huge, but it could not be guaranteed that the needy and deserving receive the payment. Several lenders were demanding immediate payment. Because of severe draught, crops have withered and many of the cultivators have sold their draught animals. Many died of hunger. This is the state of affairs right from Kashmir to the Chambal valley'. After Mahadji's death, his son, Daulatrao, succeeded him. Like Bajirao he was young and equally unworthy. Nana Phadnavis, striped of his office, was convinced that both the Peshwa and Daulatrao were planning to confiscate his vast property. It is noteworthy that Bajirao as well as Phadnavis had amassed a good deal of personal wealth, even when the government treasury was empty.

Phadnavis might have had rupees ten million in cash, besides gold and jewelry. How much Bajirao was worth? The British Residency archives had a letter written by Elphinstone to his friend, Strachey, which said that Bajirao had a habit of counting his cash everyday. He used to keep aside some amount for his expenses, and the remaining was sent to the fort under his ownership. Bajirao was receiving a yearly revenue of rupees hundred million, and his expenditure was four and a half million. He had rupees twenty million in his coffers.[1]

Daulatrao Scindia was in Pune when Holkar came with his army, and defeated Scindia's army trained by the French. This defeat forced Daulatrao to return to his troubled state. Emboldened by this victory, Holkar, who wanted to take revenge on Bajirao for crushing his brother Vithoji under an elephant's feet, challenged Bajirao. The Peshwa, therefore, asked the Company officials to help him; but Colonel Close, who was in Pune, refused, as the central authority of the East India Company in Calcatta had issued strict orders that no such help be given to any Indian ruler unless he signed a written agreement with the Company. Holkar then defeated Bajirao who fled to the Konkan area. Pune was ransacked and looted for a whole week by Holkar's army and the bands of freebooters known as Pindaries. Bajirao then had no option but to sign the military agreement with the Company in 1803 at Vasai. This helped in restoring the office of the Peshwa. The Vasai agreement made Bajirao subservient to the Company and marked the beginning of the downfall of the Maratha rule. Though the Peshwa had surrendered his authority to the Company, his other chiefs did not agree to abide by the Vasai agreement. Scindia and Bhosle of Nagpur united to jointly bring Pune and Mysore under their control. The Company, on the other hand, threatened Bhosle in Orissa and Scindia in the north. Before the year-end, Scindia and Bhosle surrendered, and large parts of their territory were ceded to the Company. General Wellseley, who was in charge of this operation, took over the fort of Ahmednagar, which secured the position of the Peshwa. He then extended his help to the Nizam in Hyderabad where he defeated the Marathas. The Company did not lose much time in bringing down both Scindia and Holkar. General Wellesley was much impressed by the courage and valour shown by Elphinstone and commended him in official dispatches. Elphinstone was then posted as the Resident at Nagpur where he spent about four years. As he had no heavy responsibility, he spent his time in the serious study of classical literature. The Pindaries came near Nagpur twice, and even Elphinstone had to flee to save himself. After four years in Nagpur, Elphinstone was asked to return to the headquarters in Calcutta. Some of the territory he traversed belonged to Bhosle, and the local residents narrated to him how miserable their lives were and how Scindia's army looted them. In a letter written to his sister, Elphinstone had described the confusion in the camp of the Scindia. He said: "Conceive a king and his court, with all their servants and retinue, a very small army of regular infantry and irregular cavalry, and a collection of shopkeepers and every other description of people that is found in a town, the whole amounting to 150,000 men, crowded into a camp in which all pitch in confusion, on all kinds of and sizes of tents; add one great street with shops of all kinds in tents on each side of it, and, in the middle of the whole, one great enclosure, of canvas walls containing a great number of tents for the accommodation of Scindia and his family; and this will give you as clear a notion of a Maratha camp as it is possible to have of so confused a thing....When I arrived, Scindia and all his ministers were confined (dharna) by a body of troops who had mutinied for pay. The Ministers were kept without eating; but the prince who was allowed to do as he pleased, was very little affected by the state of affairs, and spent his days in playing cards with his favourites".[2]

Elphinstone came from a family of landed gentry, but was not affluent. His father was a chief guard at a fort in Edinburgh. At the age of sixteen Elphinstone could secure a job in the EIC and was sent to Calcutta. His first posting was at Banares where he joined his brother. He was appointed as an assistant to one Mr. Davis who was a magistrate. Davis gave him lessons in classical Greek and Latin literature. Later, Elphinstone made a name as an efficient and studious officer who could wield pen and sword with equal ease. In Banares, he learned Hindi and Persian. Vazir Ali, the Nawab of Avadh, who was dethroned by Governor-General Shore, stormed Banares and went on killing Englishmen. Elphinstone would have been killed, if he had not been a keen horseman. Elphinstone was then sent to Pune as an assistant to the Resident, Colonel Palmer. Elphinstone met Bajirao, along with Colonel Close. About this meeting Elphinstone wrote: "The Peshwa's face is good and dignified, though there is something vulgar in his mouth". The durbar at Hyderabad, he found glittering but that at Pune was mean. "None of the Maratha chiefs were even like native gentlemen". But with further contact with them, he could appreciate the simplicity of the Peshwa durbar. Elphinstone returned to Pune as the Resident in 1811, after his stint in the north, where he had taken the measure of different local rulers and their administration. He travelled far to Kabul on a goodwill mission on behalf of the government. His book on his visit to Kabul was appreciated by readers and critics alike. The Peshwa, by then, was weaker and his Sardars defiant. He, therefore, requested Elphinstone to rein them in and compel them to be respectful to the Peshwa, and pay their dues regularly. He had no compunction in granting the power of attorney to an English Resident. Elphinstone wrote to the Governor-General Lord Minto, explaining the intricate relationship between the Peshwa and the Sardars. He said that many of the Sardars had grabbed land, taking advantage of the weakness of the Peshwa. He then asked permission of the central authority in Calcutta to intervene on behalf of the Peshwa, which would give them a foothold in the administration. This was granted and the Peshwa's authority was restored. Elphinstone assured the Sardars that as long as they paid their dues regularly, the Company would give them protection. Thus, the Company not only became the protector of the Peshwa but also of the Sardars.

What was the life of the ordinary people living under the Peshwa? T.N. Atre, an authority on the last decades of the nineteenth century rural Maharashtra, has described the all round degradation in his book titled *Gavgada* (published in Marathi). He writes: "Bajirao used to auction the posts of mamlatdars to the highest bidders. There was a time when this post had prestige of its own. Well to do people also aspired to be mamlatdars, which was taken as a mark of respect. But under Bajirao, all this changed. If anybody became rich, he would be asked whether he was the mamlatdar? The post got in auction would be 'leased' with some cut to the holder of the title. Patil was to get the last but not the least commission. There was a time when complaint against Patil was lodged with the Mamlatdar, and against Mamlatdar to the Durbar. But under the new dispensation, this practice discontinued. All these officers were in league with each other. Peasants could expect some justice if Patil was a revenue collector. But with Mamlatdar, justice was rare. He would charge not according to the standing crop in the field, but according to the income or property of the holder. In case of failure to pay the exorbitant rate, Mamlatdar confiscated the land. Money-lenders made easy money in the process."[3]

In a way it was a diarchy, and the people believed that the English had taken over. Therefore, at some places such as Satara there were minor uprisings. When the situation settled somewhat, the Peshwa's urge for a full control over his domain became irresistible. But this was not backed by sagacity and military might. As he was suspicious, he could not unite Sardars behind him. Even when his Sardars avowed allegiance to him, he suspected a conspiracy to murder him. So he asked permission from the Company to raise a platoon of guards for himself to which the Company replied that such a platoon would have to be under its control. The Peshwa agreed. Those days Elphinstone used to have frequent meetings with the Peshwa, which helped him to get a thorough measure of him. Elphinstone had written several letters to the Company's central office in Calcutta describing the Peshwa's personality and character.

In one of his letters Elphinstone wrote: "The character of His Highness the Peshwa has always perplexed those who have been interested in discovering his sentiments or calculating on his conduct. This partly owing to the inconsistencies of many of his inclinations with his ruling passion of fear, and partly to the deep dissimulation which enables him to conceal his real feelings and intentions, and to display others which are foreign to his mind. If he were less deficient in courage, he would be ambitious, imperious, inflexible, and persevering; and his active propensities would probably overcome his love of ease and pleasure, which are now so strong, from their alliance with timidity. As it is, he is eager for power, though he wants the boldness necessary to acquire it, and is tenacious of authority, though too indolent to exercise it. Even his indolence is broken in by his habits of suspicion and vigilance. And there is no part of his character that is to found unmixed and entire. His love of consequence makes him fond of company of low dependents, where he can enjoy his superiority unresisted...when it suits his purposes, there is no meanness to which he will not descend....He is vindictive in the extreme; he never forgets an injury, and spares no machinations to ruin the object of resentment...to his habitual insincerity he joins a talent for insinuation and natural love of intrigue and artifice. He is a slave to superstition: half his life is spent in fasts, prayers and pilgrimages. Though he affects great purity in his own person, scarcely a day passes that he does not spend some hours with his favourites in large assembly of women, when he enjoys the coarsest buffoonery; and witness most disgusting scenes of debauchery".[4] In another letter Elphinstone had written about Trimbakji Dengale, a low level person in the service of the Peshwa, who according to him, "was absolutely illiterate as not to have learned to read;...he was entirely ignorant of the state of India and comparative importance of master's state". Dengale came from low menial services but was elevated by the Peshwa.

Gaikwad of Baroda was not reconciled and did not pay his dues; but ultimately agreed to have some compromise after the Peshwa was restored to his authority with the help of the English. Gaikwad sent Gangadharshastri as his emissary. But the Peshwa was elusive, as he wanted to bring the Gaikwad's territory under his control, to which the English refused to be a party. After a while Peshwa asked Gangadharshastri to see him at Pandharpur. While on his way to Pandharpur, Gangadharshastri was murdered by the henchmen of Trimbakji. When Elphinstone learnt about this, he asked the Peshwa to hand over Trimbakji. Elphinstone wrote to the Calcutta office of the Company that the Peshwa's hands were not clean in this matter and he was prepared to challenge the Company as soon as he had some respite. The Peshwa's contention was that Trimbakji was not involved in Shastri's murder; and so he was putting off Elphinstone. But the Company officers apprehended Trimbakji and put him in a prison in Thane from where he absconded. Elphinstone was convinced that the Peshwa was behind this and insisted on Trimbakji's arrest. In spite of the Peshwa's reluctance, Trimbakji was eventually apprehended. Relations between the Company and the Peshwa became sour because of this episode and could not be restored to normalcy afterwards.

By now both Elphinstone and the Peshwa were wary of each other and resorted to intense surveillance of each other. The Peshwa had bribed some of the soldiers from the Company's army to be his agents, about which Elphinstone was fully aware. Between 1815 and 1816, the Peshwa was thinking of uniting the Maratha Sardars against the Company; and if that were not possible, he wanted to put an end to their domination. The Peshwa was, of course, obsessed with the idea of his own dominance and power. When he thought that the Maratha king of Satara would be a threat to him, he kept him under watch. Elphinstone had established posts—dawks—at various places, which were also useful to him to intercept the messages of the Peshwa. Some fakirs and sadhus were on his payroll and acted as his agents. Elphinstone had his informants in the Peshwa's durbar. One of the Sardars, Balajipant Natu, gave Elphinstone a list of the army personnel in Maratha army, in lieu of a few thousand rupees. A Jain trading family in Maharashtra had its offices in different parts of India and one even in Kabul. Elphinstone used this network to gather information about the Peshwa. Elphinstone's men regularly and systematically intercepted letters to Peshwa. One such letter was by Dajiba Deshmukh, a functionary from Daulatrao Scindia's court, which revealed the pathetic condition of Maratha princes whom the Peshwa was planning to unite against the Company. The letter said: "At this time the whole empire is in confusion. No person has any concert or understanding with his neighbour. You know the view of this (Scindia) Court. On what do we depend? On Scindia, Holkar and Bhosla. Of them Bhosla's hand and feet are swelled and his life is despaired. Holkar's troops are not united. His territory has been parceled out in surinjams for troops and in consequence every man has secured all that he could for himself and now makes out that he has not enough to pay his contingent and keeps up constant dhurnas for the balance. The prince is a child, and the ministers are for occupying each his place and promoting the public good among them. At the same time the overweening power of the British in all parts of the country and the general impression of it that is felt keep all other powers in awe so that each sits without energy in his own place and takes no interest in his neighbour. At present Holkar's Government is really in great disorder; do you write to Scindia and desire him to send some persons of consequence with bankers, to assemble all Holkar's ministers, some of whom are in camp, some at Cota, and some at other places and through them to make the bankers lend 5 to 10 laks of rupees and restore the stability of the government?". Conditions in Berar were not any different. Dajiba lamented in the same letter the infirmities of the youthful new raja, and disorder in the state. Pindaries were also all over the place. Dajiba concludes his letter by saying that the British had massive army which would break not only the Pindaries but might have some other plans.[5] In a dispatch to the governor-general, Elphinstone quoted this letter as a proof of a plan in the offing against the Company. He was aware that the Peshwa was in a sullen mood, as the Company did not meet his demands on the territory of the Nizam and Baroda. Besides, he was angry, as Trimbakji had not been released. The Peshwa then sent one Prabhakar Pandit as his emissary to Calcutta to make a representation on his behalf. Pandit was to get Trimbakji released and persuade the English to newly interpret the various treaties with the Peshwa.

Knowing that the Peshwa was assembling troops, Elphinstone did not waste time in gathering his forces, and received equipment from Mumbai. At that time, Trimbakji absconded from the jail again and started a rebellion against the British. The Peshwa was alarmed, and in a meeting with Elphinstone, he agreed to various conditions laid down by the English Resident. He confessed that he was planning an alliance of the Maratha Sardars against the Company, and promised Elphinstone that in future he would deal with anybody only with the help of the Company and not independently. The Peshwa also conceded a territory near Dharwad for the maintenance of the additional troops for security of his territory. In addition, the Peshwa gave up his rights over Malwa, Bundelkhand etc. which were conceded to the Company. This agreement is known as Pune Pact and was signed on June 13, 1817. Peshwa thus became a figurehead. The governor-general, on the basis of the correspondence received from Elphinstone, issued instructions to the governors of Bombay and Madras to annex the territory of Gujarat, Karnatak etc. from the Peshwa, whenever an opportunity arose. The Peshwa lay low for a while and again gathered troops in Pune. He then moved to seize the Residency by surprise. But Elphinstone made very swift moves, and retreating a little, fought with the Maratha army, which was routed. The loss of life, arms and cavalry was very large. The Peshwa then was on the run, but Brigadier General Sir John Malcolm, who asked the Peshwa to sign the surrender agreement, apprehended him. He was then sent to Vithur in Madhya Pradesh and was given some pension, and had to give up all claims on Pune administration. This pact, which sealed the fate of the Maratha Rule, was signed on June 1, 1818.

When the Maratha rule ended, England herself was not in a happy position. America already had proclaimed independence, and in fighting a war with Napoleon, England had to shade much blood and money. The royalty was facing difficulties. King George III was politically weak and had periods of insanity. This brought the royalty under more control of the Parliament. George IV and William IV followed George III. But all this did not affect the EIC adversely, which was expanding its rule in India. The English captured all the arms and armaments from the Marathas. Elphinstone dispatched his officers and men to get hold of the cash, jewellery, diamonds etc. from the forts and other places. As some of the booty was to be distributed among the searching teams, the whole campaign was carried out with extraordinary zeal. How did people react to the change of the regime? Elphinstone informed the Calcutta office that people of prestige in Pune as well as in nearby Wai met him. He gave some money to the Brahmin scholars from both places and had a talk with the gentry. The gentry or the Brahmin scholars had no special reason to love the Peshwa whose state was always in turmoil, which affected everybody's life. In addition, Holkar, Scindia and Pindaries had ransacked Pune and the surrounding areas several times. There was no guarantee of life or property in the last days of the Peshwa. In a book on Pune published in Marathi in 1868, the author, Narayan Vishnu Joshi, writes that: "Bajirao had made the people hedonists and shameless, womanisers, foolish, insolent, conspirators unconscious of their own good, indolent and glutinous. Bravery, learning and alertness, all these were at a discount. Bajirao's regime was like a house totally dilapidated. In such circumstances Bajirao became a rake and had to flee". Historian T.S. Shejwalkar, analysing the failure of the Maratha rule, wrote that: "by the time of the rebellion in 1857, the English had been in India for about two centuries, and this was a long time to understand these foreigners. The Indians who were in politics could not know why the English were superior to them in many ways. Europeans had a mastery of skills, which brought them material prosperity. Our leaders were unaware of this and did not think of emulating them. Take the case of printing. The Portuguese brought it to India, but even a wise ruler like Akbar did not understand its potential and utility. Our people had lost the sense of curiosity. Marathas were all the while on aggressive campaigns and engaged in looting. There was widespread despondency and defeatism. English found this country very easy to conquer. In the last days of the Maratha rule, the Peshwa defied Shivaji's descendent who was the ruler at Satara; and the Sardars did not obey the Peshwa; and the ordinary troopers were rebellious. Everybody aspired to be a king; and so, who could owe any allegiance to the King? The Maratha empire was not popular. Marathas had no help from anybody when they built it; and they did not get any help from anybody in the last days of the Empire as well. No one had desired that the Marathas should build an empire and no one was sorry when it ended". Major General Sir William Sleeman was one of the military officers in the service of the Company. He had seen how Scindia and Holkar administered their territories. He found that 'there was no sense of patriotism under the Maratha rule. The rulers and the ruled had no affinity for each other. The rulers who had large armies could maintain them on loot. The army was not paid regularly and would change side at the higher bidding".[6]

The superiority of the Europeans was the outcome of the Industrial Revolution, and England was ahead of many other European nations. With the Industrial Revolution, new vistas of knowledge opened up and technological innovation helped in increasing production, which required new markets. To seek such markets the adventurous Dutch, French and English started going round the world. The English who came to India were the representatives of this new era. Malcolm, Metcalfe, Elphinstone, Strachey etc. were well read in history, philosophy and political science. They did not come to India as individual adventurers, but as officers of a commercial company. India had not experienced an industrial revolution, and the big Indian traders looked after their business without thinking of combining to form a company or even establish large warehouses or the factories as the French or the English did. They had no conception of a wholesale market. Both the French and the English had an army with modern arms. No ruler in India could match Elphinstone in his knowledge and efficiency, as they did not know anything about their own country; let alone the world. They were totally ignorant of physical sciences, which were flourishing in the West. Peshwa, Scindia, Holkar or Tipu and others were the last remnants of a decadent society, which was once at the height of civilisation. As the rulers and their Sardars were morally and materially bankrupt, they were dependent on the Pindaries who indulged in looting. This looted property was then sold by the traders, which alienated the common people. They found a new dispensation under the Company. It was not that there was no competition or even enmity among the officers or servants of the EIC. They also aspired for promotion, and if they did not succeed, they sulked. But nobody revolted against the Company and went over to the Peshwa, or Scindia or Tipu.

Vasudevshastri Khare, a historian, has pointed out that "an English doctor gave medicine to a daughter of the Mogul emperor, but he did not ask anything in return for himself, but requested a license for the East India Company in Calcatta. When Clive received some amount from Mirjaffer, he used it for the welfare of his troops and officers. On the contrary, after the battle of Kharda, Nizam Ali gave thirty thousand Rs. to Nana Phadanvis, who was a mediator. Nana kept the amount for himself". This does not mean that all the officials of the Company were above board. On the contrary, they amassed money, and took advantage of the rule of the Company to trade privately. The House of Commons impeached Clive and Hastings; but their selfishness and malpractices did not harm the interests of the Company. Acharya Javdekar, a political scientist in Maharashtra, had compared the practices of the sixteenth century English traders and those of different classes in India. He wrote that: "The traders of England even in sixteenth century moved to rein in the unlimited powers of the king. In India, Brahmins, warrior and trading classes could have captured power to save religion and their avocations. But even in the eighteenth century, these classes were not at all aware that there was some relation between the faith in religion and self-government. Traders, moneylenders etc. desired that their places of worship should be protected. But they were blissfully unaware that even this required self-government. They did not feel that they had to be in politics; and therefore, did not mind inviting foreigners. The Brahmins who were to protect the religion, were no way different. There were some Brahmin rulers, but they did not think it was their duty to organise all against the aggression of the foreigners. The warring classes as well as Brahmins were bereft of national awareness and pride".[7]

The Company was facing some revolts from the local people in some parts of the country. It could not be said that the behaviour of its army of both English and Indian soldiers was proper. At places, they were rapacious. Ballhatchet quotes a letter by one of the officers, Briggs, to Elphinstone. He wrote: "The enormities committed by the Europeans and natives in this town (Trimbak), on the day of their arrival here, exceed anything. The property, the very food and clothing, and the household gods were carried off, the temples polluted, and some go so far to say the women suffered the same abomination, but certain it is, they were stripped and lying naked in the streets. Col. MacDowell did all he could to restore the property to the inhabitants, and some men were taken up, and are to be punished, if found guilty, but the fact is that the detachment at the end of the campaign is perfectly wild and there is no discipline at all in it, among the Europeans particularly, and I am sorry to say that many of the officers are as notorious for their depredations as the men, and none seems to think it essential to maintain discipline by checking it....it is in vain for us to administer the government wisely, to endeavour to gain the hearts of the inhabitant by conciliatory measures, if our army is to be the bane, instead of the support of our operations. I shall request Colonel MacDowell to have the plunderers, the Europeans in particular, punished in the streets of the town of Trimbuk, and I shall recall the Brahmins from Nassuck and other places where they had gone and give a sum of money from 500 to 1000 Rupees on account of Government to enable them to make any ceremony they may choose, so as to do away by all means in my power the unfortunate impression which is likely to go abroad of our character".[8]

Elphinstone and his colleagues were not sure about the reaction of the populace after the fall of the Maratha rule. Robertson, one of the first collectors of Pune, was doubtful about this reaction. In letters to Elphinstone he wrote on 8 April and 12 December 1818: "The Maratha character is formed of great acuteness of understanding mixed up with the absurdities of the Hindu religion. They are less religious, however, and their manners are less subservient to their faith than several other races of Hindus. Though they respect their civil obligations and they have much tenacity of caste, yet they are not overwhelmed with conviction either that the former were framed from divine ordinances or that the latter and the whole system of their society has emanated from the deity himself. They made their religion subservient to their necessities and their spirit of conquests...but with all their experience, they acquired no extensive knowledge of the world. They know nothing even in their most splendid era of the theoretical speculations, and still less of the practical application of the laws of others of other countries. They were uninformed of whatever they had not witnessed or learnt in their own land. Justice was often obtained in former times. The character of man was then valued by others and prized by himself....but in the last reign nearly all sense of respectability was lost". Of Bajirao, Robertson wrote: "No language is too strong to describe the disgraceful conduct of the prince living in affluent and luxurious ease, gave not one moment to the consideration of the happiness of the people, but on the contrary set the most profligate example of depravity and corruption....the propensity of the inhabitants of Pune to talk politics and to discriminate speculations and wit on government concerns". He also found that people held a view point that "who rules Poona rules the world". Robertson said that the people had lost all sense of morality....liquor shops and gambling dens abounded in the city. He was shocked to see the greatest evil, which prevailed was the infidelity to the marriage bed...He says that the Maratha rulers had little time to devote to cultural and artistic side of life. The Maratha regime had, therefore, not much to contribute to arts, architecture and sculpture".[9]

Elphinstone thought that with the eclipse of the Peshwa, the Brahmins might have been disgruntled. So he distributed some money to the learned Brahmins in Pune, Wai, Nasik and so on. But he also took care to humour the Marathas. He, therefore, installed a descendent from the dynasty of Shivaji on the throne at Satara. Elphinstone hoisted the Bhosle flag after the capture of Satara. He gave two months to those who were in the service of the Peshwa to join the Company's service, failing which they were to lose their property. After a while, he installed Pratapsingh Bhosle on the throne with great pomp and ceremony, which impressed the people. He himself belonged to the aristocracy. So he had some affinity for the rajas and rulers and other landed gentry in India. He was much impressed by the personality and behaviour of Pratapsingh. Elphinstone, being a keen student of literature, became emotional at times. This can be seen from an entry in his diary on March 17, 1818. He noted: "I am lodged at the Poona Palace, and am now seated in the Peshwa's closet, where our first consultation about the proceedings took place; and I have been shutting the door, the closing of which on the Sait probably first led to all subsequent misunderstandings. The Peshwa's great hall is now my reception-room and the place where we used to meet below is a dinning-room. Poona, when approached, is unchanged in appearance; but the destruction of all our houses destroys every feeling of quiet and home, and the absence of Hindoo government occasions a void that alters the effect of everything. Our respect from the place has gone, and the change is melancholy. How much the natives feel it"![10] After the capture of the territory of the Peshwas, the Company received rupees fifty lakhs and early revenue of rupees thirty-one lakhs. At Nagpur, the Company's army repulsed the attack by Bhosle and defeated him. His throne was protected for some years; but afterwards under Lord Dalhousie it was abolished. In the Central India, some of the Holkar's Sardars rose against the English, but were similarly defeated; and the Company annexed the territory adjoining Holkar's domain. The Pindaries, who in large number were with Holkar, were also crushed.

In 1819, Elphinstone was transferred as governor of Bombay. At first he was not enthusiastic about moving to Bombay, as he did not like the climate. He thought that the company of traders, lawyers etc. would not be congenial. In Pune he could entertain, but in Bombay, he thought it would be beyond his means. He was also averse to attending functions and giving speeches. But after assuming office, he found the company of the citizens quite engaging. In a letter to his cousin he wrote that unlike Pune, the atmosphere in Bombay was much relaxed. He had nothing nice to say about the English in the city. Elphinstone was surprised to learn that most of the English in Bombay had no ear for music and had the habit of making speeches and not conversation. He did not like the long debates in the meetings of his advisory council. Elphinstone occupied the post of governor from November 1819 to November 1827. No other governor had such an impact on the life of not only Bombay but also Maharashtra. With his rich experience of the state and the rule of the Marathas, Elphinstone wrote a book, which showed his keen sense of observation and objectivity. One of the objectives in writing this history was to avoid the shortcomings in the Maratha regime. In the book Elphinstone had enumerated different castes in Maharashtra and their characteristics. He did not aim at fundamental changes in the whole structure but advocated moderation. He wrote that the agricultural community, which preferred stability and peace, was not opposed to a change in the regime. Elphinstone put an end to the auctioning of the posts of the mamlatdar, and started appointing them as any other government employees. He noted that justice should not be costly to the ordinary people. Under the Maratha rule there was no written criminal or civil law and punishment was accorded according to the rank of the castes. Elphinstone wrote that the justice should not be at the whims of the judge. There were more murders under the Maratha rule, but the dacoits were fewer in number compared to Bengal. Elphinstone appointed a committee to prepare a code of the criminal law, which came into operation from 1827. He also took some steps to prepare a code, which could be said to be the code of various Hindu laws. The notes, which he had made on the subject, demonstrate his studiousness. The practice of Sati was prevalent. Elphinstone took the help of the Shastries and tried to persuade widows not to immolate themselves on the pyres of their dead husbands. He also made provision to give monetary help to such widows.

REFERENCES

1. R.D. Choksey, A *History of the British Diplomacy at the Court of Peshwas (1786-1818)*, R.D. Choskey, Poona, 1976, pp. 93-94.
2. J.S. Cotton, *Mountstuart Elphinstone and the making of South-Western India,* Clarendon Press, Oxford, 1896, pp. 55-56.
3. T.N. Atre, *Gavgada*, Varada Books, Pune, 1989, pp. 62-63.
4. J.S. Cotton, *Mountstuart Elphinstone and the making of South-Western India,* Clarendon Press, Oxford, 1896, pp. 87-88.

5. R.D. Choksey, *Mountstuart Elphinstone, The Indian Years*, Popular Prakashan, Bombay, 1971, pp. 173-174.
6. T. S. Shejwalkar, *Nivadak Lekha Sangrah*, Mote, Mumbai, 1977, pp. 39, 41, 55, 193.
7. Jawdekar, *Adhunik Bharat*, Raghunath Ganesh Joshi, Pune, 1953, pp. 20-21.
8. Kenneth Ballhatchet, *Social Policy and Social Change in Western India*, OUP, London, 1957, pp. 27-28.
9. B.R. Sunthankar, *Nineteenth Century History of Maharashtra*, vol.1, Shubhada-Saraswat Prakashan, Pune, 1988, pp.16-17.
10. R.D. Choksey, *A History of the British Diplomacy at the Court of the Peshwas (1786-1818)*. R.D. Choksey, Poona, 1951, pp. 12.

Chapter Three

ENGLISH EDUCATION

Elphinstone had asked all district and other officers to collect and preserve old books, inscriptions and artifices. Information about various dialects was also collected. William Erskin was appointed to oversee the whole operation. Grant (Grant Duff James Cunningham), collector at Satara, who was interested in history, had regular exchanges with Elphinstone on various aspects of Maratha society and its history. Though he held that Hinduism was the main hurdle in the progress of society, and Christianity would bring in desirable improvement and progress, Elphinstone discouraged evangelical work by the missionaries. He wrote to the governor-general that this evangelical work was of no consequence, as missionaries converted lowly castes, who otherwise had no influence in the society. His emphasis was on the English education. Elphinstone did everything in his power to spread education. He established schools and prepared textbooks. He was aware that the spread of English education would generate English ideas and ideals, which might induce educated people to demand more and more rights eventually. When Briggs asked him what the books in his tent were for, Elphinstone replied that it was the way for the English to go back home. Elphinstone, Malcolm etc. were of the view that the English rule was based on a very weak foundation, and in the long run was not going to last. Elphinstone had written to Malcolm that like the Romans, the English should influence the people by their learning and culture, which would be abiding. After learning that a revolt in Barakpore, Bengal, was successfully put down, he wrote to Malcolm that he had believed that the Company's empire was like glass, but it proved to be that of iron; it should be like steel. However, he cautioned that this steel in the hands of weak rulers would do much harm. He conveyed to the directors of the EIC that the ordinary people could not benefit from the new laws, as they were illiterate. He attributed their indebtedness and poor health to a lack of education. The directors saw the point, and sanctioned more outlay for education. Elphinstone also wrote to the directors that the local people should be provided with an opportunity to get higher education. This would enable them to enter into government service and take up the responsibility of administration. In 1823 he prepared a report on education. He was keen to spread scientific knowledge. For all these efforts the people of Maharashtra remained ever grateful to him, and after his retirement a school and a college were established as a memorial to him.

It was, of course, not all milk and honey under the regime of Elphinstone. There were minor uprisings in some parts of the presidency, especially in Kittur, Sindh and Kutch. Elphinstone, in a letter to his friend Metcalf, expressed distress and anxiety. He also informed him how the Raja of Kolhapur had tried to take advantage of the unrest created in Kittur area. Even Maharashtra was not peaceful. From 1823 to 1826 one Umaji Naik raised a banner of revolt against the Company's rule. He belonged to a predatory tribe known as Ramoshi, which had origins in Telangana and migrated to Maharashtra. This tribe then settled mostly in Satara and Pune districts. They had been given land, and were recruited in the Maratha army. The tribe could not reconcile itself to British rule and started a parallel administration in some parts of Satara and Pune districts. Umaji had his camps in the forest areas, and started extracting money. He and his people were marauders and indulged in violence. Vast territories from Ratnagiri to Khandesh used to be terrorised and plundered by Umaji's tribe. By distributing some of his booty among the village poor, he could enlist their support. The Company's officers were constantly hounding him, and ultimately he entered into an agreement, which gave him some land; and his people were employed as police. But Umaji went back on his word and renewed his raids. Ultimately Umaji was captured in 1830 and was hanged.[1]

After his retirement several offers were made to Elphinstone by the British government including the post of governor-general in India or Canada; but he declined. He did not want to enter an active political life. He wanted to write a detailed article on the relations between the Company and the Indian states. This was revealed by his extensive notes, which his biographer, Colebrook, found after his death. In retirement he was keeping himself abreast with the happenings in India and was distressed by the treatment meted out to Pratapsingh of Satara and was opposed to abolition of various states on one pretext or the other. In a letter to Colebrook, Elphinstone pointed out that the Raja of Satara was not an ordinary chief of a state, but a sovereign whose title was accepted by the Company in an agreement signed with him. In 1895 when Lord Sandhurst was sworn in as the governor of Bombay, he pledged that he would follow in the footsteps of Elphinstone. Lokmanya Tilak, referring to this, wrote in 'Kesari' of March 12, 1895, that "after the end of the Maratha rule, the East India Company was fortunate enough to have the services of very able and farseeing statesmen and that was why Company's rule flourished. Among them Elphinstone was unique.

Elphinstone knew the mind of the people, and administered the state without giving offence to them. He knew how to govern when the rulers were in advance state of progress and the ruled were partially progressed". Tilak concluded by saying that Elphinstone would be remembered so long as his way of administering the state would be remembered by the people.

Officers of the Company, like Elphinstone, were keen to bring about social and economic changes steadily, but they thought it prudent to keep the people and especially the upper classes on their side. Besides, they also thought that the spread of education would bring in rapid and all round change in the Indian society. Therefore, their efforts were concentrated on opening up schools and colleges. With this the question arose about the medium of instruction. Warren Hastings thought it wiser to continue with the traditional Indian system of education, while others insisted that Western one should replace it. Ultimately, the latter won. However, it is wrong to conclude that it was only the Company's officers like Macaulay who imposed the Western system of education and the study of English. Raja Ram Mohan Roy and people like him had sent a memorandum to the government, which said that it was necessary to impart knowledge of chemistry, physics and other natural sciences. They maintained that traditional education would not bring India into the modern age. Of course, some leaders also feared that with Western education, the new generation would be converted and brought under the influence of Christianity. R.C. Majumdar, a historian, has narrated how English education was spread in Bengal much before other parts of India. He says that in 1800 an English school was started. In subsequent seventeen years, English education was spread in different parts of Bengal. The Hindu College was started in Calcutta after 1817 and there were some schools imparting English education. In Bombay, the Native Education Society was established in 1815, which then spread itself in Bombay, Thane and Bhadoch. In 1846 the Grant Medical College was started in Bombay. In Bombay and Calcutta, Christian missionaries participated in establishing schools and colleges, but the local population also took an initiative. In Madras and Punjab however, it was the missionaries, who had a leading role. In Calcutta, Vaidyanath Mukherjee, a leading citizen, met the then chief justice of the High Court, Sir Hyde East, in May 1816, and requested him to take a lead in opening the English schools. A public meeting was then called, which was attended by *shastries* and pundits, and passed a resolution demanding the establishment of schools and colleges to teach English and Western knowledge. By 1835 there were twenty-five schools and more than ten thousand students.

Bengali newspapers and periodicals were publishing articles stressing the importance of the English education. In a lucid exposition of liberal ideas Raja Ram Mohan Roy wrote to the governor-general in December 1823, pointing out that the liberal ideas lay at the root of this demand for English education.

The letter said: "This seminary (similar in character to those which existed in Europe before the time of Lord Bacon) can only be expected to lead the mind of the youth with grammatical niceties and metaphysical distinctions of little or no practical use to the possessors or to the society. The pupils will acquire what was known two thousand years ago with the addition of vain and empty subtleties since then produced by speculative men, such as is already commonly taught in all parts of India...

But as the improvement of the native population of the subject is the object of the Government, it will consequently promote a more liberal and enlightened system of instruction, embracing Mathematics, Natural Philosophy, Chemistry, Anatomy, with other useful sciences, which may be accomplished with the sums proposed by employing a few gentlemen of talent and learning, educated in Europe and providing a college furnished with necessary books, instruments and other apparatus."[2] Majumdar has quoted an extract from a Calcutta periodical, 'Sudharak', which said that, "only Brahmins could learn Sanskrit and for others it was of no use. The government expenditure on Sanskrit schools was nothing but waste". The periodical told the government that it was their duty to bring the people out of the darkness of ignorance and equip them with such knowledge, which would enable them to discharge their duties to the government and the public.

India was in transition, and like any transitional period, it was also turbulent. It also saw that indebtedness was on the increase in many parts of the country. In 1823, Coats, a Bombay government officer, had surveyed Loni, a village near Pune. He found that out of eighty-four families in the village, seventy-nine were in debt. They had taken loans from the six merchants who were local residents and as they had to stay in the same village as their debtors, they were not so harsh. But under the new regime, there was no bar on the outsiders to lend money. They started charging an interest rate of twenty-five to thirty per cent. In this situation, litigation increased considerably. Ravindra Kumar, a historian, had noted that in Ahmednagar district alone, the number of cases in the court had gone up from 2,930 to 5,900. The Company was slow in deciding the land policy in the Adivasi areas. So the local officials were free to impose levy according to their whims. In Bengal, Bihar and Orissa there was a large Adivasi population, whose leaders claimed occult power and spread the belief that there was an ideal regime of the aboriginals in the remote past, which they were reviving. In Kerala, there were thirty-six riots between the Nambudri Brahmins and the Mopalas from 1838 to 1854. The Nambudris were landowners and the Mopalas the tenants. Some Nambudris wanted to resume their land, which triggered off the riots. In 1849, one cleric, Sayyad Fazal, started organising Muslims on the basis of religion, making the struggle both economic and religious. In U.P., since 1835, a large number of Rajputs lost their lands to Brahmins, Kayasthas etc. The Rajputs took this as demeaning their status and loss of face. The same Rajputs in 1857 joined the revolt against the Company.

In 1844, the tax on salt was increased from half a rupee to one. The enraged people staged demonstrations, and for three days stopped all trade and other activities in Surat. Though the government of Bombay abolished some excise duties, it did not scale down the tax on salt. The Governor of Bombay sent a report on the whole affair to the Secretary of State and a copy to the Governor-General. In conclusion he said: "This affair affords an instance of what has been so often remarked, namely, that although the people are for the most part well disposed and law abiding, and although excellence of our rule is duly appreciated by them, still events occasionally happen...which show that authority must be sustained by the presence of moral and material force...and which should serve as a warning to us accordingly".[3] To the 'Bombay Times', postponement of the tax increase was illegal, but 'Bombay Courier' asked that if the recovery of the tax had resulted in the loss of human lives, then was it not illegal?

With the acquisition of more and more territory, officers of the Company became confident and in many cases, arrogant and intolerant. Though people like Elphinstone, Munro, Metcalfe, etc. believed in their superiority over the Indians, they did not insult and humiliate them. They believed that it was their duty to uplift the local people. They were also under the influence of the ideas and ideologies then current in England and Europe. When Galileo was exploring the universe in the seventeenth century, Descartes was emphasising that human beings should be guided by intellect and not by emotion. This gave rise to agnosticism, rationalism and materialism. There was another intellectual, whose ideology widely influenced the educated class. He was Jeremy Bentham, a rationalist, who analyzed various ideas, principles and institutions. He called for political reforms. He said that though the men in power were not generally favourable to bring in political reforms, the reforms were unavoidable. However, Bentham was for a gradual change and not for revolution. That is why he did not join those in England who supported the French Revolution. He was for orderly progress. Bentham's slogan was "the greatest good of the greatest number". He believed that literate persons were competent enough to elect their leaders and rulers, and he had no objection to widen the franchise. According to Bentham, some people were endowed with exceptional qualities and even if they occupied seats of power, their role was that of a teacher. Bentham's ideology was known as Utilitarianism. The other ideology was that of Evangelism. Both of these were individualistic and wanted to liberate the people from the clutches of tradition, ignorance and also from the landlords. The only difference between the Utilitarians and Evangelicals was that the former believed that the people make the law, while the latter believed that laws were made by God. Lord Bentinck, the Governor-General, was Utilitarian, and thought it was the duty of the English officers to bring new knowledge to the people of India and thereby lead them to the civilisation. James Mill was another intellectual whose thoughts influenced not only many Englishmen but also Indian leaders like Dadabhai Naoroji, Ranade, Tilak, Surendranath Banerjea, Gokhale, etc. According to Mill, self-interest was the binding force between the rulers and ruled who require security and stability. His emphasis was on the liberty of the individual and the necessity of control on the political power. But unlike Bentham, he did not favour republican ideology, and wanted long period of constitutional monarchy. Elected representatives, according to Mill, were the watchdogs of the interests of the people; but they should also be under constant watch and only newspapers and institutions could do this. Bentham advocated freedom to the colonies, while James Mill held a view that the colonies were the beehives of corruption in the hands of the landed and feudal gentry, and advocated the continuation of the EIC's rule in India. Our first generation of leaders were influenced by the thoughts of James Mill and almost ignored his disparaging writings against the Indian civilisation and his lack of support for the representative government for Indians.

Some officials like Shore, Grant etc. were of the firm view that the Hindu religion must be contained, and Christianity must be spread in India. They thought that India would not progress unless this transformation took place. They were the followers of Wilberforce, whose sect was known after the place, Clapham, where he stayed. This sect believed that Christianity brought Europe out of the darkness of ignorance; and so science flourished and the Western countries achieved moral and material superiority. By the end of the nineteenth century, this ideology influenced some of those who were in power in India, and they allowed Christian missionaries to work and proselyte. Some missionaries and industrialists believed that it was advantageous to increase trade with India and the EIC should not waste its energy in conquering more and more territory. Ultimately, it was the Utilitarians who prevailed in India by the time the Company's rule stabilised. The idea that the English were superior and hence, qualified to govern, was akin to imperialism, and it was helpful for the protection of the Empire. The British Empire differed from the previous ones in that England's flag or the Bible did not precede the English rule.

The nineteenth century saw the advent of radical ideas and upheavals in Europe. This had cautioned the rulers of England and also those in India. Leaders like Burke and Pitt considered jacobinism, which inspired the French Revolution, dangerous. They were not opposed to reforms *per se*, but wanted them to be implemented gradually and with careful thought. They were the representatives of the new class of bankers, self-employed, traders and industrialists. This class advocated gradual and orderly reforms in political, social and economic fields. This gave rise to various organisations, which had the support of the workers. It was the Tories who had fought with Napoleon in Europe; and it became difficult for that party to oppose the demand for economic freedom to the people in England. The party made its economic policy flexible, which could satisfy the aspirations of the workers and new class of city dwellers. It was, therefore, obvious that the ideas propounded by Bentham, Mill, Chadwick and others should guide the new class. Though Mill and others advocated government intervention in matters social, political and economic, generally they were the supporters of free trade. England was enjoying political stability and economic prosperity. Leaders of England were confident that they had found the key to happiness in the doctrine of the greatest good of the greatest number. Richard Cobden was one of the prominent exponents of the free trade, which would protect civilisation. He used to say that every bale of cloth, which left the English port, was the conveyer of new ideas and knowledge; and anyone who goes back to his native land after visiting English factories, becomes the propagator of freedom, peace and goodwill. It was quite obvious that free trade was profitable to England. As Marx said, the ruling philosophy of any time is the philosophy of the ruling class.

Though England's industry and trade were at a peak, the life of workers and ordinary people was miserable. Slums sprang up in the vicinity of factories, and, in fact, there were two Englands as described by Disraeli. This was also the subject of the novels by Charles Dickens, which brought in some social legislation. People in general were living in better conditions compared to their forefathers, because of the new avenues of employment. But they were seeing prosperity all around them and were asking themselves why they remained poor and could not be rich. Robert Owen was a son of a shop-owner. He eventually started a cotton mill. Owen was the first to give more wage and benefits to his workers, who also showed profits. John Stuart Mill, who was the son of James Mill, was advocating the spread of education and organisation of labour. The new middle class organised a march on parliament making demands not only for itself but for all the working people. This was the Chartist movement. In 1849 when Europe saw great upheaval, which was revolutionary, the Chartist movement was on the ebb in England. This extra-parliamentary movement did not weaken the parliament, but helped in strengthening it.

The EIC's increasing trade and its conquests were bringing profits to some classes in England, however, on the whole, poor people not only in England but all over the empire were eking out a miserable living. Spencer Walpole, a historian, had described this misery with great details. According to him, between 1816 and 1833 the poor became poorer; but compared to the period between 1837 and 1842 it was less. In 1839, 11,39,000 people were on dole, but in 1842 it went up to 14,29,000. When those who had some basic wage suffered, one can imagine how miserable were those who had low wages. More than one tenth of the population of Manchester and Liverpool was shelterless; the condition of those in Glasgow was worse. Manchester and many other cities had too many slums, and because of open sewages, the stench used to be unbearable; heaps of garbage were found everywhere and the streets were poorly lit. In 1840 there were 10,000 coffins in the basement of a church in the Lincoln Inn area. Many of the old coffins used to be thrown in the gutters. Small children were working in mines, where safety was not assured. Children were deprived of education and human life was very cheap. This is highlighted in a poem:

> Child, is thy father dead?
> Father is gone
> Why did they tax his bread?
> God's will be done...
> Mother has sold her bed.
> Better to die than wed,
> Where she shall lay her head?
> Home she has none.[4]

Compared to European society, the characteristics of the English people were different. Marxist historian, Eric Hobsbawm, has characterised the period between 1789 and 1848 as the 'age of revolution'. He points out that: "A bad harvest, such as in 1789, 1795, 1817, 1832, 1847, still brought actual famine, even without the intervention of additional catastrophes such as the competition of the British cotton good, which destroyed the foundation of the Silesian industry. After the ruined crop of 1813 in Lombardi, many kept alive only by eating manure and hay, bread made from the leaves of bean plants and wild berries". There were many deaths in Switzerland. In East and West Prussia people had to live on potatoes. Western Europe saw thousands starving, and in the cities people were restive and not prepared to suffer without raising their voice. John Bright had described how in Rochdale, 2000 women and girls passed through the streets singing hymns. It was a very singular and striking spectacle-approaching the sublime—they are dreadfully hungry....a loaf is devoured with greediness indescribable and if the bread is covered with mud, it is eagerly devoured". With technological improvement or the decrease in demand for goods, labour was losing jobs. As the purchasing power was decreasing, there were several uprisings.[5]

In Western Europe many youth organisations sprang up and started several movements. In France between 1846 and 1847 crops failed, the prices of grains skyrocketed, and with it, riots broke out. In 1848 with the ascent of Louis Bonaparte thousands were disfranchised and many more were jailed. This brought people out on the streets. People were leaderless and the revolt did not strengthen democracy but monarchy. A revolt in Paris inspired Belgium to throw the yoke of the Dutch; and the Poles rose against the Russians. Because of the pressure from England and France, the Dutch had to free Belgium, but the Poles were not so fortunate.

Many among the Indian nationalist leaders were under the influence of the ideas of Mazzini, an Italian leader. We find Surendranath Banerjea writing a biography of Mazzini; and later on, Vinayak Damodar Savarkar also wrote one in Marathi. Italy was not a united country even in the latter part of the nineteenth century. Mazzini, Garibaldi and Cavour fought to unite their country. All three leaders not only differed, but were opposed to each other. However, in the long run their politics was complementary, and Italy became united in 1870. Dragoniti was one of those leaders, who strove not only to unite Italy, but to make it a republic. Gladstone wrote him a letter in 1854, which throws light on his political philosophy. Gladstone wrote that: "It was understandable that the Italians were wary of the chaotic conditions prevailing in some states and wanted their country to be united. English people also want them to be united and Italy to become republic. But Italy would not achieve its goal by resorting to violence and war. Political education of the people must receive priority".[6] Neighbouring Austria and Hungary were also witnessing turmoil and were under reactionary regimes. Germany was also not a united country. It became so after 1848 under Bismarck, who encouraged industries and also brought in some welfare measures.

When Europe was in turmoil, Karl Marx was asked by the Communist League of England to draft a manifesto. He did it. That is the famous Communist Manifesto. At the outset, Marx warned that a spectre of Communism was haunting Europe. The manifesto predicted that capitalism would be destroyed under its own contradictions, giving rise to the dictatorship of the workers. However, Marx believed that countries like England and United States of America would have parliamentary democracy. However European countries did not come under the dictatorship of the proletariat. England did not witness a revolutionary upheaval. There the franchise was widened and a firm basis was laid for the parliamentary democracy. Not 'revolution', but 'progress' was the watchword in the nineteenth century England. Hobsbawm has explained why 1848 uprisings failed in various countries of Europe, and workers could not come to power. "Eighteen-forty-eight uprising in various countries failed because it turned out that the decisive confrontation was not that between the old regime and the 'united forces of progress', but between 'order' and 'social revolution'. Its crucial confrontation was not that of Paris in February, but that of Paris in June, when the workers maneuvred into isolated insurrection were defeated and massacred. They fought and died hard. About 1500 fell in the street—fighting—some two-thirds of them on the government side. It is characteristic of the ferocity of the hatred of the rich for the poor that some three thousand were slaughtered after defeat, while another twelve thousand were arrested mostly to be deported to Algerian labour camps".[7]

Jonathan Parry, a historian, has described this new change and trend. He says, "by 1848 the rule of the East India Company had a firm base. But what was the political and economic condition in England? Between 1816 and 1822 ministries were unstable. Economic condition was not satisfactory and the general feeling among the people was that the government was lavish in spending their money and it was corrupt. This changed by 1822. Philanthropic societies anxious to spread Christianity mushroomed, seeking to repeat the military victory over the anti-Christ in all corners of the earth, and at home. By 1817, the Bible societies had 236 auxiliary branches and had spent 540,000 pounds in producing and circulating 1. 8 million volumes of scriptures in 66 different languages.—India was opened to missionary activity in 1813.—The two developments of 1830 intensified propertied anxiety for social stability. One was rising levels of lower-class radical activity. The Birmingham Political Union, founded in 1829, called for parliamentary reform as a means of attacking the tight currency policy of the 1820's, which is blamed for the depression.—A great debate about how best to shape individual character was under way. From the early 1850's economic progress seemed to validate the liberal thinking".[8]

When Europe was witnessing momentous events, some Indians who had received English education, came forward in India to bring in reforms in political, social, economic and religious fields. Raja Ram Mohan Roy started Brahmo Samaj, which stood for monotheism. Hindu College in Calcutta created an awakening among its students. Derozio, who was one of the professors in the college, took the initiative in inculcating the spirit of freedom. The French Revolution inspired students in Calcutta. Ram Mohan Roy was also under its spell. So a public meeting was held on December 10, 1830 in its celebration. Before this, a memorandum on behalf of the Calcatta citizens was addressed to the then Supreme Court, appealing for redress against the government restrictions on newspapers. This memorandum was signed by Dwarkanath Tagore, Chandrakant Tagore, Harchandra Ghose etc. and drafted by Ram Mohan Roy. It demanded those rights, which were enjoyed by the people of England. It cautioned the government that as restrictions on newspapers were imposed even though freedom was not abused, they might create dissatisfaction against it. Ram Mohan Roy discontinued the publication of his periodical 'Sambad Kaumudi' as a mark of protest. He also drafted another memorandum in 1827 to the government against its rule prohibiting Hindu and Muslim jurors to hear cases against European defendants. Ram Mohan Roy, who had been to England, made several efforts to make the English people aware of the conditions in India. One of his ideas was to ask the English to invest whatever they earned in India and establish colonies. He had the support of people like Dwarkanath Tagore, but students of Hindu College strongly opposed this move. According to them it was harmful to ask the English to colonise and thereby become zamindars. One of the issues of controversy was how much trust should be placed on the goodwill of the English.

R.C. Majumdar has written extensively about Bang Bhasa Pracharika Sabha, an institution established in 1830. It decided not to discuss the administration of the government and also religious subjects. From 1837 to 1843, Bengal saw two more organisations; one was the Landholders' Organisation and the other was Bengal British India Association. However, they did not attract much attention. But in 1851, the British India Association was started in Calcutta, which decided to have an all-India view and not confine itself to Bengal. Nevertheless, the Calcutta branch was considered as that of landlords and hence, the Madras branch thought it imperative to have a separate existence. In July1852 the Madras Native Association was formed. Both the Calcutta and Madras associations demanded, among others, more share in the higher government services. The petition sent by the Madras Association to the British parliament complained against the heavy taxes imposed by the Company and harassment by its officials. It also said that the system of justice adopted by the Company was dilatory and expensive. The association asked for some sort of local self-government, and more irrigation and bridges. The Calcutta association was divided, as one faction questioned the other on its reliance on the goodwill of the British; while in Madras, the social reforms became the bone of contention. Some members of the association had no objection to government intervention in social matters; while others thought it prudent for people themselves to initiate social reforms, which gave rise to another organisation, Hindu Liberal Institution. This organisation had a programme for female education and widow remarriages. The Madras Native Association continued with its work of critical appraisal of the government administration. It used to send petitions directly to the British parliament.

In Mumbai and Maharashtra, the English educated generation had stalwarts like Nana Shankar Seth, Dr. Bhau Daji Lad, Dadoba Pandurang, Gopal Hari Deshmukh, alias Lokhitwadi, Dadabhai Naoroji, Dr. Ramkrishna Bhandarkar, T.K. Telang, M.G. Ranade amongst other. Elphinstone thought that some persons from the landed gentry would come forward and provide leadership. But that did not happen. Some of them helped some educational institutes, but then they faded away. Initially, Nana Shankar Seth, Gokuldas Tejpal, Mangaldas Nathubhai, who were from the trading community of Mumbai, took the lead and petitioned the governor against the missionaries, whom they charged with proselytising the Hindus. Many English merchants were settled in Mumbai and they as well as the Indian merchants had some common problems, which they thought could get relief by united efforts. In 1836, a Chamber of Commerce was established, in which there were fifteen European and ten Indian members. The Chamber demanded the nomination of Justices of Peace, which was acceded to. This was the precursor of the Mumbai Municipality. The year 1838 saw the advent of newspapers like *Bombay Times*, *Journal of Commerce*, *The Bombay Gazette* and

Bombay Courier. At the same time people like Jamshetji Jeejeebhai and Nana Shankar Seth petitioned the British parliament and suggested that it must have at least one Indian as a member. In Bengal landlords had taken a lead and formed an association, while in Mumbai traders and merchants like Jeejeebhai and Nana Shankar Seth joined hands with the newly educated individuals.

Nana Shankar Seth was born in 1803. After the end of the Peshwa rule, Nana was of help to the Company in the fields of education, public health etc. To any institute of public interest like University, railway etc., Nana always came forward to lend a helping hand. Dadoba Pandurang and Balshastri Jambhekar devoted themselves to social reforms. Dadabhai Naoroji and Karsetji Nasarwanji Kama took the lead for social reforms in the Parsi community. They started a school for girls. Schools for Maharashtrians and Gujaratis also started at the same time. Balshastri Jambhekar, through his periodicals, 'Darpan' and 'Digdarshan' was helping social reforms and education. Majumdar says that next to Bengal the growth of political consciousness was more clearly manifest in Bombay than in any other part of India. He even says that the people of Maharashtra were more national-minded than political thinkers of Bengal because of the historical background of Maharashtra. Majumdar then quotes from some articles by Bhaskar Pandurang Tarkhadkar in the 'Bombay Gazette' in 1841. Tarkhadkar wrote: "If I were to give you (the British) credit for your having saved us from the Pindaries and Ramoshis, your trading system stands in the way which has, indeed, more effectually emptied our purses in a few years than the predatory excursions of these tribes could do in some five or six hundred years. In short it must be acknowledged that your progress in cunning and craftiness has kept pace with your advancement in knowledge and wisdom....You not only withhold from us high appointments, but you would not permit us to have a voice in your administration of our country, which latter circumstance weighs heavily upon us. Your Law Commission, composed of a few individuals, who know little or nothing of India, have absolute power to construct regulations and laws for our Government".[9] Bhau Daji Lad, who was born in Goa in 1822 and came to Mumbai, was another such person who was highly critical of the Company's regime. He was the first medical graduate of Bombay. He helped the poor in many ways and was associated with various institutions. Jamshetji Jeejeebhai started the first public dispensary and eventually a medical college. Vishwanath Narayan Mandlik was another person who was prominent in the public life of Mumbai. He was a successful lawyer and was conversant with revenue codes and manuals. As a member of the Bombay Legislative Council, he made his mark as a studious and forthright speaker.

This newly educated generation had studied the implication of the French Revolution as well as the upheavals in Europe in 1848. It was aware of the happenings in India of the recent past and prevailing situation; and charted its path with caution. It is noteworthy that Lokhitwadi should write about representative government, but his approach was cautious. Writing in *Shatapatre* on April 1, 1849 he said that after the Indian people get educated and get wise, they would politely ask the government for a parliament on the model of Britain. They would after some time ask for more power and a share in the administration. They would then demand the governorships, and after they get experience and stop taking bribes, they would be able to get self-government. The British would have to be content with trading facilities. But if they transgress the limits and resort to unpopular measures, then whatever happened in America would be repeated here. Our people would then ask the British to leave and hand over the full charge of the country.

In a meeting of the association, Bhau Daji said that India had to bear the great burden of the Company's administration. The annual expenditure on the Directors' Board in London was Pnds.13,000. The board was controlled by another committee, which spends another Pnds.250,000. The expenditure of the Government of India was Pnds.500,000. Even then, education, irrigation, public health, communication were all neglected. If this state of affairs were to be improved, so as to benefit the people, the only way was to include educated Indians in the administration. Some association members objected to this speech. Though the members were divided between the merchants and the educated, the petition sent by the Bombay Association to the British parliament in 1852 was more radical than those by the Calcutta and Madras associations. The petition was written by Bhau Daji and accepted by the association. The Bombay petition made some other points. It said that the EIC was initially a trading company, but eventually it entered into politics. The Company should have obtained the consent of the Indian people and so conducted itself as to benefit the local people. However, the Company's administration was authoritarian. Therefore, a committee responsible to the parliament must be appointed with such members, who had experience of the Indian administration and were sympathetic to India. The petition also demanded some control on the powers of the governor-general. It complained that inexperienced Englishmen were appointed to higher posts, but the legitimate claims of the experienced Indians were neglected. The Bombay Association was not happy with the choice of the people, who were selected to depose before a committee to go into the laws and other matters pertaining to India. It had pointed out that some Englishmen were critical of the way the administration of India was carried on; but these gentlemen were not invited to depose.

Some English officers of the Company serving in India as well as some members of the British Parliament like Sir Charles Wood, John Bright were sympathetic towards India, whose ranks increased later. Sir Charles Wood was for some time a chairman of the controlling board of the EIC. In this capacity he made English as the medium of instruction in India, but at the same time issued orders to give adequate importance to the local languages. In 1853 John Bright made an important speech in parliament saying that though both political parties regard themselves as the trustees of India, the EIC rules as if India was a green pasture, which could be safely exploited. The parliament had not enough control on the Company. Bright lamented that there was neither consistency nor certainty in the Indian policy. He was critical of the poor communication and irrigation facilities, adding that the system of justice was costly and time consuming. The administration was not efficient in dealing with the grievances of the people. The efficient among the local people were kept away from the higher posts and there was injustice in the appointments and promotions. While tax on salt was heavy, the revenue from opium was uncertain. Bright appealed to the members of parliament and the British government that England had a golden opportunity to serve the people of India; and by imparting English education, bring them into the modern world. They would then regard the English not as conquerors but benefactors.

Another cause of discontent was the policy of annexation of the Indian states, pursued by Dalhousie with great zeal and speed. Sir Charles Wood, who was the chairman of the Board of Control of the Company, was not opposed to the annexation of the states, but wanted to slow down the pace. He would have liked to have more and more Indian territories under the Company's rule, which would supply cotton to the mills in Manchester. The then ministry in power in England was very much under the influence of the Manchester mills. R.J. Moore, a historian, has pointed out that cotton mill-owners as well as those English industrialists and traders who had dealings with India were insisting on the speedy building of roads and railways, as they were keen to increase their trade. John Bright, who was sympathetic towards India, came from Manchester, and as he also wanted to guard the interests of the mills, he was an advocate of railways and roads. His letters make his intent clear. In December 1853, Wood wrote to the prime minister George Hamilton Gordon, earl of Aberdeen, that the Raja of Nagpur, "the finest cotton district in all India" died without leaving an heir. Wood assured the prime minister that there was "nobody who on the most exaggerated view of the case (could) set up a pretence of a claim" to the succession. He wrote, in February 1854, "I would omit no fair opportunity of getting rid of these territories which separate our districts....Nagpore and the frontiers of the Nizam's territories which we occupy give us I think pretty nearly an uninterrupted line from Calcatta to Bombay". In December Wood wrote to Dalhousie, "I hope that you will have reported on railroads before I have to bring in my bill. I am very anxious to push the railroad from Bombay into the cotton districts, if I know which is really the best line. This is in truth the only thing that the Manchester people care for, and if I can satisfy them that these points will not be neglected, I hope to keep them all in good humour. They are however a powerful body in the House of Commons, and besides this I think they are right in their object; it would be a great point to render ourselves somewhat independent of United States' cotton".[10]

When, in many parts, India was seething with discontent because of drought and other hardships, the princely states were uncertain of their future because of the policy of annexation by Dalhousie. The annexation of Avadh was the proverbial last straw. The Company's defence was that the administration of the Nawab of Avadh was in disarray and he was deeply in debt. But the Nawab was in debt for a considerable time and his administration was never in good shape. So the Company's defence of its measure was unconvincing. Vishwanath Narayan Mandlik had quoted from an article written by John Kepler, editor of 'Ceylone Examiner', criticising the policy of annexation. He warned that the government would lose the confidence of the people and it would not have credibility. But the government was in no mood for such an advice. Indeed, as the Company's policy of diarchy had concentrated all the powers in its hands and the chiefs of the states were left with no responsibility, most of the chiefs turned idlers and addicts. The Nawab of Avadh was no exception. Even then, the Resident of Avadh gave a draft of a letter of resignation to be signed by the Nawab on February 4, 1856. But the Nawab refused. The Resident himself signed it and asked the Company to take over Avadh. Some years earlier, the Nawab's ancestors had helped the Company to take possession of the state; now the Company deprived the Nawab of his possession and annexed the state. Sir John Kaye, a military historian, wrote that the behaviour of officers of the Company was atrocious. They ransacked and looted the palaces, taking away the jewellery and other valuables. The Nawab was humiliated and the Company's reputation was in the mud. As the chiefs of states were dissatisfied with the Company, and different parts of the country witnessed riots of the peasants due to penury, the soldiers from some of the military units were seething with discontent. Indian soldiers were in far greater numbers in the Indian army than the British soldiers and officers. The job of a soldier could be had for the consideration of money. The new recruit, thus, had nothing on his hand for the first few months. The salary was very low and there was discrepancy in the emoluments between Indian and British soldiers. When Company took over Sindh, the Bengal army was ordered to proceed, but the soldiers refused the orders, as they said it was a foreign country and their religion prohibited them from travelling to foreign lands. Likewise, they also refused to go to Burma. Soldiers of Barakpore and Vellore revolted because of religious reasons. Way back in 1842 soldiers in Sholapur, Sikanderabad, Cota, Sagar and some other places had refused the orders, as their demand for increased allowance was not conceded.

In such a surcharged atmosphere, a rumour that the cartridges used in the army were greased by the fat of the cow and that of the pig, spread like wild fire. This enraged the Hindus and Muslims in the army and they rose in revolt on May 10, 1857. At the same time, some state chiefs proclaimed Bahadurshah Zafar, the last Delhi emperor, as their leader and they joined the revolt. When the Rani of Jhansi's demand for adoption was rejected, she joined hands with the rebels. The rebellion was led by Nanasaheb Peshwa, Tatya Tope, Rani of Jhansi, Amanulla, Kunwar Singh and others. The rebellion was widespread in the north, but southern and western India were comparatively undisturbed.

In Maharashtra, Rango Bapuji of Satara was preparing for revolt since December 1856. His plan was to arrest all Englishmen from Satara and Mahabaleshwar and loot the government treasury and proclaim Shahu, the adopted son of Pratapsingh Bhosale of Satara, as king. He visited Kolhapur, Belgaum etc. and planned to raise an army of two thousand. But the company officials were on the lookout and they arrested one of the leaders of the revolt, Mansingh, who was hanged on June 12, 1857. By September 7, another seventeen met with the same fate. Rango Bapuji was among them. In Kolhapur about two hundred soldiers revolted and looted the treasury. But with the help of the Kolhapur maharaja, who was with the Company, the rebels were overpowered. The government of Bombay informed the Calcutta government about this incident and said that the chiefs in the Deccan supported the Company. But Sir Le Grand Jacob, who was sent to Kolhapur, reported that dissatisfaction was widespread. Jacob's notes reveal that the brother of the Kolhapur raja was actively involved in the rebellion. He had established contact with Nanasaheb Peshwa and leaders in Gwalior. There was another revolt in December in Kolhapur but was suppressed in two days. Several rebels were shot. Sir John Kaye, who wrote a history of the revolt, has said that the revolt in the Deccan, "did not come out of the greased cartridges but of the Satara lapse".[11]

The Company was successful in suppressing the revolt. There was a display of individual bravery, and both sides displayed unusual cruelty. The Company had the advantage of unified command, and was equipped with modern arms. It could also use telegraph, which was an effective innovation. V.K. Rajwade, a historian, has said: "this conflict was between the mendicants who joined hands with the irrational Hindu and Muslim leaders making common cause with the soldiers of Bengal. It was also a conflict between the theoretical philosophy and the well-oiled machine. Hindu and Muslim leaders were the advocates of the former, while Western leaders represented the latter. When all this was going on, the elite and the common people in the Punjab, Karnatak, etc. were lookers on, and when they saw who was winning, they joined them. For a long time a class of upstart and semi-literate was created, comprising that of the underlings of the foreigners, who had in its dictionary no words such as patriotism or self rule".[12] Rajwade also said that some state chiefs and kings helped the Company. Sarvajanik

Sabha's journal in 1879 also made the same point. The Government of India then proposed to reduce the army with the Indian states. The Sabha's journal, criticising the move, referred to a book by Colonel McNeal, who had said that Scindia, Holkar, Begam of Bhopal had helped the Company at the time of 1857 revolt. They had troops trained by the English, and they were loaned to the Company. McNeal said that these troops were of great help to the Company.

Reactions of some responsible newspapers are noteworthy. 'The Bombay Times' wrote on January 15, 1859: "If you chose to turn your eyes to the truth and call it, as some of your high civil officials in 1857 called it, a mere Military mutiny, the blame of keeping up a large Sepoy Army with an absurdly small number of European soldiers in the Country, with the Empire daily extending, lies at the door of the Court of Directors. If you call it by its right name, a 'deadly national rebellion', more fierce and sanguinary than ever occurred in France, the blame of annexing Oude against solemn treaties (as now admitted by every member of Parliament, but long ago ineffectually dinned into Lord Dalhousie's ears by the whole press of India, save the 'Friend') lies at the door of their pet servant whom they rewarded with a pension of 50,000 Rs. a year, to be paid out of the revenues of the very land which he had so cruelly despoiled. Who, but the Court of Directors' refusal to entertain the just and equitable prayer of the Ranee of Jhansi to have her husband's adopted son placed on the Musnud, and punished her by annexing her territory? Who but Lord Dalhousie would have annexed the large provinces of Nagpore and appropriated the Revenue of about 150,000,000 per annum, merely because the Ranee desired to place Raja's adopted son on the throne; and so we might go on tearing to tatters all those mighty acts of spoliation in India which the blind Ministers of England, misled by the Court of Directors, were wont to call great political achievement".[13]

'The Statesman' of Calcatta, in an editorial of June 26, 1876, said: "It is a very singular fact that the annexations of Lord Dalhousie have in the main proved to be very disastrous to the people of the annexed provinces. The Punjab was the legitimate acquisition. It was made under no false pretences of concern for its people, but was the result of unprovoked and open attack upon us, with the avowed purpose of subverting our empire. And the fortunate Punjabees have every reason, we believe, to rejoice at coming under our rule. On the other hand, we seized Nagpore, Jhansi, and Oudh upon pretences that were thoroughly immoral, and it is most distressing to note the miseries that our rule has brought upon them all. At the time we seized Jhansi (1853) it was probably the best governed little territory in India. It was worst of all Lord Dalhousie's annexations, and it is difficult to read the story of the wrong, as it appears in the pages of the historian, without emotion. Someone we never knew who, sent us in the depth of mutiny, the Ranee's petition to the House of Lords against the wrong that has been done to her family, and it was impossible to read it without indignation.

The petition had been sent to England, and had been thrown under 'their Lordship's table', as every other memorial of the kind was. The Ranee was the heroine of the Rebellion....And today, 24 years after the annexation, if we inquire into the conditions of Jhansi, the honest answer is, that our rule has reduced the people from a condition of the highest well being to one of deep distress and misery, which the government is its wit's end to remedy....Our rule introduced Marwarees into the little state; and as the Deputy Commissioner writes, 'They have sucked it dry'....We have the same humiliating story to tell of Oudh".

In the troubled times of revolt, the British newspapers were full of true and false reports about the upheaval. The British parliament then passed a resolution and took over the administration of India, terminating the charter of the East India Company. Queen Victoria issued a proclamation assuring the Indian people that her administration would govern justly without discrimination on the basis of caste, race or colour. The Company won the war but lost the empire. It took another twenty-eight years to establish a national organization—the Indian National Congress.

REFERENCES

1. B.R., Sunthankar, *Nineteenth Century History of Maharashtra,* vol. 1, Shubhada-Sarswat Prakashan, Pune, 1988, pp. 94-95.
2. R.C. Majumdar, (Ed.), *History and Culture of the Indian People, British Paramountcy and Indian Renaissance*, Vol. 9, Bharatiya Vidya Bhavan, Bombay, 1963, pp. 34-35.
3. M.R. Palande, (Ed.) *The Source Material For the History of the Freedom Movement in India, Vol. 1* Govt. Central Press, Bombay, 1957, pp. 45.
4. Sir Spencer Walpole, *History of England from the Conclusion of the Great War in 1815*, Longmans, London, 1912, pp. 358-363.
5. E.J. Hobsbawm, *The Age of Revolution*, New American History, NY, 1962, pp. 243-246.
6. John Morley, *The Life of William Ewart Gladstone*, Vol. 1 part 5, Macmillan, NY, pp 12-13.
7. E.J. Hobsbawm, *The Age of Capital*, Weidenfeld & Nicolson, London, 1975, p. 17.
8. Jonathan Parry, *The Rise and Fall of the Liberal Government in Victorian Britain*, Yale Uni. Press, New Haven, 1975, pp.34-35, 59-62,168.
9. R.C. Majumdar, (Ed.) *History and Culture of the Indian People, British Paramountcy and Indian Renaissance*, Vol. 9, Bharatiya Vidya Bhavan, Bombay, 1963, Part 2. pp. 456-457.
10. R.J. Moore, *Sir Charles Wood's Indian Policy 1853-66*, Manchester Uni. Press, Manchester, 1966, pp.126, 163.
11. M.R. Palande (Ed.), *Source Material for the Freedom Movement in India*, vol.1, Govt. Central Press, Bombay, 1957 pp. 258-259.
12. Rajwade, *Marathyanchya Itihasachi Sadhane*, Vol. 6, Rajawade Sanshodhan Mandal, Dhule, Introduction, 2002.
13. M.R. Palande (Ed.), *Source Material for the History of the Freedom Movement in India,* vol.1, Govt. Central Press, Bombay, 1957, p. 353.

Chapter Four

FROM COMPANY TO THE IMPERIAL RULE

Queen Victoria's proclamation was read in a public meeting called by Lord Elphinstone, the governor, on November 1, 1858, after which the Union Jack was hoisted. Dinshaw Wacha, who was present as a schoolboy, later wrote that the Union Jack was hoisted upside down, which was taken as a bad omen. This mistake was corrected immediately. The Proclamation assured the Indian people that the government would act as a trustee, and Lord Canning, the governor-general, as a representative of the Queen. However, in practice few of the British officers really behaved as trustees, who were exceptions, while a majority of them were insolent and were convinced that the Indians were inferior to them in almost all respects.

The Queen's proclamation was issued when Lord Derby was the prime minister but the hand behind it was that of the British Parliamentarian John Bright. After the 1857 revolt, speaking in the House of Commons, Bright described the miserable conditions of the Indian people and criticised the Indian administration for unbearable taxation and other inequities. He expected the administration to be responsive. Bright said that had he been in charge of the administration, he would have issued a proclamation addressing the people and the Chiefs of States to assure them of progressive rule. Bright was offered the post of Secretary of State for India, which he declined for two reasons: one, his delicate health, and the other, the insensitiveness in England, which would have deterred him from carrying on any progressive measures.

The new generation of English educated Indians was by then concerned about the conditions in the country and was appraising the government's policies and legislation. It took some time for them to come together and form a national organisation. But the beginning was made on a provincial level in different parts of the country. These efforts were the precursor of the Congress. In the turbulent times of revolt in the north, the English language newspapers were very harsh in their criticism of the uprising; while regional language newspapers were moderate in their tone, as they feared a reprisal from the government if they did not criticise the uprising. But small papers and handwritten sheets were all fire and brimstone. How were the English language papers faring? Lord Trevelyan, who was very critical of the English language papers, said that they were no less vicious than those French papers at the time of the French Revolution. He also found that they believed that every Hindu and Muslim was a murderer and a criminal because some people in Bengal joined the revolt. They might have thought that all of them had one head and it should be strangled. Acts of cruelty, arson and loot by the English were justified as they were ordained by the almighty. Lord Canning faced intense criticism, as it was supposed that not only he was responsible for the excesses against the English; but as if he was responsible for them. Canning was criticised because he did not participate in the bloodshed.

Mountstuart Elphinstone kept himself informed about the happenings in India and was distressed by the cruelty shown by both sides. After the death of Elphinstone, one John Warden, who knew him, wrote a letter to the Times, on November 30, 1859. Elphinstone had written to him: "I partake very strongly your feelings about the state of India and altered position of the natives and Europeans towards each other. It is impossible not to share in the indignation of the latter after the atrocities perpetrated by so many of one class of population, nor to feel how much its intensity must have been increased by their presence on the scene, and their distrust of the natives among whom they still live, and whose appearance of fidelity and attachment they had so little reason to rely; but the eagerness of the Calcatta press, and of others still further removed from danger, to divide all India into two parties blacks and whites, and to force every one of its inhabitants to join one or other standard, is scarcely less a proof of insanity than the panic about the cartridges which gave rise to this unhappy contest".

Elphinstone and Trevelyan were not the only ones alarmed and disgusted by the cruelty and vehemence of the English. Sir Charles Dilke also cited instances of such behaviour of the English people in other parts of the world. Dilke writes: "The great imaumbara suffered terribly in 1858 from the wanton destruction which our troops committed everywhere during the war of the mutiny.... There is too much fear that the English, unless held in check, exhibit a singularly strong disposition toward cruelty, wherever they have a weak enemy to meet. The stories of the Indian mutiny and of the Jamaica riots are but the two out of many—two that happen to have heard; but the Persian war in 1857 and the last of the Chinese campaigns are not without their records of deliberate barbarity and wrong".[1] Dilke then had quoted from some of the letters from the soldiers on the Persian campaign. But other Englishmen like James Fitzjames Stephen, a keen student of history, law, politics and philosophy, held totally different views. He firmly believed that the destiny had cast some responsibility on England. To him novelists like Dickens were carried away by emotion, describing the life of the people of England wrongly; and so the government should not enact laws depending on such depiction. He had warned that the high ideals held by England would be endangered by the people like Dickinson, Cobbden, Bright et al. He believed that every country has some duty assigned to it, and it has got to be performed, without consideration of the consequences. Stephen, therefore, justified the atrocities committed by the English army. He said that atrocities which were committed against the British had to be revenged. India was conquered by sword and must be maintained by sword.

In the surcharged atmosphere, Lord Canning clamped down restrictions on the newspapers. George Buist, editor of the 'Bombay Times', criticising the Indians, called for more stringent measures. But as the directors of his paper were Indians, they asked for his resignation. Other Bombay papers like 'Bombay Samachar', 'Rast Goftar' and 'Jame Jamshed' wrote in support of the Indians. R.C. Mujumdar says that Harischandra Mukherjee, editor of 'Hindu Patriot', kept his balance. He pointed out that the Bengal army, which was in the forefront of revolt, was not solely of Bengalis. The majority in that army was that of north Indians, Biharis and Muslims. Mukherjee tried to give a clear perspective about the Bengal army, and Lord Canning took due notice of his writings. The revolt in India had rattled many British leaders. They had realised that the British government did nothing to restrain Lord Dalhousie in his policy of relentless annexation of the states and neither did they rein in the directors of the Company whose administration was irresponsible. Even the imperialist like Disraeli criticised the Company. When in 1853 the Company's charter was to be extended, he said in the Parliament that the criticism made against the Company in 1833 had to be repeated in 1853. Succession of wars, deficits, very few public works, absence of education, and judicial system in doldrums; this was the dismal tale of the Company's rule. He compared the directors of the Company with thugs who strive hard to gain your confidence; and once gained, would take the first opportunity to cut your throat.

The revolt of 1857 saw the suspension of the activities of the Bombay Association for three years. There were clearly two groups in the association—one representing the merchant class and the other the educated elite. The merchant class was very much agitated by the income tax and wanted to lodge a protest, but they were unable to do so, as they were not proficient in English to write a petition. Accordingly, the elite class representatives were approached and a petition was sent to the government. But the elite were more interested in the share in the higher government services for Indians, local self-government, and the relief to the peasants. Their interests thus differed; but the language used by Ranade, Bhandarkar and others was always moderate. Nevertheless, papers like 'Rast Goftar', given to harsh language, called the merchant class stupid and lacking the wisdom to retire from the public bodies. When it was found that the trading class would be unable to provide leadership, a suggestion came forward that the chiefs of the states and the landed gentry should fill in the void. Dadabhai Naoroji, who went to England as a representative of the Cama and Company, which had an office in Liverpool, resigned from the company and returned to India in 1855 only to go back to England to start his own company. In 1866 Dadabhai played a leading role in establishing a branch of the East India Association in England and came under the influence of three Englishmen—John Bright, John Dickinson and Evans Bell. John Dickinson had an uncle who was a shareholder of the East India Company, and his other relative was an engineer in Mumbai. Therefore, Dickinson could correctly predict in his book, *The Government of India Under Bureaucracy* that the annexation policy of Dalhousie would lead to unrest and might bring disaster. In 1853, Dickinson and his friends established the India Reform Society, which saw significant success in bringing down the tempers of the Englishmen after the 1857 revolt in India. Dickinson wrote some pamphlets demanding more railways, roads and associating Indians with the administration. He also wanted Indians in the government service so that they would be competent enough to manage their own affairs. Evans Bell, who was a commissioner at Nagpur, was denied promotion because of his support to Bhosle. He was under suspension; but as Lord Canning knew his worth, he was appointed as police chief in Madras. Bell was of the view that citizenship rights of the Empire should be conferred on Indians and India should be a self-governing colony or dominion like others. Bell also held that the British should confine themselves to the defence of India and foreign trade, and leave the Indians to manage their internal administration.

With more contact with Bright, Bell, Dickinson and others, Dadabhai concentrated on the study of the India's economy and financial problems. In a meeting of the East India Association in 1867, Dadabhai read a paper on England's duty towards India. Three years later he read another paper on the needs of India and showed that per capita income of India was forty shillings, i.e. rupees twenty.

In those days and even some years afterwards Dadabhai was not propounding his famous 'Drain Theory'. Even in 1873 he used to say that England had a right to receive the interest on her investment in India. In 1866 when Dadabhai came to India to establish a branch of the East India Association in Mumbai, he visited the states of Kathiawar and asked the chiefs to contribute to the funds of the East India Association. He also went to Calcatta and Madras to establish branches of the association. The association had sent a petition to the British government asking for an advisory council of the representative Indians to assist the governors and the Governor General. Pherozeshah Mehta had, by this time, returned to Mumbai and plunged himself in the public life of the city. He took a lead to present a purse of thirty thousand rupees to Dadabhai on behalf of the citizens of Mumbai, to which even the Europeans contributed. Dadabhai had appealed to the branches of the East India Association to collect material about the conditions in India and send it to the association's London office along with money. Though the London office started getting material about India regularly, the monetary help was not so forthcoming.

With the establishment of the Mumbai municipality in 1865, the rift between the merchant class and the elite widened, as their interests clashed. The majority of the Indian members of the municipality came from the merchant class, who did not know the English language in which the business of the municipality was conducted. Besides, they were busy with their own affairs and could not give much time for the discussion of public causes. When the administration of Commissioner Crawford came in for public criticism for his lavishness, the 'Native Opinion' and the 'Rast Goftar' lashed out at the municipal representatives from the merchant class for their poor performance. Class interests of the trading community came to the fore when it opposed the increase in the property tax to pay for more water supply. They said that such enhancement would cut into the funds for residential buildings for the poor, and only one class had to bear the burden. They wanted an indirect tax to shift the burden to the poor. It was a strange spectacle that Governor Freer would ask for the direct tax on the rich, while Mangaldas Nathubhai, a merchant, wanted an indirect tax, which would have increased the prices of the daily necessities.

Governors of the provinces were finding it difficult to carry on the administration, as Dalhousie had concentrated powers in the hands of the Governor General. Governors of both Bombay and Madras were of the opinion that all governors should have the advisory councils consisting of the representatives of the Indians. The scope of powers of such councils was the subject of an intense discussions and exchanges between the Secretary of State for India and the governors. Sir Charles Wood, secretary of state, was afraid that the increased number of Indians on such councils would give rise to a false notion among the Indians that the councils were legislative assemblies. He did not think that the Indians were qualified for such innovation. The letter written by Sir Bartle Frere, Governor of Mumbai, to the Secretary of State, on May 3, 1860 throws much light on the difficulties of the governors while running the administration. He wrote that, "Lord Ellenborough will tell you how he found matters in both departments (military and police) when he was here, and they are far worse now...How Lord Canning got on with the old machinery is to me an accountable marvel...Since 1833 you have concentrated all law-making with most other functions here in Calcutta, and the machinery is ridiculously inadequate in every way, to the tasks it has to perform…Unless then you give us non-official Europeans in these local legislative bodies, you must be prepared to legislate in the Westminster…Then if you admit non-official Europeans, you must also admit, in at least, equal proportion, natives, who in intelligence and education are their equals, and who have a far greater stake in the country…The days are gone when you could govern India without much caring what Europeans and Europeanized community say or think of your measures, and unless you have some barometer and safety-valve combined in the shape of a deliberative Council, I believe you will be always liable to very unlooked-for and dangerous explosion."[2] Ultimately, British Parliament passed a legislation sanctioning the advisory councils for the Governor General and the governors. Accordingly the Governor of Bombay had his first advisory council in 1852. This council had members from the merchant community and some from the feudal class, which provoked the 'Native Opinion' to tell the government that these elements did not represent the people. There were other voices against the government's economic policies. 'Dnyan Prakash' of Poona was critical of the Government of India's policy to charge the expenditure of war against Abbyssinia to the treasury of India. The 'Dnyan Prakash' wrote that the people would not mind paying for the normal expenditure, but the British government decided on a military expedition against Abbyssinia for the sake of some missionaries and asked India to bear the cost. This was unjustifiable according to the paper. At the same time Dadabhai read a paper in the meeting of the East Association, London, which stated that there was a constant drain of India's wealth to England. This was done by way of salaries and pensions and purchase of stores etc. Sir Charles Trevelyan opposed Dadabhai's thesis. Though sympathetic towards India, Trevelyan did not subscribe to Dadabhai's 'drain theory'.

After the 1857 revolt, some far-reaching economic changes were taking place in India. Recently established public works department had undertaken some road building and other public works, which employed a large number of workers including supervisory staff. The railway was also encompassing different parts of the country. All such works gave employment to thousands of people. Most of the workers were unskilled, but it was the first time that people were employed on such a large scale. The wages also increased in no time, as the demand for labour went up. This raised the prices of grains and other necessities. Besides, in 1861, civil war broke out in the United States, which affected the supply of cotton to Manchester and Lancashire Mills, giving rise to an unprecedented demand for the Indian cotton; and the prices skyrocketed. The profits of the merchants jumped to two to three hundred per cent. There was a craze for getting rich quickly, and not only Indians were caught in this mad frenzy but even Europeans were not immune. Speculation was rampant and new companies were coming up like mushroom, for whose shares people were staking everything they had.

One of the banks in Bombay had reported that, "In this period every one in Bombay appears to have become wild with the spirit of speculation. Companies were started for every imaginable purpose, banks and financial associations, land reclamation, trading, cotton cleaning, pressing and spinning companies, coffee companies, shipping and streamer companies, hotel companies, lively stable companies and companies for making bricks and tiles". The government appointed an inquiry commission.

Dinshaw Wacha had written a book titled, *A Financial Chapter in the History of Bombay,* describing in detail this craze that gripped Bombay from 1863 to 1865. He cites a part of the report by the Bombay Chamber of Commerce, which came out before that of the Inquiry Commission. Chamber's report said, "The official year just closed (1864-65) will be notable in the history of Bombay, as a year hitherto unparalleled in its commercial annals for the reckless spirit of gambling speculation which possessed a great portion of the community—speculation which resulted to large numbers, as might be expected from its character, in utter ruin and disgrace. The unexpected wealth poured into the lap of Western India by the terrible incident of the American Civil War—now happily brought to a close—was not used wisely. Two years ago a mania for share speculation broke which continued to grow in intensity till it seemed to absorb the time and attention of the community. The legitimate trade of Bombay was comparatively neglected, and the energies of the people devoted to the promulgation of schemes, the utility of which to the public was probably the last thing thought worthy of consideration by the promoters. Bombay was flooded with "Financial Associations", and doubtful schemes of reclamation. Valuable works of reclamation of the greatest public utility in the course of construction, and sound banking institutions, were for a time partially discredited by the gambling that prevailed in their shares. When the mania was at its height, intelligence was received of the unexpected termination of the American Civil War, gambling speculation suddenly collapsed, and insolvency and bankruptcy followed on a scale of the magnitude unknown in any other crisis of modern share speculation."[3] Wacha also informs that between 1863 and 1865 the newly formed banks, financial institutions and companies had paid up capital to the tune of twenty-nine crores and seventy-six lacs. But demand for their shares was so great that they were sold at premium. This premium was about thirty-seven crores, i.e. more than the paid up capital. The Bombay Bank had Premchand Raichand as its chief, who was very generous. He himself took a loan from the bank and helped many to do so. The bank did not make any inquiries about the financial viability of the new companies and ultimately collapsed.

The Bombay Baroda Railway Company was selected to reclaim the land under sea and develop it for construction of buildings. But the secretary of state was opposed to a railway company spending its money on such schemes of reclamation. So a private company was given the contract. Its shares were sold at high premium. Governor Sir Bartle Frere informed the Secretary of State that even if there was no possibility of getting a dividend by the company, there was a frenzied selling of shares. This company had a tragic end and the reclamation work had to be given to the railway company. In this whole business, Sir Bartle informed the Secretary that many government servants lost their fortune. But this period also saw an increase in the number of cotton and jute mills in Bombay and Calcutta. In 1854, i.e., three years before the great revolt, a solid foundation was laid for the cotton mills. In England and other countries the lives of the working class in the initial stages of industrialism was very miserable and took several years to improve. India, however, was lagging behind. Major Moor, who was appointed to supervise the cotton mills, made a report in 1872-73, which noted that the working conditions in the mills were harmful to the health of the workers. Mr. Redgrave, chief of the cotton mills association in England, in a note said that workers in Indian cotton mills had fourteen-hour shifts and even children were employed which helped in reducing the cost of production and resulted in uneven competition. The Mill Owners Association, which was established in 1875, was alarmed by Redgrave report and petitioned the Government of India not to act on it. But Sorabji Shapurji Bengali from Bombay wrote several articles demanding the improvement of the working conditions in the mills. Bengali and Narayan Meghji Lokhande jointly submitted a petition to the Bombay Legislative Council, which demanded the reduction of working hours to nine, with one weekly holiday. The Government of India then appointed a Factory Commission, whose report did not accept all the demands of the workers. But even the moderate report was not implemented by the mill-owners. So Lokhande started organising the workers. The Bombay and East India Association, it seems, did not bother to even discuss this problem. In Bengal indigo plantation was in full swing and Assam saw the proliferation of tea gardens. Workers, however, were treated like helots in both areas. A play, *Neel Darpan*, depicted the pitiable life of the workers, but the Bengali middle class did not take any notice. It was roused only when English planters openly criticised the play.

The Sarvajanik Sabha was established in 1867 in Pune. This association came into being at a public meeting called to consider the complaints about the affairs of the Parvati temple. The meeting decided to form an association to discuss the issues of public interests. Ganesh Vasudev Joshi took the lead, and afterwards Justice Ranade was the soul of the organisation and gave it a wider base and also prestige. Both Gokhale and Tilak later served as secretaries of the Sabha. Ganesh Vasudev Joshi was known as 'Sarvajanik Kaka (Public Uncle)'. He was a government servant, but when he was wrongly blamed, he left the service. Later he was found not guilty; but instead of joining the government service, he practiced law and made enough money to spend his life in public service. He then took the vow to use Indian made clothes and other necessities. Joshi was always busy in some public work. His activities were not restricted to Poona but spread over the whole of the then Bombay presidency. In 1872 Ranade came to Poona as a junior judge and was asked to take over the Sarvajanik Sabha, which had six thousand members who elected ninety representatives and whose meeting was held on April 2, 1870 in Pune. G.V. Joshi was elected as secretary. The Sabha declared its objective to serve as a bridge between the people and the government. It aimed at communicating the government's objectives to the people, and convey the grievances of the people to the government and get them redressed. The Sabha launched a quarterly Journal, which dealt with economic, political and social subjects. It also made it a practice to review the government administration. At the time some areas of the presidency in general and Maharashtra in particular were visited by famine, and the Journal started dealing with this problem. Articles in the Journal were published anonymously and were meticulously edited by Ranade. Both Ranade and the well-known economist, Ganesh Vyankatesh Joshi, were regular contributors. The Journal was keen to keep the articles scholarly, the tone moderate and the language dignified. It was not that grievances aired by the Sabha were redressed by the government; but the Sabha impressed on the minds of its members that the petitions had a twofold objective. One was to bring to the notice of the government the shortcomings of the policy or its implementation and the other was to educate the people.

An impression was created that the Journal would create dissatisfaction against the government. 'The Times of India', while reviewing the first four issues of the Journal, dispelled this suspicion. 'The Times' wrote that after going through four issues of the Sarvajanik Sabha's journal it could safely be said that the Sabha was not a seditious organisation as it was fashionable to believe in some quarters. Though some of the government's plans had come under critical appraisal, the criticism was, according to the 'Times', precise, detailed and effective. The paper declared that no article in the Journal challenged the right of the government to expect the loyalty and obedience of the people. The 'Times' then drew attention to the article which was critical of the restrictions placed on the Indian language papers and of the prepublication censorship on some, and said that the article had compared the rule of the Russian Tsar to that of the British and expressed confidence that the British would take India on a path of progress to bring it to the level of the advanced nations of the world. Wordsworth, principal of Elphinstone College, wrote to the editor of the Journal that 'the objectives of the Sabha were commendable. There is nothing to criticise the manner in which the Journal was expressing its views on public matters to attract the attention of the people and the government. There was no doubt that in the coming years people's attention would turn more and more to the government's administration.

The government would have to take the wishes of the people into consideration'. Wordsworth cautioned that the aspirations of the people might, at times, be impractical. But, he said that the government could not afford to ignore the economic reality and aspirations of the people and necessity to hold consultations. Wordsworth said that if he were an administrator, he would have given due thought to the petitions by the Sabha about the irrigation and also about the conditions of the cultivators. According to him, many of the British administrators were shallow and did not care to consider the feelings of the people about the measures adopted by them. Wordsworth then commended the Sabha for getting to the root of the matter. He especially praised the Sabha for its work in the days of the famine. William Wedderburn (later Sir William) was then collector of Ahmednagar district. He was pleased with the work of the Sabha and wrote to say that however skillful a cobbler might be, the wearer only knows where the shoe pinches. Similarly only the people would know the good and bad effects of any government measure, and the Sabha, according to him, was representing the wishes and feelings of the people. Lord Ray, the Governor, was presented an address of welcome by the Sabha, when he declared that the critical comments by the Sabha had helped him in carrying on his administration. Lord Ray also confessed that there was a time when the Sabha was regarded not as a loyal organisation and the criticism was not welcome; but things had changed. It must also be noted here, that the East India Association in Bombay was far removed from the people, whereas the Sabha was taking up the causes close to their hearts.

Dadabhai Naoroji by then had written a sixteen thousand-word petition detailing the plight of the Indians, and presented it to the Parliament which received wide publicity in England, and the Parliament also debated this question. Gladstone, who was the Prime Minister, nominated a committee to go into the revenue problems of India under the chairmanship of Sir Henry Fawcett who had studied the economic problems of India. He used to draw attention to the dire poverty and starvation of the Indian people. Fawcett once said that Indians had no voting rights and though a railway company in England could bring pressure on the Parliament, the Indians could not. In 1867, England attacked Abyssiniya and compelled India to pay for the invasion. India also had to pay for the reception to the Sultan of Turkey in London. The British government thought that as the Suez Canal would benefit India, she should share the costs. Fawcett took the government to task for such unjust demands. When the British government wanted the Indian government to pay for the visit and the gifts which Duke of Edinburgh was to present to some Indians during his visit to India, Fawcett could not help describing it as 'magnificent meanness'. It must be noted, however, that both Gladstone and Disraeli were united in shifting this burden to India.

The Fawcett Committee, in its three years existence, collected a mass of material, and interviewed large number of people. It then published all the material in several volumes. When the Committee was in session, a huge public meeting in Calcutta passed a resolution commending its work and particularly that of Fawcett. It was Ranade, who went through all the volumes published by the Fawcett Committee and wrote a book giving the broad outline of the volumes and supplementing it with some latest information. Fawcett could not complete his task because the Liberal party and he himself suffered a defeat in the election. However, Indian people raised seven hundred and fifty pounds for him and Fawcett was elected from another constituency. When his Committee was in session, Fawcett himself made several speeches in the Commons on the Indian budgets of 1872 and 1873. The burden of his speeches was: The only source of income for government was land-revenue; as the country was poor and not industrialised, revenue could not be increased much; salt tax was unbearable to the poor and no further increase was advisable. Later too, Fawcett used to labour the point that because of the poverty of the people, the Indian government was handicapped. He drew attention to the fact that income tax was opposed not only by the Indians but also by the Englishmen. Even if the government's expenditure was reduced, its revenue would not be appreciably increased. As the income of the people was low, taxing the consumer goods would hit them hard. After the 1857 Revolt the British government had taken over the administration of India and was expected to take more interest in Indian affairs. But sadly it was not fulfilling that expectation. The Advisory Council of the Secretary of State more often than not overlooked the interests of India. Besides, even if the Secretary of State and the Advisory Council jointly made any suggestion, the consent of the British government was not assured.

Fawcett also criticised the British government of not caring to obtain the consent of the Indian government even when the latter was made a party to some projects. One of the projects was to lay the wires in the Iranian gulf for long distance communication. The Government of India was asked to share half the expenses. The latter paid two-fifths of the capital, and when that company was sold, the Indian government received two-fifths of the amount; but the company was sold at a lower price and the Government of India had to suffer a loss of 1,15,946 pounds. Fawcett also criticised the policy of spending forty-five per cent of the Government of India's revenue on defence. The Fawcett Committee report had revealed hitherto unknown facts. It was found that the Indian and British armies were merged, which increased the expenditure on the army. If the salaries and allowances to the British army were increased, the same level had to be maintained in the Indian Army. Besides, money was not wisely spent. As an example, it was pointed out that because of the defective construction, most of the newly built barracks had collapsed. Other sections of the administration were no exception. The Governor of Bombay sold his state bungalow, but the cost for the new one was five times more than that of the old. The government used to give a guarantee to the private construction companies, but many a times it incurred losses. Naturally, there was dissatisfaction about the government. Lord Northbrook, who was the Governor-General from 1872 to 1875, was aware of the sentiments of the people. Samuel Wauchope who was the police chief of Calcutta and was in the Bengal Service for thirty years had no doubt that: "Most Hindoos distrust and dislike us at present. They think the object of every Governor is to upset that which was done by his predecessor and introduce something new…The Natives look on themselves as being hustled into a state of premature civilisation and wish to settle down. Natives hate change, and they say that during the last fifteen years the whole country has been turned upside down by new laws, new taxes, and new institutions". Wauchope also reported that: "The news of Lord Mayo's death has been received with pleasure by the Mahomedan population of India, who consider Sher Ali (Mayo's assassin) to be a martyr, and also by many Hindoos".[4] Northbrook himself was of the opinion that the Indian government was going too fast and it had got to slow down. Evelyn Baring, secretary to Northbrook, was aware of the views of the Governor-General. Baring said that as India was comprised of different religions, castes and sects, and as their religion, culture, language were not similar to those of the English, it would be advisable to spread the Western culture gradually and the Indians should not be hustled.

One other government officer agreed with the Governor-General. He was A.O. Hume, secretary to the Department of Agriculture, Revenue and Commerce, who later took a prominent part in founding the Indian National Congress. In a letter to Northbrook on August 1, 1872, Hume warned that the dissatisfaction with the British rule was becoming increasingly intense. Hume maintained, "Whereas (during the Mutiny) we had the active support of some and the passive countenance of a majority of our people, …we have now between us and destruction nothing but the bayonets". He blamed the government for this. Hume further said, "A studied and invariable disregard, if not actually contempt, for the opinions and feelings of our subjects, is at present day the leading characteristic of our Government in every branch of the administration. We know, or we believe that we know, what is right and what is best for the people, and on this, strong in consciousness of the best of motives, and heedless that these are wholly misunderstood by the millions who are affected by our acts, we insist".[5] Northbrook was of the opinion that the defence expenditure of the government was unjustifiably high. He was especially opposed to charge the Indian exchequer for the expeditions of the British government for the expansion of the Empire. The Secretary of State, Salisbury, under pressure from the mill-owners of Manchester, tried to persuade Northbrook that he should reduce the duty on import of cloth from England; but the Viceroy resisted this pressure. He wrote to Salisbury that, if the interests connected with cloth manufacturers were agitating, then it was the responsibility of the British government to deal with it. He reminded the Secretary that the Government of India should look after the interests of India and not that of Manchester.

It was Ranade who wrote some articles critical of the rigid and bureaucratic nature of the English administration. Sir James Stephen, law member of the viceroy's council, made some proposals with regard to the civil and criminal law administration in 1872. Ranade, who received a copy for his comments, wrote a rejoinder criticizing the proposals for giving too much power to the district collector. He pointed out that as the collector's power was to be undivided, it would be authoritarian. Ranade attacked the collectors for their lack of understanding of the local conditions and opposing any participation of the people. He said, "The disparity between the power represented by the governing classes and the capacity on the part of subject millions to influence this exercise for good, and to check its evils or abuses, is so great that, in the interests of a good and progressive liberal government, it is essential that the two functions of sovereignty represented by the judge and the collector of revenue must be entrusted to separate officers".[6]

Malharrao Gaikwad, Chief of Baroda state, was being badly treated by the government, and hence, the Sarvajanik Sabha sent an appeal. It was not that Gaikwad was a conscientious ruler. For some time Dadabhai Naoroji was his Diwan, who improved the tone of the administration, but Malharrao did not want to give up his indulgence. The British Resident, however, imposed various restrictions and Malharrao wanted Dadabhai's help to face the Resident. Dadabhai did not oblige, but resigned. Malharrao was thus left to his wits. The standoff between him and the Resident led the latter to charge Malharrao with sedition. He complained to the Government of India that Malharrao tried to poison him. The government then deposed Malharrao. The Baroda Chief had no means to pay the fees of an advocate, in case he wanted to brief any. The Sarvajanik Sabha then decided to collect one hundred thousand rupees for Malharrao. Ranade, in fact, had not much love for the Chiefs of the States and their administration. In his correspondence and in his articles he had asked them to be more responsive to the needs of the people and to be careful about the finances of the state. Even with these reservations, Ranade, and at his instance Sabha, appealed to the Government of India, because they thought that the behaviour of the British Resident was reprehensible. They were indignant that there was no let up in the policy of annexation of the Indian states. The Sabha, in an appeal to the government, made it clear that Poona had close relations in the past with the states like Baroda, Indore, Gwalior and so on. All these states were part of the Maratha confederacy, and Poona was the seat of power of the Peshwas. The Sabha asked the government to differentiate between the Chief and the people. If the

Chief was misbehaving, he might be punished; but not the people by annexing the state, said the appeal; and told the government that there should be some limit to the powers of the Resident. Though the government did not change its decision to dislodge Malharrao, the annexation of Baroda state was stalled because of the memorandum by the Sabha.

There was a tussle between the western educated elite and the merchant class in Poona as in Bombay. The newly educated and the landholders had their differences. The landholders were represented by N.L. Noolkar who was the chairman of the managing committee of the Sarvajanik Sabha. His faction wanted the Sabha to confine its activities to interpreting the government policies to the people. Ranade, without allowing these differences to hamper the working of the Sabha, steered it to play a wider role. He, therefore, used the opportunity to criticise the Government of India's Censorship Act, which was applicable to the Indian language newspapers and publications. Though the Journal was published only in English and was not affected by the new Press Act, the Sabha sent a memorandum to the Government. It said: "The repressive influences of the Act leave the Government no resource to ascertain the genuine wishes of the people of their recognised organs". This infuriated some English supporters of the Press Act. Lionel Ashburner, who was a prominent member of the Bombay Executive Council, demanded to include the native English language newspapers. He singled out the Sarvajanik Sabha and its Journal to denounce them as seditious. Ashburner said, ('Maratha' 26 June 1878) "To be effective the press law must be thorough and if we tolerate sedition in English, the Sabhas which are springing up all over the country will find no difficulty in translating it into the vernacular...Holkar and other Native Chiefs subscribe largely to the Sarvajanik Sabha which it is not unfair to say is a seditious Association". In 1874 Ranade organised a public meeting in Poona, which ratified a petition to be sent to the government. It demanded a representative government for India, and eighteen representatives in the House of Commons. The franchise was to be limited to the persons paying the tax of fifty rupees per annum. It was the first time the term 'Representative Government' was used in a public petition in India. Ranade did not hope that the government would concede the demands, but his intention was to educate the people. The government, on the other hand, suspected that this would lead to people organising themselves, and hence, it became suspicious about Ranade.

Since 1876, Bihar, Maharashtra, Gujrat, Madras and the United Provinces were visited by severe famine. In fact, ten years since 1866 large parts of the country were experiencing famine. The Edinburgh Review had given details of famines in India since 1345. A Dutch traveller had written descriptions of famine in Orissa, Madras and other areas in 1630-31. As the communication facilities were very primitive, it was impossible to move food-grains from even the neighbourhood to the affected areas. But with the British rule, roads were built and the communication became comparatively easy. Nevertheless, starvation and deaths could not be averted because it was not enough to bring grains to the famine stricken areas, as the purchasing capacity of people was very limited. Sir William Hunter, a scholar and an editor of the *Gazetteer of India* served in different areas of India and more so in Bengal. In 1874 when he was assigned the work of collecting the details about the people of Bengal, he also wrote notes about the famine conditions. He then published his book titled *The Famine Conditions of Bengal Districts*. Hunter used to write a column called 'Indian Affairs' in the Times, London. In 1866 when he was in Orissa, he was a witness to famine. The local officers told him that if the prices of rice started rising after the winter crop, it was a warning of an impending famine. In 1876 and later, the Government of India and provincial governments were not so alert as to apprehend the possibility of famine. Consequently, thousands of people perished.

After the peasants' riots in 1875 the Sabha prepared a report and sent it to the government. The report clearly established the fact that though money-lenders might have played some mischief, the root of the whole trouble was in the long standing faulty revenue system and its implementation. The peasants could not bear the increased burden of revenue; and justice was costly. This drove them to despair and resort to violence. Ravinder Kumar studied this problem in detail and wrote a book. He has shown how the survey of rural Maharashtra had led to the enhancement of rates, which cultivators could not bear. There was great deal of correspondence on the subject between the government officials, most of whom were unmindful of the complaints of the affected people. Sarvajanik Sabha then took up the issue. It sent memoranda to the government and cogently argued the case. Ranade, in his article in the Journal, had pointed out that one of the government officers, Mr. Hope, had argued in a meeting called by the Governor-General, Lord Lytton, that the land revenue charges had increased and the revenue laws were stringent leading to the increased indebtedness of the peasants. To illustrate the point that the litigation had gone up by leaps and bounds, Hope produced an account of the stamp duty collected by various courts. Lord Lytton thought his arguments worth consideration, and wrote to the government of Bombay accordingly. But the Governor, Sir Richard Temple, was averse to reducing the land revenue.

The agitation against the increase of land-revenue assumed alarming proportions, and the Sabha advised the peasants to pay the amount, which they were paying previously, and not the increased one. The government thought that this was outrageous and also alarming, and ordered an inquiry. The inquiry demolished the case of increasing rural prosperity advanced by the authorities. Revenue had been increased on this false assumption. But the government was adamant and held that the impoverishment was due to the rise in population. Peasants were not interested in such polemics and started resisting the enhanced payment. Meetings conveyed by the government officials to explain the policy were disrupted at several places. W.H. Havelock, revenue commissioner, was inclined to consider the demand to reduce the revenue, but the collector of Poona did not support him. He asked the government of Bombay to stick to its policy and use strong measures. The government, however, was uncertain of its position, as it had realised that the new rates were unbearable and the peasants were actually impoverished. Therefore, it announced some concessions.

The peasants' feelings were assuaged somewhat but their rage then turned against the money-lenders, who were generally the traders or *vanis* in the villages. Over the years they had become wealthy and had increased their landholdings at the expense of the peasants. There was dislocation of the rural economy after the end of the Civil War in America and some years of bad harvest. The peasants then had no other option than to sell their land to the *vanis*. This was the result of the government's new rule to attach the immovable property of the peasants in case they failed to pay the revenue, which enraged the peasants who rose against the *vanis*. In the initial stage the peasants called for social sanctions against the *vanis*, which had created tension. The first outbreak of violence occurred on May 12, 1875 at Supa, near Poona. Peasants ransacked the houses of the *vanis* and then burnt them. Though there was violence in some places, on the whole, the agitation was peaceful. Peasants' main objective was to seize the documents from the *vanis* and destroy them. This was borne out by the Commission appointed by the government to inquire into the Deccan riots. The Commission said in the report: "In reviewing the character of the disturbances generally, the most remarkable feature presented is the small amount of serious crime. A movement, which was a direct appeal to physical force over a large area usually restrained within the limits a mere demonstration; the moderation is in some measure to be attributed to the nature of the movement itself. It was not so much a rebellion against the oppressor, as an attempt to accomplish a very definite and practical object, namely by disarming the enemy by taking his weapons (bonds and accounts), and for that purpose mere demonstration of force was enough".[7] The government did not reduce the rates of revenue, but passed a Debt Relief Act. It was to be limited to the riot-affected areas and therefore, the whole state could not be benefited. However, Sir Bartle Frere, who took over as the governor of Bombay, called a meeting of the state officials and told them that in view of the exorbitant rates of interest charged by the *vanis,* ceiling had to be put on the interest rate. Most of the officers agreed, but felt that the proposition was impractical. The effective remedy was to start cooperative credit societies with government backing, but the government was not inclined to accept it.

Sir Erskine Perry, who was once chief justice, supported the analysis of the Deccan riots by the Sarvajanik Sabha. On December 1, 1877, he wrote to Salisbury, the Secretary of State, that before the advent of the British power in India, money-lenders and *jahagirdars* used to oppress the peasants, who would then blame it on the providence. But when the money-lenders started exploiting the peasants, taking shelter under the laws brought in by the English, the peasants started blaming the laws of the English. Under the British the number of money-lenders had increased and their practices had also changed. The land became saleable, which was not so before; but the value of the land had not increased. In old days, money-lenders and the peasants used to reside in the same village, and Brahmins as well as *vanis* lent money. Under the British, Marwaries from outside became the money-lenders. They were protected by law and could confiscate the land. Perry's suggestion was to appoint a special judge in every district to deal with the land related cases, with no provision for appeal. The Sabha Journal supported the arguments advanced by Perry and suggested that panchayats should be given some judicial powers. What Perry wrote was not something about which the government was not forewarned. Way back in 1858 Mr. Invararity, the revenue commissioner, had submitted a report from Mr. Tytler, the collector of Ahmednagar, who was well known as an earnest and compassionate officer. The report stated: "The aid given by our courts is all on the side of the Marwari, who alone knows how to turn that aid to his own advantage. The position of the litigants is not, therefore, simply of debtor and creditor; it is the fraudulent Marwari, backed by civil courts, versus the helpless ryot, signing any bond without even a true knowledge of its content and powerless to oppose any decree that may be passed. This matter keeps up a constant irritating sore throughout the society and the whole onus is thrown by the people on the civil courts".[8]

Ravinder Kumar holds the Company responsible for these disturbances. He says, under the Company's rule, people found that they were deprived of justice; and the spirit of cooperation in the rural areas was replaced by individual interests. The government thought that the money-lenders would bring improvement in agriculture; but this hope was belied. To historian Neal Charlesworth, the Deccan riots were a reaction of the economic deprivation. He says, "In Khandesh market for cash crop had increased but the traditional landed gentry had lost their privileges. They instigated the peasants against the money-lenders. It was strange that the documents about their debts were either burnt or lost. Hundreds of such documents were sold to the merchants of the waste paper in Poona". Charlesworth does not accept the view that increase in the land assessment was the sole cause of the riots in Poona district, as the assessment was also increased in Solapur district and there were no riots. Land in Poona district was not rich and with the decline in prices the peasants feared that the money-lenders who were also cultivators themselves would not pay the amount to the treasury which the peasants had paid them. They, therefore, rose in revolt. Charlesworth also thinks that the supply of capital to the agriculture was very little and this was the root of the trouble.

After Lord Lytton's appointment as the Viceroy was announced, 'The Statesman' in its editorial wrote on January 22, 1876: "The nomination of Lord Lytton as the Governor-General of India, following the appointments of Lord Mayo and Lord Northbrook, induces us to ask whether the Viceroyalty is no longer desired by men of the first rank in England. Of Lord Lytton we know very little and that is all in his favour, but it is evident that he has hitherto been but moderately disguised. His profession is that of diplomacy, and he is far from being at the head of it, as he has reached the age of forty-four without being nominated ambassador. Of all the Governors-General of India, he is the one who, before his nomination, was the most obscure. It seems of late years it has been declined by every man of conspicuous position…It is clear, therefore, that the most responsible position in the whole world is becoming cheap. It is passing into the hands of our second and third-rate public men".

Before Lord Lytton came to India, Rajastan experienced famine. As the communication facilities were non-existent, food-grains could not be moved to the interior regions. Famine-stricken people migrated to Delhi with their animals. But thousands of people along with their animals died on the way to Delhi. After assuming office, Lord Lytton and his advisors thought that the Madras administration was liberal in spending on the famine measures. That was why Sir Richard Temple was sent as a representative of the Viceroy to Madras to report on the conditions. He reported that the provincial administration was spending lavishly and as the government was purchasing grains in the market, merchants had artificially pegged the prices. Lord Northbrook had brought in the market food-grains from the government stocks to bring down the prices. But as Lord Lytton was more concerned about the merchants and traders, he did not follow his predecessor. Lytton scaled down Madras government's expenditure on famine by twenty five per cent, which was resented by the people. Thousands of people were dying of hunger when the controversy between the two governments was going on. William Digby, who was in Madras, wrote, "While the Viceroy was travelling from Simla to Southern India during the month of August, most distressing scenes were being witnessed in the streets of Bangalore. No measure of precaution sufficed to keep 'wanderers' from flocking into the streets and thronging relief kitchen for food. The mortality, which prevailed in all relief camps, was only too notorious: in the kitchens no shelter was provided-the mortality was transferred from the sheds of a poor house to the streets and purlieus of the city…whichever way the eye turned, dead bodies were seen...when troops were marched to the shooting butts for rifle practice, soldiers were horrified with the sight of men, women, and children, lying exposed and partly devoured by dogs and jackals. People argued, not unnaturally, that if such things occurred at headquarters, most terrible scenes were necessarily be witnessed in the interior. On any spot in the streets of Bangalore, where there was temporary shelter, the poor starved creatures would creep to die: on the pials (verandahs) of houses, under the shadows of trees and walls, or in a depression in the roadside".[9]

When some of the areas of the Bombay presidency were in the grip of famine, the Sabha played a worthy role. It sent agents and correspondents to the affected areas. Based on their dispatches, the Sabha used to send reports to the government. It directed its representatives to be cautious, as the afflicted people were prone to exaggerate. It asked them to err on the safe side than to make any mistakes, as the government might pick on them, and the main objective would be defeated. Introduction to the first report of the Sabha said, "The information accessible to the Government is limited to purely official sources, and is naturally very deficient in the particular and intimate knowledge which, at such times, so sadly needed, but which is shut out to those, whose range of vision necessarily embraces whole taluks or districts, and the Sabha feels that it would be wanting in its duty to Government and to the people, if it did not supplement the official information with the details accessible only to those who, like the agents and correspondent deputed by the Sabha, live among and form part of the people overtaken by the calamity". The government of Bombay, fortunately, responded to the Sabha's efforts favourably. The secretary to the government wrote back to say, "I am directed to state that (the) government will be very receptive to receive the periodical information you propose to submit regarding the conditions of the people in drought-stricken districts of this presidency." The Sabha had described how this famine was widespread than the previous ones. In a letter to the chief secretary to the government on November 23, 1876, Chiplunkar, secretary of the Sabha, drew attention to the fact that, in 1874 drought affected area in Bihar and Bengal was forty thousand sq miles, such area of NWFP in 1860-61 was thirty thousand sq miles; while the then prevailing drought had affected sixty-four thousand square miles in Maharashtra. The Sabha made several suggestions and was willing to admit mistakes and change its views. It all along emphasised the usefulness of large relief works, which could provide work to large number of people. It regretted that the Central Government had not sanctioned a large railway work. The Sabha supported the government's policy of not entering into the markets to purchase food-grains and thus give an opportunity to the traders to increase the prices. The government of Bombay was neither liberal and nor stingy. However, Sir Richard Temple, who was appointed to supervise the works in the Bombay presidency as well as in Madras, reduced the wages of the workers on relief works. The Sabha also drew the attention of the government to drought affected areas where no relief works were undertaken. The population in those areas was four million. It demanded ten million rupees for relief work, which the government did not sanction. The Sabha warned the government against the reduction of wages and described the plight of the workers, backing up the data with statistics. But Sir Richard was not moved. Both Lord Lytton and Sir Richard

Temple had contempt for the educated Indians, and regarded them as incorrigible opponents of the government. In a letter to the Secretary of State, Salisbury, on May 1, 1877 Lytton wrote, "Politically speaking, the Indian peasantry is an inert mass. If it ever moves at all, it will move in obedience, not to its British benefactors, but to the native Chiefs and princes, however tyrannical they may be. The only political representatives of native opinion are the Baboos, whom we have educated to write semi-seditious articles in the native Press, and who really represent nothing but the social anomaly of their position".[10]

Anglo-Indian papers like 'The Times of India' and the 'The Statesman' etc. did a good job of reporting famine conditions faithfully, which found echo in 'The Times', London and aroused the British public opinion. Lord Mayor of London called a meeting to consider the famine conditions and raise funds. Florence Nightingale wrote articles, and bombarded the government and ministers with letters, memorials and reports. She suggested that unless long-term development efforts were undertaken, India would not be free from such calamities. Nightingale explained how the peasants were exploited and impoverished by the moneylenders, who were let lose under the English rule. She suggested that the government must decide to provide capital on easy terms to the cultivators through commercial banks or through the cooperatives. Lytton was furious with such attention in England; but when the Queen herself expressed disquiet, he was alarmed. Even then he tried in vain to discourage the citizens of Calcutta, when they resolved in a public meeting to collect money for the relief. Both Gaikwad and Scindia were generous in giving help for famine relief. After the famine was over, it was estimated that thirty to forty per cent of the population had been swept away. Deaths were three times more than normal, and according to the Sabha's journal in two years the death toll was twelve lakhs; and if the deaths in the Deccan were added to that, the total was two million. These horrible years of famine, though over, left a scar on the minds of the people. Hence, in early 1879 there arose in the mountainous areas surrounding Poona some groups who resorted to robberies and decoities. All these groups were then united under the leadership of Vasudev Balwant Phadke, a Chitpawan Brahmin. His main supporters were the Ramoshis, who had not recovered from the serious effects of the famine. Phadke and his followers first started raiding the houses of moneylenders and other wealthy people. But then Phadke gave a political turn to his movement and made it anti-British. Sir Richard Temple, the Governor, was all the while suspicious of the Poona Brahmins, and Phadke's movement strengthened his suspicion. On March 8, in a letter to Ashburner, he wrote, "I have seen some police reports; actually attributing these little events to treason hatched by Poona Brahmins, who organised Ramoosees against the British Raj".[11]

When the country was going through these harrowing times, British Prime Minister Disraeli proposed that Queen Victoria be conferred the title of the

Empress of India, which Lord Lytton readily and enthusiastically supported. Disraeli used to claim that his Tory party was the party of the empire. Gladstone, on the other hand, used to discriminate between empire and imperialism, and opposed Disraeli's proposal. Disraeli of course, went ahead and the declaration was made with great fanfare. Lord Lytton was directed to call a special durbar in Delhi. Most of the Indian newspapers were critical and labeled the durbar as *tamasha* (a farce). Native Opinion said that the durbar had given birth to imperialism. The Sarvajanik Sabha did not favour the idea of having a durbar at the time when the ravages of the famine were still fresh. But Ranade thought the occasion should be used as an opportunity to put forth the demands on behalf of the people of India. The Sabha, therefore, called a public meeting in Poona, which endorsed the memorandum. It recalled that in olden times kings used to grant some relief to their subjects at the time of the coronation or a birth of a son etc. In the present time, the memorandum said, that the government should announce the adoption of the 'representative government'. It also told the government that the chiefs of the states were not associated with the administration or with the army and, therefore, had no worthwhile occupation. The memorandum asked for the establishment of a council of the princes, which would advice the government. Joshi, on behalf of the Sabha, visited many cities and spoke about the memorandum. He also took this opportunity to emphasis the importance of 'swadeshi'. Joshi deplored that India was producing only raw material, and almost all manufactured goods were imported. He said that if this went on, then shortly, India would be importing even eatables and people would be totally degraded.

Lord Lytton, as announced, went ahead with the preparations for holding the durbar, which was held with great pomp and ceremony. Lytton was a vain person whose ego was satisfied by the durbar. Now onwards he would not only be a representative of the Queen, but that of the Empress. By that time many of the English officers, high and low, had become arrogant, and behaved rudely in public places. This was noticed by the Duke of Edinburgh, when he visited India in December 1869. He wrote a couple of letters to the Queen and expressed his dismay and disgust at the behaviour of some of the British officers and civilians with the Indians. The Duke especially complained against the Residents' behaviour with the states chiefs in general and that of Hyderabad, in particular. The racist attitude of these officers, he said, was creating resentment all around.

History repeated itself, and as it happened in 1865, cities like Bombay, Ahmedabad and Surat again suffered because of speculative gambling in cotton. Hundreds of companies became bankrupt and thousands of people came to grief. In 1865 Premchand Raichand gambled on a large scale in the market. In 1879 it was Narsi Keshvji who gambled in rice, opium, wheat, jute, and lost, bringing down thousands with him. The Sabha's journal wrote a lengthy article, which said, "The opinion is becoming general in India, that the English legislation favors gambler, the insolvent debtor and the wrecker of other people's fortunes, at the expense of the legitimate businessman and the creditor". The article then described how Narsi Keshavji speculated and gambled and how the banks carelessly advanced loans to him. It advised the government to assess the real need of the cotton mills and not allow anybody to artificially peg them high. It also asked to amend the Indian Companies Act. The Bombay government was annoyed over the years by the role played by the Sarvajanik Sabha and especially by Ranade at the time of Deccan riots, and his independent views about several policies and measures of the administration. The Governor, Sir Richard Temple, was obsessed with the idea that the Chitpawan Brahmins were hatching a conspiracy against the government. When at the end of Ramoshi uprising and the deportation of Vasudev Balwant Phadke to Eden, two Peshwa palaces in Pune were burnt, government decided to act and Ranade was summarily transferred to Nasik, a smaller place than Pune. It was a virtual demotion. The name of the arsonist in Pune was K.K. Ranade who was later found to have no relation with M.G. Ranade. It took more than a year for the government to revise its attitude towards Ranade, and he was transferred to Bombay as second presidency magistrate.

REFERENCES

1. Sir Charles Wentworth Dilke, *Greater Britain, a Record of Travel in English Speaking Countries during 1866-67*, J.P. Lipponcott, Philadelphia, 1869, p. 192.
2. John Martineau, *Life and Correspondence of Sir Bartle Frere*, John Murray, London, 1895, pp.300, 338-340.
3. D.E. Wacha, *A Financial Chapter in the History of Bombay City*, A.J. Combridge and Co., Bombay, 1910, pp 7-8.
4. Edward C. Moulton, *Lord Northbrook's Indian Administration, 1872-1876*, Asia Publishing House, Bombay, 1968, p. 13.
5. Edward C. Moulton, *Lord Northbrook's Indian Administration, 1872-1876*, Asia Publishing House, Bombay, 1968, p. 12.
6. Sabha Journal, Vol. 7, 1874
7. Ravinder Kumar, *Western India in the Nineteenth Century*, Routledge and Kegan Paul, London, 1968, pp. 186-187.
8. L. Natarajan, *Maratha Uprising: 1875, in Peasant Struggle in India*, edited by A.R. Desai, OUP, Bombay, 1979, p. 161.
9. William Digby, *The Famine Campaign in the Southern India*, 2 Vols., Longmans, London, 1979, pp. 467-468.
10. Lady Betty Balfour, *The History of Lord Lytton's Administration, 1876-1880*, Longmans, London, 1899, p.109.
11. Richard P. Tucker, *Ranade and the Roots of Indian Nationalism*, Uni. of Chicago Press, Chicago, 1976, p. 91.

Chapter Five

DISSENTING FORCES

After the suppression of the 1857 revolt, the internal situation in India was mostly trouble-free. But the British rulers were apprehending invasion by an external enemy. Initially they laboured under the idea that America would be the aggressor. But they overcame this fear and started imagining that the Tsar of Russia had designs against India and might invade anytime. They were also wary about Germany, which had defeated France. Since 1870 Tsar had consolidated his position by annexing areas near the southern border, and extending the railway. The British feared that the Indians would revolt to synchronize it with the invasion by Russia. But this fear was unwarranted, as the Indian leaders had no affinity towards the Russian emperor. They preferred the British rule to that of the Tsar. Germany was not strong enough to mount any move against Britain and threaten her Empire in India. England then apprehended that Russia and Germany would combine against her, which led her to enter into alliance with Italy, Austria and Spain.

Gladstone was opposed to the imperialist policies of Disraeli. In 1879 he made several speeches, which are known as Midlothian speeches. They were regarded as the policy statements of the Liberal party, the burden of which was: "The loyalty of the people of India was proclaimed at the time of conferring the title of the Empress of India, on the Queen; but strangely, they were prohibited to keep arms. Every year about twenty thousand people die in India because of the attacks by the forest beasts and snakes. Hence, their need for the arms. Explosives were useful for the public works such as roads etc. But there were restrictions. This only showed that the Government did not trust the Indians. Special tax was levied to create a fund for contingencies such as famine, but that amount was spent on the war in Afghanistan. Because of the war, India would suffer a revenue deficit of six million Pounds. Was it the way to win the minds of the Indians? Many sordid things would come into open, if the roots of this policy were investigated. But as the empire had come into our possession, it was the duty of the British to uplift the Indians who were peaceful people. That the Asians should accept the rule of law was amazing. What was the purpose behind the Afghan war? Those who had served there deliberately adopted the policy to keep Afghanistan under the Afghan rule. But this policy was abandoned and in the name of the probability of Russian invasion, Britain took to arms against Afghanistan. This was not a policy, but simply imagination. We went into Afghanistan, divided it and ruined the people. We went to war because the Russian ambassador was welcomed by the Amir and our emissary was not received by him. The Amir had no other option than to welcome the Russian ambassador. Blame lies not with the weak Amir, but with the strong Tsar. The most disgusting thing was that the British government had the habit of accepting the lame excuses of the Tsar, but punish the Amir. The objectionable part of this affair was that not England, Wales or Scotland but India was to pay for this war", regretted Gladstone.

Annie Beasant was at that time working with Charles Bradlaw, a liberal leader. She wrote a book titled *England, India and Afghanistan*, in 1878. The book was very critical of the Afghanistan policy of both Disraeli and Lord Lytton. 'The Statesman' had opposed the Afghan policy for a long time. On December 7, 1875, the paper wrote: "We believe that Russia had about that much serious thought about invading India as we have of storming St. Petersburg, and that our attitude on this subject must be a matter of constant amusement in the inner circles of the Russian Court. We further hold that Russia has a true and legitimate mission in Central as we have in Southern Asia…The Government is heavily to blame for having ministered to the popular belief of a Russian invasion of India; heavily to blame indeed". 'The Statesman's' editorial on April 26, 1877, was more stinging. It said: "It is becoming clearer almost everyday, that Lord Lytton was selected for the Viceroyalty of India in order to commit this country to a repetition of the same policy of sin and shame that led us into Afghanistan in 1839, and that after a course of almost incredible business, treachery and violence, resulting from the straits to which we were reduced, ended in massacre of the forces that were the instruments of our sin. Englishmen talk of the intrigues of Russia, and her duplicity and breaches of faith in utter forgetfulness of the fact that the course of Russia has been purity itself, compared with the perfidy, treachery and violence of our own". It was not that only official circles were apprehensive of the Russian invasion, but some newspapers and periodicals were also fearful. 'The Economist', for instance, wrote on November 2, 1878: "The question is not whether the Amir has any plausible excuse for being hostile to us, but whether his hostility can with common prudence be disregarded under the existing circumstances. Let the Russian mission be withdrawn from Cabul as publicly as it was sent…it is the duty of English statesmen to prefer the security of India to the convenience of the Amir and even to the patriotic sentiments of the Afghan freebooters".

However, some members of the Commons, like Henry Fawcett, were warning the government of the harmful effects of war against Afghanistan. He had quoted statistics to show how the useful public works in India were suffering because of the war.

Lord Lytton frowned on the critical newspapers and suspected sedition everywhere. His government, therefore, clamped down restrictions and pre-censorship rules on the Indian language newspapers. In fact, some English language papers were more carping in their criticism. But Lytton's administration decided to limit the new legislation to the Indian language papers. The publishers of 'Amrit Bazar Patrika' found out the way to bypass this law by converting it into an English paper. This legislation came under nationwide criticism. Lord Lytton held that the semi-literate Indians who were managing Indian language papers were irresponsible and must be curbed. He was supported by the English officers and industrialists, who were numerous in Calcatta, and were annoyed by the criticism against them and enthusiastically welcomed the new measure. Lord Northbrook was also advised to bring such press restrictions though he rejected that advice. Lord Lytton had a supporter in Sir Richard Temple. He thought that if Calcutta had a need for such press restrictions, Bombay needed more of that. The United Provinces governor, Sir George Cooper, was another governor who asked for stringent measures against the Indian language papers. He wrote to Lord Lytton that the English should not be blind to the reality. If the Indian language papers were to be treated on equal terms as the English ones, then there was no necessity for them to be in India. He disapproved the pace of imparting English education to Indians, which he thought was harmful to the English rule. But there were others who disapproved of the measure. One was the law member of the viceroy's council, Hobhouse, who told Lytton that the Press Act was against the policy of the British. The governor of Madras wrote to Lytton that the excerpts given in the newspapers as an annex to the bill might be construed as objectionable; but any independent newspaper could be expected to give critical articles, which are not objectionable. The truth in their writings might not be palatable, but they were not seditious. Some members of the advisory council of the Secretary of State were uneasy with the Press Act. Pointing out that there was fundamental difference between the imperial policy of the British and the Dutch, they asked whether they were now on to follow the Dutch? Sir Erskine Perry, a member of the Council, wrote a note to the Secretary of State that the Secretary's consent was requested as if there was an emergency and it was given by a telegram. He said the Act was retrograde and based on the wrong ideas, which was bound to be a stumbling block in the future progress.

Two years before, i.e. on July 31, 1876, Robert Knight, editor of The Statesman had written a letter to Sir Owen Burne, private secretary to Lord Lytton, explaining the importance and usefulness of cordial relations between the press and the government. He asserted that as the Government of India was authoritarian, only check was that of the press. In England there was Parliament besides newspapers. Knight asked the government to be more considerate and liberal. In India it was inevitable that the press had to play the role of an opposition party. Under Lord Northbrook only loyal journalists were privy to the important news. But Knight reminded that the journalists were not courtiers. He suggested the creation of an information department in the administration whose chief would help the press and not direct or control it. The newspapers editors' conference in Calcutta created an atmosphere conducive to the establishment of such other organisations with all India base. Some British officers did anticipate this outcome. W.B. Jones, a commissioner at Hyderabad, wrote to his superior on February 28, 1878 that the sense of nationality, which was absent before, had taken root in India. Before, if Marathas were angry, the Bengalis did not mind. But this had changed in twenty years. Newspapers had become critical. Indians could now come together and converse. This was the fruit of the efforts of the English and was a reality, Jones concluded.

Lord Lytton justified the Press Act as necessity to defend the British Empire. He said that the Indian language papers were indulging in vicious campaign against the British rule, which he could prove from numerous clippings from the papers. Lytton further argued that the British started some new institutions in India, which were never there. Such institutions were helpful in securing the well-being of the society; and the government had a duty to see that they play the same role in India. When the administration itself was threatened, the government had no other option than to restrain the Indian language papers. Lord Lytton asserted in his speech to the Council on March 14, 1878, "It is not in the resentment for injuries that we propose to legislate. It is in the firm conviction that the maintenance of our Raj is for the good of the people, that we seek to save the people from the ruin in which they would involve themselves by seditious agitation against it." Less than a week after passing of the Press Act, Pherozeshah Mehta wrote a letter to 'The Times of India'. He assured that: "The vernacular press was guilty of no disloyal hostility to British rule. The worst that could be said of it was that it was on occasions guilty of angry recriminations, exaggerated generalisations and vulgar personalities. But such effusions conveyed no treasonable idea to a native reading them with his natural knowledge of native modes of thought and expression". Warning the government that the Act would defeat its purpose and annihilate honest criticism, he said: "And while thus the sound and healthy political growth of the people would be indefinitely retarded, the Government would be deprived of all trustworthy sources of keeping itself well informed of the real inner feelings and thoughts of the people towards it. Deprived of free and sincere criticism, it would hardly know to steer its way through servile adulation or scurrilous abuse".[1] The Sarvajanik Sabha's Journal criticised the Press Act and told the government that the press was an instrument to create public opinion about the government laws and measures. If that were to be muzzled then both the people and the government would be ill served. Sensing the mood in the country, Lord Lytton called a conference of the editors in Calcutta. Joshi attended the conference, along with about three hundred editors from all over the country. After the conference it was mooted to have an all India organisation of the editors. Joshi then came to Bombay to attend a meeting of the editors called by the Sarvajanik Sabha in March 1878, which was attended by Pherozeshah Mehta, Telang, and Jeejeebhai among others. The conference passed a resolution demanding the withdrawal of the Press Act.

Lytton's regime came to an end with the electoral defeat of the Tory party and coming to power of Gladstone and his liberal party. With Lytton, Sir Richard Temple also retired as governor of Bombay. A review of their rule by the Sabha's Journal represented the views of the Indians. About Lytton the Journal wrote: "The faith of people of India in the 'honour' of England has been considerably shaken, and 'the authority and prestige of its august sovereign' sullied in the eyes of millions of subjects by the untruthfulness and mean jugglery of Lord Lytton's attempts to over-reach them; the progressive well-being of the millions, both material and moral, has been successfully thrown back for many decades, the former by the suspension of works of public utility, and the increase in taxation and national indebtedness, and the latter by such measures as the Press Act, the Arms Act, and the Native Civil Service rules; 'the just rights and hereditary privileges' of the Princes and Chiefs of India have been violated by the salt and opium negotiations and by the threatened disbandonment of the arms of the native Princes; and those of 'our allies beyond the frontiers' have been infringed in the case of Afghan ruler by an unprovoked and wanton invasion of his country by our forces, and in the case of Burmah by the needless withdrawal of the Resident at his Court". The Journal also admonished Lytton and his finance member, Sir John Strachey, for sacrificing the interests of India for those of England. About Sir Richard Temple the Journal said: "He always loved to advance his own interests and never sacrificed them if it was in conflict with public well. It is true that he cared for popularity of a sort, but it was a cheap popularity. He was always in the theatrical attitude, and was always looking about him in his most heroic moods for the applause of the pit of his own countrymen. He had the proverbial faults of the new broom, which thinks to sweep clean the muddled brains of all who are subordinate to him, or who crossed his purposes. He had no love for the people, and his most pliable moment was always fishing a bait for the credulous to swallow. His pride of Englishism was intense to overbearing, and he thought the native races were all to be patted like children, and had no other purpose in life, but to remember gratefully the hired services of every white man in the country. He had no policy of his own, but veered like a weather-cock with every change of views of the power that dispense patronage and applause. His rule was essentially one of self-seeking and self-laudation and eminently demoralizing in its consequences".

When the Sarvajanik Sabha was moulding the public opinion in Maharashtra, some new organisations were coming up in Bengal. Keshav Chandra Sen activated the Brahmo Samaj. He not only toured Bengal but also many parts of India. Surendranath Banerjea formed the Indian Association in July 1876. He was in the ICS; but for technical reasons was relieved. Surendranath then joined Hindu College as a professor. He was a powerful orator and was disposed to social work. He was influenced by the life of Mazzini. His speeches on Mazzini made impact on the people of Bengal and gave rise to the Mazzini cult. R.C. Mujumdar says that this cult was at the root of the militant groups, which in later days spawned in Bengal. Like Mazzini, Surendranath's objective was a united country. The government had then reduced the age limit of the candidates appearing for the ICS. Calcutta witnessed a huge rally to protest against the decision which also demanded holding of simultaneous ICS examination in England and India; change of rules for the civil service etc. This meeting was followed by a similar meeting which decided to awaken the people of India, and elected representatives to go round the country. Surendranath was one of them who visited many places. This was the precursor of the national organisation, which was to be formed later.

What was the thinking in the Muslim community? Muslims played a prominent role in the 1857 revolt. In the same period Syed Ahmed was a judicial officer in Bijnaur, United Provinces, who gave protection to many British people, which helped him in getting an access to the official circles. As the Muslims were at the forefront of the revolt, British officials and people had a grudge against them. Syed Ahmed thought that his community must establish cordial relations with the British and their salvation lied in the English education. He then started a high school in Gazipur, in U P. To him science had a great priority and hence, he established a science institution. In 1864, Syed Ahmed visited England, where he was received in high circles and even had an audience with Queen Victoria. After his return he started a college at Alighar with Theodore Bake as the principal, who posed himself as the defender of the Muslims. In his articles in the college magazine and in other periodicals, Bake used to preach that Hindus and Muslims could not live together, and it was in the interest of the Muslims to be with the English. As Syed Ahmed shared his views, he warned the Muslims that they would get nothing by the elections to the municipalities and other bodies, as Hindus would dominate. He went so far as to write that Hindu and Muslims were like animals, and the English were superior who had the natural right to govern. In his opinion the Hindus and the Muslims were two swords and could not be accommodated in one scabbard. Syed Ahmed feared that with the representative government, Muslims would have to be subservient to the Bengalees, who were not a fighting race. William Hunter's book on the Muslims in India came out by this time, which was critical of the role of Muslims in the 1857 revolt. He thought that the Muslims were not loyal to the British rule. He, however, advised the government to cultivate and bring them round. That Hunter should be supportive of Syed Ahmed was obvious. The British politicians and government officials taking note of this new trend gradually took steps to assuage the feelings of the Muslims and cultivate them. Wilfrid Blunt was another Englishman who claimed to be a champion of the Muslims. He came from an affluent family and had felicity for writing and moved in high political circles. Blunt opposed the English invasion of Egypt. In his autobiography he mentions that in his visit to India in 1883, many Muslims complained to him about the Hindu dominance and he told them to cooperate with the Hindus without depending on the British. But this was not palatable to many Muslim leaders who decided to side with the British and to advance under their protection.

By the time Gladstone came to power in 1880, England had made progress economically. Helped by the new inventions, production had increased; and the country did not have to depend on cotton-mills alone. There was a talk of bringing in the social welfare measures. With the 1886 political reforms, graduates from universities, bankers, men from industries as well as professionals entered the political arena. This class was against an aggressive foreign policy and desired peace and stability. It did not advocate withdrawal from the Empire; but expected that those who were in charge of the administration of the colonies must run them efficiently and for the well-being of the people. Politicians belonging to this class favoured the Liberal party but were not necessarily supporters of Gladstone. His religiosity was not to their liking and they were insistent that with the scientific progress, sociology should not lag behind. It was, therefore, imperative to undertake social and economic surveys and make suitable policy and administrative changes. The new class demanded priority for such changes, which Gladstone did not favour. The Liberal as well as the Conservative parties were not well organised and were fractious. Only handful of Liberals were of the view that it was time to take steps to gradually wind up the Empire, while a sizeable number opposed the oppressive policies and advocated efficiency as well as welfare measures. Those, who were opposed to grant Home Rule or its equivalent to Ireland, and forced Gladstone to adopt cautious approach, could not be expected to give autonomy to India. On the other hand Gladstone ministry could not follow the high-handed policy of the imperialists like Disraeli or Lytton. So with the assumption of power, Gladstone replaced Lytton with Lord Ripon as viceroy.

Ripon had liberals in Sir Courtney Ilbert as Law member and Evelyn Baring in charge of finance. But several governors and high officials were traditionalists and were opposed to the liberal policy. In the Gladstone ministry Hartington became the Secretary of State for India followed by Kimberley. Both wanted to go slow with the political reforms. The Executive Council and Advisory Council attached to them were dominated by the traditionalists. Lord Ripon, who was assistant to the Secretary of State for India two decades earlier, was aware of the conditions in India. After taking over the reigns of office, Ripon realised that the conditions in India had changed to a considerable extent. The class of university graduates had swollen, and it was demanding more opportunities and a large share in the administration. He had brought this to the attention of Hartington. The Indian elite class had high hopes about Gladstone who had his limitations, and so also the party, which he headed. Indeed, Gladstone started his political career as a Conservative and then switched his loyalty to the Liberal Party. Besides, he was rather passionate about Ireland and Egypt, but did not have much interest in India. It was, therefore, no surprise that Gladstone did not back Ripon in later years. However, it was because of Gladstone and his ministry that Ripon could do away with the aggressive policy of Lytton against Afghanistan and first suspend and then abolish the Press Act. Indian politicians welcomed both decisions. But conservatives in the advisory councils of the Secretary of State successfully scotched Ripon's move to abolish the Arms Act.

While dealing with Afghanistan, Ripon was shocked and aghast to read the correspondence and documents of Lytton. He found that Lytton was playing a deep game and had the support of his C-in-C, Sir Frederick Haines. Ripon wrote to Hartington: "The root of the evil appears to me to lie in the fact that Lytton has all along shut his eyes to the liabilities, political, military and financial, in which he was involving himself. You are perfectly right when you say in your letter of May 21, that 'he (Lytton) is more anxious to retire from Kabul and Northern Afghanistan without leaving behind him any settlement than we are…" In February Ripon sent Hartington 'a set of curious documents' showing that in 1876, Lytton and the commander-in-chief were discussing whether in the event of a war with Russia, they should, or should not, annex the whole of Afghanistan. The idea seems to have been to attack Russia in Central Asia; but the force proposed (30,000 men) was so palpably inadequate for the purpose that Ripon suspects that, in Lytton's mind at least, the idea was to use the pretext of a Russian scare to cover the preparation of a force to conquer Afghanistan. "No man who reads these papers", he adds, "can doubt that the annexation, virtual or actual, of Afghanistan was a foregone conclusion when Lytton came out, though he was anxious not to fix public attention on his schemes".[2]

Ripon then examined the structure of the Indian Army and came to the conclusion that the power given to the governors of Bombay and Madras to control divisions in their respective regions were ill-conceived and creating problems. He abolished those powers. Opposing the suggestion to increase the number of British recruits in the army, he told the Secretary of State that it would be a harmful step, which would increase the burden on India. If the number had to be increased, then Britain should bear the extra cost. But Ripon was astonished when he was told that the British government, including Gladstone, wanted India to pay for the Army, which was sent to Egypt to put down the local rebellion. The secretary of state for India, Hartington, wrote to Ripon that many of the policies of Gladstone were vague; but about the payment by India for the Egyptian expedition, he was quite clear. Gladstone was of the view that England had to pay heavily for the Indian Army. Besides, the Suez Canal was a great help to India and that was why India should pay for the expedition to Egypt in proportion to the Indian troops sent. Ripon repudiated this argument. He wrote to Hartington: "You say that the British taxpayer is enormously saddled with military expenditure on account of India, and that but for India, large reduction could be made. What is there in it to justify you in making the Ryot...pay an anna for military expenditure, more than is absolutely necessary, I will not say for the maintenance of the tranquility in India, but for the utmost needs of the English government in this country? The truth of the matter is, I fear, very simple; you have got a Parliament at home, and you do not like either to ask it for more money or to face the outcry which would be raised against large military reductions...therefore, you impose a wholly unnecessary burden on the people of India where there is no parliament to ask awkward questions or to make inconvenient resistance. The cabinet, I admit, has got the giant's strength and it is using like a giant".[3]

Lord Ripon considered how Indians could be associated with the administration. He was helped by Finance Member Baring when the usual five-year review of the grants to the provinces by the Central Government was due in 1880. Baring suggested that it was much more convenient for the municipalities and district boards to collect the local duties and the taxes and to expend them. This might help the local self-institutions, to add to their revenue. Baring also suggested that instead of appointing administrators for such institutions they should be allowed to govern themselves; at least the progressive municipalities should be given such power. This stimulated Ripon's thoughts, and he concluded that the way to political progress lied through the development of local self-government. Ripon, then, called for notes on the local self-institutions in the provinces. The governors of Bengal, Bombay and Madras, while complying with the request, expressed their dissatisfaction, and said that those institutions were worthless. However, the administration of the Bombay Municipality was efficient and had the benefit of the services of the prestigious citizens who were clamoring for more powers. Ahmedabad and Poona were asking for more elected representatives on their municipalities. But the government was not willing to concede the Poona demand, as it believed that it was a seditious city. After going through the reports, Lord Ripon came to the conclusion that the Act itself was restrictive and defective and the provincial governments did not like to share power. He, therefore, published a resolution on May 18, 1882 indicating the objective of the government. The resolution said that the number of municipalities and district boards would have to be increased; government should not control them from within but from outside; the district boards should have the elected presidents. It was made clear that it was not the intention to make these institutions fully elected bodies; but to give more scope to the representatives of the people. It was felt that as the number of educated people was increasing, it was imperative to give them opportunity to show their ability. The resolution expressed the hope that the development of the local self-government would be an instrument of political training.

Ripon had not provided any draft of the legislation to the provincial governments and had given enough freedom to fashion their own scheme. Baring had made it clear that the resolution had a limited objective and that was to reform and develop the existing local self-institutions; and not open a forum for political debate. He thought the Bengali Babu would give his time to think about the roads and lightening of his city. Indian leaders welcomed this move by Ripon. Ranade wrote an article in the Sabha's Journal and dwelt at length on the importance and the paradigm of the local self-government. Though Ripon wanted to impress on the Indians that the problem of political rights was to be discussed in the remote future with Ranade and others, it was very close to their hearts. Hartington and Kimberley, who succeeded him as Secretary of State, advised Ripon to be cautious and in no case curtail the controlling powers of the government. Some provincial governments enacted laws as desired by Ripon, but Bengal and Bombay governments did their best to limit the powers and the number of the non-official members. Lt. Governor, Revers Thompson, of Bengal did not pass any law creating district boards. He was afraid that giving Bengalees freedom to speak their mind would be harmful to the establishment. Baring wrote back: "If Bengalees talked freely about the civic problems then they would be tied down and would have no time for any other mischief". The governor of Bombay, Sir James Fergusson, was a Tory who openly opposed Ripon's scheme as he firmly believed that the existing policy should not be changed. He wrote to Ripon that the demand for the right to send representatives was voiced only by Brahmins from Poona. Besides, Indians would never be satisfied. They would demand more, if their present demand was accepted. Present state of local self-institutions, if changed, would invite trouble. With the governor opposing the Ripon scheme, the Bombay legislation was bound to be more reactionary than that of any other province. Madras was no better. Hartington also was not happy with the Ripon scheme, but when Ripon threatened resignation, he relented.

By January 1883, Bombay saw the birth of a new monthly magazine, 'The

Voice of India'. It was Wedderburn who suggested that a monthly magazine should be published which would reproduce some news-items as well as editorial opinions of the vernacular papers in English. Dadabhai, with the help of Behram Malabari, brought out such a magazine. Later, as Dadabhai was residing in England, Malabari, editor of the 'Indian Spectator' remained the sole editor of 'The Voice of India'. The first issue of this magazine carried articles from 'Subodh Patrika' etc., which supported the Ripon scheme. But the 'Bombay Chronicle' was not favourable. It said that if the carpenters and such others were to elect the representatives to the municipality, then it would defeat the purpose of the Central Government. On December 26, 1882 in a letter to Kimberley, the deputy Secretary of State for India, Ripon said, "Two policies are lying before the choice of the Government of India; the one is the policy of those who have established a free press, who have promoted education, who have admitted natives more and more largely to the public service in various forms, and who have favoured the extension of self-government; the other is that of those who hate freedom of press, who dread the progress of education, and who watch with jealousy and alarm every thing which tends, in however limited a degree, to give the natives of India a larger share in the management of their own affairs. Between these two policies we must choose; the one means progress, the other means regression. Lord Lytton chose the latter. I have chosen the first".[4]

When Ripon learnt how some governors and members of the India Council reacted to his scheme, he asked Hartington, "What is the use of a liberal government, as far as India is concerned, if it is to give itself up, bound hand and foot, to the guidance of a set of old gentlemen, whose energies are relaxed by age, and who having excellent salaries and no responsibility, amuse themselves by criticising the proposals and obstructing the plans of those, who have the most recent knowledge of the real state of India, and who have upon their shoulders the whole responsibility for the good government of that country".[5] Ripon had to dilute some of the provisions of the local self-government bill. But the Calcutta correspondent, of the 'Times', as his wont, criticised the bill, for which he came under trenchant criticism by the 'Maratha' on 4 February 1883. It advised the 'Times', 'to go through the books on the local self-Government which were available in large number. 'The Times' challenged that the local self-government institutions would rein in the bureaucracy, which, the 'Maratha' said, was narrow minded and self-seeking. The bureaucrats were expected to oppose the bill. But those who had the benefit of modern liberal education should have welcomed it'. Ripon's bill was opposed not only by the bureaucracy, but also by the English planters and industrialists, who were pressurising the British government to slow down the process of anything which was remotely liberal. When Ripon decided to increase the age limit for the entrance to the government engineering college at Rurki, and to appoint graduates from the college in the

Public Works Department, the Englishmen in India put up a fight. They insisted that the monopoly of the Englishmen in the department must not be disturbed. Ripon had to revert his decision but then appointed a senior Indian judge in place of Sir Richard Garth, the Chief Justice, in a leave vacancy. Garth registered his disapproval, but the appointment could not be withdrawn.

Gladstone, the prime minister, was a different politician than Gladstone, the opposition leader. This was again demonstrated when the Indian Penal code was to be amended. In 1882 Bihari Lal Gupta, a civil servant in the Bengal service, suggested that the Indian magistrate and the sessions judge should have equivalent powers as his English counterpart. Both the government of Bengal and Viceroy's executive council supported this suggestion. Even the Secretary of State gave his consent. The law member, Sir Courtney Ilbert, then brought a suitable legislation, and Lord Ripon gave a detailed reply to the debate in his council. But this legislation generated tremendous controversy outside the council. Official and non-official Englishmen united against the bill. In numerous public meetings they criticised it and many Anglo-Indian papers joined the chorus. The government was warned that if Indian magistrates and Sessions judges were empowered to try Englishmen in their courts, then there would be a repetition of 1857 revolt. This scare was raised by J.C. Macgregor of 'The Times'. 'The Times' editorial criticised the Ilbert bill on Feb 5, 1882. It said: "If Lord Ripon is resolved to clear Indian administration of every anomaly he can discover in it, the best thing he can do will be to pack up his trunks and come home at once. He is himself the greatest of anomalies, the head and the front of the office he is seeking to remove. English rule over India is an anomaly in itself, not in this or that point of detail, but in every point. We must accept it for what it is, or we must give it up altogether and leave India to the full enjoyment of the natural rights of man". Sir James Fitzjames Stephen, in a letter to 'The Times' wrote: (March 5, 1883) "It is impossible to imagine any policy more fearfully dangerous and more certain, in case of failure, to lead to results to which the Mutiny would be child's play than the policy of shifting the foundation on which the British Government of India rests. It is essentially an absolute Government, founded, not on consent, but on conquest…Implying at every point the superiority of the conquering race, of their ideas, their institutions, their opinions, and their principles and having no justification for its existence except that of superiority". Pointing out that India was never a unified country, Sir James Fitzjames Stephen again reverted to the same subject; this time in the October 1883 issue of 'The Nineteenth Century'. He said that if the English or any European power had not taken it over, India would have been divided into many kingdoms. He then proceeds to add: "the expression 'absolute government' has an unwelcome, not to say terrible sound, in English ears, but does it mean anything which Indians regard with aversion or terror? To the natives of India substantive would appear to involve the adjective. They have never had any experience of any government which is not absolute in the only sense in which the government of India is absolute: that is to say, in the sense of being vested as far as the law is concerned in a single person, or in a small number of persons not chosen by those whom they rule, and not checked in the exercise of their powers by any elected body which is so chosen". Stephen firmly believed that only the British government could guarantee the security of life and property to the Indians, and the British magistrates alone could do this job. He warned if handful of Irish members could stop the proceedings of the Parliament, then Parliament in India could be very well imagined to bring chaos. Muslims would attack everybody else with Koran in one hand and sword in the other.

To his English critics Ripon's reply was that England had given some promises to the people of India and it was incumbent on her to fulfill them. If the Indians were to be associated with the administration, then the criminal law had to be amended to appoint Indians as magistrates and to allow them to hear the cases of the English. With such an onslaught on the bill, Ripon had no other option than to amend it. The amendment defeated the objective of the bill. It must be noted that neither Gladstone nor the Secretary of State supported Ripon. The Viceroy could not anticipate the ferocity of the opposition to the Ilbert bill. The most vociferous opposition was from the planters. They were united and were used to treating the workers with cruelty. They did not want their 'rights' to be infringed in any way. Planters' case was that, it was not correct to assume that the magistrates from the rural areas would behave as those in the cities; and they feared that the evidence would be cooked up. British soldiers and officers also joined in opposition to the Bill. Macgregor was the villain in this whole affair; and 'The Times', which wielded influence on the government, editorially carried on a campaign against the Ilbert bill. Lord Ripon was aware of this, and wrote to Lord Northbrook: "He is a small Calcatta barrister, by name Macgregor, who knows nothing of this country or its affairs, except what he picks up in the bar library and the Bengal club. He lives in a narrow set of lawyers and represents their feelings and prejudices only. We have offered to give him information upon any subject on which he may want it, but he never asks for it, and prefers to telegraph such inaccurate stuff as he sent it to the 'Times' lately about our financial condition. It is a great pity that as the 'Times' goes to so large an expense about its weekly telegrams from India, Mr. Chenery should not employ a really good correspondent here who should reside at the headquarters of the Government and whose business it would be to supply his newspaper not with his personal crochets but with accurate and trustworthy information. The present system is very mischievous as a great many people at home know nothing of Indian matters except what they see in the Monday telegram in the 'Times'.[6]

Ripon had an eminent defender in Florence Nightingale. In August 1883 issue of 'The Nineteenth Century', she wrote: "The natives of India ask for no new concessions. They simply claim the fulfillment of the pledges and assurances already given. But the public in England are perhaps not aware of the very important steps which Lord Ripon has already taken to deal with these and other evils of the same class which had not been mentioned. How does Lord Ripon's policy seek to deal with the grievances complained of? The chief grounds of complaints are (a) the unsuitability of our institutions, (b) the great cost met by excessive taxation. Lord Ripon has struck at the root of both these evils by his measures of decentralisation and local self-government; and by the steps he has taken for the employment of the natives. Under the local self-government scheme, much of the work now done by highly paid foreigners and low paid corrupt native underlings will for the future be done for little or nothing by the villagers themselves; while by the due employment of natives in official positions great economy in salaries will be effected and the administration, it is said, will be gratefully brought into conformity with the needs and wishes of the various races. The measure known as Ilbert bill is an integral, by no means the most important part of this policy; offices of responsibility cannot be conferred upon natives unless they are at the same time granted the powers required to perform the duties of these offices". The amendments to the Ilbert Bill provoked the 'Maratha' on June 6 and 13, 1884 to comment that Lord Ripon had come to India to remove the anomalies in the administration and not to add new ones. The finance member of the viceroy's council, Evelyn Baring, later Lord Cromer, was all for the Ilbert bill. Lord Zetland, his biographer, quotes some extracts from Baring's farewell speech in Bombay, in which Baring reiterated his support. At the same time he said that he was much more concerned with the lot of the peasantry. He was determined to amend the land law in Bengal. Baring was pained to see that Permanent Settlement policy of Lord Cornwallis had left indeterminate relations between the landlords and their tenants. Result was that the lot of the peasantry became worse. An inquiry revealed that in one district of Bengal, landlords had levied twenty-seven different cesses. One of the objectives of Cornwallis was to save the peasants from illegal cesses. As this objective failed, an amendment to the act was a necessity. Baring asserted that that was not the breach of faith on the part of government; and he was keen to get that bill passed by the Council.[7]

Hobhouse, a historian and a political scientist, in his article in June 1883 issue of the 'Contemporary Review' wrote: "The question raised by the non-official English community in India and their abettors in England, is between the two methods of governing India. What goal shall we aim at? What ideal shall we set before our eyes? 'Our own superiority', says one set of thinkers; 'The welfare of Indians', says another. This difference of view underlies controversies, not only as to the employment of Natives, but as to their education, as to the freedom of their press and occasionally as to the treatment of their neighbouring states…The men of great eminence have insisted on the nobler and more generous principles of government for the welfare of the Indians; the English Parliament has always recognised that principle as its guide". It should be remembered that Ceylon or present day Sri Lanka had passed a similar legislation and the Ceylonese magistrate was given the power to hear the criminal cases against the Englishmen. That was why this discrepancy added to the fury in India. Public meetings were held in most cities criticising the opponents of the Ilbert Bill. Sarvajanik Sabha Journal, reviewing the agitation by the Englishmen against the bill, wrote: "The first great lesson of the political turmoil of the past few months which we wish our people to lay to heart is that they should never cherish any more the fond day-dream that the Anglo-Indian community will ever make a common cause with them in their struggle for higher power and privileges. A very large, we might well say, over-whelming majority of their races will occupy the position of conservatives of India, whatever may be their political partisanship in their own mother country. The official and non-official Europeans are as a body bound by the very reason of their privileged existence to resist all attempts to level up the native populations, and with them the time will never come when freedom and equality may be safely conceded. Any misunderstanding on this fundamental condition of our political life can never fail to be attended with disaster and disappointment. The educated minority of the native population, with their free press, and their Associations unconsciously sympathized with by the mass of their countrymen, represent the soul of Indian liberalism and their strength lies in the justice of their claim".

The speeches and writings, especially the tone of racial superiority, of the opponents of the Ilbert bill both in India and England hurt the feelings of Indians. The movement against the Bill was termed by many as 'white mutiny'. But the Indians were not disheartened. They decided to accord a grand farewell to Lord Ripon who by then had decided to resign and go home. From Simla to Calcutta Ripon was felicitated at various places. Not only kings, states chiefs, advocates, journalists but everybody who was anybody participated in these functions. In Madras a huge meeting was held and decided to send representatives to the Bombay meeting, which everybody wanted to be a grand success. When Ripon arrived in Bombay, his train was stopped at Parel and the mill workers felicitated him. Dadabhai who took the lead in arranging felicitations for Ripon, impressed on the people that instead of having functions in different places it would be better to pool the resources and arrange a huge farewell function in Bombay. He invited Kathiawad princes to contribute; and they did. In a letter to Malabari, Dadabhai said that it was not important what the Indians received under Ripon's rule, but the manner in which he ran the administration and his expression of warm feelings must be recognised. Ripon was felicitated by the University of Bombay where Vice Chancellor and Chief Justice Sir Raymond West presided.

The next day a public meeting was held in the Town Hall where representatives from Madras as well as Pune, Khandesh, Gujarat etc. attended. It was a huge success. Ripon in his reply expressed his indignation at the trend to break the promises given by Queen Victoria in her Declaration. He criticised the principles enunciated by Stephen, which he regarded as opposed to the Queen's Declaration and the tradition of England. Ripon declared that the rule of England did not rest on the valor of the army or the power of the arms, but on the trust in goodwill.

These unprecedented functions evoked different reactions from different quarters. Anglo-Indian papers like 'The Pioneer' said that the functions were not for what Ripon did, but to express anger at the superiority of the English. It reminded its readers that those who arranged these functions were opponents of Britain and did not have the support of the Indian people. Sir Auckland Colvin, finance member, posed the question in an article, if it was true, what it meant? His opinion was that the people were now becoming politically conscious and were aware of their strength. It was for the English rulers to decide whether this awareness was to be utilised as Ripon did or to suppress it, and like Lytton, invite danger to all. To him the Indians had given their verdict by way of the functions for Ripon. The people of Bombay were so engrossed in the memories of the grand functions held in honour of Lord Ripon that they did not take much notice of the arrival of Lord Dufferin who came to replace Ripon. In Calcutta, newspapers were discussing the farewell functions rather than the reception to the new viceroy. Lord Lytton writing in the 'Saturday Review', London, took the opportunity to vent his frustration and anger by criticising Lord Ripon's regime, for which 'Maratha' upbraided him.

Ripon, while laying down the office, wrote three notes for his successor. In the first note, Ripon emphasised the importance of the government consulting the leaders of the educated India. In his opinion the British officials in India were administrators and not politicians. His conviction was that the best way to win the confidence and friendship of the Indians was to increasingly involve them in the administration. To him, it was a folly to ignore this class. Ripon's second note advised Dufferin that he should not be persuaded by those who wanted to revive the vernacular Press Act. He said, "More mischief is done by some of the Anglo-Indian newspapers in a week than is done in a year by the vernacular journals put together." The Third note warned Dufferin against the arrogant Englishmen. He said, no Englishman be allowed to come to India who would not hold his interests subservient to those of the Indians.[8]

Lord Dufferin decided to take the middle path. Addressing a meeting of the Chamber of Commerce, he assured the people that his government would give justice to everybody without discrimination on the basis of race, creed or castes. But Lt. Governor Rivers Thomson, in his speech, spoiled the effect of the viceroy's speech. Thompson said that the Hindu civilisation had lost all vitality and it was the mission of the British to restore it. But in the recent past these efforts took a different turn, and the imagination of some people had run riot. They started making all sorts of demands. Thompson declared that he had no sympathy for such people. He said that it was very difficult to wield a nation of the people so divided by religion, race, castes and tongues. Next day, instead of the viceroy, Thompson got the publicity. As expected, his speech was severely criticised by the Indian press, and Governor-General Dufferin's position became awkward. Secretary of State Kimberley had advised him to take steps to bridge the gap between the Indians and Anglo-Indians. But Thompson at the outset threw a spanner. However, Dufferin used his discretion and decided that his priority was to get the amended landholding bill passed; and for this he required Thompson's help. This bill was accordingly passed.

The mutiny of the Anglo-Indians against the Ilbert Bill and their exhibition of racial superiority awakened the educated Indians to the urgency of some national forum. Most of the existing associations were busy with the local problems. Those in Calcutta, Madras, Bombay were more advance. So Surendranath Banerjea and his colleagues called a conference to discuss the issue of a national organization, which would have an annual session in different parts of the country. In Madras, a four day conference was called in 1884 which also discussed national problems and was attended by Nagendranath Sen, Surendranath Banerjea and A. Bose from Calcutta. East India Association and Sarvajanik Sabha jointly sponsored a meeting in Pune on January 18, 1885, which was attended by Ranade, Dadabhai, Telang, Pherozeshah Mehta etc. to discuss the national problems. Two years earlier one such meeting had decided to send a weekly newsletter to 'Pall Mall Gazette', London, as a counter to the biased reporting of India by Macgregor of the 'Times'. The provincial associations, thus, were deliberating about the necessity of having a national organisation; but no definite steps were taken.

It was Allan Octavian Hume who had already initiated a move to establish such an organisation. He was secretary to the Government of India in charge of agriculture, forest etc. and had cordial relations with Lord Northbrook as well as Lord Ripon. As the secretary of agriculture, he was aware of the conditions of the peasantry from the government reports and also by touring the country. He had also seen some intelligence reports reaching the government. Hume was alarmed by the degree of the public dissatisfaction and had already conveyed his views to Sir Auckland Colvin and warned Lord Ripon about the dire consequences, if the situation was not handled properly and promptly. Hume then circulated a letter addressed to the graduates of the Calcutta University on March 1, 1883. The letter opened with kind and encouraging words. Hume said, "Constituting, as you do, a large body of the most highly educated Indians, you should, in the natural order of things, constitute also the most important source of all mental, moral, social and political progress in India. Whether in the individual or the nation, all vital progress must spring from within, and it is to you, her most cultured and enlightened minds, her most favoured sons, your country must look for the initiative." Hume then stressed the need and urgency to have an organisation. For this, Hume proposed, "If only fifty men, good and true, can be found to join as founders, the thing can be established, and further development will be comparatively easy." Hume suggested that the constitution of such an organisation should be democratic and free from personal ambition: the head should merely be the chief servant, and his council, assistant servant. Hume's appeal had an excellent response from many parts of the country. This appeal helped the consolidation of the idea of forming a national conference. Hume did not wait after issuing an appeal; he visited some cities and conferred with prominent Indians. It was then decided in a meeting in December 1884 at Madras that an organisation by name of 'Indian National Union' be established. Those who attended made it clear that this new organisation would be loyal to the British government, but if any injustice was done to India, would strive to get the grievances redressed by constitutional means. Another decision of the Madras meeting was to establish branches at Calcutta, Bombay, Madras, Ahmedabad, Allahabad, etc. and to enlist those men with character and with service as their motto, as members. The first session of the organisation was to be held in Poona and the branches were authorised to select the delegates. Hume then went to England and held discussions with Bright and others.

It was decided to send a delegation to England, as elections to the Parliament were due. At the same time the Bombay Presidency Association circulated a manifesto to prominent persons in India. It was, in fact, a charter of demands, which drew the attention of the English electorate to the fact that the whole of India had a common legal system and an official language; the education was spreading and the Indians were enjoying individual freedom. But they had no share in the administration, and as long as this right was not accepted, it would be difficult to elicit cooperation from the people. It reminded them that the British Parliament had given many promises to the Indians, though many remained unfulfilled. The manifesto then enumerated different demands. Chief among them were: more representation in the government service; fixed land revenue; India's wealth was drained to England by way of salaries, allowances, expenditure on Secretary of States office in London, purchase of stores etc., which had to be remedied and India had to be given a share of this amount; representation in the provincial and central legislatures to the Indians; England to bear the expenses of the intervention in Afghanistan etc. Ranade and Telang prepared the draft of this manifesto. When it was discussed in a meeting in Bombay, Baddrudin Tyabji suggested that the Indian delegation should not participate in an election campaign on behalf of any single British political party.

Dadabhai, Pherozeshah and Wacha did not support Tyabji. They held the view that the Indians had a right to tell that not Richard Temple but William Digby should be elected, and that right must be exercised. Madras and Calcutta leaders also held similar views.

In England the delegation realised that the Liberal Party neither supported all of their demands nor thought them practical. Tory press was critical of the delegation as it was considered to be close to the Liberals. It was Dadabhai, who insisted that the Indian delegation should support the Liberals. This was not approved of by T. Madhavrao who, therefore resigned. He did not want Indians to associate with the radical elements in England. In Bombay Dadabhai Framji took a similar position and like Madhavrao, wrote a letter to the 'Times of India'. The paper then suggested that following the example of these two gentlemen, Jeejeebhai should also resign from the Presidency Association. Macgregor, in a telegram to the 'Times' "emphasised the decisions of the Bombay Presidency Association, the Indian Associations of Calcatta and other three to disregard Madhavrao's advice and to intervene in the General Election by having the Indian delegates oppose certain Conservatives and support certain liberals for Parliament..." Macgregor added that the lists had led to the resignation of Framaji, whose letter he quoted, and that 'The Times of India' had urged Jeejeebhai and other leaders of the Bombay Presidency Association to resign. In conclusion Macgregor stated that: "neither the Bombay Association nor the delegates with their Appeal spoke in the name of the people, but were merely agitators whose words were not understood by the dumb millions or by the wealthy landlords...the real leaders of the people".[9] 'The Time's editorial objected to the support to the Liberal candidates by the Indian delegation. The delegation had to suffer a set back, as no candidate it supported was elected. Lal Mohan Ghose, who fought the election, lost by a narrow margin.

To whom should go the credit for the establishment of the Indian National Congress, was a subject of discussion for some time. Raosaheb Mandlik gave it to Ganesh Vasudev Joshi ('Public Uncle') and S.B. Govandye, secretary of the Sarvajanik Sabha, as they circulated a letter in 1876 emphasising the need of a national organisation. N.C. Kelkar had an interview with Ranade in 1896, in which Ranade told Kelkar that the credit should be shared by Hume and Wedderburn. Ranade also praised the services of both of them to India. It can now be said after the lapse of so many years and after having so much material available that the credit for the establishment of the Indian National Congress does not go to any one individual or organisation. The need for such a national organisation was felt by many in different parts of India; however it was Hume who took a lead and gave to 'airy nothing a local habitation and a name' and acted as a catalyst. Hume had a meeting with Dufferin and told him that he was planning to have some voluntary organisation. He also wanted a governor of a province to preside where the annual session of the organisation was to be held. But Dufferin disagreed and advised Hume that the organization, which he had in mind, should confine itself to discuss the social problems.

The first session of the national conference was to be held in Poona, but due to cholera, the venue was shifted to Bombay. Surendranath Banerjea had called a conference in Calcutta at the same time. He, therefore, could not attend the conference in Bombay on December 28, 1885. It was also true that there was intense controversy going on among the Bengali leaders, and several of them did not see eye to eye with Banerjea. The result was that for the first session of the national conference in Bombay only three delegates from Bengal were present. As each provincial association had been allotted fixed number of representatives, total number who attended was seventy-two. There were twenty-five observers. Ranade and Dr. Bhandarkar, being in the government service, were among them. W.C. Bonerjee was elected as the first president and it was resolved that the new organisation should be known as the Indian National Congress. Bonerjee was a successful lawyer in Calcutta, who in later years was a generous donor to the Congress. He was also known as 'every inch an Englishman'. Dadabhai, Hume, Pherozeshah, Wedderburn, Telang, Badruddin Tyabji etc. played a leading role in the deliberations, and Hume was appointed secretary of the Congress. 'The Tribune's correspondent was much impressed by the dress as well as the fluency in English of the delegates from Madras. He wrote, "Madras sent the greatest number of delegates, all of good education and high social standing. They completely enchanted the audience with their liberal views and impressive eloquence. Clad in conservative Hindu garments, with their shining foreheads rubbed with sandalwood after the orthodox Hindu fashion, and speaking in eloquent English about the various ways in which India should improve her political status, they exhibited a spectacle at once charming and instructive".

Bonerjee, in his presidential address, stressed the need to establish cordial relations with the politically conscious individuals in India and in the British Commonwealth. He appealed for unity. The session passed a resolution expressing loyalty to the British government. Almost all speakers acknowledged the benefits of the British rule. The resolutions in the sessions demanded more representation to the Indians in provincial councils and the Viceroy's council. It wanted councils to be established in Avadh, Punjab and NWFP. Congress suggested that a standing committee of the House of Commons be formed to consider the complaints received from India. Simultaneous ICS examinations to be held in England and India, was another demand. It expected reduction in the government expenditure.

Hume had made explicitly clear that the Congress would not be a parallel organisation to the government, but would supplement its work. He declared that though the Congress would discuss the shortcomings of the administration, it would not be an opposition party. For some years to come the Congress did not deviate from this path. Even after the establishment of the Indian National Congress, some provincial or regional institutions continued to work and flourish; but the need for a national organisation was felt and accepted by all. India, thus entered into a new era.

REFERENCES

1. Homi Mody, *Sir Pherozeshah Mehta*, Asia Publishing House, NY, 1963, pp. 55-56.
2. Lucien Wolf, *Life of the first Marquess of Ripon*, 2 Vols., John Murray, London, 1921, pp. 18-19.
3. Ibid, pp. 55-56.
4. Anil Seal, *The Emergence of Indian Nationalism*, Cambridge Uni. Press, London, 1968, p. 149.
5. Ibid., p. 151.
6. Edwin Hirschmann, *White Mutiny, the Ilbert Bill Crisis in India*, South Asian Books, Columbia, 1980, p. 51.
7. The Marquess of Zetland, *Lord Cromer*, Hodder and Stoughton, London, 1932, pp. 80-83.
8. R.S. Mehrotra, *The Emergence of the Indian National Congress*, Barnes and Noble, NY, 1971, p. 378.
9. Briton Martin. *New India 1885*, Uni. of California Press, Berkeley, 1969, p. 228.

Chapter Six

THE INITIAL PERIOD

Gokhale did not attend the first session of the Congress, the organisation, in which he later played a prominent part. In 1885, the year when the first session of the Congress was held, Gokhale had started his career as a teacher in the New English School of the Deccan Education Society. He could not attend even the next three Congress sessions. In the initial period the organisational details of the Congress were not decided and the nature and the scope of various committees took some time to be finalised. It could only be done by 1888 when it was decided that the provincial conferences should be held regularly. Accordingly, the Bombay Provincial Conference was held in Pune in 1888. Though it was a Bombay Provincial Conference in name, the initiative was taken by the leaders of Pune. Dinshaw Wacha wrote to Dadabhai to complain against the Pune leaders for their defiance.

Gokhale was the secretary of the Provincial Conference for the first four years. In the second session of the conference he made a speech decrying the reduction of expenditure on higher education by the government. He emphasised the importance and usefulness of the English education, which he said would usher in an era of progress in India. He firmly believed that if India's case was properly explained to the English people, they would get justice. This, of course, was also the position of Ranade, Dadabhai and Pherozeshah Mehta. The fifth Provincial Conference was presided over by Pherozeshah Mehta, and then onwards the leaders from Bombay and Pune started to hold such sessions jointly.

The first session of the Congress evoked opposite reactions from different newspapers and quarters. 'The Hindu' of Madras commended the restrain shown by the political leaders and also in the deliberations. Even if there had been any festivity, it would have been justified, but the leaders convened the Congress session as any other public function. 'The Hindu' was confident that this would give prestige to the Congress, and gradually the public opinion in India would also be influenced by the new organisation. 'Hindusthan' of Lucknow remarked that the Anglo-Indians did not consider India as one nation, but the Congress session in Bombay had given a fitting reply to them. 'Hindu Patriot' declared that the session had clearly shown that the Indians could act collectively. It was confident that eventually those castes and races, which were distant from the Congress would come round in spite of whatever the Anglo-Indians do. 'The Times of India' advised the government that the demand for more seats for Indians in the Viceroy's Council should be rejected in the interests of Indian people. It feared that elected representation in the Provincial and Viceroy's Councils would be the next most important demand which should firmly be denied.

Based on the newsletter of its Bombay correspondent, the 'Times', London, wrote an editorial on December 31, 1885. It said that the 'lawyers, teachers, journalists dominated the Congress which did not represent the Indian masses'. Kashinath Trimbak Telang, a prominent lawyer and afterwards a judge, replied to 'The Times' in its issue of March 9, 1886. He wrote, "Although it must be admitted that the Mahomedan community was not adequately represented at our meeting, your remark is not altogether an accurate one. Two leading Mahomedan gentlemen did attend the Congress, viz., Mr. R.M. Sayani and Mr. A.M. Dharmsi. Both of these gentlemen are graduates of the University and attorneys of standing at the High Court of Bombay. Mr. Sayani held the office of the Sheriff of Bombay. Further, the Hon. Badroodin Tyabji, a member of the Legislative Council of Bombay, and Mr. Cumroodin Tyabji would have attended the Congress, had they not been absent from Bombay at the time the Congress was seating. And it must be remembered that this Congress was the first of its kind, and naturally, therefore, there were some shortcomings. But we feel confident that next year, when assemblage would be at Calcutta, Mahomedan community will be represented as it befits its numbers and importance. The second point relates to the omission of social reform from the proceedings of the Congress. As regards this, it is to be observed that the main object of the Congress was a political one. But when the programme for business was informally discussed by the members, they decided that after the subjects for which they had specially assembled were disposed of, the questions of social reform should be considered if there was time. But on that (last day) earnest social reformer, Diwan Bahadur Raghunath Rao of Madras, gave an eloquent address on social questions, and he was followed by another eminent reformer, the Hon. M.G. Ranade, of this Presidency". 'The Times', in the years to come, made it a point to emphasize that the Congress had no support of the Muslims. It was also the constant refrain of many of the British officials and opinion-makers. In the December 1886 issue of the 'Nineteenth Century', one W.H. Jeffrey wrote to advise the government to grant more facilities to Muslims and keep them on 'our' side. He reminded that Lords Mayo and Dufferin did something to cultivate the Muslims, but under Lord Ripon's regime Brahmins and Bengalees were given more importance.

After the first session of the Congress, Dadabhai went to England. Some in the Congress, and especially Dadabhai, were demanding that the Indians should have some reserved seats in the Parliament. This, of course, was not accepted by the British government or political leaders. Nevertheless, Dadabhai thought it worthwhile to contest an election to the Parliament. So he and Lal Mohan Ghose entered the fray in 1886, but were defeated. 'The Statesman' was of the opinion that the Liberal Party did not support both Dadabhai and Ghose as it should have. Dadabhai then came back to India to preside over the second session of the Congress in Calcutta. This session of the Congress differed from that of the first in many respects. The exuberant report of the secretary says, "In regard to the second congress, the greatest enthusiasm prevailed, especially throughout Bengal. At many places, large crowds accompanied delegates to the ships or railway stations on their departure for the Congress, giving them ovation". Preparation for the Session began in the rainy season. In many cities some institutions organized meetings and discussed the subjects, which they thought ought to come up in the Congress session. The report of the secretary, giving the classification of the delegates, asserted that every two delegates represented one million people. One of the striking things was a total absence of the landed aristocracy and also of the shop-keeping class. But higher landed interests as talukdars and zamindars were represented. Bankers and merchants were fairly represented, but petty moneylenders and shopkeepers were absent. He also says that there were very negligible representatives of peasants and agricultural classes. But to him it was no surprise, as they had very imperfect knowledge of political problems, and they were poor. Legal profession mustered strong. Referring to the poor representation of the Muslims, the secretary argues, "The Mohammedans were inadequately represented; which is just as if the nationality of the House of Commons in England were denied, because it contained the smaller proportion than the population of Great Britain as a whole, of Methodists or Roman Catholics". This inadequate representation of the Muslims was the subject of comments by many newspapers. 'The Hindu' attributed this to "an insidious attempt...made to discord and foment sectional jealousies among the Mohamedan community".

In his presidential address Dadabhai laid all the emphasis on eradication of poverty. He also repeated the Congress demands for more representation for Indians in the Provincial and Viceroy's Councils and in the government. The session passed a resolution on the subject when Surendranath Banerjea and Ambika Charan Muzumdar pointed out that poverty was due to absence of industries and also due to the large population. Bipin Krishna Bose, who was a judge in Nagpur, in his reminiscences narrates an incident at Calcutta. He writes: "I had a talk with Mr. Bapu Rao after his return from Calcutta. He said that Mr. Chitnavis and he were among those whom the Viceroy, Lord Dufferin, had graciously received, not as delegates of the Congress, but as distinguished visitors to the Capital. In the talks which His Excellency had with the president, Mr. Dadabhai Naoroji, the matters soon came to a crisis, and when Mr. Naoroji said that he and his friends were determined to carry on the propaganda vigorously until success was attained, His Excellency said, what if in the public interests he were to stop their dangerous activities by putting into operation both his ordinary and extraordinary powers in that behalf, Mr. Naoroji promptly replied that His Excellency might please himself and he and his friends never expected to reach their goal except through many troubles and tribulations. No publicity was given to the incident by any of the delegates present".[1]

'The Times', as expected, severely criticised the Calcutta session of the Congress. A 'National Indian Congress, composed of three hundred delegates from all parts of the country, holds its first meeting in Calcutta today. It is organised, of course, upon the model of the societies, which discuss political and social affairs in this country. The subjects discussed are the representation of the Natives in the Legislative Councils, the admission of Natives to more numerous and responsible posts in the civil service, and generally, the objections to British administration which naturally occur to persons of considerable imitative powers, of great fluency of speech, and of total ignorance of the real problems of the Government and the means by which they have to be overcome by practice. The Mahomedan community appears to be aloof from this kind of thing, on the ground that they prefer not to hamper the Government at a time when it is doing its best for the natives of India. We have produced an extensive class of talkers and equipped them with a second-hand knowledge of English history and literature. Thus, we have to deal with the public opinion of a kind, but it is important to remember that it is the public opinion of a class whose aims and interests are not by any means identical with those of the great masses of Indian populations for whom we have to care. These societies and the newspapers they control represent a very trifling percentage of the people of India".[2] The demand for more representation in the Councils and administration by the Congress was not favoured by many Muslim leaders. But even the Kayasthas in the north India were also wary of this demand, as they feared that it would lead to the dominance of the Bengalis. Nevertheless, unlike Muslim leaders, the Kayasthas in the north, without much loss of time, joined the Congress.

Both Tilak and Gokhale shared the platform in the first session of the Provincial Conference. Gokhale's first public speech was on the scandalous behaviour of Crawford, who became notorious in his capacity as a collector and commissioner. He was efficient but unscrupulous; a great spendthrift, he was careless about other peoples' money. Crawford spoke Marathi very well; and N.C. Kelkar said that with a dhoti on he could have passed as a Chitpawan Brahmin.

As a commissioner of the Bombay Municipality, he executed some useful schemes, but spent lavishly on them. There was, therefore, a public outcry and the government had to appoint an inquiry committee. But Crawford's most reprehensible behaviour was with some Mamlatdars under his jurisdiction when he was the commissioner of the Central Division of the Bombay Presidency. It was freely said that Crawford had taken bribes from Mamlatdars. When the government decided to inquire into this scandal, it assured the Mamlatdars that they would not be charged for the bribery, if they produced concrete evidence against Crawford. Mamlatdars took the bait and after the inquiry Crawford had to leave, as he was found guilty. Crawford then left for England, where he wrote a book viciously criticising the Indians in general and Pune Brahmins in particular. However, the Mamlatdars found themselves in soup, as the government went back on its promise and sent notices asking for the explanation of their behaviour.

When the government proceeded against the Mamlatdars, it was Tilak who raised a hue and cry. He wrote several articles and addressed meetings. Gokhale joined in protesting against the government's action in a public meeting in Pune on September 1, 1889. The government had no doubt about the culpability of Crawford. Viceroy Lord Dufferin, wrote to the secretary of state that the behaviour of Crawford had brought shame to the English regime. But many of the Englishmen were angry with the government, as they believed that the governor, Lord Ray, blundered in instituting an inquiry against Crawford.

'The Times', London, avoided any criticism of Crawford but came down heavily on the Mamlatdars; while 'The Times of India' said that the whole affair had proved that the Indians were incapable of holding responsible positions. In his public speech Gokhale took both these newspapers to task and said that 'The Times' could be depended upon to justify any untruth. The government then decided that the Mamlatdars should be compensated; but did not bother to pay a farthing for two months. In critcising the government's action or inaction, Gokhale wrote in the January 29, 1890 issue of 'Sudharak': "When there was some slight unavoidable delay in communicating to Mr. Crawford the conclusions at which those three worthy gentlemen—the Commissioners—had arrived with regard to his guilt, a terrible hubbub was made in about every quarter and great sympathy was expressed for his being liable to be done to death by that delay. While here are about fifteen to sixteen persons who have, in the first place, been most unjustly dismissed, and who are not again as yet even informed of the decision of the Government, arrived at about two months ago, to compensate them in some measure, for the pecuniary loss they have sustained. But these persons are only Natives and that makes all the difference in the world".

Ronald Smith, in an article in the 'Westminster Review' of June 1890, criticised the bias of the government with regard to Crawford. He also provided some interesting details of Crawford's methods of raising loans recklessly. Smith said: "One of his agents, a Native, called Hanumantrao turned the loan-raising into blackmailing. The Indian magistrates having savings or friends with means, were subjected to pressure by Hanumantrao. And by suspending some on trifling pretext and transferring others to districts far away from their own people, scruples were removed and money was found... Inquiry was held and Mr. Crawford was suspended from duty. Having remitted large sums through the French bank to Europe, he made preparations for flight. He wrote two letters addressed to his brother, who was expected to arrive at his bungalow the same night; then, disguising himself he disappeared". One of the letters disclosed that he was to commit suicide at Holkar bridge in Pune. Crawford then disguised as a tramp, boarded the third class compartment of a train and travelled to Bombay without knowing that he was followed by police. In Bombay he stayed in a hotel near the dock and requested the purser for some information. But he was then apprehended by the police.

In his capacity as the editor of the English section of 'Sudharak', Gokhale had decided to follow the policy laid down in the first sessions of the Indian National Congress. The national organisation had expressed its faith in and loyalty to the British rule. It believed that the English rule was in the interests of the Indian people. At the same time the Congress made some demands. It felt the need for some control on the powers of the British Parliament. To this end it suggested forming a standing committee of the Parliament. The Congress also demanded an increase in the number as well as the powers of the Indian representatives in the councils of the governors and the Governor-General; reduction on salt duty and acceptance of the elective principle to be adopted for the councils of the governors and that of the Governor-General. The secretary of state for India, Lord Cross, was opposed to accepting the principle of election for the membership of the councils, even in a limited form. Gokhale in his article in 'Sudharak' of March 10, 1890, took exception to this attitude. He referred to the fact that all the governors and the Governor-General, Lord Lansdowne himself had concurred with the secretary of state. The governor of Bengal wanted additional thirty members on his Council, but the governor of Bombay would like to have less than eight members. The Viceroy's Council was opposed to any increase. Gokhale reminded the government that the former Viceroy, Lord Dufferin, had conveyed to the secretary of state that an increase in the number of members was overdue and quite in order. He also suggested that without disturbing the majority of the official members, non-official members should be elected from the electoral college of the municipalities, district boards etc. In the Lords, Ripon, Northbrook, Kimberley generally supported this suggestion. But Prime Minister Lord Salisbury, opposing the introduction of elective principle, said that adoption of such principle in an oriental country was a mistake. He reminded the House that this experiment failed in Turkey and Egypt before.

Besides, Indian people were divided by castes, race and religion. Gokhale alluded to the opposition by some members of the House of Commons, who were known as promoters of Congress and advised them not to throw the bill lock stock and barrel. He thought it would be madness to reject the bill altogether because it did not incorporate an elective principle. Gokhale would have been happy to have the reforms with elective principle, but was ready to accept the limited reforms, which Lord Cross offered as a compromise.

But it was not only the high government dignitaries who were opposed to elective element; William Hunter, Principal Selby, Sir Richard Garth etc, though sympathetic to India, also had reservations. Hunter had a compromise solution. He suggested that the number of members of the governor's Council should be increased to eighty, fifty per cent of which should be elected by the municipalities and district boards. He was afraid that some areas, which were also thickly populated, were backward than others, and they would send more members. To Hunter, second chamber would act as a check on the lower one and that would be more effective than a veto power of the viceroy. Gokhale did not agree with Hunter's misgivings that members from Bengal and the north would outnumber and dominate the Governor General's Council. He felt that the veto power of the viceroy was quite comprehensive and there would be few occasions to use it. Gokhale thought that it would be difficult to elect only fifty per cent of the members from the municipalities and district boards. Hunter scheme did not require the Governor's prior consent for the admission of any member on Governor's Council; but it had to be obtained for those who would sit on Viceroy's Council. Gokhale pointed out that it was exactly what the Congress members of Maharashtra had suggested.

Professor Selby of Deccan College was an Irishman and was generally in sympathy with aspirations of the Indians. Ranade invited Prof. Selby to express his opinion about a scheme, which he called 'graduated election', which Selby disapproved. He thought that each part of Ranade's scheme would increase the distance between the representatives and the constituents. Selby concluded his letter to Ranade by declaring, "I am by no means prepared to admit that the remedy for India's ills, whatever they may be, is the importation of English institutions. It seems to be too often assumed that liberalism in politics means the anglicizing of India. English institutions are good in England. But with regard to India the question is, as it must be with regard to all other countries; what do the present times and circumstances require?" Gokhale, criticising the stand taken by Selby (June 30, 1890), thought that the present requirements were met by the freedom to express the views of the people through different institutions like Sarvajanik Sabha. Gokhale argued that Selby was raising questions, but not offering remedy. Selby feared that by conferring the voting right, people of the calibre of Ranade and Telang would be left out and non-entities would come to the forefront. Gokhale was reminded of the clamouring against the lowering of the franchise by the Tories, but Gladstone had shown that political reforms had in no way brought about the deterioration of the quality of the House of Commons. Gokhale then asked whether Ranade and Telang would always be nominated? He also asked, if Selby held members of the Sarvajanik Sabha in such a high esteem, then what prevented him in allowing them to elect members to the Council? Sir Richard Garth was the retired chief justice of the Calcutta High Court. He agreed with Hunter that elections would give too much representation to people from the backward regions of India. Sir Richard also feared that the elective element would give overwhelming majority to Hindus. Gokhale did not subscribe to these fears. He was emphatic in saying (July 14, 1890) that people like Dadabhai or Tyabji would not be discarded by Hindu voters simply because they were Parsi or Muslim. At the same time persons of the calibre of Ranade or Telang should not be debarred to give place to some inferior persons simply on the basis of religion.

Gokhale wrote three articles in support of the Congress demand for holding ICS examinations simultaneously in England and India. The opposition to this demand was voiced mainly by the British ministers and high civil servants. They objected on the grounds that the level of education in India was not suitable to prepare the candidates for such examination. Besides, the viva voce was equally important and Indian students would not be able to match the British candidates. Gokhale refuted all these arguments. He said that if there was any deficiency in the educational system in India, it was the responsibility of the government to take appropriate steps. Gokhale also said that in Macaulay's time it might have been all right for the civil servant not to have knowledge of the vernacular languages, but with the passage of time, this knowledge had become necessary. He even suggested bringing some examiners from England.

The year 1889 proved to be a turning point in the life of Gokhale. He became the life-member of the Deccan Education Society and attended the session of the Indian National Congress for the first time as a delegate from Pune along with Tilak. Gokhale was also nominated as the secretary of the Sarvajanik Sabha and the editor of its prestigious journal. The Congress session in 1889 in Bombay was known as the 'Bradlaugh session'. Bradlaugh, the British MP, was held in high esteem in India. His sympathies for India were well known, for which he was nicknamed as a 'Member for India'. In the session Gokhale supported an amendment moved by Tilak, and then was asked to make a speech on a resolution about the simultaneous examinations of the ICS in England and India. His brief speech was much appreciated, and then onwards Gokhale became one of the permanent speakers in the Congress sessions. Gokhale in his first appearance on the Congress platform reminded the British of the Queen's Declaration of 1858 assuring the Indians that they would be treated on equal footing of race and religion. He hoped that the majority of Englishmen would not support the views of "a famous or infamous judge (James Stephen)" who advised the British to ignore that declaration. Gokhale asked, what was wrong in demanding the implementation of the assurances, which were given to Indians?

'The Times' correspondent on January 22, 1890 derisively said, "The term India is not to lead us astray. It is nothing more than a geographical expression. Not a single test of the nationality is fulfilled. Congress delegates who numbered two thousand came from all parts of the country, but they have nothing in common. What then brought these divergent elements together? Two hundred millions under the British rule had not sent them. The Indian ryot has no political aspirations, nor has the workman in the town. Nor has the Native aristocracy cared to agitate; nor do the 40 million Mohammedans. Few Mohammedans appear at the Congress but they were handful with no representative character. The real leaders of Islam not only hold aloof, but they have organised a Patriotic Anti-Congress League. The Parsis hold a similar attitude. Few have joined but the main body has followed the two leaders of the Parsi community—Sir Jameshetjee Jeejeebhoy and Sir Dinshaw Petit. The movement is a Hindu movement carried by the advance section of the Hindus". 'The Times' concluded by saying that Hume was the main inspirer without whom the Congress could not have come into being. Writing to Queen Victoria, Viceroy Lord Lansdowne, informed: "He (Lansdowne) believes your Majesty is quite right in thinking that Mr. Bradlaugh's visit has to some extent disappointed the advance party, which expected him to take a much more pronounced and aggressive line. Mr. Bradlaugh's public utterances were on the whole cautious and more moderate than was anticipated. Lord Lansdowne believes that his attitude has to some extent had a salutary effect in undeceiving those who believed that the Radical Party in Parliament was ready to take up anything and everything, which the agitators in this country might suggest. On the whole, the general impression of the last meeting of the Congress fell flatter than those held in previous years".[3] The Viceroy, however, betrayed his bias by not dealing with the reality.

'The Times' Calcutta correspondent had sent a malicious newsletter to his paper. He said: "The Hindu Congress, that cave of Aladdin for government pensioners, unsuccessful pleaders and impecunious graduates, opened its session in Bombay, Thursday. The whole proceedings in spite of Mr. Bradlaugh's presence have fallen flat and save locally, have attracted little or no public interest. Though a few individual Parsis and Mohammedans attended, both these influential communities have declared against the Congress. Both the general secretary and the president are ex-government officials, drawing from the Indian government yearly pensions of one thousand Pounds. They are faddists of a very pronounced type. The president is essentially a man of half knowledge. He is possessed of a very ordinary range of intellect". This criticism of the correspondent was directed against Hume and Wedderburn.

In the Bombay session, Bradlaugh was given a draft of a bill outlining the political reforms for India. Bradlaugh assured that though he was derisively described as a member for India, he was proud of this title. Though the Congress constitution could not be passed in this session, some rules for selecting the delegates were approved. The Sabha Journal, writing about the session, asserted that it was the proof that the Congress has struck its roots firmly in the soil of this country. The article said that: "many of the critics had by then realised that their opposition to the Congress would be futile. But the Indians should take note of what critics had to say. The greatest opponents were the Anglo-Indians, who were narrow minded, and their selfishness was enormous unlike their conscience. They did not want Indians to make progress in education and politics. They would even go to the length of hitting us under the belt to achieve their objectives. It was better not to pay attention to those people. There were some others who were timid and afraid of change, who should be persuaded and cultivated". 'The Statesman' of Calcutta took 'The Times' to task for its virulent criticism of the Congress and the educated Indians. The paper wrote on February 5, 1890: "That the Indian National Congress has fastened itself on the attention of the English public is shown by the criticism showered on it by the leading London journals, who whether speaking for or against the movement treat it as an imperial theme. Of course, the idea has been ridiculed; but ridicule does not in every case kill. Those who have ridiculed the Congress and the aspirations of the educated portion of the people of India belong to the least intelligent section of the English public—flippant, flashy, supercilious, and astonishingly ignorant and stupid. 'The Times' is contemptible for its lack of all principle, the St. James Gazette is a jingo monomaniac. Yet these are the journals that attempt to cast ridicule on the Congress movement. The flippancy and coarseness displayed by some of these so-called Conservative journals in their comments on the Congress are beneath notice".

One of the demands of the Congress was to scale down the tax on salt. The economist, G.V. Joshi, in an article in the 'Bombay Gazette' pointed out that there was a surplus of rupees two crores in the Indian budget. Gokhale, alluding to this in 'Sudharak' of February 10, asked the government to use that surplus to relieve the hardship of the poor people and reduce the tax on salt. He reproduced a dispatch by Lord Cross, the Secretary of State, to the government of India that the increase in tax on salt proposed that time was temporary and should be scaled down as soon as possible for the benefit of the common people. Gokhale asked the government to follow that advice. Gokhale dwelt on this subject several times later. In the Calcutta session of the Congress in 1890, one of the resolutions was about the salt tax, and Gokhale's speech was effective and well appreciated.

R.D. Rusden, an Englishman, was moved by the hardships suffered by poor

Indians due to the tax on salt. He wrote a letter to the editor of the 'Maratha', which was published on July 21, 1889. Rusden said: "I should think your 'policy' as regards the salt tax should be to agitate for its total extinction as opposed to mere 'reduction', that is what our anti-corn law men did and you know that they won in the end. I think the time has come to say to the Government: The whole thing is hateful and shameful and scandalous, and we insist upon the sweeping away of the tax; and if you do not repeal it, we will try and make it so hot and disagreeable to you that before long you will have to drop it whether you like it or not. As I have often written, it's no use going to a Government with a plea of justice. They know all about that—the principles of justice are like the principles of Christianity, very well-known, but never acted on, certainly not by Government, but go to them and show by good evidence that unless a certain course is taken, there will be a danger to the 'Rulers' and see how quickly they change".[4]

In 1890 the Industrial Conference was established and its first session was held in Pune in May of the same year. It was Ranade and G.V. Joshi, who took the initiative to establish the conference and hold the session. Addressing the session Ranade said that as there would not be any difference of opinion about the need to industrialise, everybody could cooperate. Gokhale supported this plea in his editorial in 'Sudharak'. Sarvajanik Sabha, in a statement issued about the session of the Industrial Conference, said that with the import of mill cloth, the indigenous handloom industry had suffered. Bombay and Calcutta have seen the growth of new mills. But the Government of India's inquiry about the industrial progress of the country has revealed that it was unsatisfactory. India is very backward in technical education. The Industrial Conference did not hold the view that there was only one way to industrialisation. It would encourage small and big industries. It appealed to the industrialists, traders and the government that they should all cooperate to foster industries.

Congress, by now, was facing increasing opposition from Syed Ahmed. When the third session of the Congress was convened at Madras and Badruddin Tyabji was selected as president, Syed Ahmed mounted an attack on the Congress and did his best to persuade Tyabji to disassociate with the Congress. It was Lala Lajpat Rai who crossed swords with Syed Ahmed Khan on this issue. He wrote two articles citing Syed Ahmed Khan's previous writings showing how he became a turncoat. Syed Ahmed had written a book in Urdu about 1857 revolt. This was translated by Sir Auckland Colvin in English, which was published in 1873. Syed Ahmed's thesis was that the revolt was not religious and was not a planned affair. He maintained that stability and prosperity of any nation were dependent on the scope which was given to the people to advise and participate in the administration. Syed Ahmed pointed out that as the rulers did not know the language of the people and the people did not have the right to send their representatives to the Councils, it had created misunderstanding about the government's laws and intentions. Lala Lajpat Rai also cited the views expressed by Syed Ahmed in his speeches at Muradabad and Lahore in 1884. In both these speeches Syed Ahmed appealed to Hindus, Muslims and Christians to join hands and cooperate. He complimented the Bengalis for bringing in the light of western knowledge. He declared that by nation he meant the one that consists of Hindus and Muslims. Lala Lajpat Rai expressed his surprise at the volta face by Syed Ahmed in the following four years when Syed Ahmad published a book—*The Present Discontent In Indian Politics,* to which Mr. Bake, the Principal of the Alighar College started by Syed Ahmed Khan, wrote an introduction. Bake had contempt for the Congress and Hindus. In the introduction, Bake described the Congress as a debating society and not a political organisation representing the whole of the country. He asserted that the Congress represented a section of the people of some castes in India. Bake appealed to the people of England not to be carried away by the Congress propaganda. Syed Ahmed's book carried some of his speeches. In one such speech he asserted that Hindus and Muslims not only belonged to two religions but they were two nations. Muslims had ruled India for some centuries and the Bengalis who were afraid of a table knife should not be allowed to rule over the Muslims. Syed Ahmed opposed the representative local self-organisations and more representation in the higher echelons of the administration. His fear was that, it would lead to the Hindu domination. To Syed Ahmed, it was the right of the government to decide the size of the army it needed for national security and it was totally unnecessary to discuss this with the people; the Bengalis who had never ruled were incapable of understanding this. Syed Ahmed's original speech in Urdu was much more vituperative.

The English officials were pleased with Syed Ahmed Khan's speeches. The secretary of state had conveyed to Lord Dufferin that some fetters must be created in the way of the Congress to which the viceroy was not averse. Syed Ahmed even opposed the reduction of salt tax. He said that the government needed to maintain an army and hence it had to levy taxes. It was, therefore, natural that Syed Ahmed was peeved by the selection of Badruddin Tyabji as the president of the Madras session of the Congress. Tyabji was of mild disposition. He impressed upon the Congress leaders that any decisions regarding the Muslims should be taken with the consent of the Muslims, to which the Congress leaders agreed. Madras session of the Congress was much more disciplined than the previous two. The preparations started quite in advance, and Congress workers spread themselves in small towns and collected whatever money they could. There was tremendous enthusiasm for the session and everything was orderly. The local leaders made special efforts to muster Muslim support, which resulted in an impressive attendance of eighty Muslim delegates at the session. 'The Times', reviewing the Madras session, referred to the speeches of Syed Ahmed Khan, and stressed again the unrepresentative character of the Congress. According to 'The Times' it was an organisation of the Parsis and Bengalis. In fact, delegates to Madras session had come from different parts of India. 'The Times' on December 22, 1887 published a letter by 'An Indian Mohammedan', which declared: "that the Indian National Congress was got up by a handful of Bengali and Parsi gentlemen"; the Calcutta Mahomedans had refused to send delegates because, "they had perfect confidence of the government of India". This anonymous letter referred to the Anglo-Indian papers who were discussing whether in view of the absence of the Mahommedans, the Indian National Congress should be called National or not. Ten days later, Syed Ahmed Khan made a speech at Lucknow, which was reported by 'The Times of India' on January 18, 1888. The similarity of views between the anonymous letter and the speech by Syed Ahmed Khan was striking. Three days after the speech Syed Ahmed Khan was made a Knight Commander of the most exalted order of the 'Star of India.'

In his speech to the Mohammedan Educational Congress, Syed Ahmed claimed that the people had a due share in the making of the laws and the government did not act without regard to the opinion of the people. He did not think that competitive examinations were suitable for India, as there was no one nation. He referred to the Congress as a 'stupid agitation', and the Congress session as mere scribbling of the pen, "Zig, Zig, Zig, Zig, Zig" and more talk—"Buk Buk Buk Buk". The 'Times of India's editorial praised the speech as 'slashing address' and characterised the Lucknow meeting as "a great meeting of the intellect and aristocracy, the brain and muscle of Mohamedan community." Hume was furious with the speech by Syed Ahmed and asked Tyabji to issue a rejoinder and also sent a draft. Tyabji advised patience. Hume then wrote a long letter to Tyabji on January 22. He said, "Having been patted out on the back for it, he (Syed) would go further and make it impossible to hold the next Congress at Allahabad." Hume was convinced that Syed Ahmed's speech had been put up to throw out the suggestion of suppression of the Congress. He then added, "Doubtless, though it may be hard to realise—just as mosquitoes and cockroaches perform a useful part in the universal workshop, so men like Syed Ahmed and creatures like 'Muslim Herald', perform useful parts in the evolution of the nation, so, I never for two minutes bear any of these people any personal ill will".

Tyabji had written to Sir Syed before the latter made his vituperative speech. He expressed his regret that on matters affecting all of India, a section of the Mussalman community should keep aloof from the Hindus and thus retard the national progress of India as a whole. Tyabji assured Sir Syed that the intention of the Congress was not to subject Muslims to Hindus. Sir Syed in reply to Tyabji reiterated his views about the Congress, which he thought was not only harmful to the Muslims but to the whole of India, because it was based on the wrong assumption that India was a one nation. Tyabji again wrote to Sir Syed stating that the Congress could not be stopped, and by resolute action Muslims could direct the course that the Congress should take. Sir Syed did not reply to Tyabji but in a speech at Meerat on March 16, 1888 he made a reference to the letter by Tyabji and repeated his arguments. In the end Sir Syed cited Koran and said that the God had commanded that the Muslims could not be friends with non-Muslims. If they could be friends, it could be only with Christians as they were men with a book like Muslims. Sir Syed's tirade against Congress evoked sharp reaction from some quarters, while some others expressed their sorrow and dismay. Pherozeshah declared that Sir Syed was not on the right path. However, all Muslim leaders were not following the lead given by Sir Syed. Sheikh Raza Hussain, president of the Anjuman-i-Rifa-i-Am, one of the most prestigious associations in the North, declared that he had full sympathy for the Congress and was ready to furnish fifty thousand signatures of the Muslims in support. He also said that India was one nation. The Sheikh wrote to Tyabji saying that Muslims should come out openly to support the Congress. It was then decided that the Congress should invite the Anjuman to send delegates to the next session to be held in Allahabad.[5]

Wacha, Dadabhai and Malbari had reacted to the criticism by Sir Syed against the Congress. Wacha in a letter asked Dadabhai whether he had read a newspaper report in which Sir Syed was supposed to have said in one of his speeches in England that he was ashamed to be an Indian. On January 20, 1888 Wacha sent Dadabhai a clipping from 'The Statesman' carrying Sir Syed's speech, and remarked, "The old man is a fool and pretends to lead. But it is blind leading the blind. Badrooddin's presidency has been the most fortunate thing at the juncture". Wacha in another letter (May 29, 1888) told Dadabhai that, "No doubt the Allahabad Congress must be viewed with grave apprehension. Theodore Beck is braying in the columns of 'The Pioneer'. He is being answered valiantly by almost all the vernacular papers. In one respect Sir Syed Ahmed's tirades have done good. The Congress is so much talked about that even our arch enemy, 'The Times of India' suggests to Syed to allay the fury, and suspend his activity for a time."[6] Dadabhai thought that Sir Syed had the backing of only the Muslim zamindars and would not be able to influence the ordinary Muslims. Future events have proved that Hume, Dadabhai, Wacha were all wrong in their estimation of Sir Syed and the forces he unleashed. Sir Syed had appealed to the religious feelings and invoked the past glory of the Muslim rule, and frightened them about their present and also future.

Before the Allahabad Congress a great deal of controversy raged at different levels. Muslim organisations were divided, especially those in the North. Sir Auckland Colvin, the lieutenant governor, by his expression of displeasure, was frightening the Muslims. Tyabji took stock of the situation and held talks with many Muslim leaders as well as with Pherozeshah, Telang and some others, and wrote to Hume: "As an ardent friend of the Congress desiring nothing but its success". He said that whatever he was suggesting had the approval of Pherozeshah, Telang etc. Tyabji then suggested that in view of so much controversy, it was better to postpone the Congress session for five years and then review the situation. He said, "Friction and bitterness which are caused by the agitation every year outweigh the advantages gained. If after the end of five years, our prospects improve, we renew the Congress, if not, we can drop with dignity, conscious of having done our utmost for the advance of India and for the fusion of different races into one". But Hume disagreed. In a lengthy reply he wrote, "Out of eight millions (Muslims) we have one million distinctly with us, and there are not one hundred thousand really opposed to us. In the Punjab we are sweeping Syed Ahmed away. In Bihar and Eastern Bengal we have an overwhelming majority. In Madras it is the same. The upshot is that they (the Moulovies) consider that in all probability, within the next two or three years we shall have every single Moulavie of any real influence in India...and with them the great bulk of intelligent adults, and we shall within this period win at least half of the intelligent of the eight millions". It was to be a daydream. For the moment Hume carried the day; and the idea of postponing the session of the Congress was given up.[7]

The Allahabad Congress session had to encounter difficulties created by Sir Syed Ahmed who considered the United Provinces to be his area of influence. Lt. Governor Sir Auckland Colvin, in order to harass the Congress leaders and workers, made them change the venue several times, and the provincial governments asked for bail from those attending the session. In spite of all these difficulties, Congress session attracted a large number of people; and 221 Muslim delegates participated. This was more than those present at Madras. Hume in his letter had written that Sir Syed Ahmed and Deoband Muslim leaders were jointly conspiring against the government. This was nothing but his wild imagination, as Deoband leaders were angry with Sir Syed because of his insistence on English education for the Muslims. Maulana Rashid Mahmod Gangohi, the chief of the Deoband, had issued an edict that Muslims should cooperate with the Congress purely for secular purpose. But some other sections were withdrawing their support to the Congress even before the Allahabad Congress. They were the zamindars from Bengal and several Parsis from Bombay. Letters by Wacha and Malabari to Dadabhai made clear that Parsis were deserting the Congress. Wacha wrote to Dadabhai on Oct. 5, 1888, "Bombay is no doubt cutting a sorry figure in every way. The spirit of political activity which was so visible and strong three years ago is nowhere. A sort of languor is supervened. Our leaders are taking it coolly with but little forethought or even counting the present odds at stake". Wacha wrote on November 23, "'Rast Goftar' is worse. In last Sunday's article (November 18) it openly incites the Parsis to refrain from joining the Congress, if the Congressmen become revolutionists and irreconcilable. Pherozeshah told me that he had to remonstrate to Kabraji against such a mischievous article said to emanate from the pen of Bhownuggeree". Wacha wrote on June 18, 1889, "There is this disturbing element of the Mahomedans and the Parsis. The rabid writings of the 'Rast' are a disgrace to that paper. The attitude of Mahommedans, is as you know, hostile. For these considerations we thought that Poona might be pitched upon. In Bombay absence of Parsis and Mahomedans, if bent upon holding aloof, may be most marked and will certainly commented upon adversely".[8]

At the Allahabad session of the Congress, George Yule, an industrialist from Calcutta, presided. In his address he regretted that there was no control over the Indian administration, especially, the Finance Department; and not only Indians could not participate in the administration, but even the Englishmen who were outside the official circles, like industrialists, traders etc., were kept out. Mr. Yule then gave some interesting statistics. He said, India's export trade was about rupees fifteen crores. England's foreign trade in 1837 was of the same order. But the British government had no authority to spend a farthing without the consent of the Parliament. The school-going population in India was 3. 3 million, same as it was in England in 1821. But even with the spread of education, the government could not find Indians to participate in the administration. Anybody from India staying in England and paying taxes could get the voting right, but such a person, on returning to India was disfranchised. In the session, Gokhale was asked to move a resolution on the question of Public Service Commission. This was in a way promotion for him and with that he moved into the higher echelon of the Congress. Gokhale pointed out that the number of seats for Indians in the government service had gone down as per the report of the Public Service Commission. The Indians should have 125 seats, but the Commission had given 108 seats, which belonged to the provincial cadre. Even then the right to fulfill these seats rested with the secretary of state who had not given any promise. Gokhale sarcastically said that no doubt the change was taking place, but progress was in a reverse direction. In this session many complaints were made against the treatment given to the delegates from Punjab, Madras etc. by the officials. The secretary's report denounced such intimidation and reminded the government that repression gives rise to the secret work and secret societies. The report declared that the idea of the Congress had taken deep roots in India and even if ten thousand congressmen were deported, the organisation would continue to grow. Because of the repressive measures under Lord Lytton, some secret societies came into being. Those who had studied history would know where these societies would lead. The report in conclusion said that if the Viceroy and the government would look to the Congress and people with contempt and resort to repression, then that would spell danger to both India and England.

There was a discrepancy between the public utterances of Dufferin and the official correspondence with the secretary of state. Dufferin had great expectations about the state chiefs, zamindars and the landed gentry. He bestowed titles and honours on them lavishly. He was also thinking of having a Council of these chiefs. He had realised that political reforms were unavoidable in India. In 1886 he wrote to the secretary of state that there were several movements going on and the demands emanated from them would have to be considered in seriousness. Whatever was to be given should be given without loss of time and with grace. He advised that it should also be made clear that within the next fifteen years there would be no changes. Dufferin was confident that if the energies of some of the efficient people were harnessed, then many good schemes could be implemented. Dufferin had some discussions with Surendranath Banerjea. Moreover, he had asked his officials to prepare a scheme for social reform. The committee of the officials had suggested that all castes and religions should be represented. Property was to be the criteria for the selection of a member. The Committee suggested that the members of the Councils should have the right to see the government documents and to ask questions. The right for discussion should be accepted. Two fifths of the members should be elected and government would have overriding powers to go against the majority opinion. Dufferin was aware that his scheme would not be accepted by the British government as it was. Therefore, he wrote to the secretary of state an explanatory letter. He said that his scheme aimed at enlarging the provincial legislatures and giving them some additional powers. Some elective element could be introduced. At the same time it should be made clear that it would not be on the model of the British Parliament. Dufferin wrote that the British had the responsibility to protect the interests of various castes and religions and of the administration of the Empire in India; and as the government in India was responsible to the Queen and the Parliament, the newly created legislative councils could not follow the Parliamentary model. If that model had to be followed, then in the event of loss of majority, the opposition would have to be invited to form the government. As that was not possible in India, there could not be legislatures on the model of the Parliament and that was why the government majority was assured in the scheme. India might be a backward country in many respects, but it had also a large educated population. Some of these should be associated with the government, Dufferin concluded.

Though Dufferin initiated this move on official level, he was very critical of the Congress politics while speaking at the farewell dinner in Calcutta. He asked the Congress to concentrate on social work, as government was doing its best to safeguard the interests of the people. Dufferin was convinced that it would take hundreds of years before India would have parliamentary democracy. His speech provoked a controversy. Umashankar Misra wrote a piece in the July 1889 issue of the 'Westminster Review' and supported Dufferin. He wrote: "When we reflect calmly over the arguments adduced by the late Viceroy in support of his proposition on this subject, we are forced to admit the truth of his assertions. We admit that India has made great progress in education, and the growth of an intelligent public opinion, and the number of men of Western culture and Western thought is increasing rapidly. But we do not think that they have as yet a representative character. The Mohammedan community, with its distinctive characteristics, whether religious, social or ethnological, which has shown no sympathy for the movement, is a great drawback to political unity. One of the methods lately employed by the Congressionists has been to issue two pamphlets in the form of catechisms, with third report of the Congress meeting held at Madras. The object of these indiscreet publications-not to use a stronger term-is to hold the Government of India to the contempt and indignation as "unjust, inconsiderate, ill-informed, and reckless of the consequences of their actions. We all know how much inflammable material there is in India, and we can easily conceive what evils will ensue if such pamphlets are circulated amongst the credulous and ignorant masses".

Pandit Bishan Narayan Dar, one of the eminent leaders of the Congress from the United Provinces, countered every argument of Misra in the June 1890 issue of the 'Westminster Review'. He referred to Dufferin's statement that English brought the legal codes, which secured to Her Majesty's every subject equality before the law. Refuting this argument, Dar said that this was all very well on the paper. "There is a sharp line of demarcation drawn between the rulers and the ruled; the trial by jury is conceded to the one but refused to the other; Indian magistrates, whatever their experience and ability, are not allowed to try European offenders; but a young English civilian, who probably knows as little about India as he does about the other side of the moon can try Indians for the most serious offences. This is not our idea of equality before the law". Dar castigated the Indian legislatures as sham. Citing statistics, Dar showed how Indians had very little scope in the government service. "Nobody will deny that Russia is despotic, but one of the chief secrets of her remarkable expansion is, as soon as she annexes a territory by force of arms she removes the bitterness of conquest from the minds of the conquered people, by, at once, extending to them the laws and principles which govern the people of St. Petersburg. On the contrary inequality is the keynote of the English constitution". Dar reminded the English readers that this trait had alienated the colonists in America as well as in Canada. Proceeding further, Dar said, "It is human nature to love liberty and equality. It is certainly untrue to say, as is always implied by those who say that the demands of the Congress proceed from a discontented educated class, and not from the masses. Britain is civilized, is just, is humane, but it is not sympathetic. I think that it is creditable rather than otherwise to the Congress that it is under the guidance and control of the educated classes".

When Misra mentioned in his article, that inflammable material was circulated in India, he was echoing what Sir Auckland Colvin had said in his correspondence with Hume. This was the new line, which was then adopted by the British officials. Colvin had objected to the language used in the Congress pamphlets, which according him would spread disaffection about the British rule among the people. Colvin advised Hume to ask the Congress to take up social problems. Objecting to the demand for a representative government, Colvin said that that demand was confined to the educated class, as the masses were not aware of such representative government and the conditions were not ripe for it. Hume, in a lengthy reply, refuted Colvin's arguments. He said that the Congress had as many true representatives of the people as there were representatives in the British Parliament. Hume asserted that the Congress was a growing organisation and spoke the minds of the people. He also told Colvin that many Congressmen were involved in many other fields to further the cause of their country.

Nobody was aware of the shape of the impending political reforms, though everybody was expecting some. Dufferin had asked for very limited reforms, but the secretary of state, Lord Cross, was a diehard Tory and did not approve of the scheme proposed by Dufferin. He and his Advisory Council raised many questions and objections. Aware of this, the Congress leaders felt an urgent need to do everything in their power to assert and propagate their demands. Dadabhai and other Congress leaders had already agreed that the propaganda campaign had to be undertaken in India as well as in England. They were convinced that as the government of India was under the control of the bureaucracy, it was necessary to convince the Parliamentarians and the British public of the justness of the Congress demands. Congress had earlier decided to start an agency and a magazine or a weekly to undertake this job in England. In 1888, Dadabhai had started an agency named Indian Political Agency, which was renamed as British Committee of the Indian National Congress. Sir William Wedderburn was appointed president, and Dadabhai, MacNeill etc. were the members. William Digby, a journalist and a writer, was the secretary.

It was recognised by the Indian National Congress in 1889. Forty-five thousand rupees were sanctioned for the expenses. The British Committee started a periodical, 'India', in 1890 under the editorship of Digby. From 1892 it was converted to a monthly magazine and after six years it became a weekly. Dadabhai's correspondence reveals that this venture was facing financial difficulties for a long time. Dadabhai, Hume and Wedderburn were raising funds and spending their own money. Malabari also lent a helping hand. It was decided that every Congress Committee should collect a certain amount of money and enrol subscribers. But this was seldom done. Most of the provincial Congress committees found it difficult to enrol subscribers or raise the amount, which was expected of them. They found that it was beyond their capacity to sell definite number of copies of 'India', which were allotted to them. The Madras Committee had informed Dadabhai that fifty per cent of the copies allotted to them should be kept in the London office, and the Committee would pay for them so that they would save on postage. At one time, the British Committee came to the conclusion that it was better to close down 'India'. When Gokhale agreed to raise money for 'India', Wedderburn was happy and wrote to Dadabhai, "The news that Mr. Gokhale will undertake this work is indeed cheering. As the favourite disciple of the great and good Mr. Ranade, he is thoroughly 'sound' and has also the energy and ability necessary to make his work fruitful. Mr. Hume will be very glad to hear the news". [9] As was his wont, Gokhale undertook this job seriously and made it a point to collect money and enroll subscribers for 'India' wherever he went. In the Gokhale papers there are several letters in which Gokhale could be seen giving the details of his collection to Dadabhai. On the other hand, Wacha informed Dadabhai that both Pherozeshah and Telang were not enthusiastic about his work in England and thought that Dadabhai should return to India.

Dadabhai did not listen to Pherozeshah and Telang and continued his work in England. He also decided to contest election to the Parliament from Finsbury, in 1892. British Liberal Party accepted his nomination after great deal of efforts by Dadabhai and his friends. Malabari seemed to be serious about sending money to Dadabhai for the election. Dadabhai's task was not easy, as he was facing a stiff opposition in England. Prime Minister Lord Salisbury called Dadabhai a 'black man'. But it was Gladstone and newspapers like 'The Guardian', which took strong exception to such a racist expression. Ultimately, Dadabhai won the election by razor thin majority. Whole of India celebrated this victory with great enthusiasm and joy. Lokmanya Tilak, congratulating him in an editorial said that: "when Dadabhai was castigated as a 'black man', everybody in India was amazed and saddened by the thought that a prime minister of a progressive country in the nineteenth century should think in such racial terms. It was also feared that the assurances by the Queen, of equal treatment, would be of no avail. But the voters in the Central Finsbury had demonstrated to the whole world that their hearts were not 'black' and they would be remembered for a long time, both in India and England. If out of the twenty crore people of India only one was to be selected to contest the election in England, on the basis of intelligence, character and high moral qualities, then all India would have unanimously selected Dadabhai as their representative. Dadabhai's election had also shown that the English people were not adamant, rigid and narrow minded like English bureaucrats in India". Writing in the Sabha's Journal in the January, 1894 issue Gokhale said, "We all remember how for six long years a whole nation's eyes were watching with anxious suspense the unequal and unprecedented struggle which Dadabhai was carrying on in England on India's behalf, and how our hearts constantly rose and sank accordingly as we heard that his prospects were getting brighter or darker. And gentlemen, to my mind, it has always appeared that the one secret of the unique, unparalleled success which he has achieved has been the great faith that if only he did his duty honestly and manfully, success must follow no matter when it came".

Before the Indian people celebrated Dadabhai's victory, Hume threw a bombshell by a circular addressed to the Congressmen on February 16, 1892. Hume reminded them that they should take a serious note of the poverty, which was on the rise. He said that the poverty was the mother of anarchy and the government was unable to protect the people. Hume told them that they and especially the rich were oblivious of the conditions in India, while the government of India was pauperizing the country and inevitably paving the way for a terrible cataclysm in the history. The Indian people were mild and humble but so were the people of France; but they rose in revolt and executed their Sovereign and practically the bulk of the better classes. History shows that hunger and poverty drive even peaceful people to violence and revolt. This violence might be met with by force; and thousands will die; "but when there were millions and millions who had nothing to look forward to but death…nothing to hope for but vengeance, there would be no lack of leaders". Hume expressed his frustration about the smugness of the government, which did not want to implement any essential reform measures. He, however, thought that the only ray of hope was the conscience of the British people, which had to be appealed to and roused. He suggested that Britain must be flooded with articles, pamphlets and other propaganda material…the way followed by the Anti-Corn Law League, which triumphed. This would require money; but though the common people were generous in contributing to the Congress fund, the rich were blind and miserly.

Hume's circular was denounced by several members of the House of Commons. Mr. Maclean said that under the less mild rule than that of the British, Hume would have been shot or hanged as a traitor. The officials in India were furious and there was panic in the Congress circles. Anglo-Indian press savagely attacked Hume. The Allahabad, Madras and Bombay Congress Committees refused to circulate the letter by Hume on the ground that it would be seditious. Even the British Committee disowned the circular by issuing a statement signed by Caine, Dadabhai and others. On April 1, a letter by Dinshaw Wacha was published in the 'Bombay Gazette', which said that immediately after the receipt of the circular, Pherozeshah Mehta sent a telegram begging Hume to withdraw the circular. As Hume did not do so, the standing committee of Bombay Congress met and passed the resolution deciding not to circulate Hume's two letters; the second being declination to withdraw the first.

But Wacha was in two minds. This is clear from his two letters to Dadabhai and his articles, which were collected in a book eight months later. In a letter to

Dadabhai on March 19, 1892, Wacha wrote: "It (Hume's circular) somewhat borders on seditious, though the facts cannot be gainsaid. Hume embodied these sentiments of the circulars in a more amplified form in the concluding portion of his usual introduction to the Congress Report. Now this Report is an authentic document. It has the imprimatur of all Congress delegates who therefore become responsible for its contents. Imagine the disaster, which might befall the Congress, if government took into its head to discredit it. They could easily do so, and suppress the Congress as a body, which under the guide of loyalty was endeavouring to sow the seeds of sedition and inflame the popular mind. Owing to the remonstrance from more than one quarter, Hume informs all Congress Committees in a letter...that he has entirely omitted from the Report the whole of the introduction. This he carries to England where he means to publish it. I am entirely in one with Hume's facts which none can gainsay. They are notorious, but there are ways of expressing them. Between *ourselves* we must say that Hume is sometimes too impulsive". On April 2, Wacha again referred to Hume's letter informing Dadabhai that all friends of the Congress were apprehensive that Hume's most "ill advised action" had harmed the cause. Wacha also feared that it might affect adversely the India Council Bill then before the Commons.[10] It was only Lokmanya Tilak, who through 'Kesari' and 'Maratha' openly supported Hume. He said that it would have done no harm if those Congressmen who issued statements criticising Hume's circular, had kept quiet. Hume had correctly described the situation in the country. 'Maratha' recalled that some years ago there were peasants' riots in Maharashtra, and asserted that the failure to improve the situation would create such a situation, which Hume had envisaged. Tilak followed his articles endorsing the views of Hume by two more editorials under the title, '*Would the Indian peasants have to revolt?*' Afterwards when Wacha published his articles giving great deal of statistics about the impoverishment of the people and specially the peasants, Tilak congratulated him in the editorial columns of 'Kesari'. Agarkar, editor of the 'Sudharak', in his characteristic impassioned style denounced those Congressmen who criticised Hume's circular and called them cowards.

Though the Congressmen betrayed their cowardice by distancing themselves from Hume, it is equally true that Hume was impulsive and given to imagine things. Nobody doubted his contention that there was abject poverty in India; but the situation was not inflammatory and there was no immediate danger of any large-scale revolt. About his suggestion to wind up the Congress, it must be recalled that it was Hume who strongly opposed Tyabji who had suggested two years earlier that in view of the controversy raised by Sir Syed Ahmed Khan, the annual session of the Congress should be postponed for five years. But in 1891 Hume himself suggested the disbanding of the Congress altogether. In a circular letter to all Congress Committees, he said that the objective of the Congress was to create awakening in the people. The government had been approached and demands were placed before it. As nobody knew when the Liberals would come to power, it was uncertain when the session of the Congress could be held in England. Under the circumstances, it was futile to spend hundred or hundred and fifty thousand rupees every year on a Congress session. It was a sheer waste of money. Agarkar wrote two editorials in July 1891 opposing Hume's suggestion. He thought that the suggestion might have come from Hume, who might be disgusted with the behaviour of the Indian elite. They were selfish, cowardly, and not prepared to sacrifice for the good of the country. In the second editorial, Agarkar disagreeing with Hume suggested that the people of India should raise a memorial for Hume in the form of a hall to be named after him. At the same time all was not well with the political agency established in England, which was looked after by William Digby, as a secretary. He was paid for this work. Digby also looked after the interests of some Indian princes. Moreover, the information that Digby provided about the probable government policy towards the states like Kashmir had eventually proved to be incorrect, which created bitter feelings among the members of the British Committee. The 'Amrita Bazar Patrika' was also angry with Digby. He, therefore, was relieved from the responsibilities of the secretary and as the editor of the 'India'. J.R. McLane, a British Member of Parliament in his book, *Indian Nationalism and the Early Congress* has discussed in detail disagreements and the differences in the Congress.

REFERENCES

1. Sir Bipin Krishna Bose, *Stray Thoughts or Some Incidents In My Life*, G. A. Natesan, Madras, 1923, pp. 186-87.
2. Palande M.R., *Source Material for the History of Freedom Movement in India, Vol. II, 1885-1920*, Government of Bombay, Bombay, 1968, pp. 37, 38
3. George Earle Buckle, *The Letters of Queen Victoria*, Vol. 1, Longmans, NY, 1928, p. 572.
4. Ram Gopal, *Lokmanya Tilak*, Asia Pub. House, London, 1966, pp. 47-48.
5. Hussain B. Tyabji, *Badruddin Tyabji*, Thacker and Co., Bombay, 1952, pp. 196-213
6. R.P. Patwardhan *Dadabhai Naoroji Correspondence*, Vol. 2, Part 1, Allied Publishers, Bombay, 1977, pp. 62, 98.
7. Hussain B.Tyabji, *Badruddin Tyabji*, pp. Thacker and Co., Bombay, 1952, pp. 224-225.
8. R.P. Patwardha, *Dadabhai Naoroji Correspondence*, Vol. 2 Part 1, Allied Publishers, Bombay, 1977, pp. 127, 133, 168.
9. *Dadabhai Papers*. (these are unpublished papers from Dadabhai Naoroji Trust).
10. R.P. Patwardhan, *Dadabhai Naoroji Correspondence*, Vol. 2, Part 2. Allied Publishers, Bombay, 1977, pp. 281-284.

1. Gopal Krishna Gokhale

2. Founding of the Deccan Education Society in Pune

3. Lokmanya Bal Gangadhar Tilak

4. Gopal Ganesh Agarkar

5. Fergusson College, Pune

6. Justice Mahadev Govind Ranade

7. First Indian National Congress

8. A. O. Hume

9. Dadabhai Naoroji

10. Surendranath Banergea

11. Pherojshah Mehta

12. William Wedderburn

13. Wacha, Dadabhai Naoroji, Gokhale

14. Lord Curzon

15. Gokhale's Residence in Pune

16. Memorial to the foundation of Servants of India Society, Fergusson Hill, Pune

17. Servants of India Society, Pune

18. *Sir Ratan Tata*

19. *V.S. Srinivasa Sastri*

20. *John Morley*

21. *Lord Minto*

22. *Gokhale and Gandhi in Africa*

23. *Mahatma Gandhi*

Chapter Seven

UPHILL TASK

Before Dadabhai decided to contest the elections to the British Parliament, there was a move to have an understanding with the Irish Parliamentary Party to get some seats for the Indians from the Irish constituencies, and members so elected to support the Irish party's agenda in the Parliament. Those who were involved with this move had some talks with Dadabhai, who showed no enthusiasm. Though Dadabhai had cordial relations with the Irish Parliamentary Party, he did not favour the cooperation with it politically. However, forging some ties with the Irish Party was an old idea. It was Maharaja Ganendra Mohan Tagore, who was the first Indian in 1878, to moot such cooperation. Hugh O'Donnell, a member of the Irish Parliamentary Party, was friendly with Tagore who was then staying in London. O'Donnell also had correspondence with some leaders in India. The Indians then asked whether it was possible to send four of their countrymen to the British Parliament as candidates of the Irish party. The Indians offered some monetary help in return. O'Donnell discussed this with the Irish leader, Parnell, who like Dadabhai was not eager for such an arrangement.[1] This was expected, because most of the Congress leaders were disturbed by Hume's circular and feared that their organisation would be banned on a charge of sedition. Hence they could never think of having any cooperation with the Irish Parliamentary Party.

Radical English leaders like Hyndman frowned upon this moderation of the Indians. He wrote to Dadabhai to express his disappointment with the extreme moderation of the Congress leaders. Dadabhai, replying to him, asked him to consider the reality of the situation as well as the government's policy and the mindset of the Congress leaders. In 1890, Dadabhai wrote to Hyndman, "With reference to my visit to you, I have carefully considered the matter again and I remain of the same view as I then expressed to you that after reading your article in 'Justice' I cannot any more work with you and the SDF on Indian matters. My desire and aim have been not to encourage rebellion but to prevent it and to make the British connection with India a benefit and blessing to both countries, which it can certainly be, but which unfortunately has not been the case owing to an evil and unrighteous system of government being persisted in by the executive authorities, in spite of the wishes of the sovereign, the people and the Parliament of this country to govern righteously".[2] Dadabhai thus avoided the path of radical politics. In the circumstances what was the achievement of the Congress? Hume, who was felicitated in Pune, declared that the Congress was successful in breaking the back of the British bureaucracy. Some district collector or any other officer might be boasting that he did not pay any attention to the Congress, but he would think twice before taking any step as he was aware that his action would be taken note of by the British Parliament.

The secretary of state was under the impression that though Lord Dufferin had supported the acceptance of the elective principle with some limitations for the members of the Legislative Councils; the new Viceroy, Lord Lansdowne who succeeded Dufferin would not endorse such a scheme. But he was disillusioned and had no option but to bring in a legislation for political reform, which the responsible opinion in England was already advocating. 'The Edinburgh Review' of January 1889, reviewing the regime of Lord Dufferin, said, "The manifestations of National Congress have accordingly been met by a counter movement quite sufficient to prove, what the conservative party steadily affirms, that the Congress delegates actually represent no more than a party organisation in the country, and that there is much worth, weight, and intelligence directly opposed to their views. Now it must be clear that to all the irresponsible discussion of the native press, some counterpoise, according to the English principles, ought to be found in responsible education. The affairs of government have become multiplied and complicated; they are discussed much more widely and vivaciously…and it is known that Lord Dufferin has been constantly in favour of strengthening and extending the provincial legislative councils. The enlargement of the provincial councils would indeed be a measure in accordance with the spirit of the England's policy, it would also multiply the supports and lighten the burden of the supreme government." The question of political reforms in India was under consideration of the British government for a fairly long time. Lord Dufferin believed that it would have been proper to announce the increase in the power of the legislative councils at the time of the jubilee celebrations of Queen Victoria in 1887. He thought it would be better to empower the members of the councils to discuss the economic problems. Some other Englishmen in power and some members of the Parliament had also supported such a move. N.J. Raynolds, a member of the viceroy 's Council suggested that the number of members of the viceroy's Council should be 104. To him it was proper to keep an equal number of official and non-official members and also nominate some state chiefs. Ultimately, the reform bill was adopted in 1892.

This bill was an amendment to the 1861 act, and thereby the government indicated that it did not intend to make any radical changes. The bill authorised the Viceroy to nominate 16 members to the Council in place of ten; he was also empowered to change the rules of nomination from time to time with the approval of the secretary of state. The Secretary of State, Lord Cross, took pains to stress the fact that the new councils were in no way related to the elected legislatures in the Western countries. In a letter to the Viceroy, Lord Cross made it clear that the existing councils were to be expanded so that they might be more representative of the Indian public opinion. He was agreeable to resort to the elective principle wherever the local conditions were suitable. At the same time all members would be subject to the approval of the government. The new bill was moved by the assistant secretary of state for India, Curzon.

Bright's non-official bill before the House was to raise the limit of the number of members to all Councils in the country to two hundred and fifty. Curzon, opposing the bill, said that it was not possible to get so many qualified persons, and if found, it was not known how many of them would spend their time for the work of the Council. Curzon's arguments were not convincing, as there would have been more than two hundred and fifty eligible persons from all over India. Moving the bill for the expansion of the Councils, Curzon rejected the demand for the electoral element to be introduced in forming the Councils. He asked who the Indian people were, and replied that they were the millions who were dumb and could not read or write their own language. They were even unaware that it was the English who were ruling them. These people were cultivators, and so poor that they did not have any political ambitions, but were concerned only about their daily bread. The policies and program of the Congress party did not touch the life of the poor in India; and though the party might have several public spirited and intelligent individuals, they represented their own class. This class might have known Western culture, but had nothing to do with the millions in their own country. In the circumstances, representative administration was impossible, asserted Curzon. Later in his capacity as viceroy, he ran his administration with this ideological baggage.

Some Indians were also opposed to the elective principle. 'The Times' had reproduced an editorial from the 'Bangvasi', which expressed the fear that, "The introduction of the elective system into the legislative council will make that Congress more dangerous than it now is. He who can flatter and walk about and spend money profusely will be elected. Introduction of English system in India will do great harm. Under this system butchers, coolies, bearers and milkmen have been elected in municipalities. Only the sweepers and undertakers have not as yet been elected. Competent men will never condescend to beg for votes from door to door".

Schwann, a member of the Commons, moving an amendment to the bill tabled by Curzon, clarified that the Congress did not demand majority for the non-official members in the Councils. He said that those who demanded political reforms in India, and their friends in England, wanted the members of the Councils to have the right to see the official documents and ask questions. The members of the Advisory Councils of governors and the viceroy were not expected to ask for political reforms, and that was why the members of the Parliament should take an initiative. But the Liberal Party leader Gladstone was satisfied with the explanation given by the government. So the amendment was withdrawn. John Morley, a follower of Gladstone, toed his leader's line. Thus, both Gladstone and Morley gave a jolt to the Indian leaders, who had been much enamoured by their liberal professions. Gladstone himself did not consider that the Indian leaders were representatives of the Indian people. He had said that these leaders' claim that they were the true representatives of the people was a very dangerous assumption. Wacha, in a letter to Dadabhai on April 23, 1892, said, "Yes, we are all sorry that Mr. Gladstone should have been so extremely cautious in letting us have the elective principle in the way we wanted. What seems rather strange (is) that after having given adhesion to our proposal fourteen months ago, he should now have gone a step backward. Could it be that the telegrams regarding Hume's Circular which reached London about the same time have influenced his mind? To me this seems more likely. John Morley was never in our favour and I fear that Gladstone's mind may have been at the last moment biased by him also. He is a cold and calculating politician and sadly wants the warm and generous impulse of Gladstone who has a burning desire to give greater freedom to the struggling nationalities".

The Liberal Party, in its manifesto at the time of the elections for the Parliament in 1892, did not make any mention of the political reforms for India. Drawing attention to this significant omission, Wacha wrote to Dadabhai, on May 21, 1892, "I am now convinced that the GOM (Grand Old Man—Gladstone) played a double stroke of policy. (1) He evidently desired that the Indian affairs should not find a plank in the Liberal programme of the coming elections. For that would have committed his party to more liberal measure than now conceded. (2). By being relieved of doing anything for India in this line in power, his party would not bear the odium of any grievances which might arise in future. So the Liberals should be thanked by India even for what they have done. This is *Jesuitical* enough, is it not? You know some of his lieutenants, John Morley specially, are also dead against giving the elementary representation we want".[3] While Gladstone was soft about the elective principle, diehard Tories like Sir Richard Temple opposed it vehemently. He denounced the Congress, and said it was not representative of the Indian people. He said that if the British had not been there, those who were clamouring for representative government would have been wiped out. Temple described the Congress leaders as people having no influence with the masses. He was pretty sure that the administration under the elected representatives would nullify all the advantages, which the Indian people had gained till then. To Temple it was only the British who could bring cooperation among several races and castes. He did not forget to demand adequate representation to the Muslims. The secretary of state had informed Queen Victoria about the nature of the bill and assured her that enough care had been taken not to introduce the elective principle. Victoria on her part, in a letter to the viceroy emphasised this point. She admitted that if moderate reforms were not undertaken, radical elements in India would come forward and then the situation would go beyond control.

It is interesting to note the views of some of the contemporary British public men about the Congress and the Indian people. Sir Charles Dilke himself was an administrator and had travelled widely. He warned that it would be dangerous to despise the Congress and the Indian people. He wrote, "Argument upon the matter is to be desired, but not invective, and there is so much reason to think that the Congress movement really represents the cultivated intelligence of the country that those who ridicule it do harm to imperial interests of Great Britain, bitterly wounding and alienating men who are justified in what they do, who do it in reasonable and cautious form, and who ought to be conciliated by being met half-way. The official class themselves admit that many of the natives who attack the Congress, do so to ingratiate themselves with their British rulers and to push their claims for decorations; and while I am on this point, I may add that it is an almost universal opinion among the officials themselves that some of the recent appointments in the various classes of our orders have been unfortunate. Our first duty in India is that of defending the country against the anarchy and invasion...but our other greatest duty is to learn how to live with what is commonly called the Congress movement; namely, with the development of the new India which we have ourselves created. Our past work in India has been a splendid task, splendidly performed, but there is still nobler one before us, and one larger even than that labour on the Irish problem to which our public men on both sides seem to much inclined to give their whole attention.[4]

Seymour Keay, a member of the House of Commons, in his speech on the India bill, supported the introduction of the elective principle. He criticised Sir Richard Temple's administration for increasing taxes on the poor people and adding to their misery. He was confident that the elected representatives would work for the eradication of poverty. On the other hand Lord Northbrook, a Tory, was liberal in his views, but did not favour principle of election, and supported the bill as it was. He suggested that the members of the new Councils might be permitted to ask questions, but should go no further. He did not want to give the right to move a non-official resolution and rejected the demand by the Congress to refer the resolution so rejected by the Viceroy to the special committee of the

Parliament. Lord Northbrook said that the speeches and the resolutions in the Congress sessions were detrimental to the interests of the Muslims. He was, however, in favour of introducing elective principle in the provincial Councils but suggested that the governor must have the authority to accept or reject the membership of any candidate. George Jesney was sometime a member of the defence department in the Viceroy's Advisory Council and was prejudiced against the Congress. His opinion was that the Congress was promoting the interests of some classes.

Samuel Smith, who visited India four times, raised an alarm about the danger facing the English and their administration in an article in the July issue of the 'Fortnightly Review'. He deplored that the English had not learnt any lessons from the 1857 revolt. To him the Cantonments, railway stations etc. were insecure and could be besieged by the mob and taken over. He also thought that Russia and Afghanistan might combine and invade India. In such an eventuality the Indians would not give help to the British. He said, "The division of parties in our own country upon the Irish question, and the rebellious tendencies of that unhappy portion of our dominion are most damaging to our reputation for good government. Upper classes in India ask—if England cannot govern a small island like Ireland, close to her own door, why should she hold 'interior', the two hundred and fifty millions of Indian Empire?" Smith was against the principle of equality, which according to him would spell doom for the Empire. His remedy to save it was to befriend Muslims and confine recruiting in the army to Muslims, Parsi and the Gurkhas. 'The Quarterly Review', in its editorial, opposed the introduction of the elective principle in India and called the Indians 'liars'.

The British government hedged the bill by many safeguards. The act gave the power to the municipalities and some social institutions of long standing, to decide on the members. In exercising their right they had to resort to some sort of election; but government was not willing to accept the principle of election. The government was unnecessarily scared and feared that the acceptance of the principle would bring in revolution. In fact, Ramswami Mudliar, in the Allahabad session of the Congress had pointed out that in Pondechari and other French colonies elections were regularly taking place; and there were legislative assemblies, which were functioning very well. The Assembly was elected by adult franchise. The budget was discussed in the Assembly and then passed. Indian leaders were astonished by the position taken by the Liberal leaders about the elective principle to be introduced in India. But if they had seriously taken note of the political ideology prevailing in England, they would not have been so shocked. In England, franchise was based on property and it was gradually widened. For twenty years the Tory party did its best to stem any efforts to widen the franchise and some of the Liberals supported them. In the nineteenth century the representative government was synonymous with the government of the representatives of the educated middle class and the propertied class.

After the industrial revolution, industry, trade and foreign trade increased many fold. Wealth and empire expanded. Industrialists, traders, self-employed and professionals, all were aspiring for political power and retaining it in their hands. This was of course, inevitable. 'The Times' had predicted that the people of the new aspiring class would turn to social and public work after retirement; and the Parliament would witness their enthusiasm, and after a while everything would come to normal. With the expansion of industries there was massive expansion of labour. With the improvement in the communication and transport there was great deal of influx of people in the cities. All this transformation alarmed people like Carlyle, Ruskin, Mathew Arnold and some others. Benjamin Lippincott, while discussing the thoughts of Ruskin, Carlyle, Mathew Arnold, Stephen, Lecky etc., calls them Victorian critics of democracy. According to Lippincott all these intellectuals were disturbed by the radical changes in the society with the rapid progress of industries. Rejecting democracy Carlyle argued for benevolent democracy whose leaders would be drawn from the best English stock, which would rule in the military fashion. Ruskin was the disciple of Carlyle and he was afraid that the middle class values of liberalism would spell political disorder. He probed the economic and intellectual foundation of the industrial system and insisted on the abandonment of capitalism and replacement by cooperation. The remedy advanced by both Carlyle and Ruskin was regressive. But their critique of capitalism created ground for socialism. Mathew Arnold was not an opponent of democracy as Carlyle and Ruskin, but he was advocating moral education and upliftment. He was disgusted by the materialism of the upper classes and vulgarity of the middle class and brutality of the lower. He, therefore, insisted on a national system of public education. Stephen, Maine and Lecky held that the middle class democracy had failed, and so they opposed the extension of suffrage to the lower classes. They were opposed to the principle of equality inherent in democracy. All of them believed in the rule by the wisdom of the few, as democracy might lead to anarchy. Carlyle thought that the Parliament was useless as a ruling body, it should be restricted to advise the sovereign. In such a biased atmosphere it was a tall order to expect radical reforms from the British government.

After the bill about the expansion of the Councils became law, various rules were framed. They were more restrictive. The Viceroy received numerous petitions. Burma and the Central Provinces had no Councils and so they could not have any benefit under the new law. The secretary of state replied that as the Act would not be amended, the viceroy would try to find whether he could do anything. Some judges and advocates demanded representation, but their demand was turned down. The Central Mahommedan Association and its branches passed a resolution criticising the provisions of the Act. The resolution said that the structure of the local self-institutions was such that the Muslims would not get adequate representation in the Councils. The viceroy replied that he was fully aware of their grievances and it would be his endeavour to appoint some prominent Muslims on the Councils. 'The Spectator' published a report of a meeting of the Muslims in Pune in January, which adopted a resolution disfavouring any expansion of the Councils. Indeed, the meeting did not want any Councils at all, as it was satisfied with the local self institutions in the Deccan Division. The Sarvajanik Sabha, on the other hand, sent a petition on June 3, 1893 to the viceroy, pointing out how the Deccan Division, i.e. Maharashtra, was discriminated against. The petition said that the area of the division was three times more than the Northern Division and thirty per cent more than the Southern one. Population, number of villages and cities in the Deccan Division were also larger than the other two. The Division paid more revenue than others but it would not have a single representative on the Council. Responding to the Sabha's appeal, public meetings were held in Pune, Satara, Solapur, Nasik, Dhulia etc., expressing dissatisfaction with the regulations under the new Act. The viceroy found that there was a substance in the petition of the Sabha, and directed the Bombay governor, Lord Harris, to find out some way to meet the demand of the Sabha. Accordingly, rules were amended and in 1895 the Deccan Division was given one seat on the Provincial Council, and Lokmanya Tilak was the first member followed by Gokhale in 1899. On the viceroy's Council, Pherozeshah Mehta and the Maharaja of Darbhanga were the first members to be selected.

Dadabhai, in his presidential address to the Lahore session of the Congress in 1893, criticised the amended Council Act for discarding the principle of election. He also said that the objective of the Act would not be achieved by the rules framed under the Act. Surendranath Banerjea welcomed the Act in 1892, but in his presidential address to the Pune session of the Congress in 1895 criticised it. He said that, "the members were free to speak on the Budget and make suggestions but had no right to move any resolution. Non-official members must be eager to move amendments to the budget provisions, but Act did not permit them to do so. The principle of any modern government was no taxation without representation. Indians had not demanded this right, but they must have the right to move amendments. Government was free to veto such amendments which they did not approve of. In no way the government would have been defeated or embarrassed". Under the Act the number of members of the viceroy's Council was sixteen. Out of the ten non-official members four were to be sent by the four provincial Councils, the fifth by the Chamber of Commerce, Calcutta. The other five were to be nominated by the viceroy. The Act gave powers to the viceroy to decide the rules of the procedure. The permission to a member to move a resolution was at his discretion.

As the Congress decided to cooperate with the government in running the Councils under the new Act, Sir William Hunter, in his column, 'Indian Affairs', in 'The Times', welcomed this change of attitude. On June 22, 1894, he said, "The political movement represented by the Indian National Congress passed through critical stages during the viceroyalty of Lord Lansdowne, but has steadily gained ground. Soon after the accession of Lord Lansdowne it gave support to a scheme, which would have divided India into cut and dried electoral divisions, a scheme, which in the hands of Mr. Bradlaugh, become the reductio-ad-absurdom of the principles that the wiser members of the Congress advocate. But the Congress, however, extracted itself from the false position into which it had slipped, and since then has held its annual meetings in various great cities of India. Representative institutions grow up all over the world wherever the British ideas are sown, and to deny their cautious extension to India would be to falsify the traditions of our race. But the murderous animosities which darkened the last months of Lord Lansdowne's rule prove how shallow is still the soil in which the tree of religions and civic liberty has been planted in India." The Columnist's reference to the murderous animosities was to some communal riots in some parts of the country and the incidence of laying mud cakes on the mango trees in some parts of Bihar, which reminded the officials of the uprising in 1857. 'The Times', taking notice of this, wrote on May 14: "The mango stems in Bihar have made a deep impression on the average British news-reader than the recent sacrifice of the Indian interests to Manchester clamour against which all India is indignantly protesting. There is not an Englishman in India and scarcely an Englishman who cares anything about the matter at home, who does not feel, that we have late been acting wrongly by the Indian peoples. The conscience doth make cowards of us all, and any unusual occurrence in India is magnified into a portent of the dangers which we ourselves have provoked".

One of the demands of the Congress was to hold ICS examinations simultaneously in England and India. Gladstone again failed to support this demand. In June 1893 an unofficial resolution in the Commons had accepted this demand. But when the secretary of state sent the same resolution to the viceroy for his comments, his Advisory Council opposed it. The secretary of state was informed that if the resolution was accepted, the number of the British in the ICS cadre would go down and that would be harmful to the security of the British. It was also conveyed that not only the number of the English officers would be reduced, but that of Muslims and Sikhs would also be affected. The secretary of state conceded and rejected the unofficial resolution. However, he assured that whenever any high posts in the government fell vacant, the most competent Indian ICS officers would be considered to fill them. Thus, a long standing demand of the Congress was rejected by the government of Gladstone.

The selection of the members of the Councils was done on the basis of religion, castes etc. In the session of the Congress in 1889, Tilak moved a resolution demanding that the members of the Councils should be elected and not selected on the basis of religion and castes. The resolution was seconded by Gokhale, but the Congress rejected the resolution. The Sarvajanik Sabha suggested that the territory should be the basis, which the government did not accept and introduced the religious element and reservation. It was Lord Dufferin, who suggested this provision, which was then incorporated in the 1892 Act. Dr. B.R. Ambedkar, discussing how the principle of religion was accepted, says, "It was in the legislature that were constituted under the Act that the principle of separate representation for Musalmans was for the first time introduced in the political constitution of India. The Introduction of this principle is shrouded in mystery. It is a mystery because it was introduced so silently and so stealthily. The principle of separate representation does not find a place in the Act. The Act says nothing about it. It was in the directions—but not in the Act—issued to those charged with the duty of framing Regulations as to the classes and interests to whom representation was to be given that the Muslims were named as a class to be provided for. It is a mystery as to who was responsible for this provision. The scheme of separate representation was not the result of any demand put forth by any organised Muslim Association. Where did it then originate? It is suggested that it originated with the Viceroy, Lord Dufferin, who, as far back as year 1888, when dealing with the question of representation in the legislative Councils, emphasised the necessity that in India representation will have to be, not in the way the representation is secured in England, but a representation by interests. What could have led Lord Dufferin to suggest such a plan? It is suggested that the idea was to wean away the Muslims from the Congress, which had already started three years before. Be that as it may, it is certain that it is by this Act that the separate representation for the Muslim became, for the first time, a feature of the Indian constitution. It should, however, be noted that neither the Act nor the regulations conferred any right of selection upon the Muslim community, nor did the Act give the Muslim community a right to claim a fixed number of seats. All it did was to give the Muslims the right to separate representation".[5]

As the Congress was striving to get more political power and had to contend with some Muslim leaders who wanted to go by the separatist way, it also was driven by internal controversy over the question of social reforms. Behramji Merwanji Malabari who was a friend of Dadabhai and a writer and a journalist, wrote some articles in 1884 describing how the child-marriages were harmful. He was also an advocate of widow-remarriage. He gave several speeches in England describing the plight of the widows and the harmful effects of the child-marriages among the Hindus. Malabari then started a campaign to increase the age of marriage. Ranade, in an article in the Sarvajanik Sabha Journal in 1878, had discussed the evil consequences of the over population and said that the child marriages were one of the causes of over population. In 1881 he gave a speech in Pune, and suggested that the people should take a lead in increasing the age of marriage of the daughters. He wanted people to take the initiative and Tilak supported the voluntary efforts. But when Malabari started a campaign asking for a law to be enacted, Ranade and Tilak fell apart and a bitter controversy ensued. Tilak did not want any government interference, while Ranade argued that as the society had accepted several laws of the government and it was the duty of the government to secure the wellbeing of the people, there was nothing objectionable if government passed any law regarding child and widow marriages. Dr. Bhandarkar, Telang, Agarkar and several others supported Ranade. Tilak was not an extreme orthodox. His daughters had some school education and were married not at the age of eight as those of orthodox Hindus. In fact, in 1889, he had signed a circular, which appealed the people to raise the marriage age limit for boys from sixteen to twenty and for girls from ten to fourteen. But he was opposed to giving any authority to the government to enact laws relating to any social customs. It was quite characteristic of him to wage a furious campaign. A century later, the whole controversy seems irrelevant and futile; but in those days the upper caste Hindus all over the country were disturbed over the enactment.

It was not that Tilak alone opposed the government interference and asked the Congress not to deal with any social problems, but stick to the political work. Dadabhai was also of the same view. He had publicly advised the social reformers that they should not expect the Congress to take up the social issues, as that would divide the ranks. Moreover, he observed that the leaders of one caste were ignorant of the traditions and customs of the others. His emphasis was on unity of all Indians to secure wider political rights. In a letter to Malabari on December 15, 1887, Dadabhai advised him to continue working for social reforms; but he asked why he was criticising those who were working in the political field. One thing was clear to Dadabhai that those who were on the lower level politically, would not be able to achieve anything socially; only the politically advanced would have sufficient courage for social reforms. When Malabari asked for the support for his campaign, Hume wrote him two letters. Hume was not against the widow remarriage or abolishing the custom of child marriage. But he, like Dadabhai, was not prepared to relegate the political issues to the secondary level. He clarified that the Hindus should come forward and even support legislation for the marriages of the child widows, but for other widows he thought it better to educate the public. Hume wrote, "But to me it seems you put forward these two unquestionably desirable reforms as if they were the most momentous questions of the day, and as if on them hinged the national regeneration, whereas they are mere fractional parts which can never be successfully manipulated by themselves. Moreover, pressing these isolated points so strongly, as if they were obligatory and stood by themselves, and not as mere optional sections of a general enterprise, has certainly, temporarily alienated some who would cordially have cooperated in many other sections"[6].

Lord Dufferin had moved a resolution and not a bill on social reforms; and Malabari asked Hume's opinion on the resolution. Hume wrote back to say that he could support Malabari if he wanted the government to pass an enabling legislation. That might soften his critics, but Hume was not prepared to suggest to the government to bring a bill. He said: "Were I a Viceroy at this moment with virtually only European colleagues, I should reply to you just as Lord Dufferin has done, viz., that the Government was not in a position to legislate on such subjects".[7] Hume, writing to the Viceroy, said, "Many district officers have been setting the people up to oppose. They have been saying: 'Oh yes. You were all so fond of the Congress people, and you believed the English people would help you, and now see it is the English people (back home) who have forced this on the Government of India, on our Government, who are your true friends and the Congress people and your friend, Mr. Hume are backing up this attempt to interfere with your religion'".

'The Times' published a newsletter by its correspondent on June 6, 1891which was written after the Age of Consent Bill had been passed. It said, "In the first place, this was a social reform carried at last by the Hindoos themselves. Mr. Malabari, who initiated the movement, wisely stood aside at the last, and his community with equal good sense, did not interfere. The Mahomedans maintained a neutral attitude. Those (propertied classes and zamindars) who were loyal to the British rule supported the bill; those who foment discord and disloyalty opposed the bill...The controversy has incidentally had very important effect...It has broken up the Congress. The Congresswallas are now divided into two camps". For the correspondent it was an opportunity to further divide the Congress by accepting the limited demand of the moderates granting the expansion of the Councils and introducing some element of election which would satisfy them and isolate the agitators. "Lord Lansdowne's government, thus, by the recent Age of Consent reform, has not only put an end to an immoral and cruel practice; it has also ruined that Congress party which, only four years ago, in Allahabad, threatened to lead a formidable seditious movement, by distributing and broadcasting throughout India, the famous seditious pamphlets. The abolition of the annual Congress, such as it was likely to become, is almost as important as the abolition of the cruel marriage itself".

The bill definitely generated strong feelings and animosity between the two contending groups in the Congress. But the organisation itself, contrary to the wishes and prediction of 'The Times' and its correspondent, did not split. The intense controversy resulted in a stormy public meeting in Pune, which ended with violence. Tilak did not condemn those of his associates who indulged in violence on the plea that he was not present at the meeting. Gokhale was disturbed by such show of force and intolerance. In this mood he wrote a letter to G.V. Joshi on March 3, 1891 expressing his disgust. Gokhale said, "The conduct of 'leading men' of Poona which culminated in disgraceful rowdyism of Wednesday last has fairly sickened me. It has exercised a deciding influence on my wavering mind and I am now most exceedingly anxious to be relieved of the necessity of keeping up any kind of connection with them. I am longing for the time when I shall have nothing to do directly with these people".[8] This was followed by another stormy meeting which resulted in passing the reins of the Sarvajanik Sabha into the hands of Tilak from Ranade, as Tilak proved his majority. Gokhale then sent in his resignation of the office of the secretary and also that of the editor of the Journal. Tilak wrote in 'Kesari' that Gokhale would be able to devote more time for the Fergusson College. The Sarvajanik Sabha had received recognition not only in Maharashtra but all over the country. This was due to the untiring efforts of Ranade and the band of workers under his guidance. Whatever happened with regard to the Sarvajanik Sabha was a part of the grand strategy of Tilak. He wanted to fight with the social reformers and also to defeat them politically in the Congress. It was not that Ranade and his friends were spoiling for a fight on the question of social reforms. Even when the controversy about the Age of Consent bill was at its zenith, the Sabha's Journal had published several articles from people of Madras, Calcutta and Bombay who had made suggestions for a compromise. Several scholarly articles also discussed other social problems. Thus the intent of the moderates like Ranade and Bhandarkar was clear. But Tilak did not want to part company with his orthodox followers and associates. He, therefore, mustered majority in the Sabha and captured it. However, for about the next twenty years he could not succeed in establishing his leadership in the Congress. He remained popular with the masses because of his sacrifice and uncompromising zeal in espousing the people's causes and his incarceration. In Maharashtra, he widened his base by starting the Ganesh and Shivaji festivals. Gokhale, on the other hand, could easily relate to the Congress leaders. Thus, it was not a personal rivalry but the temperament and political outlook that made them pursue different paths.

The year 1893 also saw riots in Bombay, Yevala and other places. In Yevala and some other places Muslims objected to the playing of music in front of the mosques. Tilak, disapproving government's order, suggested that the government should with the consent of the Muslims regulate the hours of music to be played. His criticism was directed more against the government than the Muslims. He said that the dispute was not confined to two parties; but there was a third party involved. He was hinting that this third party, which was the government, directly or indirectly was helping in fomenting the riots. Governor Lord Harris, without waiting for the report of the inquiry committee, blamed the Hindus for the riots in Bombay. However, the Bombay government in a confidential report to the secretary of state, on October 26, 1893, drew a different picture. It said,

"On both occasions (1873 riots between Muslims and Parsis, and 1893 Hindu-Muslim riots) the first resort to violence must be laid to the door of the Mohammedan community, and on both occasions the scene of the outbreak was the neighbourhood of the Jama Masjid. Your Lordship will observe that Mr. Vincent (the Commissioner of Police) lays the blame primarily at the door of the cow-protection societies of Bombay and elsewhere, while he admits the religious riots in other parts of India, especially at Prabhas Pattan, and the meetings held at Bombay by both communities with these last were contributory causes. Mr. Vincent's opinion, in a matter of this kind, is of the highest value, but it is to be observed that while the cow-protection movement has undoubtedly been pushed of late with growing vigour, the movement itself is not a new one. We hesitate to adopt the opinion that the cow-protection movement is the principal cause of the violence".[9] Ranade and Gokhale were disposed to take a more liberal view of the whole matter and thought that some leeway must be given to the Muslims. However, on November 29, 1894, Gokhale, on behalf of the Sarvajanik Sabha, sent a note to the government which charged some government officials with partiality towards Muslims. The note said that these officers adopted a biased attitude even in cases where Muslims were the offenders.

Lord Harris was highly prejudiced against the Indian leaders and more so against the Pune Brahmins. That is why even in the communal riots he saw conspiracy against the British government. 'The Times of India' supported this theory. Gokhale refuted the argument in a letter to 'The Times of India' under the pseudonym 'Poona Brahamin'. He wrote: "A great deal has recently been said of a conspiracy in the Deccan. Yes, I too believe that there is a conspiracy in the Deccan, but it is for discrediting not the Government, but the people in Deccan in general and the Poona Brahmins in particular. I admit that some of the vernacular papers in the Deccan wrote much too strongly. Did they write like that during the Lord Ray's time? Has Lord Harris ever shown the least regard for the press or the Presidency? But is there no provocation to write strongly? Has he ever moved even so much as by the breadth of a hair, to conciliate public opinion? The entire press opposed the Mhowra Bill; the entire press disapproved the exclusion of the Central Division from the elective franchise, the entire press condemned the Provincial Services rules. Has Lord Harris shown the least shred of respect for these unanimous expressions of opinion?"

It was Pune's turn to host the session of the Congress in 1895. The bitter controversy about the age of consent bill and the rivalry in the Sarvajanik Sabha had culminated in capturing of the Sabha by Tilak and the resignations of Ranade and Gokhale. But both groups had to cooperate for the Congress session to make it a success. Thus, they formed a committee and Tilak was appointed as the secretary. Before the session, Hume visited Pune where a public meeting was held in his honour. Gokhale in his speech praised the services of Hume and affirmed that whatever Congress had achieved from its inception was due to Hume. He added, "Hume had enabled India, for the first time in its history, to breathe and feel like one nation by bringing together men of enlightenment and patriotism from various parts of the country to work in a common cause. He had tried to steady their faltering footsteps and turn their weak accents into firm speech. He had set them a high and glorious example as to how they (India people) should labour for the regeneration of motherland."[10] Tilak eulogizing the services of Hume in the columns of 'Kesari', alluded to Hume's famous circular and said that "if there was dissatisfaction about the existing system, then it must be openly ventilated. It was waste of time and energy to call a session once a year and make mild speeches. That was not the way to get the demands fulfilled. It was obligatory to work both in India and England all the year round and by incessant propaganda compel the government to accept our demands. Government would not yield unless pushed in a corner".

Though moderates and radicals jointly formed a steering committee for the session of the Congress, a new controversy erupted and the committee was paralysed. Radicals were opposed to allow the use of the pandal for the session of the social conference, which was the custom followed in all previous sessions of the Congress. It was a convenient arrangement as those delegates who wanted to attend the social conference did not have to move to some other place. But the radicals maintained that the resolutions and deliberations in the social conference were not acceptable to large number of Congressmen and they did not want to be identified with it. Tilak led the radicals and demanded that the social conference be shifted to another venue, and resigned as secretary of the committee. Gokhale took his place. Tilak even called a public meeting and registered his opposition. Some hotheads even threatened to burn the Congress pandal. It was not that the radical congressmen alone were opposed to holding of the social conference in the Congress pandal, but even many social reformers held the same view though for different reason. They thought that by using the Congress pandal the social conference was demeaning itself. 'The Social Reformer' writing in 1892 remarked: "If it is still insisted to hold the Conference with the Congress, then the future of the Conference is not hopeful. It is only another way of proclaiming to the world that the Conference cannot stand on its own legs".[11] But the holding of the Conference in the Congress pandal was a part of the larger controversy and that was about the role of the Congress. In the second session at Calcutta, Dadabhai as a president advised the Congressmen to avoid social subjects, as they were sure to divide the organisation. Pherozeshah Mehta endorsed Dadabhai's opinion. Badruddin Tyabji laid down the condition that all decisions relating to Muslims must be taken with their consent. Ranade then assessed the general consensus of the Congressman and found that overwhelmingly it was against holding the Social Conference in the Congress pandal. To avoid further complications and probable disruption of the Congress session, he withdrew and decided to shift the venue of the Social Conference.

But the differences about the Congress session persisted. Ranade's letter to Pherozeshah Mehta apprising him of the happenings in Pune is revealing. He wrote: "Mr. Tilak has not been able to accept your advice and he has on third or fourth time during the past three weeks demonstrated that he is not the sole master of his own movements. Soon after my coming here about three weeks ago, I arranged to get him round to sign a joint circular with Mr. Gadgil. But after signing the circular and taking it home, he refused to issue it. A few days latter, I again persuaded him not to go in for sentimental meeting of the extremists. He allowed himself to be persuaded; and both parties signed a joint and non-contentious programme, speeches, resolutions and all. On going home again, he changed his mind and called his people's meeting and broke finally, as it seemed to me, with the moderate party and joined the extremists. There the reference to your intercession came on and he appears to have again promised to follow your advice, and join other friends, together with the three Bombay secretaries. He changed his mind and obtained time to make up his resolution finally. Coming here, he resolved to stand out. Then Mr. Wacha and Mr. Khare came here on Sunday, and at his instance, Mr. Wacha and Khare persuaded the other group to give up their part about the Social Conference so far as to refer the decision of that question not to the Reception Committee, as was previously arranged, but to the Standing Congress Committees all over India and to abide by their advice. He agreed to all their points at the meeting and then again obtained 24 hours time from Mr. Wacha. At the end of that period, he sent in his resignation yesterday morning".[12]

It must, however, be noted that Moderates tried to out maneuvre by passing a resolution which would have enabled only those who pay rupees fifty or more to get voting rights along with their family members. This resolution was in super cession of the previous one, which permitted one vote per head, irrespective of the amount paid. Tilak then called a meeting and condemned this move. Because of the public pressure, the Committee was dissolved and a new Committee was formed with three members from Bombay, which did away with the equal status to Tilak's group. This became the bone of contention. Tilak clarified his position through a letter to 'The Times of India'. He wrote: "A Congress in Poona cannot be regarded a success unless the majority of the people in Poona join it enthusiastically. We must approach the trader, the artisan and the working man as well as the educated classes and make all of them subscribe to the Congress fund, and in order to do this we must appeal to each of them in a manner so as not to offend their susceptibilities unnecessarily. The Congress eventually aims at being a Congress of the people and the object cannot be achieved, unless, every year, an effort is made to approach more and more classes that have not taken hitherto much interest in the movement".

As the venue of the Social Conference was changed, Surendranath Banerjea expressed his satisfaction and indicated how he was not happy with Ranade's position regarding the Social Conference to be held in the Congress pandal. Surendranath's presidential speech was on the usual line of such speeches made so far. The dispute between the radical and moderate Congressmen was settled and the session was conducted peacefully. But the dispute had deeper roots. It was mainly about the objectives of the Congress and the method of achieving them. After the session was over, Tilak wrote in *Kesari* drawing the attention of the Congressmen to a picture of a poor peasant, which was put up by somebody outside the pandal. He warned that if the Congress did not pay attention to the grievances of the poor peasants, it would defeat its own purpose. It was, however, clear that both Tilak and moderates in Pune lost opportunities to compromise and the impression went round the country that Pune congressmen were quarrelsome and obstinate. A letter by Virraghava Chari, a Congress leader from Madras, to Dadabhai, on November 13, 1895 speaks for itself. Chari said, "I am really sorry that Poona people are unnecessarily quarreling among themselves. Poona is always a bad place and Mr. Hume was always averse to have any Congress there. Namjoshi and Tilak are bad people. Justice Ranade has been doing his best to smoothen matters. Had it not been for him we would have by this time resolved the Congress in Bombay".[13]

At the end of a decade of existence, Congress was thus facing a crisis. There arose sharp differences about the objectives of the Congress and the methods to persue them. Arvindbabu wrote some articles in *Indu Prakash*, Bombay, lampooning the Congress leadership. He called them cowards and slavish and declared that the Congress had completely failed to achieve any of its objectives. This was a new tone; and in future Congress was to face such rebellious tendencies.

REFERENCES

1. Hugh O'Donnell, *A History of the Irish Parliamentary Party*, Vol. 2, Longmans, NY, 1910, pp. 427-431.
2. *Dadabhai Papers.* (these are unpublished papers from Dadabhai Naoroji Trust).
3. R.P. Patwardhan, *Dadabhai Naoroji Correspondence, Vol. 2, Part 2*, Allied Publishers, 1977, pp. 285-86, 289-90.
4. Sir Charles Dilke, *Problems of Greater Britain*, Macmillan and Co., London, 1890, p. 434.
5. Dr. B.R. Ambedkar, *Pakistan or Partition of India,* Thacker and Co., Bombay, 1946, pp. 240-41.
6. William Wedderburn, *Allan Octavian Hume*, Peagasus, New Delhi, 1974, pp.152-154.
7. William Wedderburn, *Allan Octavian Hume*, Peagasus, New Delhi, 1974, pp. 152-154 and 164-65.

8. *Gokhale Papers.* (these are unpublished papers from Gokhale institute).
9. Ram Gopal, *Lokmanya Tilak,* Asia Pub. House, London, 1966 pp. 86-87.
10. Gopal Krishna Gokhale, *Speeches*, G.A. Natesan, Madras, 1920, pp 755, 756.
11. S. Natrajan, *a Century of Social Reform in India*, Asia Publishing House, Bombay, 1959, p. 90.
12. Govind Talwalkar, *Virat Dnyani ; Nyayamurti Mahadeo Govind Ranade*, Prestige Prakashan, Pune, 1990, pp. 70-71.
13. *Dadabhai Papers* (these are unpublished papers which from Dadabhai Naoroji Trust).

Chapter Eight

WELBY COMMISSION

The second decade of the Indian National Congress—1895 to 1905—was turbulent in the life of Gokhale. In the year 1895 he was bereaved of his two valued colleagues in the Deccan Education Society. One was Waman Shivram Apte, who was efficiently running the society and its college. Gokhale shared a close relationship with him. Apte was followed by Gopal Ganesh Agarkar, who was Gokhale's senior. Moreover, he also had an ideological affinity with Gokhale. Because of the demise of both Apte and Agarkar, Gokhale had to devote more time to the Deccan Education Society and Fergusson College.

Gokhale had to raise funds for the college building and also select suitable staff. It was Gokhale who invited D.K. Karve, who later blazed a new trail in the field of female education in Maharashtra. After Gokhale's death, Karve, in paying tribute to Gokhale, eulogised his contribution to the society and the college. Karve said, "It was really Gokhale who found capable men for the College and collected a substantial part of the funds for the first building of the College which was really the best of the whole set of buildings. If there was one man, more than any other, whose labours went to establish the reputation of the College, it was Gokhale…it was also he who placed things on a stable footing. It was also he who steered the ship of the Society clear off rocks on which it might have floundered during the great crisis following Government's hostility to private institutions in Poona after the Rand murder in 1897, persuading the life-members on one side to accept apparently hard and unjust conditions and on the other inducing the outside members of the Council of the Society and especially Mr. Selby and Dr. Bhandarkar, the Chairman and Vice-Chairman of the Council to put the case of the life-members before the authorities in proper light. The Government desired to place the Society in the hands of its nominees. Owing to the advocacy of the men like Gokhale and Selby, Bhandarkar and Ranade, Government finally agreed that a Governing Body consisting of non-life-members, fellows and patrons of the Society should be set up to control the affairs of the Society's institutions".[1]

In 1895, Gokhale was disturbed by the controversy in the Sarvajanik Sabha and the exhibition of bitterness over the Age of Consent Bill. He had expressed his anguish in a letter to G.V. Joshi on February 8, 1896. Gokhale wrote, "Our recent misfortunes make it incumbent on me that I should devote as much of my time as I possibly can to my school and college. I have besides grown absolutely sick of the public life of Poona. Recent events have opened my eyes very wide indeed, and I am anxious to be relieved of all public responsibilities and to lead hereafter entirely retired life". He also sent a letter to Dadabhai. He wrote to Dadabhai from Poona on September 3, 1896, "Developments of distressing character have already taken place in the political life of this city. God's curse seems to be resting on this country. Else how should it always be that directly when some good and useful work is begun, dissentions arise to undo it? Sarvajanik Sabha, a child of Justice Ranade's for which he has worked so nobly for a quarter of a century has been taken out of his hands and for a whole year the Sabha had done absolutely no work. The whole attempt here is to drive out of public life all workers who sympathise with the cause of social reforms by discrediting them with the masses by all manner of means. Excuse me for writing so freely of the situation here. Perhaps it is not right that I should add to your anxieties by sending you such distressing news. But in a way it was necessary to write all this to prepare you for possible disappointments as regards Poona in future".[2]

After Tilak took over the Sarvajanik Sabha, Gokhale on the advise of Ranade withheld his resignation for six months and then submitted it. His resignation as the secretary of the Sabha was accepted on August 15, 1896. Ranade and his colleagues after waiting for more than a year established a new institution—the Deccan Sabha. As their attitude, objectives and method of working differed totally, it was inevitable that Ranade and Tilak should part company. The Deccan Sabha issued its manifesto on November 4, 1896, which made clear the direction which should guide the political and social work of the moderates. The manifesto said, "For some time past, the conviction has been forcing itself on many lovers of political progress in the country that it was necessary to take effective steps to give adequate expression to the spirit of moderate liberalism which animates the most thoughtful leaders of public opinion on this side of India. The (Sarvajanik) Sabha always aimed at securing the cooperation of all classes and it scrupulously avoided identifying itself with any preponderant sectional interests".

The manifesto then made note of the new turn taken by the Sarvajanik Sabha and the necessity of the new organisation. It declared its ideology, which would guide the new organisation. "Liberalism and moderation will be the watchwords of the Association (Deccan Sabha). The spirit of liberalism implies a freedom from race and creed prejudices and a steady devotion to all that seeks to do justice between man and man, giving to the rulers the loyalty that it is due to the law they are bound to administer, but securing at the same time to the ruled the equality which is their right under the law. Moderation imposes the condition of never vainly aspiring after the impossible or after too remote ideals, but striving each day to take the next step in the order of natural growth by doing the work that lies nearest to our hands in a spirit of compromise and fairness. After all, political activities are chiefly of value not for the particular results achieved, but for the process of political education which is secured by exciting interest in public matters and promoting the self-reliance of citizenship. This is no doubt a slow process, but all growth of new habits must be slow to be real".

Lokmanya Tilak was furious at the formation of the Deccan Sabha and especially by its manifesto. His editorial in 'Kesari' was spitting fire, and the language was at times undignified. But it must be admitted that both the Sarvajanik Sabha and the Deccan Sabha could not achieve the prestige and influence that Sarvajanik Sabha had under the guidance of Ranade, before it split up. Both organisations did their utmost to help those affected by the famine in 1896-97. Gokhale had the added responsibility of the Deccan Education Society and the College as well as the Congress organisation. Besides, he was elected as a member of the Provincial Council. Gokhale, therefore, could not devote much time to the Deccan Sabha as he did for the Sarvajanik Sabha. Tilak was imprisoned and the Sarvajanik Sabha was left with no effective leadership. As predicted in the Deccan Sabha manifesto, Maharashtra suffered a severe famine in 1896-97. The Deccan Sabha, under the guidance of Ranade, did a yeomen service in gathering information about the famine and sending detailed memoranda to the government and undertaking relief work.

Lord Lansdowne was replaced by Lord Elgin as viceroy who was not sympathetic towards Indians. It was Lansdowne who made the Council Act more rigid by various regulations. While laying down the reins of office, Lord Lansdowne declared that it was futile to expect laws in England to be replicated in India. He was critical of the practice of approaching the British Parliament directly. He pointed out that though the Parliament was sovereign, it had to use the authority with great circumspection. Lord Lansdowne said, those who administer India had practical experience and if the Parliament did not make use of them, it would endanger the security of the empire. 'The Statesman', reviewing the Lansdowne regime on January 21, 1894 said, "The foolish tradition of spending millions on our impregnable North-West Frontier was his by inheritance; but the exercise of a truly independent judgement would have suggested a doubt of the urgency if not the necessity of the works, or at least have insisted that the annual expenditure thereon might be, if not curtailed, at least distributed over a long term of years, to the sensible relief of the finances of the Empire. But the ruinous waste has gone on, unaffected for good or evil, by Lord Lansdowne's presence...for to dispel so time-honoured a delusion as that with which Simla has invested our North-West Frontier would require an exceptional man; and our departing Viceroy has been exceptional in nought save the opportunities he has enjoyed. Turning now to Lord Lansdowne's internal administration, we are forced to observe that with the one exception it has been a record of failure".

Two years after Lord Elgin took over as viceroy, the 'India' observed that the attitude of the government about the Congress was getting modified. But this optimism was unfounded. Lord Elgin was a weak viceroy and was subservient to the secretary of state. In 1894, when Lord Elgin took over as viceroy, the Government of India had a budget deficit. In a letter to the Secretary of State Sir Henry Fowler, on March 7, 1894 the viceroy wrote, "As regards finance everything is in most critical position; I doubt, indeed, if the position has parallel. As it stands, the Import Duty Bill, if every one were free, would not, I Suppose, secure a single vote. When it does come in, every unofficial member will vote against it. The members of the Executive Council will, of course, vote for it, although they do under protest. If other Imperial duties are to be imposed, why is not this one, and is not accepted from the consideration of home interests alone? I do not think that it can be argued that it is more distinctly protective, especially if you may insist, upon Excise Duties, and the opinion seems prevalent that an Import Duty on Cotton Goods would not really affect the volume of trade. On the other hand, the money is absolutely required, and I am assured that there is no other source of revenue which would not be both inadequate and dangerous". After retirement, in his speech in the Lords on July 20, 1894, Lord Lansdowne justified the import duty on cotton goods imposed by the government of India. He said that the central government had taken over the surplus of the provincial government in view of the deficit budget. Because of this, building of the barracks for the Army had stopped. In the cantonments in India many projects of the water supply schemes and scavenging were abandoned which was dangerous to the health of the people concerned. Many railway projects were also stopped. In the circumstances, duty on cotton was unavoidable and mill-owners in Lancashire should not raise a hue and cry. When other colonies impose duties on the English goods, why India should be made an exception and criticised for the cotton duties levied to bridge the gap between income and expenses? Lansdowne also pointed out that as India was producing coarse cloth, it was not competing with Lancashire. He said that it was an opportunity to show that India was governed with a view to promoting the Indian interests. He warned that if the British government did not accept those duties, then agitators in India would be provided with a cause.

This problem of import duty on cotton goods was discussed in the Parliament and the British press for a considerable time. 'The Times' supported the duties on cotton goods and was critical of the Lancashire mill-owners. On March 5, 1894, the paper referred to the Indian budget, which carried a deficit of three and half crore rupees. The finance minister had made provisions to meet half the deficit by levying tax on petrol and the export of rice, but he avoided duty on Manchester cotton goods. 'The Times' wrote: "In regard to the export duty on rice, the Finance Minister does not fear the Indian peasants. In regard to import duty on petroleum he had not consulted the wishes of the foreign producer. In regard to the cotton duties he is compelled to consider the interests of the British manufacturer". 'The Times' then criticised the practice of charging India to pay for the salaries of clerks and officers of the Commonwealth Office and so also those in the India Office. There was much criticism in the Lords against the practice of charging India for the expenses on Military. The paper also added: "It is not a question of account; it is a question of principle. It is often said that Great Britain holds India by a spell. That spell has been nothing more nor less than slowly natural belief that the British rule is, in the main, a just rule. Signs are not wanting that the spell is losing something of its power. If ever it should be altogether dissolved, no ancient mantras or modern political shibboleths will ever reward for us that moral ascendancy which we shall have lost". In another editorial on March 12, 1894, the paper pointed out the tariff, which India placed on the cotton goods, was for revenue purposes and not a protective duty. The Indian affairs correspondent of 'The Times', told the government of India that it should govern to promote the Indian interests and not that of Britain. On January 8, 1895, he quoted an editorial from 'The Times of India' which said that there would be many who would prefer the abolition of the legislative councils than allowing it to function by the wires from the White Hall. It also said that even if the secretary of state took over the administration of India he would, at least, be assisted by a council whose members would speak their mind, unlike in India where there was no such council.

The Secretary of State, Sir Henry Fowler, speaking in the Commons on February 21, 1895 quoting statistics nailed the lie that because of the duty the Indian import of cloth had gone down. In fact, it had increased. He also pointed out that in Canada, duty on the imported yarn was twenty-three per cent and on cloth twenty-two per cent; in New Zealand duty on cloth was twenty-two per cent. Chesney asked why the Manchester mill owners should grumble against the duty of five per cent when Indian tea had to pay a hundred per cent import duty in England? 'The Economist' in its editorials on January 12, February 12 and March 2, 1895 emphasized the same point. It maintained that the critics of the Indian import duty on cloth were entertaining false notion that the income from the duty wiped out the deficit. India had levied countervailing duty on Indian cloth. It also said that, in 1894, England received 31 lak and 42000 pounds by way of import duty on tea from India and Ceylone, i.e. Sri Lanka. It was maintained by some that, though some colonies were imposing duty on British goods, the trade itself was very small. 'The Economist' did not see any logic in criticising India for levying duty on the British cloth and not criticising the colonies because their trade was small. "Lancashire, in short, has been treated with unjustifiable excess of consideration, yet she assumed the air of injured innocence; complains of unfair treatment and demands that the finances of India shall be regularised with a single eye to her particular interests".

In July, a delegation from Lancashire waited upon Kimberley, Secretary of State, and warned him that the people of Lancashire from all parties would launch an agitation against the Indian duty on the cotton goods. On July 21, 'The Times' referring to this warning wrote: "As Lord Kimberley admitted, the feeling in India was strongly in favour of the duties, and if it was strong then, it has been growing since. India believes, rightly or wrongly, that it has been sacrificed to the interests of Lancashire. Lord Roberts, as a soldier, insists on the imperative need of maintaining in India our military and naval supremacy; but he speaks even more strongly on the value of the firm reliance, which the Natives have been accustomed to place on our integrity and honesty of purpose, and our determination to do what was right and best for them..." Even the 'Quarterly Review', which never displayed any sympathy for the Congress movement, objected to the countervailing duty on cotton goods by the government of India as beneficial to England and not to India. At the suggestion of the British government, the Indian government levied a countervailing duty on the cloth made in India and thus the deficit was wiped out. The Indian leaders were supporting the import duty on cotton goods to encourage the indigenous industry. But as the British government was the advocate of the free trade, it opposed such a protective measure. Elgin followed the instructions of Lord Kimberley and levied countervailing duty on Indian cloth and thus protected the interests of Lancashire mill owners. This was another blow to the Indian leaders who believed in the fairness and liberalism of Gladstone. In 1896, India had a surplus budget because of the improvement in the exchange rate; the railways also brought more revenue. But the government reduced the import duty on cotton goods from five per cent to three and half per cent. Wacha wrote to Dadabhai saying that this reduction would benefit Manchester industry by four million rupees. Government at the same time imposed duty on coarse cloth and cancelled that on the yarn. This duty on coarse cloth was to be on the Indian mills. Thus, profit of the Manchester rose by thirty per cent and the burden on Indian mills increased by seventy per cent.

Another irritant was the Gold Standard adopted by England while India continued with Silver Standard. When prices of silver went down India had to pay more to England. This fluctuation in the exchange rate was disadvantageous to India. 'The Times' on April 2, 1894 discussed this problem along with the duty on cotton goods and criticized the British Government's policy. The discussion on Gold and Silver continued for a few years. In 1898, the British government decided to purchase gold worth twenty million Pounds and send the quarter of it to India. At the same time government purchased whatever rupees available and turn them into silver. Government thought that it would stabilise the exchange rate and the gold would flow into India.

The year 1896 was the year of famine in Maharashtra and some other parts of the country, which continued till 1900. After the 1876-77 famine the government, under the public pressure appointed a Famine Commission, which prepared a Famine Code. This code defined the rights of the famine-stricken people and the responsibility of the government. As the Sarvajanik Sabha had come under the control of Tilak, it assumed a bold posture and made demands on the government on the basis of the Famine Code, as Tilak was keen to organise the people and make them conscience of their rights. The government was disturbed by the aggressive attitude of the Sabha and became suspicious. Tilak's emphasis was on the implementation of the provisions of the Famine Code. He also used to exhort the people to complain against those officials who were reluctant to implement the provisions of the Code. At some places the public meetings were stormy and when one of the workers of the Sarvajanik Sabha made some unfounded statements, the government informed the Sabha that it had cancelled its recognition and would not entertain any communications. Tilak wrote in reply that the Sabha was not started with the permission of the government and it was not dependent on its recognition. Famine in India was the subject of intense discussion in the Parliament. When MacNeill, a member of the Parliament, pointed out that 94,299 people died in Madras in 1891 famine, Curzon who was the deputy secretary of state disputed this figure, but did not disclose the official figure. He claimed that because of the Famine Code, the number of deaths had been reduced. But MacNeill was not satisfied and castigated the attitude of the government, which, he said, was more concerned with the revenue than the lives of the people. He also said that India was not only fleeced of its wealth to sustain the bureaucracy but even the life of the people was also robbed.

Viceroy Lord Elgin tried hard to lessen the seriousness of the famine; but when the people in England came to know the severity of the calamity, Lord Mayor of London appealed for funds. When Queen Victoria publicly expressed concern, Elgin was alarmed. 'The Statesman' on January 5, 1897 wrote: "It is a significant fact, and one which in any case might well furnish food for reflection to Lord Elgin, that the conference, British Indians held a few days ago in London to consider the situation created by the famine in this country, rejected a resolution thanking the Government of India for its energy in combating the calamity, and passed one on calling upon the Lord Mayor to open a famine fund. How far, in refusing the former resolution, the Conference was influenced by the sense of inadequacy of the measures taken by the Government of India and its subordinates to combat the famine, and how far by the disgust of the attitude adopted by the Government in the matter of Lord Mayor's recent offer to appeal to the British public for subscriptions, the telegram does not enable us to say. In any case, it is clear, the resolution appealing to the Lord Mayor is an emphatic condemnation of Lord Elgin, who, only a few days previously, reiterated the bland assurance that the time for opening a famine fund had not arrived and might not arrive. In Bombay, at a public meeting presided over by the Governor, it was unanimously resolved that time had come for further subscriptions to alleviate the sufferings caused by the scarcity". B.M. Bhatia in his book, *Famines in India,* referred that a Russian newspaper had appealed to its readers to contribute to the famine fund for the relief work in India. In the next two years, area under famine spread to one hundred and forty thousand square miles and drought in another two crores and twenty lakh square miles.

The report by the Inquiry Committee on the 1891 Famine said, that wherever the members of the committee went, they found that within eight years two fifths of the land had been sold to the moneylenders. The chief secretary of the Bombay government, while deposing before the Committee, revealed that twenty-eight per cent of the land from the Bhadoch district was taken over by the money-lenders. In the Bombay presidency one forth of the peasants had lost their land. The Famine Commission had noted that even where the Debt Relief Act was in force and other relief measures were applied, land on large scale was sold to the money-lenders or it remained fallow. The Commission suggested, that some other measures must be adopted. Sir Antony MacDonnell suggested that in view of the dire poverty, government should remit the debts and establish agricultural banks. Sir Anthony drew the attention of the House to the fact that forty million people in India were starving while another fifty million were half starved and most of the people had to subsist on the coarse grains. In the five years of famine, the government revenue instead of going down had actually increased.

Famine in India was discussed by various organs of public opinion in England. Van Nash, a correspondent of the 'Manchester Guardian', writing in the 'Contemporary Review' criticised the Government of India for its policy. Lord Salisbury justified this policy of drift and Nash said that this policy was evident in the days of famine. He warned that this policy of drift was bound to be wrecked on a rock. Nash deplored that the peasants were impoverished and the traders and moneylenders had amassed unprecedented wealth. Rural economic and social life was completely dominated by the money-lenders, which was disrupting the social fabric of the society. Nash had visited four famine stricken districts. He found that in twelve villages, 444 families out of 742 were completely bankrupt and fifty per cent were steeped in debt. In the four districts fifty per cent of the land had been acquired by the money-lenders; in another district this percentage was twenty-eight and in the third it was seventeen. Nash suggested a flexible revenue policy.

Famines in different periods of time had been discussed by various inquiry committees and commissions as well as some economists. The glaring facts which came out of all this discussion could be summarised as follows: in the years 1876 and 1878 famine took seven million lives. The expenditure on the relief work was a hundred million rupees; and loss of revenue to the government was thirty million. In 1896 almost whole of the country was visited by famine. It was severe in the Deccan districts of the Bombay presidency and Hissar district of Punjab. The Famine Commission under the chairmanship of Sir James Layal had noted that of all the provincial governments, that of Bombay was much more rigid and very stingy. The commission was also critical of the Bombay government's policy about the food supply and the rates paid to the workers on the relief works.

Secretary of State Lord George Hamilton told the public meeting called by the Lord Mayor of London, on January 16, 1897 that one hundred sixty four thousand square mile area was famine-stricken and three hundred million people were affected. Besides this, more than four hundred million were in the drought areas. Henry Hyndman was to move an amendment to a resolution, which was to be placed before the public meeting called by the Lord Mayor of London. But he was prohibited from attending the meeting. 'The Times', referring to this incident, said, that raising a fund for the famine stricken people was a temporary measure; the important question was why India remained so poor. It gave the answer by saying that India was exploited by the British government; and the country would not be so impoverished if the exploitation stopped. Dadabhai was vindicated now that the forum of the establishment like 'The Times' was supporting his view. William Digby had calculated that four and half million people died of hunger. In the famine years between 1899 and 1900 twenty-eight million people were affected by famine. About one million and two hundred thousand people died in the famine of 1900. Famine also took the toll of the animals, and hence, after the famine was over, peasants found it difficult to cultivate their land. Michelle Burge McAlpin, in her book on the food crisis in the Western India, between 1860 to 1920, gives the figures of death due to famine. For the decade 1891-1901, the figures are in accord with the rates of change of population derived from the census for all three divisions; Gujarat's deaths from famine were 381,000; Deccan's, 259,000 and Karnataka's 47,000. Famine was followed by plague; and deaths by plague in the entire Presidency including Sindh and Bombay city were 265,000 in 1896-1900.[3]

B.M. Bhatia in his seminal work on famines in India has quoted statistics from various surveys and inquiry reports about the miserable conditions of the peasants who could not face the famine due to their debt. Bhatia concludes that heavy burden of the land revenue in the Bombay Presidency left almost nothing for cultivators who were unable to face the famine. All over the country indebtedness of the peasants was on the increase and they had no other option than to sell their land to the money-lenders. Thorburn, the financial commissioner of Punjab, had surveyed some villages from the four divisions and found that from twelve villages 566 families out of 742 were destitute; 650 were in debt. The divisional commissioner of Bengal had found that 120 families out of 156 from the twenty four *parganas* were in debt. After the riots in 1875 in Ahmednagar, Solapur and other districts government passed a law for the relief to the peasants; but Woodburn did find that the objective of the law had not been achieved. Bhatia after giving these statistics concluded that by 1890 total debt on the rural India was about three hundred crores, and as the rate of interest was eighteen per cent, the amount of interest alone was fifty-six crores. Thorburn in a speech before the Fabian Society stated that the Indian peasant was impoverished not because of the drain from India to England but because of the British administration. Because of this administration there was no duty on the imported cloth and other reforms could not be implemented. George Bernard Shaw, who presided over this meeting, confessed that he was under the impression that Hyndman was drawing a picture of India in dark colour, but after listening to Thorburn's speech he thought that Hyndman was a supporter of the Indian government.

Among those who were raising funds for the famine was the prince of Jamnagar. Dadabhai wrote to him (March 4, 1895) to draw his attention to the larger question of the poverty of India of which the famine was one of the manifestations. Dadabhai wrote: "You have to distinguish the appeal for the relief of the present calamity from the necessity of preventing such calamities in the future, and if you can in some way impress upon your hearers their great duty to see that this is looked into, you will do a service both to England and to India. You will also be able to impress upon them that during the last fifteen years since the last great famine, this country (England) has added to its wealth from India four or five hundred million sterling. Even one per cent of this will mean four or five million. There are people who do not, and cannot come to relief works—women, children, old and infirm, and, more pitiful still, the respectable—who would on no account seek relief and would prefer to starve and die. Private charity is most needed".[4] It was inevitable that the Congress session, in 1896, should devote its attention more to the famine and overall economic condition of India. The speeches in the session and the resolutions stressed how India was drained of its wealth and how she had to pay through her nose for the top heavy administration. The session suggested some short term measures to ameliorate the conditions of the common people. As a long term plan the session suggested establishment of industries; stopping the drain from

India to England; reducing the government expenditure; spread of technical education; fix rate of revenue and revised and increased wages for the workers on relief works.

Famines in India in the nineteenth and twentieth centuries are the subject of research even in recent days. Mike Davis, an American researcher, has taken climatic conditions into consideration. He has also quoted extensively from the diaries of Missionaries, reporters and travellers and also newspaper reports. 'The Christian Herald', an American publication, had published various reports about the famine in India. Davis states that in the last quarter of the nineteenth century and even some years after, large areas of the world were affected by famine; which included India, Russia, Sri Lanka, Indonesia, North and South Africa and Brazil. In that period rain was either totally absent or was very scanty. Large part of this area was under the control of England. Davis supports the criticism against Lord Lytton and Sir Richard Temple for their handling of famine in 1876-77. In spite of famine, large quantity of food grains were exported, which increased the prices, and large section of the population was unable to purchase the food grains. Navtej Singh has described the conditions in Punjab. Davis quoting him says, "Thus the enormous amount of wheat was purchased at high price to be exported to Europe, resulting in a general depletion of stocks within the province. One European company namely Rally Brothers and Company, purchased even the standing crops for the purpose of export to Europe. The local trader or bania as usual raised the prices of grains, thereby causing distress in almost all districts of Punjab." When Julian Hawthorne, son of the famous New England writer and the 'Cosmopolitan' special correspondent, reached Jabalpur in April 1897, conditions in the Central provinces had grown even more nightmarish. Hawthorne was horrified by families of corpses seated in the shade of the occasional desert trees. "There they squatted, all dead now, their flimsy garments fluttering around them, except when jackals had pulled the skeletons apart, in the hopeless search for marrow." Hawthorne heard it was conservatively estimated in London, that a total of more than one hundred millions of Dollars would be expended directly and indirectly upon the Queen's jubilee ceremonies.[5]

Lord Elgin had admitted that in 1897 famine four and half million people died. But he had not taken into account those who died of cholera, malaria, and plague, which followed the famine. If that is taken into consideration, then it came to eighteen million, which was the number given by Malabari. The severity of famine induced great deal of discussion about the economic conditions of India, in the British Parliament and the media.

Why India remained so poor was the question which was raised and discussed in various quarters. Naturally Dadabhai's drain theory came to the fore. Dadabhai quoting lot of statistics pointed out that large amount of wealth was drained towards England by way of duties, dividends, and numerous cess and salaries and pensions. Dadabhai called it a tribute. He said that every year India paid two hundred and four million rupees by way of tribute. He added that in 1905 the amount was increased to five hundred and ten million.

In the initial period justice Ranade supported this theory. In 1872 and 1873 he gave two lectures in Poona, in which he propounded his views. Late Prof. N.V. Sovani, in his critical introduction to the collection of these lectures, pointed out flaws in the theory. Ranade, however, changed his views later and never again talked about the drain. Ranade thought that the poverty of India was not solely due to the drain. India was poor for some centuries and did not have industrial revolution like England or some European countries. Ranade discussed his revised views about the drain theory in his address to the Industrial Conference session in Pune in 1890. He said that some people were of the opinion that two hundred million rupees, which were exported each year, was a drain and hence nothing could be done to increase the wealth of the country.

He pointed out that one portion of the drain was the interest on the borrowing and the dividend paid on the invested capital. Instead of complaining against it, we should thank ourselves that we had a moneylender who was advancing cheap credit. Another part of the drain was by way of expenditure on the stores for the army and on the administration. But the stores could not be had in India as there were no manufacturing facilities available indigenously. Ranade also maintained that the expenditure on the administration, pensions etc could not be said as unwarranted. He then said, though we were paying for the administration, we also were receiving sizeable revenue by exporting opium to China, which was made possible under the same administration.

Analysing the causes of poverty in India, Ranade time and again said that our village industries could not compete with the manufactured goods imported from England. In the process, our craftsmen lost their employment and consequently, pressure on the land increased and became unbearable. When an advanced industrial country rules the one that had no technological facilities, then the people so ruled start giving undue importance to politics, and economic problems are relegated, regrets Ranade. He drew attention to the fact that there was little scope for capital formation in any agricultural country. That was why Ranade emphasized the importance of industrialization. It must be noted that though Gokhale toed the line of Ranade about industrialization, unlike his mentor, he did not give up the drain theory.

According to Dadabhai's calculation, the per capita income of India was rupees twenty. Though he had limited resources at his disposal, Dadabhai's calculations were nearer reality. This subject of per capita income was much discussed then and also some years afterwards. Lord Curzon did not agree with Dadabhai. According to him per capita income was rupees twenty-seven. After he became viceroy, he declared in 1901 that it was rupees thirty. He also said that in any agricultural country per capita income rises much less, as the pressure on land increases year by year. Later K.T. Shah, Dr. V.K.R.V. Rao concluded that the per capita income was rupees twenty-three or twenty-four.

With this background the British Parliament appointed an inquiry Commission under Lord Welby. Dadabhai, Caine, Wedderburn and Courtney were some of the members. After the announcement of the Commission, Dadabhai wanted Ranade to be one of the representatives, but the government declined to send Ranade on the plea that he was in the government service which of course, was a lame and unconvincing excuse. It was then decided that Gokhale should go to England on behalf of the Deccan Sabha to appear before the Welby Commission. Other delegates were Wacha, Surendranath Banerjea and Shankaran Nair. For eight years Gokhale had studied the administrative, economic and political problems of India under the guidance of Ranade. But Ranade thought Gokhale should study the economic problems in depth and so asked G.V. Joshi, the economist, to guide Gokhale, which the latter did with great enthusiasm. Gokhale then sailed for England in March 1897. During his travel Gokhale spent most of his time in preparing for the deposition before the Welby Commission.

Depositions by Wacha, Surendranath and Nair were well received, but Gokhale surpassed them all. He had submitted a written note to the Commission, which examined it. His written submission filled fifty-seven closely printed pages and his whole deposition came to 137 pages, which reveal how closely the Commission examined Gokhale. If anybody wants to understand the economic and administrative problems facing India, then, Gokhale's deposition is a sure guide. It is comprehensive and in depth. It reveals his honesty and transparency. If he did not have any written evidence to support his assertion, he stated so. He did not make any remark without evidence and statistics. The burden of his deposition was: "There was no provision for any constitutional control on the Indian administration. Every government department was dominated by English officers. The Finance Committee of 1886, appointed by Lord Dufferin's Government, consisting of men like Sir Charles Elliot, late Lieutenant-Governor of Bengal, Mr. Justice Cunningham, Sir W. W. Hunter, Sir James Westland, Justice Ranade and others, observed that the Public Works department was reorganised because of the agitation by the Europeans employed in it, which should have been disapproved by the government. This reorganisation was done to improve the salary and allowances of the class one and middle level officers. Government of India was under the control of the Secretary of State and both of them were responsible to the Parliament. The Advisory Council of the Secretary of State almost always supported him. Besides, whole of the administration was bureaucratic and at no stage there was any control by the representatives of the people. At the time of the East India Company, Parliament used to supervise its administration every twenty years. Annual budget which the Company forwarded was scrutinised by the Parliament. But when the British government took over the administration of India from the Company, this stopped and the taxes increased. Provinces had no authority in financial matters.

After the government of India was taken over from the Company by the Crown, the expenditure had increased by two and half times. Whereas the capacity of the country to bear increased burdens was growing particularly less, the expenditure was rising higher and higher. The expenditure on the Army had considerably increased and the Army was always on the war footing. It was the India government which paid for the war against Afghanistan and the conquest of Burma. In 1859 the Royal Commission had laid down the proportion of the European and Indian soldiers, but it was never followed. Out of senior 2337 officers in the Army and Civil service only 60 were Indians. All the officers in the Railways were Europeans. In the other levels in the civil administration, Europeans were 1207 but number of Indians were only 421. Why Europeans should be appointed to register the ownership of land?" Gokhale produced several sheets of statistics in support of his contention and in the end described how the policy of discrimination of the government of India had affected the morale of the people. He said: "The excessive costliness of the foreign agency is not, however, its only evil. There is moral evil which, if anything, is even greater. A kind of dwarfing or the stunting of the Indian race is going on under the present system. We must live all the days of our lives in the atmosphere of inferiority, and the tallest of us must bend, in order that the exigencies of the existing system may be satisfied. The upward impulse, if I may use such an expression, which every school boy at Eton or Harrow may feel, that he may one day be Gladstone, a Nelson, or a Wellington, and which may draw forth the best efforts of which he is capable, is denied to us. The full height to which our manhood is capable of rising can never be reached by us under the present system".

Gokhale suggested that the method of selecting the members of the Advisory Council should be changed and their tenure should be five years and not ten, as it was then. Moreover, the secretary of state should not alone be authorised to select the members of his council; but judges and the unofficial members of the viceroy's Council may be associated with such a selection. Members of the secretary of state's Advisory Council were generally selected from those who had served in India and retired. But they had had their prejudices and bias. So their mind could not be receptive. Gokhale's cross-examination went on for two days and never for a moment he faltered or avoided an answer. One of the members of the Commission asked Gokhale whether tea plantation and other enterprises required capital and when it had to be imported, could it be said that the export of dividend on the same was a drain from India? Dadabhai who was one of the members of the Commission intervened at this stage and asked Gokhale was it not true that because of the drain the scope for capital formation was limited. Gokhale replied in the affirmative. When another member tried to show that the severity of the famine was not as much as it was made out, Gokhale corrected him. He said that he had been to famine affected Sholapur district and narrated the miserable conditions of the people. Gokhale also told the Commission how the special fund created for famine was utilised by the government for other purposes. He was lucid in his exposition and firm in his conviction. Though he had been briefed by both Ranade and G.V. Joshi, he had studied the subject thoroughly. And even though he had a train accident and was not well, he worked tirelessly.

Gokhale was naturally elated by his performance and wrote to G.V. Joshi, "Everything passed off first class—far better than I had ever ventured to hope. On Tuesday, after the whole thing was over, Sir William Wedderburn came up to me and said, 'you have done most splendidly. Your evidence would be the best on our side. Let me congratulate on the signal service which you have rendered to your country. Our minority report is based particularly on your evidence.' Sir W. Wedderburn added that I had made a great impression on Lord Welby and other members of the Commission, good old Dadabhai is also quite pleased. Mr. Caine who attended only for a few hours on the first day writes to me as follows, 'I have spent about seven hours in a careful study of your evidence. Permit me to say that I have never seen a cleverer or more masterly exposition of the views of an educated Indian reformer on all subjects dealt with. And though I do not agree necessarily with all your views, it must be of necessity to have very great weight with the Commission. You and Wacha have rendered splendid and unique service to your country; for which your countrymen ought to be ever grateful.' Mr. Courtney was much struck by my evidence and all through he was very sympathetic, always ready to help me with questions as against Peile or Scoble. On the whole, everything passed off in a most grateful manner. And now let me say that I have thought it my duty to tell you all this because all this high praise belongs really to you and Raosaheb (Ranade) and not to me. And if it had been bestowed on me, I have received it only as your representative, and now I lay it at your feet and Raosaheb's as our ancient *gurudakshina*. For most part my work has been that of a mere conduit pipe or Edison phonograph, and I have told Sir William and Dadabhai so. Pray accept once more this expression of deepest gratitude for the splendid assistance which you so cordially, so cheerfully gave me and which has enabled me to discharge satisfactorily a great national duty".[6]

Wacha's performance was splendid but he was generous enough to admit that Gokhale surpassed all of them. In a letter on April 16, 1897 to G.V. Joshi, Wacha said, "He (Gokhale) has most splendidly come out of the ordeal and you and Mr. Ranade will be delighted. He manfully stood the cross-examination, so much so, the papers have thought fit to give a part of it—touching railways and poverty—in the shape of question and answer with the sensational heading, 'Startling the Royal Commission'. You and Ranade deserve whole credit in the first instant. He held your brief; but the brief has been admirably handled by the advocate".[7] Indian newspapers were all praise for Gokhale for his masterly performance. Tilak in his *Kesari* summarised the important points from Gokhale's evidence and concluded by saying that Gokhale has proved to be a worthy disciple of a worthy master (Ranade).

Dadabhai was one of the members of the Commission who had submitted some detailed notes to the Commission. But he thought that it might not take sufficient notice, and so he appeared before the Commission to depose. Some of the exchanges between the chairman of the Commission and Dadabhai were sharp, if not heated.

It was clear from the exchanges that the Welby Commission would not come out with a unanimous report. Gokhale rightly believed that his evidence would be helpful to the minority of Members while preparing their report. As expected, Majority members restricted themselves to three subjects, namely administration, increasing expenditure and financial relation between India and England. They thought the financial machinery was satisfactory but slow, compared to that in England. They expected more revenue in view of the increasing population and recommended some economic assistance to India. To the minority members, the Commission's inquiry into the government expenditure was shallow as it accepted the statistics given by the government and had not taken into consideration the increase in the revenue which was already an intolerable burden. They also stated that the Commission did not pay any heed to the statistics given by Dadabhai about the distribution of revenue between India and England. They maintained that there was no scope for any increase in the taxes and reiterated various other demands of the Congress in their report.

Some periodicals like the 'Quarterly Review' were irritated by the evidence given by the Indian representatives before the Welby Commission. In January-April 1899 issue it said: "The evidence given by carefully selected specimens of these 'Flowers of Progress' before the Welby Commission, showed pretty well the value of their opinion and their capacity to deal with public affairs. The same flimsy arguments, baseless insinuations, and vamped up statistics were repeated by all, with parrot-like iteration, to illustrate the same text, which as stated by their leader—one of the handful of Parsis who have joined the Congress movement—reads somewhat as follows: First, India is so crushed by taxation and impoverished by the withdrawal of her wealth to England that the people are ground down and reduced to starvation; secondly, that the British Services and inordinate and arbitrary employment of Europeans are India's greatest evil, and the cause of all its economic misery and losses; and thirdly, the Government of India is an unrighteous system of selfishness and despotism. It is easy to see the thread running all through this fustian. In other words, replace the British Civil Service of India by Brahmans and the money will not go out of the country, nor will foreign capital be wanted in it. The masses care nothing for the vapourings of the press, for they cannot read. They find the grass under the British oak fairly succulent, so they silently chew the cud".

Ranade desired that Gokhale should address some meetings in England and suggested to Wedderburn to arrange them. Accordingly, Gokhale addressed several meetings at different places, which were well attended, and received a good response. Gokhale made a favourable impression by his moderation and studied exposition. Sir William Wedderburn introduced him to some English politicians and also to Morley, for whom Gokhale had high regard. Gokhale came in close contact with Dadabhai, Hume and Wedderburn and was very much impressed by their kindness towards him.

REFERENCES

1. Gokhale Digest. (This is an unpublished collection of obituaries on Gokhale).
2. Dadabhai Papers. (Dadabhai Naoroji Trust. These are unpublished).
3. Michelle Burge McAlpin, *Subject to Famine, Food Crisis and Economic Changes in Western India 1860-1920*, Princeton Uni. Press, Princeton, 1983, pp. 75-78.
4. Dadabhai Papers (From Dadabhai Naoroji Trust. These are unpublished).
5. Mike Davis, *Late Victorian Holocausts*, Verso, London, 2002, pp 123, 157-158.
6. Gokhale Papers (unpublished papers).
7. V.S. Srinivas Sastri, *Life of Gopal Krishna Gokhale*, Bangalore Printing and Publishing Co., Bangalore, 1937, pp. 16-17.

Chapter Nine

PARALYSED CONGRESS

On his return to India, Gokhale would have been enthusiastically welcomed with many receptions where he would have been publicly acclaimed. But the interview he gave to the 'Manchester Guardian' about the brutality in handling the plague operations in Poona by the English soldiers involved him in the vortex of bitter controversy. The plague was in an epidemic form in Poona and some other places even when Gokhale sailed for England. To control this epidemic government had called the Army for help and had appointed Rand as special officer to direct all the operation. Rand was a disciplined but an unimaginative officer. The citizens of Poona had no experience of plague before and were unaware of the medical treatment. At the same time Rand and the soldiers were ignorant of the customs of the people and insensitive to their sentiments. They were behaving arbitrarily and running roughshod. Tilak wrote several editorials condemning the behaviour of the soldiers and even the moderate weekly like 'Sudharak' had some fiery articles, which exhorted the people not to submit to the arbitrary behaviour of the soldiers. After Agarkar's death 'Sudharak' was taken over by the Deccan Education Society and was edited by G.K. Deodhar. Gokhale had read these articles and he also had received letters from some trustworthy persons. They had given very lurid descriptions about the brutalities in Poona. Gokhale was naturally upset by these letters and instead of making some general criticism in his interview with the 'Manchester Guardian' on July 2, 1897, he made specific charges against the Army. He even mentioned two instances of molestation of women. Before leaving for India, Gokhale published a letter in July 15 issue of the Guardian, explaining that he made those allegations on the basis of letters which he had received from persons whom he trusted.

The Governor of Bombay, Lord Sandhurst, then appointed one Mr. Lamb to inquire into the complaints against the government's handling of the plague menace. Gokhale questioned the propriety of the governor's statement in denouncing the allegations when the inquiry was not concluded. When Gokhale disembarked in Bombay, a police officer met him to ask explanation. Gokhale told him that he would do so only after he sees the gentlemen who had written letters to him. In Poona, he realised that his correspondents were not prepared to come forward to testify whether the allegations they had made were true. Years back, Tilak and Agarkar were the victims of fake letters, which had sent them to prison. Now Gokhale found himself in the same predicament. The letters he received were not fake, but they became so as their writers did not vouchsafe.

Ranade then advised Gokhale to apologise and that too without any reservations. Accordingly Gokhale sent a letter of an apology to the governor on August 1. He said that he had received some letters and had also seen Indian newspapers, which had published some vehement criticism of the measures adopted by the government to control the plague epidemic. He had also seen memorials of the Deccan Sabha describing unusual panic and had read in a sober paper like 'the Spectator' that a deaf ear had been turned "even to verified complaints of wanton damage to property and injury to body and mind". He then heard the news of the assassination of Rand in Poona and stringent measures adopted by the government. But he did not make any public statement. Then the news about the riot in Chitpur heightened the feelings of exasperation in England. Most of the Englishmen suspected that the Hindus and Muslims were acting in concert against the government. Some British newspapers published news, articles and letters warning that serious trouble was brewing in India. As the assassin or assassins were not apprehended soon; the people in England became impatient and summary methods were freely advocated. The collector of Poona imposed a heavy punitive force and warned of dire consequences if the culprits were not found. Gokhale said in the statement that: "Our loyalty is our only claim on England for a sympathetic, progressive and enlightened rule, and I feared that if our character for loyalty was lost, our best national interests would be injured beyond repair. And as I honestly believed that the irritation caused by the plague operations and not dissatisfaction must have been at the bottom of the tragedy of 22 June, (assassinations of Rand and Ayerst), I felt it was my duty to endeavour to avert the impending misfortune". Gokhale therefore, decided to make public the information in his possession. He then placed all the material, including the private letters he had received, before the Indian Parliamentary Party and to a representative of 'the Manchester Guardian.'

On return to India, as Gokhale found he could not substantiate his criticism, he withdrew it. On the basis of the letters received, he had alleged the violation of two women, one of them committing suicide. It was suggested to him that he should disclose the names of those who sent him those letters. But Gokhale, a gentleman, did not think it was proper. He, therefore, accepted both moral and legal responsibility. "I own I have shown much more credulity and much less judgment than may have been expected from one in my position". Gokhale then tendered unqualified apology to the governor, the members of the Plague Committee and to the soldiers engaged in plague measures.

On August 4, 1897 Lord Sandhurst, the Governor, made a statement in the legislative Council and denounced allegations made against the plague measures. He then referred to Gokhale's statement of apology without naming him. The governor said, "Then it is true that an apology, and a withdrawal has been made by a gentleman whose name was prominently for a few days before the public, but it is very easy thousands of miles from here to make statements which have not a shred of foundation, but which such a man may deem good enough for the English people—statements which show this and show that. That is very easy. It is also very easy to come back and say, 'I was misinformed, and I apologise'. But the harm is done in spreading abroad these foul unfounded accusations and attacks, and while I recognise that the apology has been made I might tender the advice that in future when it is thought it necessary as it may be at times to offer criticism— if it is necessary to make statements of that kind they should be made here where they may be inquired into, and if untrue, contradicted and not made so that they get currency all the world over before an answer can be given." Lord Sandhurst was also critical of the Deccan Sabha. He referred to the memorandum sent by the Sabha, which claimed that it was signed by Hindus and Muslims against the plague measures. The governor informed the Legislative Council that he ascertained who the 721 were from the 1699 signatories and he found only 144, and remaining 577 could not be found or traceable. Of the 144, fourteen denied their signature and the rest said that they were induced by the Deccan Sabha and the Dnyan Prakash newspaper to sign some petition about the plague measures. Fifty of them did not know what they were signing and half a dozen different objects for which their signatures were required were held out. Raobahadur Bhide was the principal signatory of this affair. He was the chairman of the Deccan Sabha and admitted that he worked with the troops from first to the last, never missing a day of his turn to accompany the search parties, and that he never saw any misconduct. Nawab Abdul Khan, another signatory, said he signed merely in his private capacity, never having seen the memorial, not knowing any of its contents, and never having seen any misconduct. The Mahommedans denied they had any complaints to make against the plague operations, asserted the governor. He had sent the communication to the secretary of state on the same lines. Thus he debunked the Deccan Sabha. The government had already disqualified the Sarvajanik Sabha.

Not being aware of the letter sent to the governor by Gokhale, Morgan-Brown wrote to Gokhale advising him to disclose the names of his correspondents who alleged misconduct. He told Gokhale to keep the statement very short. There were several military officers who had written home that the soldiers had performed excellent job and so Morgan-Brown felt it would be a hard task to convince the family members of those soldiers and other British citizens. Sir William Wedderburn told the Commons that it was he who introduced Gokhale to some members of the Commons in a meeting in which Gokhale informed them that he had received some letters from Poona about the plague operation. Sir William expressed his regret but also reminded the Commons that Gokhale had already tendered his apology explaining that he was misled by the correspondents. Mr. Bhownaggaree, an Indian, elected to the Commons with help of the Tory Party was always eager to please the powers that be. He was severe in his criticism of Gokhale. In his speech in the Commons he said that Wedderburn had committed an error in putting a blind reliance upon the statement of a man who had confessed that he perjured himself in a despicable manner. He also asserted that so long as the letters received by Gokhale were not disclosed, they must be treated as fake.

The general consensus was that Gokhale should not have put trust in the letters he received and he should also not have tendered such an unqualified apology. Wacha held this view and wrote to Dadabhai on August 6, "It has been generally felt in our circle, and I am informed that the same is the impression outside of that circle, that Mr. Gokhale has blundered for the second time in giving an unqualified apology *in reference to those matters on which there was no controversy.* The statement challenged was with reference to the alleged outrages. If he had recanted that portion nothing might have been said. But he has in a most abject way apologised for everything. In doing so, it has rendered incalculable mischief to our cause. The moral effect of it on your side, especially among our Parliamentary Committee will be extremely prejudicial to us. Apart from the humiliating position to which Sir William has been reduced, there is this fear that in future our friends will not help us. Sir W.W. and his friends will be greatly discouraged and we shall fare infinitely worse in parliament in future than we do at present".[1] Wacha's apprehension was unfounded. Wedderburn and his friends did not change their position about India and the Congress. Gokhale was so disheartened that he thought of retiring from the public life. Sir William wrote back: "Please do not speak of withdrawing from the public life. The very ferocity of the attack upon you testifies the importance and value of the work you did in England on behalf of your countrymen". Hume told Gokhale, "I don't care two pence about this incident. I don't think you have injured the cause *at all.* I see no earthly reason for your withdrawing from public life. Have done away with despondency and with the talk of withdrawing from public life. Be more zealous than ever; only be more cautious than ever. Do not fancy you have lost any ground with us. Do not apologise to us. We look upon you as martyr to the cause and are more ready than ever to aid, and so far as we can, to stand by you". Dadabhai as an elder statesman consoled Gokhale and wrote him an encouraging letter. He wrote: "You are young, you have a long, earnest and by no means easy work before you. Never say die. Do your duty perseveringly. You are excitable and I shall be consoled even for your present troubles if you can now, after the present painful experience learn to be cool and calm and to consider a matter before acting. But do not despair". Gokhale replied: "How kind of you to write as you have done. I was prepared for a much more severe reproof and you have written in such gentle and encouraging terms. All I can say is that all my energies will be devoted to making amends for what has happened".[2]

Poona suffered from plague epidemic even in 1898 and Gokhale who was then president of the Poona municipality did his level best to help the people affected and cooperated with the government in controlling the disease. Lord Sandhurst, the governor, was all praise for Gokhale and thus closed the old chapter. But the storm created by the plague and the assassinations of Rand and Ayerst continued to affect the life of Poona. Deccan Education Society had to face internal problems created in the wake of the troubled situation. Professor Selby, who was the chairman of the Society, sent in his resignation in protest against the highly critical writings against the plague operation in the 'Sudharak' and a speech by Prof. Bhanu of the Fergusson College, who defended the murder of Afzulkhan. Selby was in the government service. On his insistence, the Governing Council asked the editor, Deodhar, to go on a long leave. It was also agreed that the 'Sudharak' should not be used for political purposes by the life-members of the Society. Selby was pacified and withdrew his resignation. Bhandarkar, Ranade and Gokhale helped to bring about the reconciliation. Selby was also satisfied by the letter of apology from Gokhale. After the reconciliation took place, the Society received a lengthy dispatch from the director of Public instruction. It said that four members of the Deccan Education Society were closely associated with certain political events of the preceding few months, which were not in accordance with the original objects of the Society. The letter pointed out that grants-in aid were given under some procedure securing the confidence of the government. It was made clear that the government was dissatisfied with the management of the Society. No educational institution should have any connection with political writings, political speeches and political assemblies. The director said that the Governing Council of the Society was not effective and the managing board enjoyed much power. He, therefore, suggested some changes in the constitution of the Society. If accepted that would have deprived the Society of its independence. So after some protracted negotiations, the director was satisfied with the changes proposed by the Governing Council and the Life-members, and proposed to the government to accept the amended constitution of the Society.[3]

At the end of the year, Amravati in Maharashtra, hosted the annual session of the Congress, where as usual, Gokhale would have moved one of the important resolutions, but slogans were raised against him which made it impossible for

Gokhale to participate actively in the session. Gokhale on his return then issued a clarification through the columns of 'The Times of India'. As a reply to his critics, Gokhale in this letter on January 8, 1898 said, that after his return from England he issued a retraction, which he thought was the only honourable course to follow. He expected the storm that broke out after the retraction would subside. But he felt that in some quarters misunderstanding was deeper. He then clarified how he rushed to the press with the conviction that it was in the best interests of the Indians. About his abject apology he reiterated that it was the only honourable course to follow as the aggrieved party had no recourse to get redress. Gokhale expressed regret that friends like Sir William Wedderburn were put in an awkward position by his interview to the 'Manchester Guardian'. In conclusion he said: "My countrymen must not confound an apology with the traditional prostration to save one's own skin". Gokhale had confessed that long after people forget this apology incident, he himself would not forget it. This was true, as it rankled in his mind for quite a long time. N.G. Chapekar, a writer on social subjects, had written that Gokhale told him that Tilak would have come to his rescue if he had not been in jail at that time. When Atul Ghose wrote to Gokhale that he was satisfied by his public clarification, Gokhale told him how he was touched by the kind letter and said: "Thanks to the teaching of Mr. Justice Ranade, I have long learnt to make my conscience—and not popular applause—the spring of my actions. Moreover, remember that the best part of our nature is manifest not in what we enjoy, but what we endure. There is sublimity and moral elevation in undeserved suffering which nothing can equal and which is almost its own reward".[4]

After Gokhale's death one of his friends, V.G. Apte, wrote an article in the 'Modern Review' wherein he noted that on a September morning, in 1897 he and Gokhale had their tea and Gokhale asked him what the newspapers in general were saying about his apology. Apte told him that many were critical and gave his own opinion. He wrote: "I could not withhold from him the truth and rather indiscreetly added that his (Gokhale's) conduct had brought no little humiliation on the country to whose service he had consecrated his life. My remarks only deepened his sorrow and depression and to my surprise he said in a low tone, 'Vasudevrao, you can scarcely have an idea how sorry I feel to hear from you that my conduct on this occasion has brought no little humiliation on my country. I accept that as your frank and honest opinion, and I take it for what it is worth. But I tell you, you will, I hope, live to see that a day will come when I shall cover my country with glory by way of compensation for the wrong of which I am alleged to have done, and the critics of your type who are running me to death will be converted into my admirers'". Apte admits that Gokhale's prophecy came true. Srinivas Sastri in a biographical article on Gokhale in the 'India Review' wrote, referring to the apology that the episode was an instance where public opinion was more in the wrong, than the unfortunate victim of it. Sastri says: "The grammatical implication that the unfortunate victim was also in the wrong hurt him deeply. He was anxious, he said, that I should understand the matter in its full bearing on the proprieties of public life. He had not made the apology without consulting the best and the wisest men of the time. It behooved a critic of other men's conduct to hold their honour as his own. When one has aspersed another's character in public and found himself unable to substantiate the charges, the proper course was to own up manfully. To leave a sting behind in the apology was neither righteous nor sportsmanlike. I felt edified and expressed my gratitude. A feeling of relief seemed to come over him when he said, 'I don't as a rule talk to people on this subject and I promise not again to refer to it in our conversation.' And he kept his word to the end".[5]

The whole episode weighed on Gokhale's mind and so he made some resolutions, which he noted in his diary. His diary entry reads: "By the grace of Sree Guru Dattatreya, I will endeavour humbly but firmly, to acquire or achieve the following:

1) I will practice *yoga* regularly
2) I will acquire a good knowledge of:
    (a) History—Ancient and Modern
    (b) Philosophy—Ancient and Modern
    (c) Astronomy
    (d) Geology
    (e) Physiology
    (f) Psychology
    Now no more "ology!"
    (g) French
3) I will try to become a member of—
    (a) The Bombay Legislative Council
    (b) The Supreme Legislative Council
    (c) The British Parliament
    In all these assemblies I will try to do good to my country and by all means in my power.
4) I will try to become a preacher of the highest philosophical religion and I will preach this religion to the *whole world*."

Gokhale became the member of the Legislative Council and afterwards that of the Supreme Legislative Council. He could not fulfill his ambition to become a member of the British Parliament as he had a short span of life. Had he lived longer, he might have entered the British Parliament like Dadabhai. He could not spare time to learn French, but as he stayed for a long time in Calcutta for the Supreme Legislative Council's meetings, he learnt Bengali to read Tagore's poems. One day Gokhale told Gupta that he could read Tagore's poems but his pronunciation was not like Bengalis, and so he asked Gupta to recite some of the poems.

Poona was seething with discontent because of the harsh measures resorted to control plague and after the assassination of the two officers—Rand and Ayerst —when government imposed punitive police. Tilak wrote fiery editorials and asked whether the government had lost all its senses. The government, on the other hand, was convinced that assassinations were part of a larger conspiracy and Tilak was the moving spirit behind it. Natu brothers were detained without any inquiry and S.M. Paranjpe, editor of the 'Kal' was arrested on the charge of spreading discontent against the government. Tilak was arrested. The prosecutor failed to convince the judge not to grant bail to Tilak. Judge did not find any convincing evidence of any conspiracy. So he granted the bail. When the case opened against Tilak, the jury consisted of six Europeans and three Indians. European jurors voted for conviction for Tilak and the Indians against it and Tilak was sentenced for a year and a half. 'The Times of India' had no love for Tilak and when he was arrested, it started a vicious campaign against him. Some anonymous letters were published criticising Tilak who then sent a rejoinder to the paper: "Your continued malicious remarks about me and the journals published by me compel me to write this letter. I do not expect any praise from you, but I once believed the 'Times' under its present editorship would at least be fair; but your recent articles have more than disappointed me in the matter. The shocking tragedy at Poona, which we all deplore, may have obscured your judgment. But I have little to do with your motives. What I want to show is that you have entirely misrepresented my position both as a journalist and a private gentleman during the time the plague operations were in force in Poona.—I think that you are doing me sheer injustice by representing that either myself or my paper did anything to excite feelings of disaffection amongst the people. It was my firm conviction that stringent sanitary measures would do considerable good, if they would stamp out the plague altogether; and I have not only expressed this conviction in the paper, but have done as much as a single citizen of my position practically could do to show how people should help themselves and not blame the plague committee for everything. But unlike yourself I could not shut up my eyes to complaints and grievances which from personal knowledge I was convinced were real and well founded."

Tilak's conviction became the subject of discussion in the country as a whole. In Calcutta a newspapers' association was formed in which most of the leading Indian papers participated. On August 28, 1897 Banerjea wrote an editorial in Bengali, entitled 'The Olive Branch for Peace', which advised the government that it would be unwise to bring Tilak to trial, because if he were sentenced his popularity would reach the height of martyrdom. The article impressed upon the government that "recent events have vastly added to Tilak's popularity and if developed further he will be elevated to the rank of a demi-god". The article was followed up by a letter by Banerjea to the officiating lieutenant-governor of Bengal which proposed that whenever the government intended to prosecute an editor for seditious writings, it should first refer this case to the Press association which would act as an unofficial censuring body and would reprimand the concerned editor. In the event that the offending editor would ignore the warning of the Press Association, the government would prosecute him with the full support of the Press association. After Tilak was sentenced funds were raised to pay for the advocates which had a good response from Calcutta, Madras and various places from Maharashtra but Surendranath did not think that it was the test of Tilak's popularity. He wrote: "It is a testimony of the united India…the soundest triumph of British rule, a crown of glory to the British government".[6] The Government of India amended the Penal Code and also the Post and Telegraph Act, which showed how both the government of India and that of Bombay had lost balance. Englishmen in India were furious because of the assassinations of Rand and Ayerst and so Sir Cawasji Jahangir, a Sheriff of Bombay, was not allowed in the cemetery where the body of Rand was to be buried. It was not that only the Indian publicists thought the Bombay government had lost its head, but according to C.Y. Chintamani even the lieutenant-governor of the United Provinces, Sir Antony McDonnell, also could not understand the harsh measures. "He asked to Pandit Bishan Narayan Dar, 'what is this talk of unrest? Let them send me to Bombay and I shall restore peace in a fortnight'".[7]

Pherozeshah Mehta and Wacha had different perspectives on the conviction of Tilak. Wacha thought that the charges against Tilak were not sustainable. At the same time he was opposed to Tilak's politics. In a letter to Dadabhai on April 15, 1899 supporting Pherozeshah, he said, "You will no doubt read all about the agitation which that wretched paper the 'Kal' of Poona has created here. I must say some of the Poona Marathi papers which are either directly or indirectly under the influence of Tilak, are still writing in a way which makes the Government keep its sharp eye on them. The 'Kal' which is known to be an organ influenced by Tilak, is edited by a graduate of the University named Mr. Paranjpe. Lately, he wrote an article in which he tried to justify—in a sort of metaphysical way—the murders of Rand and Ayerst. The whole tendency of the article as well others was to preach an open doctrine of sedition to the effect that State murders are not wrong in the eyes of God and can therefore be committed with impunity. The Calcutta (Congress) Committee at once passed a resolution condemning the writings. Mr. Mehta seriously considered the situation and urged on the Bombay Committee through me to pass a resolution also repudiating the writer.—Mr. Mehta observed that if any one has done the greatest mischief to the Congress it is Tilak. I also trust that you will send to Mr. Tilak a few words of wisdom and advice and make him see the error of his ways and of his friends.

But Tilak is already spoilt.—He thinks he is the coming Saviour of India. When people have got such notions in their head you can understand to what limits that may go. Altogether his conduct is inexcusable and he is using his talents to a most objectionable and mischievous purpose".[8] A columnist of 'Indian Affairs', in 'The Times' referred to the case against Tilak and said, "Mr. Pugh (Tilak's advocate) sought to show that the language for which his client stood in the dock was the natural outcome of the language taught in our Indian schools". The columnist then quoted some of the passages from some of the textbooks and then remarked, "For the natives, educated in our schools and colleges, still derive their conceptions of England's action in India during the last century from the misleading word-picture of Macaulay and the partisan vituperation of Burke".

The conviction of Tilak and restrictions on the press generated heated debate in the Indian Press. 'The Statesman' of October 10, 1897 came out against the judgment of the High Court. It did not approve of the construction, which Justice Strachey charged the jury, and the decision of the full bench. It said, "We ventured to predict that, when the present excitement has passed away and the recent incidents are regarded in the dry light of reason, Englishmen generally, whether in England or in India, will not only recognise the harshness of the punishment meted out to the defendant but will feel it to be absolutely essential to the good government and the public safety that the law should be placed on a sounder and more intelligible basis than that on which it now stands. In speaking of injustice involved in the sentence of Mr. Tilak, we are referring, not to the verdict of the jury, but to the severity of the punishment. Assuming, however, for the sake of the argument, that he (Tilak) might have been so (justly) convicted, then, it seems to us a multitude of considerations might reasonably have been expected to dispose the court to weigh his offence mercifully. In the first place, far from the incitement to disaffection of which, on that assumption the defendant was guilty, being of a flagrant and palpable kind, it was only by placing the wildest possible construction on the law that the language on which thc charge was based could be brought within its scope, and then only by taking the more injurious of two possible interpretations of the word used as representing the meaning that they were intended to convey". Many newspapers gave the news of Tilak's conviction with black border. 'The Hindu' wrote, "In the conviction of Mr. Tilak the country beholds the beginning of a most mischievous and most deplorable struggle between the Indian people and their enemies in their own country, for, they have enemies who are very powerful, who have free access to the rulers, and who command the services of the Tory press in England. There will be rejoicing among them, no doubt." However in the opinion of 'The Times of India', "the sentence does not err on the side of the severity, but it carries a lesson with it which every good citizen must hope will not be lost upon the followers of and imitators of the 'Kesari'. Some Muslim papers justified the sentence. The 'Rast

Goftar' was totally with the government. It felt the sentence should have been more severe.

The House of Commons discussed the arrest and the conviction of Tilak on February 17, 1898. At the same time some prominent people in England had issued a statement demanding the release of Tilak. In the Commons debate some members suggested that the government should take cognizance of the statement by Tilak and release him. In a letter to Sir John Lubbock, on February 17, 1898 Max Muller wrote, "My interest in Tilak is certainly that of a Sanskrit scholar, for though I do not agree with the arguments put forward in his *Orion, or Researches into the Antiquity of the Vedas,* (Bombay, 1893), I cannot help feeling sorry that we should lose the benefit of his labour. I sent him my edition of the *Rig-veda*, but I am told that now he is not allowed to read even the Bible and the prayer-book in prison. You see from the wording of our petition, that we do not question the justice of the sentence. Personally, I have wondered for years at the license allowed to the native press. But the warning has now been given, and none too soon, though I do not believe that there is any sedition lurking in India at present, not even in the hearts of such men as Tilak. I thought the Government might possibly like such a petition at the present moment. It seems odd that the murderer was an ignorant fanatic, who could not even read. Such fanatics will always exist in a country like India, but it would be dangerous to identify them with the loyal, or, at least, contented population of India".[9]

While participating in Commons debate, Dadabhai asked, what measures government took to pacify the people who were angry by the handling of famine and the plague? He added that the government appointed punitive police put restrictions on the newspapers and resorted to detention without trial. These measures were against the educated classes, which would not be in the interest of the British regime. Sir William Wedderburn pointed out that there was no conspiracy in Poona. He said Tilak was a scholar and had distinguished himself by his work in the educational field. Wedderburn suggested that the government should release Tilak or otherwise he should be treated well in the jail. But the Secretary of State, Lord Hamilton was not moved by such speeches. He asked Sir William whether he was referring to the few persons in Poona or the common citizens of the city. He then criticised Lord Ripon, who, as he maintained that it was Ripon in his regime as the viceroy, began thinking in terms of race, which became a practice. Lord Roberts castigated the government for convicting Tilak and detaining Natu brothers without trial through sheer panic. He said that letters written by Natu brothers were mild. The government had confiscated their property and then released it. He said the only course for the government was to prosecute Natu brothers but detention without trial was indefensible. Lord Roberts drew the attention of the government to the fact that Tilak had expressed his loyalty several times, and as the murderer was already convicted, Tilak should be released. He also referred to an article written by Sir Richard Garth, a retired chief justice of the Calcutta High Court, which said that he did not find seditious writings in the Indian language papers for quite some time. Nor did he come across writings, which were spreading dissatisfaction against the government. Garth had found some critical writings against the government officials, which he himself liked and did not think that they should be stopped.

The Commons also discussed amendment to the Indian Penal Code, which brought restrictions on the press and the freedom of speech. Lord Roberts reminded the government that such restrictions were put by the Lytton regime, but they were of no avail. Nothing had happened to change the policy, which was in force for half a century. The amendment had given a right to the government to prosecute a person for his speech given in England if it found the speech objectionable. For the same speech he could not be prosecuted against in England, but on his return to India, government could do so. Government had assumed the power to prosecute those whose writings would be deemed to spread disaffection about the regime. But the clause itself was vague and dangerous. The clause in the Penal Code, which was used to prosecute criminals and undesirable elements was to be used against the editors which, to Lord Roberts, was highly objectionable. It was pointed out that as the jury system was abolished, the bureaucrats would be prosecutors and also judges. Secretary of State, Lord Hamilton, defended the amendments and informed the House that the Mahommedan Association in Calcutta had welcomed the amendment. It so happened that under the amendment government prosecuted Malabari for a poem written ten years earlier. In the House of Lords, Lord Reay who one time was the governor of Bombay vouchsafed that Malabari was never disloyal.

The Congress session at Amravati at the end of the year was marred by the conviction of Tilak. The session itself passed a resolution expressing dissatisfaction about the amendment to the Penal Code giving more power to the officials. The Congress also demanded the release of Natu brothers who were in detention without trial. Speaking on the resolution, Surendranath Banerjea criticised the conviction of Tilak and some other editors. He said that the British constitution guaranteed freedom and as the citizen of the Empire, Indians should enjoy the same freedom fully.

As Gokhale was advised by Ranade, Dadabhai, Hume and Wedderburn, not to think of withdrawing from public life, he accepted the presidentship of Poona municipality. He did his best to reform the administration of that body. But he could not implement schemes for increasing water supply, drainage and sanitation as they required more money, which could be had only by increasing the taxes, which the majority of the members opposed. Gokhale was also a member of the Senate of the University of Bombay. But Ranade wanted Gokhale to play on a wider platform, and the opportunity came when an election was announced for a seat in the Provincial Legislative Council. Tilak was a member of the Council from 1897 and also wanted to contest the election. Gokhale did not leave any stone unturned. His correspondence gives an ample proof to show how he strove hard to get a seat in the Council. It was obvious that even if Tilak had won the election, which was doubtful, the governor who had the veto power, would not have accepted Tilak as a member of the Council. The Governor Lord Sandhurst had made his intentions clear in a letter to Lord Curzon who was the viceroy. He wrote that even if Tilak got elected, he (governor) would use his special power and overturn Tilak's election. He also said that Gokhale had made some unfounded charges against the plague operation, but later he rendered an apology and as a member of the plague committee Gokhale had rendered splendid service. Lord Curzon agreed. Tilak, therefore, withdrew from the contest. Viceroy Lord Curzon was pleased at the prospects of Gokhale's victory and he conveyed his feelings to the Secretary of State.

Gokhale was a member of the provincial Council for two years and worked conscientiously. That was the year when many areas of the province were again visited by famine. Gokhale had experience of the previous famine and knew where the government efforts fell short. When the Council discussed the famine conditions, Gokhale was very eloquent and constructive. The government had started some big public works as relief measures. Gokhale drew the attention of the government to the fact that such large works could be undertaken in some definite places as they were difficult to manage. Affected people had to leave their places to work on these schemes. Since a large number of people were concentrated in one place, sanitary facilities were inadequate, giving rise to epidemics. Gokhale also said that the norms laid down by the Famine Commission were rigidly followed by the government officials, which deprived the workers their dues. Gokhale made several constructive suggestions and compared the measures with those in other provinces. Council also discussed the bill about the municipalities.

Gokhale, as a president of the Poona municipality, had enough experience to pin down on the shortcomings of the local bodies. His speech on the amended bill, as expected, was full of information and suggestions. He reviewed the previous laws and made clear the expectations of the representatives of the people. He then suggested that the bill should be sent to the Select Committee so that it would be discussed in depth. His suggestion was accepted. As a member of the Committee Gokhale complained that the law gave the government the power to appoint one or two experts on a municipal body, but this right was not exercised. He criticised the government officials on the Municipality for misusing their authority. Gokhale regarded the municipal bodies as the training ground for the representatives of the people to enable them to discharge the increased responsibilities in future; but he regretted that the government, instead of giving more power to the municipalities, was curtailing them. Some of the suggestions by Gokhale were accepted by the government. However, the amended bill provided for the communal representation, which was opposed by Gokhale and some other members, but it was not withdrawn by the government.

The amended land revenue bill was opposed by Gokhale as well as others on the ground that it was restricting the right to transfer land. Gokhale clarified that he for one was all for giving protection and incentive to the tenants. Gokhale with his usual flare for statistics pointed out how the peasants have become more indebted under the British rule. The remedy was to fix the revenue and not increase it thirty years after the assessment. He, like his mentor, Justice Ranade, proposed Ryotwari system. The amended bill, according Gokhale, was helpful only to the government and not to the agriculturists or money-lenders. Money-lenders or the *inamdars* were resuming the land in case the agriculturists did not pay the rent. The amended bill empowered the government to restrict this right and take over the land itself. Though Gokhale pleaded for full assistance to the agriculturists, he did not want to restrict the rights of the money-lenders and *inamdars* and transfer those to the government. Ranade and Pherozeshah had also expressed the same view. After the lapse of time this problem could be viewed dispassionately. Though our leaders had called for establishment of cooperative credit societies and also demanded protection and assistance to the agriculturists, they did not want the rights of the money-lenders to be restricted. Late P.V. Gadgil, a scholarly and respected editor in Maharashtra, pointed out how this position was unjustified. He wrote that Raobahadur A.B. Joshi, a member of the Council, who had served in the revenue department, had supported the bill. He pointed out that the rate of assessment in Kolhapur was more than in the Bombay Presidency. Joshi said that the money-lender used to advance money to the agriculturists to get interest on his investment. If the assessment was too excessive to render the whole land cultivation unprofitable, why would he give money?

Agriculturists were borrowing money at the rate of thirty-seven per cent interest. It was said that in the regime of the Peshwa, agriculturists were not so much in debt. That was because there was instability and the agriculturists had to be protected. It was the land, which was in need of cultivators and not the other way round. Agriculturists were invited to colonise and cultivate the land. Under the British, peace was restored and the rule of law prevailed. The bill under discussion authorised the government to take over the land. But it was only paper transaction. Ultimately, the land with the government was to be sold to the cultivators. So why this provision was to be opposed, asked Joshi. The amended bill would have restricted the rights of the money-lenders and *inamdars, Khots,* etc.[10] It was strange that the British government wanted to restrict the rights of the vested interests in the rural areas while our leaders including Gokhale were indirectly supporting the same interests, though they were also keen to protect the cultivators.

There was no let up in the political rivalry between Tilak and Gokhale. When the Provincial Conference met at Satara, Tilak and his associates made a deft move. They wanted to move a resolution condemning various harsh measures used by Governor Lord Sandhurst. This would have embarrassed both Gokuldas Parekh, president of the conference as well, as Gokhale. Ultimately, when Parekh threatened to resign, the resolution was withdrawn. This showed the fractious state of the Congress organisation in Maharashtra. But Maharashtra was not an exception. In almost all provinces it was the same story. When different areas like Maharashtra, Gujrat, Madras etc. were visited by famine, organisations like Sarvajanik Sabha, Deccan Sabha did a splendid job in organising the relief measures. But Congress as a political party was nowhere on the scene. Several local organisations were having liaison with the government and continued to do so. Some of them were involved in the famine relief works and also helped the government at the time of plague epidemic. But the Congress leaders did not think it as their duty to come forward and help the affected people. If the Congress insisted in playing this role, its organisational structure would have to be changed and become more formal with constitution and definite rules and regulations. As the Congress organisation was informal, leaders like Pherozeshah Mehta, Surendranath and their associates wielded unlimited power and influence; and the local leaders, who were jealous of their power, also did not want to disturb the existing arrangements.

Wacha's letter to Dadabhai throws light on the state of the Congress in its second decade. Writing on October 22, 1898 he said, "I cannot understand *why* our people are so apathetic even when their most cherished interests are at stake. The well to do and the wealthy are in the same boat. And I cannot excuse their conduct. To pay even Rs. 6 a year is to them a heavy tax as if they do not spend perhaps sixty times as much in a month on less useful objects or objects of no use. I have very bitter experience of my own subscribers in the city of Bombay. I employ active agency to collect arrears. But even my patience is exhausted. Nine-tenth of the excuses made by the committees are pure shams. The fact is nobody works. Nobody takes a personal interest. It might be wise thing if it could happen if all 60,000 rupees or at any rate 50,000 are paid down in advance in cash *when the Congress meets,* instead of having to wait for the year or even for years. But who is to *enforce* this golden rule? And how are you to *force* the committees? The more I have thought on the subject the more I have come to the conviction that the raising of a *permanent* fund by each Committee is the only and the *soundest* solution of the present chronic embarrassment of the British Committee. Even here, I fear, nothing substantial will be done until either you or Mr. Hume come down and spend four months on the business".[11] This indolence or lethargy in the Congress continued even after 1900. So Dadabhai, Hume and Wedderburn wrote an article in the 'India' and circulated it to all Congress Committees. The article admitted that Congress had failed in some respects, but in the other it had achieved success. It also explained what was achieved by the Welby Commission. In conclusion the article said that the work of both the Congress and the British Committee was important and appealed to make both wider and more energetic.

After the defeat of Both Dadabhai and W.C. Bonnerjee in the election to the British Parliament, most of the Congress leaders in India lost their interest in the British Committee. Even then the idea of holding the Congress in England was alive but it was found impracticable, as in England the Tories had come to power replacing the Liberals. This had dampened the enthusiasm of the British Committee, though Dadabhai, Hume and Wedderburn were leaving no stone unturned to collect funds for the Committee. But they were finding it difficult to raise enough money. Because of the murder of the two British officers in Poona, many people became wary of the Congress. Mr. Mudholkar conveyed this response of the people to Dadabhai and said that if that continues, then the Congress would face a difficult situation. John McLane discussing the finances of the Congress in detail writes, "The amount of money budgeted for the British Committee each year was often larger than that spent by the Reception Committee of the annual Congress session. The newspaper, 'India', was the chief expenditure, costing about two thousand pounds a year from the time it became a regular monthly, in 1892, until 1898, when it was converted into a weekly. After that the expense was even greater. The activities of the British Committee itself cost another 1000 pounds. In the seven years between 1894 and 1900, the total amount transmitted to the British Committee was 2,25,800 Pounds or 32,237 per annum. This was Rs. 58,200 less than the amount pledged for Congress work in those years. The failure of the Congress standing committees to collect subscription for 'India' became a crucial problem only after the death of the Maharaja of Darbhanga in 1898. The government of Bengal reported that he had given Rs. 10,000 annually to 'India', and he was also said to have paid for the conversion of 'India' into a weekly. But even before Darbhanga's death, a major portion of the British Committee's funds was coming from England. W.C. Bonnerjee, who lived with his family near London, gave "ten to twenty thousand rupees" every year, according to Pyarelal. In October 1899, Wedderburn and Hume sent a tart letter to the Congress standing committees. The British Committee became so exasperated by the indifference of Congressmen in India that it announced that it would give up its rooms and discontinue 'India', if the outstanding balance of Rs. 37,500 was not received by the end of June 1901. At the last moment Dadabhai deposited Rs. 25,000 with Wedderburn as a guaranty against the losses".[12]

Members of the British Committee were somewhat divided and there was lack of harmony. Jonathan Schneer, disclosing this, wrote, "The organisation was riven with personality conflicts. 'Wedderburn is a good generous fellow, but terribly weak in a crisis'. Cain confided to Gokhale: "Hume was once a man of energy, but his day has passed. J.P. Goodridge, a member of the executive committee, resigned late in 1898 because, 'as at present constituted (it) performed no useful purpose, and did positive harm to the cause. 'His' dear friends 'Dadabhai and Wedderburn' Goodridge judged to be 'impracticable men without much tact'. Meanwhile (Motilal) Ghose had fallen out with his INC cofounders Bonnergee and Hume, 'men who are serving their own interests by means of the organisation'".[13] Earlier, it fell to the lot of Dadabhai to criticise Sir Henry Fowler, one time regarded as a friend of India. Wacha had written to Ranade on October 24, 1896 giving a summary of Dadabhai's letter to him, which warned him to be wary about Fowler as he had become a turncoat and was a wolf in a sheep's clothing. Fowler, Dadabhai said had become a henchman of the secretary of state and was out to harm 'our' cause.

The British government had instructed the Government of India to find out the source of the Congress funds. Its findings were not different from those of McLane. Government of India was closely watching the Congress affairs after the murders of Rand and Ayerst in Poona. It surmised that the Congress was a divided party and its influence had diminished. Government officials were of the opinion that as the government was not responsive to the demands of the Congress, voiced through its resolutions, it helped in diminishing the influence. Some other officers concluded that as some more members of the Congress were elected to the Provincial and Central Legislative Congress, the organisation had become indolent. Lord Curzon, no friend of the Congress, could not help expressing his elation to the secretary of state, Lord George Hamilton. In a letter on November 18, 1900 Lord Curzon wrote to Lord Hamilton that Congress was tottering and he would be happy to lend his hand to bring about its demise. Curzon also conveyed that best among the Indians had realised the futility of the objectives of the Congress. Lord George Hamilton was pleased with the information and gave credit for the poor state of the Congress affairs to Lord Curzon. He said, Curzon had genuine love for the common people of India and had always scoffed at the claims of the Congress leaders. According to Hamilton this had brought about the weakening of the Congress organisation. Lord George Hamilton had discussed his views about India in some of his letters to Curzon. He wrote that problems in India were the creation of the British government itself. It was the British who gave Indians English education, which gave rise to an educated class. Queen Victoria had promised through the Declaration that Indians would be treated on equal footing without prejudice of race or religion and the Indians always cite this to justify their demands. But, Hamilton felt that

1858 Declaration should be set aside forever. Present British administrators were troubled by this pronouncement. But in the course of time this trouble would turn into a danger. Hamilton firmly believed that Indians should never be given a representative government.

In the September 1888 issue of the 'Contemporary Review' Sir William Hunter had written, "It is a difficulty that underlies our whole position in India; a difficulty to be encountered not by heroic remedies but by timely precautions, a problem not of reconstruction or of substitution; but of transition and development. For we have not only given pledges, which we are asked to fulfill; we also nurtured aspirations, which we are expected to satisfy. I prefer the more simpler and more honest course of admitting that the speed in the proportion of ideas and in their political realization must be different". But this difference became the bone of contention. There was discrepancy between Queen Victoria's 1858 Declaration and the behaviour of the British administrators. Dadabhai and most of the Congress leaders had firm belief in the benevolence of the British regime and regarded it as divine dispensation; but at the same time they were very critical of the administration and held it responsible for the poverty of India and thus were facing a dilemma. Hume and some Englishmen of his persuasion felt that the radical elements would not have been strengthened if the British government had accepted some of important demands of the moderate leaders. However, the very nature of the British administration was such that it could not satisfy the moderates. Besides, many of the Englishmen, who were obsessed by the racial superiority, had contempt for the educated Indians. They thought that they alone knew what was best for India and Indians, and without them, India would not have any future. Therefore, they believed that British should administer India for a very long time.

People like Hyndman were critical of the division among the moderates and the radicals in the Congress. He criticised the demands of the Congress published in the issue of the 'India'. He did not approve of its too mild tone. He wrote to Dadabhai telling him that when he was with Mazzini, a representative of Manuel, the King of Italy, came to see Mazzini. Hyndman was impressed by the dignity with which Mazzini conducted himself. Hyndman felt it was a dialogue between the two powers. Mazzini was fully conscience of his power. Hyndman advised Dadabhai to take the Congress to the revolutionary path, which Dadabhai rejected. Some other Englishmen were of the opinion that the British should administer India with due consideration of the changing times and make changes accordingly. Sir Charles Dilke belonged to this school of thought. He wrote that though the Congress had considerably weakened, there were enough indications that it was bound to take a turn in the direction of the radical politics. It was a correct forecast as immediately afterwards Arvindbabu Ghose, who was a professor at Baroda in 1893, wrote some articles in which he came down heavily on the old guards. In his opinion enemies of the national movement were not without but within. He said, old Congress leaders were cowards and politically emotional and the Indians had become weak. Arvindbabu said, the Congress leaders were demanding more share in the government service and did not concentrate on gathering support from the lower middle classes. He, therefore, demanded a departure from this practice. Radical thoughts were taking roots in different parts of the country, especially in Bengal and Punjab. Since 1893 the delegates from Punjab to the Congress session started demanding the adoption of a constitution for the Congress. Thus they wanted to clip the wings of the Congress leaders from Bengal and Bombay, who were wielding great deal of influence. Under this pressure All India Congress Committee was formed in 1899, but within two years Pherozeshah made it almost defunct. In spite of all this, Curzon was not to see the demise of the Congress. In fact, because of his authoritarian rule, he strengthened the Congress and was indirectly helpful in the rise of radical politics in India. In this changed atmosphere Gokhale was to play more important role in Indian politics and not restrict himself to the precincts of the Bombay Legislative Council.

REFERENCES

1. R.P. Patwardhan, *Dadabhai Naoroji Correspondence*, Vol 2, Part 2, Allied Publishers, Bombay, 1977, p. 563.
2. T.V. Parvate, *Gopal Krishna Gokhale*, Navajivan Publishing House, Ahmedabad, 1959, pp. 81-2.
3. P.M. Limaye, *The History of the Deccan Education Society*, Deccan Education Society, Poona, 1935, pp. 159-64.
4. V.S. Srinivas Sastri, My Master Gokhale, Model Publications, Madras, 1946, p. 142.
5. *Ibid.*, pp. 74-75.
6. Daniel Argov, *Moderates and Extremists in Indian Nationalist Movement, 1883-1920*, Asia Publishing House, NY, 1967, pp. 76-77.
7. Sir C.Y. Chintamani, *Indian Politics Since the Mutiny*, George Allen and Unwin, London, 1940, p. 51.
8. R.P. Patwardhan, *Dadabhai Naoroji Correspondence*, Vol. 2 Part 2, Allied Publishers, Bombay, 1977, pp. 689-91.
9. Mrs. Max Muller, Ed., *The Life and Letters of Frederick Max Muller*, Longmans, London, 1902, p. 390.
10. Govind Talwalkar, *Naoroji te Nehru*, Majestic Prakashan, Bombay, 1989, pp. 104-5.
11. R.P. Patwardhan, *Dadabhai Naoroji Correspondence*, Vol. 2, Part 2, Allied Publishers, Bombay, 1977, p. 656.
12. John R. McLane, *Indian Nationalism and The Early Congress*, Princeton Uni. Press, Princeton, 1977, pp. 134-39.
13. Jonathan Schneer, *London 1900*, Yale Uni. Press, New Haven, 1999, p. 193.

Chapter Ten

AT THE ZENITH

In 1905 Gokhale was at the zenith of his political life, which began in 1899 when he was elected to the Bombay Provincial Legislative Council. For two years he could develop his parliamentary skills in the Provincial Council. By that time Pherozeshah Mehta had decided to give up his seat on the Central Legislative Council. Gokhale wrote him a letter on January 15, 1901 appealing him to consider him as a possible candidate. This letter was, as Srinivas Sastri had described, full of eloquent words, charged with emotion and at the same time conveying to Sir Pherozeshah the feeling of reverence.

In the letter, Gokhale conveyed at the outset, that he was about to retire from the Fergusson College and dedicate the rest of his life in the service of the country. He wanted to go by the path, which Dadabhai had chosen himself. He then wrote that he had heard that Pherozeshah was to retire from the Supreme Council. Gokhale told Pherozeshah that he should continue to represent Bombay presidency as long as his health and energy vouchsafe. But if what he heard was true, then Gokhale wanted Pherozeshah to consider his candidature sympathetically. Gokhale writes, "Everyone feels—I state what I honestly think—that on the score of gifts, natural and acquired, on the score of prestige, on the score of those numerous qualities which are indispensable in a political leader, there is no equalling you or even coming near you. The same cannot be said, of course, of the men who aspire to succeed you, and there being little difference between the qualifications of the various candidates, I ask for your sympathy and encouragement. In 1897, when perfect storm of fierce criticism broke over my head in connection with my unhappy share in the incidents of that year, nothing wounded me deeper than Bhownaggree's denunciation of me in the House of Commons as a 'despicable perjurer'. The words burnt into my heart, and the night I read them, I made up my mind to devote my life, as soon as I was free from my pledge, to the furtherance of our political cause in England, to which I had, without meaning it, done such a serious injury. And for this work a brief period of membership of the Viceregal Council will be useful. I have written frankly and without reserve, and hope I shall not be misunderstood. I already owe much to you in public life, and I feel I may lay bare to you the aspiration as well as the wounds of my heart without being repulsed for doing so".[1]

Pherozeshah readily accepted Gokhale's plea and told him that he would fully support his candidature for the membership of the Central Legislative Council. After Gokhale's election Pherozeshah wrote to Sir Bipin Krishna Bose, who was a high official in the Judicial Department and later became a judge of the High Court at Nagpur, that in Gokhale, "We would have a colleague who would soon make a mark in the public life of the country". Though Pherozeshah had resigned his membership of the Council for reasons of health, Sir Bipin was not convinced that it was the real reason. He thought Pherozeshah resigned to open for Gokhale a wider field of service to India.[2]

Unfortunately, the day after Gokhale wrote to Pherozeshah, his master, Justice Ranade, died after a few days of illness. Gokhale had great devotion for Ranade and he regarded him not only as a guide and a philosopher but also as his father. He was impressed by high intelligence, patriotism, liberalism and moral personality of Ranade. Gokhale felt like an orphan by the death of Ranade. His letter to Dadabhai and later his speeches show how deeply he felt the loss of his mentor.

Gokhale then decided to commemorate the memory of Ranade by having memorials in Poona and Madras. He involved many people in this endeavour and made several speeches to collect funds. His efforts bore fruit and suitable memorials were erected accordingly.

After his election to the Central Legislative Council was announced, Gokhale resigned as a professor at the Fergusson College. His farewell speech is memorable for his honesty, sincerity and dedication. For some years this speech was memorised by hundreds of educated people, at least in Maharashtra. Explaining the most important reason which influenced his decision to retire, Gokhale told his colleagues and students in a meeting on September 19, 1902, "Years ago I remember to have read the story of a man, who lived by the side of the sea, who had a nice cottage and fields that yielded him their abundance, and who was surrounded by a loving family. But to him the sea had a strange fascination. When it lay gently, heaving like an infant asleep, it appealed to him; when it raged like an angry and roaring lion, it still appealed to him; till at last he could withstand the fatal fascination no longer. And so he disposed of everything and putting his all into a boat, he launched it on the bosom of the sea. Twice was he beaten back by the waves—a warning he would not heed. He made a third attempt when the pitiless sea overwhelmed him. To a certain extent this seems to me to be my position today". Gokhale thus launched his boat on an uncharted sea. He faced several storms and had to strive hard to take the boat to the safe harbour. There were periods of exultation and also of depression. But Gokhale did not falter in his resolve and never wavered from his goal.

Two years before Gokhale took his seat in the Central Legislature, Lord Curzon had taken over as the viceroy and the governor-general of India. Curzon was no stranger to India. He had visited it earlier on his tour of South Asia and aspired to be the viceroy of India. He also was aware of the problems of the country, as he had served for some time as the deputy secretary of state for India. He had firm convictions and never budged from them, though in politics for a long time, he did not believe in flexibility. Curzon believed that the British Empire in India was divinely ordained and the British were to hold that in trust. He regarded himself as a trustee and exerted without regard to his health. Efficiency and duty were his watchwords. He wanted everybody, who served in the administration, never to be slack or waver from duty. So when he found that some of the soldiers were involved in the atrocities in Burma, he sent the whole company to Eden as punishment. This infuriated the Englishmen, who thought the punishment excessive; but the Indians were elated. Curzon did not mind the criticism of his countrymen, as he never cared for popularity. Curzon believed that as rulers, the English must be above board and establish themselves as morally superior. This alone, he thought, would enable them to be acceptable to the Indians. He also believed that England and India had been united by the almighty God.

In another speech Curzon assured that in India he would combine duty with sympathy. He also said that those who had visited Eastern countries had known that it was a different sort of a university where education was continuous. No degree was conferred. It was like a temple where you learn somthing and forget something. However, Curzon had not forgotten anything, and displayed sympathy on very few occasions. His ambition was limitless which was also accompanied by egoism, which led a political commentator to state that Lord Curzon would have been great, if he could have occasionally forgotten that he was Lord Curzon.

After assuming the reins of office, Curzon spent about three months in reading the files of all departments and came to know how his predecessors dealt with numerous problems. After his study of the files was completed, Curzon wrote to the secretary of state that the Government of India was caught in the vortex of files and papers. In a given file, detailed notings were made right from a clerk to the highest officer, which ultimately resulted in a large file. In the process, there remained much less time to read the documents and take decision. Curzon thought that the pen was more oppressive than the bureaucracy. He decided to give priority to fortify the frontiers of India. Like some of his countrymen he was convinced that Russia had aggressive designs against

Afghanistan and would occupy it any time. Lord Salisbury had said that if Curzon's arguments were to be accepted, then an army of fifty thousand had to be deployed, which was not possible. However, Curzon's first move was to remove the troops from the more dangerous areas and station them in secure positions. He told the tribals in the frontier region that they should defend themselves, and the British army would support them from the rear. This reduced the expenditure on the army. But his Afghanistan policy and his plan for the occupation of Chitral generated much debate and criticism in the British Parliament.

Curzon had realised that the Bombay and Madras governors were enjoying much power than any other governors. After the assassination of Rand and Ayerst in Poona, many were arrested and Natu brothers were detained without trial, which invited much debate in the Parliament. To Curzon's query about the detention of the Natu brothers, Governor Sandhurst gave some casual replies. However, later both brothers had to be released. Even six months after the arrival of Curzon, the governor of Madras did not send him any letter, and refused to take any notice of him. Taking affront, Curzon wrote to the secretary of state demanding the curtailment of the powers of governors of Bombay and Madras. This proposal was accepted, and then Curzon sent a communication to that effect to both governors and gave publicity to his communication. The administration of Madras Presidency in general, and the police department in particular, was rife with corruption. "The rules of service in the ICS notwithstanding, a Chief Secretary was found taking bribes to provide for his forthcoming retirement. The First Member of the Governor's Executive Council was caught in a lie to the Secretary of State and in land speculation. 35 civilians, including the whole of the Board of Revenue and half of the Governor's Executive Council, were discovered speculating in plantation and gold shares in the native states; two leading officials, D. Carmichael and W. Huddleston, were accused publicly of nepotism; a Collector was dismissed for bribery".[3] These and other details are given by D.A. Washbrook after examining the Madras government records. He has also described how the collector of Madura became law unto himself and indulged in nepotism and all sorts of malpractices. But the Madras administration being very lethargic, the collector escaped any punishment. Both the viceroy and the secretary of state were amazed to see that the Madras administration, instead of punishing these officials, was protecting them. As Curzon insisted on duty, he advised the Talukdars to behave as the trustees and not as autocrats. In a circular to the chiefs of states, he told them not to visit Europe often, and commended the practice of the Maharaja of Gwalior of touring the various parts of the state and understanding the problems of the people. Addressing a gathering of the students of the Rajkumar College, Curzon advised them not to aspire to become Europeans. Such activities and utterances of Curzon took everybody by surprise.

Curzon was put to test in 1899 when Gujarat, Central and United Provinces were affected by famine. The severity of this famine was felt more, as there had been another famine two years earlier. Curzon, then, came down from Simla and toured Rajasthan, Gujarat and Central Provinces in the smoldering October heat. While visiting the famine areas, he found that the government of Bombay was very tardy in providing relief to the affected people. He then admonished it and put the matters straight. By 1900 three and half million people were on the famine works and by July the number rose to six and half million. Never were so many employed on famine works. Thousands of cattle died of the scarcity of fodder. The tribals living in forests started crowding in the cities and towns. Water scarcity brought in cholera. Speaking on the budget in 1901, Lord Curzon gave the details of the ravages of famine. He said that an area of almost four hundred thousand sq. miles was famine-stricken. Loss was to the tune of rupees seventy five crores. Gujrat, Berar, Hissar and Chattisgarh (present day Madhya Pradesh) lost all the crop, while in other parts some crop could be saved. Curzon estimated that one fourth of the Indian population was affected by famine. The government spent rupees ten million on relief directly; while land-owners and cultivators received aid to the tune of rupees thirty eight lak. He said that half of the land revenue from the Bombay and Central provinces would be lost. Punjab used to contribute rupees four million as revenue, which also had to be given up. Lord Curzon appealed for generous donations from the public who responded readily. But the sordid side also came to light, when B.G. Khaparde, a friend of Lokmanya Tilak, visited London in 1909 and met Wilfrid Blunt who had large number of friends in the political circles. Khaparde told Blunt how the accounts were manipulated on the provincial level in famine years. Khaparde said, "In Berar, no accounts were kept by those entrusted with the distribution of relief, the money wanted being drawn from a fund at Hyderabad, which consisted of the surpluses of six or seven years paid from the Berar and kept there in hand, but when the famine was over, those who had administered the relief were called together and were told to write out the accounts; so much for one thing, so much for another, so as to make up the sum taken from the Fund; thus there was no real check at all upon the expenditure".[4]

Lord Curzon did not accept the criticism that excessive land revenue was responsible for the poverty of India. However, some officials who served in the revenue and other departments, in a memorial to the secretary of state on January 20, 1900, controverted the viceroy's contention. They said that irrigation was helpful to the cultivators but most parts were dependent on the rainfall, as irrigation was confined to limited areas. The officers then wrote, "We consider it essential that the share taken as the Government demand on the land should be strictly limited in every Province. Where the Land Revenue is paid directly by the cultivators, as in most parts of Madras and Bombay, the Government demand should be limited; to 50% of the net profit after a liberal deduction for cultivation expenses has been made, and should not ordinarily exceed one-fifth of the gross produce. No revision of the Land Tax of any Province or any part thereof should be made within thirty years of the expiration of any former revision. A limit be fixed in each Province beyond which it may not be permissible to surcharge the Land Tax with local cesses. We are of opinion that Bengal rate of six and one forth per cent is a fair one and that in no case should the rate exceed 10 per cent".[5]

The other measures that Curzon adopted were of far-reaching consequence. He asked his Advisory Council to pass a resolution stating the policy to be implemented in the time of famine and drought. He found that there was no uniformity in different provinces with regard to the suspension of revenue and also the relief works. The resolution brought all the provinces on the same level and did not give any discretionary or special powers to any province. But the long term measure that Curzon adopted was to start an Agriculture Department which established a research centre at Pusa and agricultural training schools and colleges at many places. To improve irrigation facilities, Curzon appointed an Irrigation Commission. He also established a Forest Department. To provide credit to the cultivators, he brought out an act under which cooperative credit societies were to function. Madras took a lead in establishing these societies. Curzon also established a Railway Board, which was helpful in making the railways profitable. The British government stood for free market and so it did not believe in the government intervention in the economic matters. But Curzon, with all these measures, reversed the policy. The other measures he adopted were to appoint Police Commission to improve the police administration and an Archaeological Department to preserve and develop the ancient and historical monuments.

When famine was raging in many parts of India. Vaughan Nash, a representative of the 'Manchester Guardian' was on a tour of the country and his newsletters were published by his paper and later in a book titled *The Great Famine*. His newsletters gave the other side of the picture presented by the government. He wrote that because of the reduced demand due to famine, many of the cotton mills in Bombay were closed. Bombay was also crowded by the famine-stricken people whom police tried in the initial period to oust, but ultimately they gave up, as they found that the exodus could not be stopped. Other parts of the Bombay Province also saw an influx of people. From Hyderabad alone ten thousand came in one week. Government had issued instructions under the Famine Code, but most of those orders remained only on the paper. Those who were working on the relief-work were not getting prescribed wages. And those who were unable to work, were getting limited relief. Officials were keen to deduct from wages and relief under one pretext or the other. But bye and large, officials worked very hard and did help people. The main work was that of stone-breaking, and at various places rubble was piled up in huge quantities. Some small and medium irrigation works were undertaken and many others were only on paper. Besides, some of them were left uncompleted. About nine hundred million famine-stricken people were spread over Bombay, Central province, some princely states and the Punjab. Because of the shortage of fodder, hundreds of thousands of cattle perished. Thousands of people left their children and went in search of work and food. There was nobody to cremate the dead bodies, which were left on the streets unattended. Bombay government did not remit the land revenue, which added to the misery of the people. Central province and Punjab were much liberal than Bombay. A district in Bombay province, which had been free from the Banias, came under their clutches. Banias made large profits, as they charged heavy interest and also acquired land by way of mortgage.[6]

Several Indian leaders appreciated various measures adopted and innovations made by Lord Curzon, and they publicly praised him. In the annual session of the Congress in 1901 in Calcutta, Wacha, in his presidential address, complimented Curzon for undertaking various schemes beneficial to the people and suggested that his term should be extended. Gokhale in his maiden speech in the Central Legislative Council expressed confidence that Curzon in the near future would occupy higher positions and help the people of India. But it was not all milk and honey, as Curzon brought in a bill to amend the University Act, which aimed at reducing the members of the Senate, which infuriated the educated Indians. His bill amending the Municipal Act also aimed at reducing the number of the elected representatives and curtailing their rights. After calling a meeting of only the officials, Curzon appointed an Education Commission comprising of all government officials with an exception of Syed Hussain Bilgamy, who was in the service of the Nizam. When this Commission came under much criticism, the name of Justice Gurudas Banergee of the Calcutta High Court was added. The Commission thought that in order to improve the working of the University and also the quality of education, the membership of the Senate should be reduced. In Allahabad it was 82, Lahore 104, Calcutta 180, Madras 197 and Bombay 310. The Commission also recommended the increase in the fees of colleges and more restrictive conditions for affiliation. Before the Bill was passed, Curzon had prohibited any new additions to the Senate of the Calcutta University. He made it clear that the main task of the university was to impart high quality education and thus prepare the students, to qualify them to face the future. After a lapse of a century one can take an objective view of the measure to reduce the number of the Senate members. It was not objectionable then and neither it is now. Of course, Curzon did this not only to improve the educational standards, but to spite the educated Indians for whom he had contempt. That was the crux of the matter; and so opposition to the Education Bill gathered strength. When the Bill was introduced, Pherozeshah Mehta was the member of the Central Legislative Council and Gokhale was that of the Bombay Legislative Council. Pherozeshah succeeded in forming a committee in Calcutta on which some Europeans agreed to serve. There were some meetings of the citizens of Calcutta where some Bengalis made highly critical speeches, which Gokhale did not like. He felt that some of the members of the committee would not stay together because of the criticism. But he also thought that Pherozeshah would prevail upon them to stay united.

Gokhale in a letter to Pherozeshah congratulated him on forming a committee to oppose the Education Bill. Gokhale wrote, "That you should have got the European members of the committee to join in all your criticisms proposals except one, is a remarkable triumph for us all; and everybody must recognize that it has been achieved mainly owing to your great tact and influence and your powerful personality. It is felt here that, if the Bombay Senate adopts this report, as most probably now be the case, the opposition to the Commission's recommendations will be enormously strengthened. They have no hope here of getting their own Senate to condemn the Report as ours has done, or rather will shortly do, and the difference in calibre and political grit between their leaders and ours is, therefore, at present being freely recognised here. You know how emotional these people are, and how easily swayed. The very men who, after the Congress of 1901 were violent in their denunciation of your and Mr. Banerjee's high-handedness in extinguishing Nundy's Congress Committee, are now praising you to the skies and recognizing in you—very justly—the greatest political leader of our time".[7]

While Curzon was moving fast, what was the state of affairs of the Congress? It met three days in a year and passed almost same resolutions. In 1899, compared with the speed with which Lord Curzon was acting, the inactivity of the Congress was conspicuous. In Maharashtra, the imprisonment of Lokmanya Tilak and apology by Gokhale paralysed the political life for two years. After his release Tilak wrote in 'Kesari' on July 4, 1889 that "'in the days of plague, government became hauteur which paralysed the social life of Poona. Now everybody should strive hard to activate the institutions. But this could only be done by putting an end to the divisions among the leaders and in the institutions. Reformers of different hue and those, who were opposed to them, had their own quarrels, and the moderates and radicals were also equally divided; but the government trashed them all. We might think anything of ourselves, but the government was there to put down all of us. Poona suffered for the last two years because of the factions in the society". It was not that Poona alone was divided; Bengal and other provinces did not fare better. Congress leaders had become lukewarm about the organisation. Wacha conveyed this to Dadabhai in a letter on February 14, 1901.

He said, "My position has grown very awkward, and I really wish I may be relieved of a duty which is so difficult to discharge amidst conflicting bodies. A section of the Bengal element, a greater portion of Lucknow and Allahabad, and almost all from Madras are rabid. Your big leaders nowadays don't care to attend the Congress. So we have a minor crew—most of whom try to boss themselves without judgment and wisdom. And you know in a body where cliquism is prevalent to a large degree, it is impossible to make a head. In short, I am disgusted with many of them and were I to relate all I know of the Congress in public, I would certainly damn it forever. The leaders are much at fault. I cannot excuse their studied absence at Congress time and their perfect indifference to its cause all the year round. This is not the way to carry on the Congress organisation. We cannot afford to lose these leaders for that would be even a worse calamity and the Congress would drift goodness knows where". In another letter on February 28, 1903 Wacha wrote to Dadabhai. "There was the captious Punjaub which has been fretting and fuming and fanning flames of sullen discontent. They are screaming aloud yet, that the whole Punjaub is disaffected! Why? It is simply the cry of 'wolf". The Punjaub has never been in my opinion a source of strength, politically or financially, to the Congress".[8]

In fact, this was the case of lady protesting too much. The person to be blamed for the Congress' malice was Pherozeshah Mehta. He did not want to abide by the rules adopted by the Congress, as he wanted to keep the Congress organisation under his thumb. Even in his absence, he saw to it that the 'election' of the Congress president and resolutions to be adopted must have his approval. Wacha at times might have been exasperated by Pherozeshah's attitude, but he always stood by him. The Congress constitution was adopted in 1898 and Chandawarkar was nominated as president because Pherozeshah backed him. His election was not according to the provisions of the constitution. The constitution also created three tiers sub-committees. The All India Congress Committee was to be the highest committee. The constitution put restrictions on Bombay and Bengal Congress Committees, which for long had enjoyed the monopoly of power. Leaders of Punjab along with some others were insistent on adoption of the constitution and that was why Wacha was complaining against them. N.N. Ghose, writing an editorial note in the September-October 1902 issue of 'Kayastha Samachar', a prestigious monthly from Allahabad, edited by Dr. Sacchidanand Sinha, criticised the attitude of some Congress leaders. He said that "a committee was appointed in 1899 to draft a constitution for the Congress, but Bengal was opposed to it. Only one representative from Bengal attended a meeting of the Committee held in October 1900. At the Allahabad meeting in October 1901, Bengali was conspicuous by its absence. Now in 1902, successful efforts were made to disband the committee altogether. This was the victory for Bengal." Surendranath, Mudholkar, Khaparde in a statement blamed the committee for not doing the assigned job. But Ghose pointed out that it was not given sufficient time. He said that "an impression had been created that the committee was disbanded under pressure and if the matters would stand as they were, then the educated Indians would be angry with the Congress". John McLane was correct when he wrote in 1903, "The Congress had little to show for its existence in 1903, nineteen years after it was founded. It had no money, no permanent organization, no sustained activity. It had failed to find any significant support among the masses and the Muslims. It was a house divided, with little confidence in itself and enjoying the confidence of few others. It was ignored or ridiculed by British officials. It received moralistic and condescending lectures on its shortcomings from its British friends. Yet in its own torpor and demoralization lay the seeds of revival".[9]

Earlier, Malabari had warned in his January 14, 1901 issue of 'Spectator' that a handful of leaders did not represent the mass of Congressmen. The majority of the Congressmen wanted the organisation to take a radical posture. This majority might one day take the moral leadership, which was unavoidable. Wacha was complaining to Dadabhai on behalf of this handful of leaders who were coming under criticism in the Congress sessions. In 1900 in the Lahore session, many delegates from Punjab and some other provinces complained that they were not getting adequate representation on the All India Congress Committee, and succeeded in getting it increased. But, when the session was held in Calcutta, in 1901, Bombay and Calcutta leaders jointly saw that the new AICC was not appointed. This infuriated the Punjab delegates, who warned that if the new constitution wasn't implemented, they would boycott the session. As the next session was held in Ahmedabad, which was the sphere of influence of Mehta, no opposition to him was possible. Wacha, without consulting any provincial Congress Committee, saw to it that Chandawarkar was nominated as president. At Madras, where the session was held in 1903, president Lal Mohan Ghose, without naming Pherozeshah Mehta, criticised him. Ghose said that the Congress demand was to bring in representative government and so the Congress should not be under the thumb of few leaders. Pherozeshah by his rejoinder hurt the feelings of many delegates. This session was poorly attended. 'The Hindu' as well as 'The Indian Nation' of Calcutta made critical comments against the method of nomination of the president of the Congress by few, and warned that that would spell ruin of the organization. As the feelings of the delegates were hurt by Mehta, Gokhale visited the city to assuage the feelings of the Madras leaders. Gokhale cited the example of the Japanese, who he said, obediently followed their leaders. Gokhale's intention was honourable, as he did not want any rift in the Congress, but his argument was faulty and misleading. The seeds of a split in the Congress were laid in Madras and even earlier in the Calcutta session. Pherozeshah, Surendranath Banerjea and some of their associates like

Wacha had started behaving as if the Congress was their personal property. They feared that if they lost the control of the Congress, it would be radicalised and also communalised. Gokhale, however, did not want to control the organization, as he was not power-hungry; but as he did not want Congress to be dominated by the radicals and communal elements, he was supporting Mehta and other moderates.

Dadabhai, on the other hand, was adopting radical views. That was why when the British people contributed to the fund for the famine-stricken people in India, Dadabhai impressed upon them that it was the duty of the British government to donate considerably large sum. By the end of the century Dadabhai thought it was advisable to convince the English working class that India was being exploited by the British ruling elite. He, therefore, addressed several meetings of the workers, telling them that it was in their interest to raise the standard of the Indian people, so that they would buy more English goods. After seeing a report of one of his speeches, 'Amrit Bazar Patrika' wrote that such utterances in India would be a cause for a case under the sedition law. Dadabhai was also alarmed by the increasing controversy in Congress and feared that if unchecked, it would split. So he wrote to Lokmanya Tilak not to precipitate the matter. Tilak in his reply on December 6, 1904, assured Dadabhai that he was not opposed to the constitutional agitation. At the same time he asserted that Congress must increase its efforts and go to the logical conclusion. Tilak said, "I have never been, nor am I in any way against the Congress. Constitutional agitation, I shall be the last person to decry. But I am rather sanguine by temperament, and think that we must push our efforts to their logical extreme. I firmly believe—and let me tell you that you yourself have been the principal cause of this belief—that if we wish to get any rights or privileges, we must agitate in England in a missionary spirit. The Anglo-Indians here will not listen to what we say. The pressure must come from England and this is possible only if we follow your example, establish a permanent political mission in England and work there persistently after the fashion of Christian missionaries in India or elsewhere. What a grand thing it would be, I said, if Sir P.M. Mehta, Mr. Surendranath Banerjea or Rai Bahadur Ananda Charlu were to go to England and stay there for some years agitating the Indian questions like your noble self? But I am sorry to say that there is no prospect of these great men taking up the agitation in right earnest and pushing it home. My scheme is that either the elder leaders of the Congress should themselves follow your example and spend the last few years of their lives in agitating Indian questions in England, or failing this, we should select half a dozen younger men and maintain them in England for ten years at least, by paying them their expenses".[10]

At the time of the third session of the Congress, in 1887, Bipin Chandra Pal was working with 'The Tribune' in Lahore. He decided to attend the session.

He was aware that many delegates disapproved of the way in which the whole programme of the session was worked out. Pal writes, "I was not as yet known to Mr. Hume, but Mr. Namjoshi was. So it was decided that immediately upon our arrival in Madras, Mr. Namjoshi would go and see Mr. Hume and place this proposal (to decide upon the programme in the open session) before him. This was done, but did not receive the serious attention of the General Secretary. The evening before the public session, the leaders had a meeting in Mr. Hume's bungalow, and the programme was settled there, as noted. When the Bengal leaders came back, we asked them what was to be the programme of the next day. One of them, I think, Surendranath Banerjea, said that the programme had been settled. This was the signal for a combined attack on them. 'Who settled them', we asked. 'We did' was the reply. 'But who are these "we", we asked". One of them replied, 'Mr. W.C. Bonnerjee, Mr. Guruprasad Sen, Mr. Narendra Nath Sen, Dr. Trailokya Nath Mitra, Mr. Surendranath Banerjea and others from Bengal'. 'But what was their authority'? This question staggered our friends". Pal then said that Surendranath Banerjea assured that the programme would be finalised only after their approval. But next day there was no such move. Instead, the delegates received copies of the resolution. At this, Pal got agitated and went to Namjoshi's place where other delegates from Bombay were housed. Pal told Namjoshi that he would not tolerate what was happening, and warned that after the presidential address he would move a resolution and challenge the circulated notice. Justice Ranade happened to be there and listened to what Pal had to say. He complained against the behaviour of Hume and the manner in which resolutions were accepted for consideration by the open session. Ranade, then admitted that wrong was indeed done. But he advised not to express the grievances openly and asked what was the alternative. Pal suggested that after his address the president should announce to form a representative committee, which would go through the resolutions and make recommendations. Ranade acted as a conciliator and the compromise was accepted to the satisfaction of all, according to Pal.[11]

As the Congress had been drifting some years past, Hume, Dadabhai and Wedderburn, in 1899, had sent a circular to the Congressmen in India noting the achievements of the organization but it had no effect. They also reminded them to arrange to pay the amount pledged by the Congress to the British Committee and its periodical. This appeal also failed to evoke any response.

Gokhale took his seat in the Central Legislative Council, when Lord Curzon was enjoying popularity among most of the educated Indians. When Curzon visited Bombay, the municipality presented him with an address. In reply to this, Lord Curzon said that as in other countries, it would be helpful, if the rulers in India received support of the popular opinion. If the administration came under criticism, it should not be construed that the critic was always wrong. He might be in the right, at least there would not be any harm in making inquiry. It was easy to denounce the criticism in a country of a continental proportion like India. Native opinion could be characterised as that of some groups like educated class, business community etc. Curzon then appealed for the cooperation of all citizens. But Curzon himself did not live up to the sentiments he expressed publicly. His behaviour was that of an autocrat. He regarded himself as a very 'superior person' and had contempt for the educated Indians whose opinions he started increasingly to discard. This attitude of the viceroy gave scope to Gokhale to ventilate the feelings of the educated Indians in the Central Legislative Council. A bill based on the Report of the Education Commission was moved in the Council in November 1903. Participating in the debate, Gokhale referred to Curzon's remarks in the course of his speech on the budget of the previous year, that the educated Indians had unnecessary grudge against the government. Gokhale told the viceroy that if that was the case, then it called for the introspection on the part of the government.

Gokhale then discussed the University Bill thoroughly. He began by asking whether the conference in Simla, called by the viceroy, was of officials, as only one non-official European educationist was present. Gokhale also asked whether it was of the European educationists? Gokhale said that the official view, that the Universities had created discontented BAs and an army of the failed candidates, was wrong. These people were not a curse. They proved that the supply was more than the demand. Gokhale then said, "The truth is that this so-called discontent is no more than a natural feeling of dissatisfaction with things as they are, when you have on one side a large and steadily growing educated class of the children of the soil, and on the other a close and jealously-guarded monopoly of political power and high administrative office". Gokhale reminded the government that the graduates coming from the English Universities are more dissatisfied than those from the Indian ones. He advised the government to adopt a friendly tone and absorb more and more Indian graduates in the administration. Gokhale said that the bill would not improve the quality of education. He characterized it as more on the French model than the English. There was no provision to give equal representation in the University to the government, people and those whose children were enrolled in the University. The bill was sent to the Select Committee, but no radical changes were made. Gokhale criticized the curtailment of the rights of the Senate and the number of the members of that body. He also told that it was not the way to improve the standard of education. To achieve that objective, government should spend more on education and increase the grants and facilities to the colleges. After passing of the third reading of the bill, Gokhale confessed that the critics of the bill were defeated and whatever education was given in half a century had been laid waste. Though some of the provisions of the bill were baneful, there was nothing in it to reject it totally.

Srinivas Sastri, speaking on the life and times of Pherozeshah Mehta, did not endorse such rejection by both Pherozeshah and Gokhale. He said, "I should like to mention that the University Act was not as baneful a measure as Pherozeshah and Gokhale and others made it out to be. Upon the whole, subsequent events have shown, that while excessive enthusiasm was displayed by Government in bringing the University Act into effect, a good deal of benefit did follow it; and it was, from the point of efficiency and concentration of effort, a measure in advance. But from the point of view of popular element showing itself in educational matters, it was certainly a little retrograde".[12] After the enactment, various appointments were made for different faculties, and some other measures were taken by the Chancellors. Some of these measures might have been declared illegal by the courts. So the government brought a bill which made all such measures legal and outside the purview of the courts. Gokhale strongly objected to this bill. He said if the measures taken by the chancellors were illegal, then the best course was to withdraw them.

On December 1903 a Bill to amend the Indian Official Secrets Act was moved, which the 'Englishman', a pro-government daily, said, if passed, would bring in the Russian model of administration. It naturally came under scathing criticism by Gokhale. He pointed out that the Bill proposed to place civil matters on a level with Naval and Military matters. It had not put English and Indian editors on the same footing. Gokhale said, "I would like to see the official who would venture to arrest and march to the police *thana* the editor of an Anglo-Indian paper. But so far as Indian editors are concerned, there are, I fear, officers in this country, who would not be sorry for an opportunity to march whole battalion of them to the police *thana*. The responsibility of the Government to the people in this country is merely moral; it is not legal, as in the West. The criticism by the Indian Press is the only outward check operating continuously upon the conduct of the bureaucracy, possessing absolute and uncontrolled power. The proper and only remedy, worthy of the British Government, for whatever is really deplorable in the present state of things, is not to gag newspapers as proposed in this Bill, but discourage the issue of confidential circulars which seek to take away in the dark what has been promised again and again in Acts of Parliament, the Proclamations of Sovereigns, and the responsible utterances of the successive Viceroys. Of course with our Legislative Councils, as they are constituted at present, the Government has the power to pass any law as it pleases. But never before, I think, did the Government disassociate itself so completely from all public opinion—including Anglo-Indian public opinion—as it has done on the present occasion". R.C. Dutt was very much pleased with Gokhale's speeches on the University Bill and the Bill to amend the Official Secrets Act. Dutt wrote to Gokhale on March 22, 1904, "You have performed a noble and patriotic duty, both with the Official Secrets Bill and the University Bill and a grateful country will not forget your services. You have lost all along the line, as you yourself put it, but there are defeats which are more brilliant and more honourable than victories—and the fight that you have made during the last and worst years of a heartless and ungenerous Imperialism will be historic and will never be forgotten by our countrymen. I have myself fought this battle in another sphere for the last seven years of a blatant Imperialism, and I have failed in every single endeavour that I have made. But I have ever felt, and I feel it today that every blow which you and I have struck will have its effect and I have more hopes from the increasing efforts and persistence of our countrymen rallying around us than I have fears from repressive acts of despots".[13]

In August 1904, the government brought Cooperative Credit Societies Bill. Gokhale, speaking on the Bill, said at the outset that though he had various occasions to oppose the government, he would welcome this Bill. Gokhale said that Indian agriculturist was very poor and it was the duty of the government to make every effort to instill confidence in him and help him to stand on his feet. Speaking about the Bombay province, he said that there were three categories of the agriculturists. In the third category was the large mass of them who were so indebted that there was no hope for them to get out of it. Gokhale regretted that this category would not be helped by the provisions of the Bill. He cautioned the government that those who were not indebted would not be members of the Credit Society; only those in the second category who were not hopelessly indebted would join them. He suggested that if any measure was taken to remit the debt, only then the second category would be members of the Credit Society. Provision to confiscate the property was discouraging. The remedy he suggested was to affiliate the Societies to the banks as in Germany and Italy so that they would not be short of funds.

Gokhale's great contribution to the Legislative Council was his budget speeches from 1902 to 1914. With his first speech he achieved the status of an all India leader. Curzon was the viceroy between 1902 and 1905 when the budgets were surplus. For two years earlier also the budgets were surplus. Speaking on the budget of 1902, which was his first, Gokhale said that it was unprecedented to have seven years of continuous surpluses, but they constituted the double wrong to the community. That means the government had taken so much more from the people, when there was depression and suffering. It was wrong again because it led to misplaced optimism and so, secretary of state thought all was 'best in this best of the land'. The surplus was the result of continued high level of taxation which was introduced when the rupee was at its lowest. As that was not the case now, taxation level should have been scaled down. Nine years out of twelve were of increased taxation. In sixteen years the increased taxation brought an additional rupees one hundred three million to the treasury. If amount from the land revenue were added, it came to one hundred and fifteen million. In the circumstances, even if tax on salt was reduced by half a rupee and the duty on cloth was reduced and the minimum rate of the income tax was raised slightly, still the budget would be surplus. But the test lied in the economic condition of the country. It would be seen that the land under cultivation was reduced, high quality agricultural produce had gone down; while birth rate was low, death rate increased. Import-export trade was also less than before. Gokhale blamed the external policy of the government, which compelled it to increase the expenditure on the army. India was sufficiently armed to defend itself against the supposed intended aggression by Russia. Expenditure on the army had gone up because of the expansionist policy of the government. Gokhale pressed for more provision for education and recasting of the policy of revision of the land revenue every thirty years.

Next year when the duty on salt and cloth was reduced, Gokhale welcomed the government measure. He, however, criticized the government for neglecting the interests of India to safeguard those of Lancashire. He again pleaded for more expenditure on education and suggested that if teachers and professors were to be brought from England to raise the quality, then it was advisable to bring in experienced and recognised scholars. Budgets for next two years were surplus and Gokhale repeated his demands. Quoting a good deal of statistics, Gokhale pointed out how municipalities and District Boards were in need of more grants. In 1905, Gokhale welcomed a raise of one rupee in the salary of an ordinary policeman. But dealing with the report of the police commission just released, he reviewed the police administration in general. He criticized them for being brutal and largely corrupt. He said they were generally partial to the vested interests and treated the ordinary people with great deal of brutality. When rivers in Assam and Bengal changed courses, dispute about the land ownership invariably arose and the police sided with the landlord and not the tenant or the small landholder. However, the government did not implement the report of the Police Commission, as it required more expenditure.

The first budget speech by Gokhale was hailed all over India including the official members of the Council. The 'Amrit Bazar Patrika' wrote on March 29, 1902, "We had ever entertained the ambition of seeing some Indian member openly and fearlessly criticizing the Financial Statement of the Government. But this ambition was never satisfied. When members had ability, they had not the requisite courage. When they had requisite courage, they had not the ability. For the first time in the annals of the British rule in India, a native of India has not only succeeded in exposing the fallacies which underlie these Government Statements, but has ventured to do it in an uncompromising manner". 'The Times of India' expressed gratification that in Gokhale Western India possessed a representative of so much distinction and individuality.[14] R.C. Dutt wrote to Gokhale, "I am not in the habit of saying more than I mean—and I can honestly assure you that I consider your budget speech to be the ablest and the best that has ever been made by our point of view in the Viceroy's Council. The Viceroy must feel today—strong and self-willed as he is—there are stronger forces arraigning themselves in India in the popular cause. And I dare prophesy knowing all the eminent men in India, you will be the strongest, the foremost and the most irresistible leader among them, because you are inspired by truest and honestest zeal for our country".[15] Finance Minister Sir Edward Law was much impressed by Gokhale's speech and next year he invited him to be his guest at Simla so that he could discuss many subjects and get acquainted with the views of Gokhale. 'The Statesman' praised Gokhale for his eloquence and the mastery over English language as well his marshalling of facts. Sarala Ghoshal, who was the wife of a Congressman in Calcutta and a relative of Rabindranath Tagore, wrote to Gokhale on March 11, 1902, that she read his speech in the Council with great relish. She thought the reply by Lord Curzon was shallow. She also felt that India would benefit by the efforts made by people like him. She referred to Gokhale's resolve to dedicate all his life in the service of the country and hoped Bengal would also have such men.

Gokhale, thus, became the centre of attention of the people in Calcutta and even the prestigious among them would take opportunity to attend the Council meetings as visitors when Gokhale was to speak. Gokhale, by nature and by the style of his speech, was bound to be effective in a small gathering like the Council. He would substantiate his argument by statistics and extracts from reports. His appeal was to the intellect and not to the emotion. That was why he was not able to sway the masses which orators like Surendranath Banerjea could. Srinivas Sastri gives a graphic description of Gokhale's style and manner of public speech. He writes, "As he spoke you saw on his countenance a glow that people did not naturally catch on his face. For when he sat at a public meeting, he was generally glum and serious and when he began to speak, there was animation in his countenance, which communicated itself to the listeners. It would almost seem that his chief power lay in his earnestness. Every word he spoke was charged with sincerity, you could see his soul as it were trying to escape through his lips".[16] B.G. Horniman, narrating his experience, had written that Gokhale's voice was very soft and it could not be audible in the press gallery of Viceroy's Council. So when Horniman and some of his fellow journalists told this to Gokhale, he arranged to give them the gist of his speech in advance.

Lord Curzon could not be expected to be pleased with Gokhale's speeches in the Council. But he realised his worth and then on December 31, 1903 in a letter to Gokhale he said, "I hope you will allow me to make an announcement in tomorrow's Gazette of the CIE bestowed upon you. HM the King by a personal line from myself to say that the honour is offered to you in recognition of abilities which are freely bestowed upon the service of your countrymen and of which I would ask no more than that they should continue to be so employed. I wish India produces more of such men".

Curzon, contrary to his public utterances, did not heed to the public opinion; and that was why he decided to hold a durbar in Delhi on December 31, 1902. In fact, only one or two years had passed after the horrible experience of famine that the large parts of the country went through. It was a totally uncalled for ceremony and it was also insulting to the feelings of the Indians who had lost so much in the natural calamity. But Curzon had a romantic streak and relished the medieval pomp and ceremony. Added to it was his belief in the divine destiny of the British power and himself. It was no wonder that Curzon had come under severe criticism from the Indian press. 'Kayastha Samachar', in an editorial note, ridiculed the Maharaja of Reva for bringing a white elephant for the Delhi Durbar whose thousands of citizens had to take refuge in Delhi in the famine years. While 'Review of Reviews' reminded the participants of the durbar that, behind the glitter of the jewelry and diamonds of the Maharajas there were millions of invisible hungry and destitute Indians. Lokamanya Tilak was scathing in his criticism. He wrote in his editorial that instead of this unjustified ostentatious expenditure, if the government had remitted the debts of the cultivators, the expenses would have been much less and the people would have blessed the government. It should be remembered that the very ground on which this durbar took place, had seen so many empires and also their demise; and the seven cities which comprised the present Delhi were reduced to ashes. England had a history of about one thousand years, and so persons like Lytton or Curzon could not be expected to go beyond such period. But Indians who had a history of more than five thousand years, remember how Hastinapur and before that Ayodhya came to a sorry pass. So any number of such futile ceremonies would not be able to obliterate this historic memory of the people of India, warned Tilak.

In spite of much publicity that accompanied the Durbar, how were the guests, other than Maharajas and some very important persons treated? B.G. Khaparde, who was one of the invitees, had very sad memories. He wrote indignantly in his diary that December 23rd was a bad day. His train reached Delhi by midnight, which was six, hours late. The English guests had conveyance and reached their destinations without having to wait. Other guests like Khaparde were not provided with such facility. They had to wait in the waiting room at the railway station. It was bitterly cold but the railway staff showed no courtesy. He reached his camp by ten in the morning. Roads were full of dust and at the camp there were no proper arrangements. They were far worse than at the annual sessions of the Congress. But an incident, which was narrated by Khaparde later to Blunt, was hilarious. He told him that when everybody present was waiting for Lord Curzon to arrive, a terrier from the Scottish band broke his leash and ran straight to the gilded chairs and climbed on to one of them. He was removed before Curzon and Duke of Connaught and the Duchess arrived. Some three soldiers from the Scottish Company fainted due to heat and later died. The Begum of Bhopal prostrated herself before the viceroy, which the assembled Maharajas resented. They were annoyed that the viceroy did not visit their camp even once.

Durbar was not an easy affair for Curzon or Secretary of State and his Advisory Council. Correspondence between the Viceroy and the Secretary of State was acrimonious and at one stage Curzon offered his resignation. After the death of Queen Victoria, Prince Edward was crowned in the summer of 1902 in London. Some Indian troops were sent for the occasion. Besides, some officials as well as invited guests had to attend the ceremony. Problem arose as to who was to pay for the travel and stay. There was to be a march of troops on the grounds of the India House and the guests from India were to be entertained. The Secretary of State's Council took the stand that it was obligatory on the part of the Government of India to pay the expenses, which Lord Curzon resented. He told the Secretary of State that the Government of India was asked to pay for the troops which were sent to fight in the Boer War; now if India was to bear the cost for the participation in the coronation ceremony, it would not only be unbearable but also unjust. Prime Minister Arthur Balfour was a personal friend of Curzon. In a letter to Balfour, Curzon told him that when no other colony was asked to bear the expenses for the participation in the coronation ceremony, India should not be made an exception. This would not become an imperial power. In the Boer war some thousand Indian troops were sent; besides many prisoners were kept in India. But the then prime minister, Lord Salisbury, had not expressed a single word of appreciation or thanks. Now if India were asked to bear the expenses, people would resent it. Secretary of State, Lord George Hamilton asked Curzon to take back his letter. He warned, otherwise relations between the Secretary of States' Council and the viceroy would be adversely affected. Curzon replied that there was honest difference of opinion and it should not be a cause for estrangement. The Council itself on many occasions took the view, which was contrary to that of the Government of India. Lord Hamilton then realised that he had no convincing argument against that of Curzon; and the King himself held that Curzon's position was sound. Lord Hamilton then had no other option than to take back his letter and agree to bring India on the same level as other colonies in regard to the sharing of expenses for the coronation.

Though Curzon came out successful in this controversy, on the other score he suffered a defeat. He had suggested to the Secretary of State that reduction in the tax should be announced at the time of the Durbar. He said this was customary in India, and as India had suffered much for the cause of the Empire, this reduction would be appropriate and would be appreciated by Indians. Lord Hamilton rejected this suggestion, which, according to him, would lay a precedent, which the British government did not approve of. He said, that Curzon could announce such reduction at the time of budget session of his Council. Curzon was furious and threatened resignation. But in the end he had to retreat. Lord Curzon by then thought that unless he continued to be the viceroy, many of the schemes, which he had undertaken, would not be successfully completed. He, therefore, in 1903 wrote to the prime minister, Balfour, that his term should be extended for another five years. As Curzon had rubbed some ministers and officials the wrong way, most of them were against acceding to his request. Correspondence between Balfour and Curzon on this subject was not very pleasant. However, the ministry agreed to grant an extension to Lord Curzon.

In 1904, on the suggestion of the British Committee, the Congress had resolved to send a delegation of four to England to put before the English people and their representatives the case of India. One of the delegates was to be Gokhale. It was Wedderburn who wanted Gokhale to visit England because the Tories were losing ground and elections were a possibility. He thought, if Gokhale and some Congress leaders visited England and addressed meetings, it would have a salutary effect. Gokhale then started making preparations. But when he with his friend Lallubhai Samaldas met Pherozeshah Mehta, he disapproved of the visit of an Indian delegation to England. It was obvious that Pherozeshah was not against Gokhale's visit, but was against the British Committee, as he thought the Committee was irrelevant and Dadabhai was wasting his time in England. Besides, Pherozeshah was directly and indirectly criticised in the Congress session, which had resolved to send the delegation. Though Gokhale had not recorded how he was treated by Mehta, Sir Lallubhai in a letter to Gokhale on May 10 had done so. He wrote, "We were both so much excited last night that I did not like to add fuel to the fire by speaking out mind about the disgraceful (I use the word in calm state of my mind) conduct of Sir Pherozeshah Mehta. You should not give up the idea of going as a delegate to England. The public has elected you, and you should not disappoint the public. I feel that an apology or at least an explanation is due to you from him. You may treat him formally as a recognised leader of the party; the private relations will of course cease". Gokhale, however, did not defy Pherozeshah because of his reverence for him. But in the end, Pherozeshah relented under the pressure from Dadabhai, Hume and Wedderburn and Gokhale sailed to England in September 1905.

The year 1905 was important in the life of Gokhale and also in the history of India, as on June 12 of that year Gokhale established an institution, which played a historical role in the years to come. As he was playing his role as a member of the Central Legislative Council, Gokhale felt the need of an organisation of young men who would dedicate their lives in the self-less service of the country and study various problems facing her. He held long discussions with his friends like, Dr. Dev and then decided to start an institution to be named 'The Servants of India Society.' On early morning of June 12, 1905 Gokhale along with three of his colleagues went to a ridge near Fergusson College. First Gokhale took seven vows and administered them to N.A. Dravid, A.V. Patwardhan and G.K. Deodhar. Gokhale was designated as the First Member. The object of the society as mentioned in the memorandum was to train men for the work of political education and agitation, and to promote by all constitutional means the national interests of the Indian people. This was changed and the objective was then defined as "to train national missionaries for the service of India and to promote by all constitutional means the true interests of the Indian people". The seven vows which all the members had to take were:

1. That the Country will always be the first in his thoughts and he will give to her service the best that is in him.
2. That in serving the country he will seek no personal advantage to himself.
3. That he will regard all Indians as brothers and will work for the advancement of all, without distinction of caste and creed.
4. That he will be content with such provision for himself and his family, if he has any, as the Society may be able to make. He will devote no part of his energies to earn money for himself.
5. That he will lead a pure personal life.
6. That he will engage in no personal quarrel with any one.
7. That he will always keep in view the aims of the Society and watch over its interests with utmost zeal, doing all he can to advance its work. He will never do anything which is inconsistent with the objects of the Society.

In order to train the members, a library was established and Gokhale himself took pains to select books on subjects like politics, history, economics as well as parliamentary reports and reports on various subjects. The constitution was drafted by Gokhale. After consultations with many of his friends, he made amends. One of those friends was Professor Selby for whom Gokhale had high regards. After reading the draft, Selby objected to the article five of the constitution. That article said, "Every member on admission be under a vow of absolute obedience to the First Member for five years". Professor Selby wrote on June 15, 1905, "I have read through the rules of your new Society. It is rather an awful thing that you should ask a man to surrender absolutely to you, his conscience and the right of private judgment for five years. This popularly was supposed to be the first condition of admission to 'the Society of Jesus' and the main ground for Protestant condemnation of that order. It reads to an Englishman rather like a rule of a Russian secret society". Gokhale pondered over this letter and modified the article five. It then read, "Every member under training shall, during the time that he is under training, place himself under entire guidance and control of the First Member and do such studies as the First Member may direct". Gokhale had anticipated that the absolute powers to the First Member would invite objection, and so in a circular letter along with the pamphlet about the proposed Society, Gokhale had said, "It may perhaps appear to you on a perusal of the rules that the position of the First Member during the first five years is much too dominant. But after very careful consideration we have come to the conclusion that it is necessary to make it so. The work of the Society will often involve questions at the utmost delicacy and requiring the greatest introspection. Men with unformed judgments in political matters and unaccustomed to the responsibilities of public life cannot be permitted to determine important issues without exposing the Society to grave risks. The five years special discipline which we propose for every member of the Society is intended to mould alike his character and judgment and enable him to comprehend an ideal for the nation, complete in all respects". But when Gokhale received Selby's letter, he saw the point and amended the Article five.

Krishnaswami Iyer advised Gokhale to consult the governor. He wrote, "Can you not take the Governor and any of his Councillors into your confidence? They are sure to disapprove of your scheme, but they will know what it is and won't suspect. Secrecy endangers suspicion, and suspicion of the authorities in India means danger to individuals. The Servants of India Society must face it. But unnecessary risk must be avoided. I am not for unnecessary publicity. But few at the head of the government may know. No serious harm can then befall anybody". Gokhale received very good response from many of his friends in India and abroad and he did not find it difficult to collect money. Sir Lallubhai Samaldas, sending a cheque, suggested that those who subscribed largely should have some voice in the management. Sir Ratan Tata sent the first installment of Rs. 5000 and wrote to Gokhale, "I give my personal support to the Society, because I see in it a constitutional and rational alternative to the violent methods which some people adopt for the progress of our people and country. In the statement of your little pamphlet of the objects of the Society, I notice one omission. There appears to be no reference to stimulate industrial development of the country".[17] Srinivas Sastri was sworn as a member of the Society at Calcutta in 1906, when Gokhale took Sastri and two or three others to meet Dadabhai, who that year presided over the Congress session. In 1935 when a memorial tablet was erected at the place where Gokhale and three other members took the vows, Sastri in his speech narrated the conversation, which Gokhale had with Dadabhai. Gokhale told the Grand Old Man that some of those who sat beside him were the members of the Servants of India Society. Dadabhai threw his hands in surprise. He said, "That's right. This is the idea which I have long held in my mind and I congratulate Mr. Gokhale on having had the good fortune to embody it in an actual organisation". The construction of the building of the Society started in the 1905 itself, as it had by then received donations of about rupees seventy thousand.

Before his departure to England, C.Y. Chintamani informed Gokhale that Benares and Allahabad Congress Committees had decided upon his nomination for the presidentship of the Congress session to be held in Banares later in the year. In England Gokhale had a whirlwind tour of the country. Besides London he addressed several meetings in different cities and towns and gave interviews. Gokhale met Morley, Brodrick and several other politicians. After meeting Gokhale, Morley thought he was close to Cavour, an Italian leader. The burden of Gokhale's speeches and interviews was that India's objective was to reach Dominion Status; to reach that goal, provincial as well as the Central Legislative Council should be made more representative of the people and the elective principle should be adopted. He did not ask for the reduction of the majority of the official members in the Councils. He made it clear that he or Congress was not asking for the far-reaching changes in the immediate future. He impressed upon his audience that a new generation of the English educated people had come up and it was growing. This generation, naturally, demanded English institutions and equal treatment, which were guarantied by Queen Victoria's Proclamation in 1858. Viceroys like Lord Ripon adopted a liberal policy and tried to bridge the gap between the Englishmen and Indians. But these efforts were thwarted by his own countrymen, giving rise to the suspicion and resentment among the educated Indians. Lord Curzon had adopted the policy of repression, which was bound to fail. Indians had, therefore, lost faith in the British rule.

Wedderburn, reviewing Gokhale's tour, wrote, "In 1905, four Delegates from India were expected. Only two Delegates, Mr. Gokhale and Mr. Lala Lajpat Rai were able to come; and much of Mr. Lajpat Rai's time was taken up by a visit to America, where he addressed meetings at New York, Boston and Chicago. But Mr. Gokhale's campaign in Yorkshire and Lancashire was a brilliant success. His visit to Lancashire was specially opportune, with reference to the Partition of Bengal and boycott of Manchester goods. At Manchester he addressed four important meetings. At each of these meetings he made a different speech. The Chairman of the British Committee, who accompanied him can bear witness to the profound impression produced on his hearers by the accuracy of his information and the cogency of his arguments. Good meetings were also held in London, and he had a gratifying reception by the undergraduates of the 'Union' at Cambridge, where his motion in favour of more popular institutions for India was carried by 161 to 62. The Fabian Society also held a special meeting to hear an address from him".[18]

In one of his speeches Gokhale had posed the question whether India had progressed morally and materially under the British rule. He said under the British peace and stability were established and the English education had spread. But it was evident that the English occupied all high government posts. As the Indians were not appointed on any responsible position, their growth had been stunted and there was frustration. Among the 2400 government officers who received a salary of 700 pounds, only 60 were Indians. A voter in England enjoys a right, which three hundred million Indians did not. When Natal and Transvaal were under the Boers; some of the ordinances which the government had promulgated were against the Indian settlers but were never actually implemented. But after the British defeated the Boers and those colonies came under their rule, the same repressive laws came into force. That was why an Indian in those colonies could not walk on the footpath on which an Englishman was crossing and he could not get reservation in the hotel or dine in a restaurant along with an Englishman. Gokhale then compared the relative income of the British and the Indians. He pointed out that whereas average per capita income of England was forty-two pounds, that of India was two pounds. The per capita import of England was thirteen pounds and that of India was five shillings. According to William Hunter, forty per cent of Indians went hungry, as they were unable to afford two meals a day. During the previous eight years, produce worth two hundred million pounds was lost due to famine. In the last twenty years the death rate per thousand had gone up and not down. One third of the revenue was spent on the salary, pension and allowances of the English officials. Even then, Gokhale said, that India's demands were moderate. They were: fifty per cent of the non-official members on the Councils; more Indians to be appointed in the higher government posts; right to move an amendment to the annual budget etc.

On November 15, 1905 Gokhale addressed the New Reform Club. He alluded to Morley's book on Gladstone where one expression of Gladstone's repeatedly occurs. Gladstone used to say that though Oxford had taught him many things, it had not taught him an appreciation of the profound principle of liberty as a factor of human progress. Gokhale then said, "Well, it seems other Oxford men, too, have not learnt how to appreciate that principle. Lord Curzon is no believer in free institution or in national aspiration. I believe if he were allowed a free hand, he would hand the people of this country back to the rule of the aristocracy that governed here before 1832. Well, Lord Curzon sees that the educated classes of India are pressing forward more and more to be associated with the government of their own country, and he thinks it is not to the interest of England, as he understands that interest, that this should be so. He has tried to fetter the Press by his Official Secret Act. In regard to higher education, he has transferred the control to the hands of the officials and of such Indians as will always agree with the officials. Then as regards the few fairly high offices open to us in our own country, he has abolished competition and made everything dependent upon the pleasure of the official patronage. Now the main part of the responsibility for this state of things must rest on Lord Curzon, after all it is your system of administration in India that has enabled him to attempt all this repression. My quarrel, therefore, is less with him personally, or with the officials, than with the system—this bureaucratic system—this monopoly of power by officials". Gokhale's speeches and interviews had good press coverage, and newspapers like 'The Daily Star' and 'The Daily Chronicle' praised him. Dadabhai was pleased with his performance. But Pherozeshah was not reconciled, and so Gokhale, on his arrival in Bombay, was not accorded a welcome. It was expected of the Bombay Presidency Association and the Congress Committee to arrange a meeting to honour Gokhale. But it was Lokmanya Tilak, who arranged a reception in Bombay. When Gokhale arrived in Poona, Tilak invited him to his residence, which was also the office of 'Kesari' and 'Maratha'. Tilak praised Gokhale for his speeches and efforts in England. He said, "Gokhale was the suitable person to put the case of India before the English public by his sweet tongue and effective arguments. His task was difficult, because there were powerful advocates of the officials in India; but Gokhale was not deterred and came out successfully".

Before the Benares session of the Congress, Dadabhai congratulated Gokhale on his nomination as president of the Congress and reviewed the political situation as he saw it. Dadabhai said that when fifty-two years ago three associations were started in Calcutta, Bombay and Madras, they had limited political ideas and aspirations. They also had no knowledge of the extent and causes of poverty in India. The formation of the Indian National Congress in 1885 was the fruit of the efforts of these three organisations. Dadabhai then stressed the importance of awakening the Indian people of their rights and also to educate the English public of their duty to grant such rights. This double work both in India and England was absolutely necessary, reminded Dadabhai. He again expressed his faith in achieving equal rights for India as those of other colonies, and make India prosperous. Dadabhai gave credit to the Congress for awakening in India, which was manifest in protest against oppressive measures of Lord Hamilton and Lord Curzon. At the same time Dadabhai expressed his gratitude and appreciation for the help, which Hume, Wedderburn, Sir Henry Cotton and Martin Wood had given to the Congress. He desired that in each province there should be a band of young people who would work to educate the people about their rights as free British citizens and they should do this work in a missionary spirit. He wanted more Indian members to be elected to the British Parliament and also stressed the importance of unity among the people. Dadabhai was, however, disturbed by the differences in the Congress and the rise of radicalism among the youths. He wrote to Gokhale, "We have now around us a new generation of well educated and prepared (persons), thanks to past work, for the great task before them. Theirs is now the responsibility. Let the youth of the rising generation rally round the Congress with that energy and enthusiasm which youth can most furnish. Let them discuss them and then abide by, and undertake the burden of carrying into effect, the decisions of the majority. Let those who cannot agree take their own course in their own way towards the same goal, and not hamper and destroy each other's work".[19]

Dadabhai had referred to the rise of the youths who were inclined to follow a radical path. This new trend was due to the partition of Bengal and also due to the new wave of self-assertion generated by Japan's victory over Russia. That an Asian nation could defeat a European nation had enthused the people of Asia. Gokhale had welcomed this victory of Japan. William Digby, in a speech in London, appealed the British to take cognisance of this new awakening in Asia and India. The enthusiasm of the Indian leaders was understandable, but one does not know whether they were fully aware of the happenings and also the way the Government of Japan was ruling the country. The victory was costly to Japan. It had lost one hundred ten thousand soldiers. United States of America had brought about the cease-fire; and under the terms of the peace, Japan had to surrender her right over the Sakhalin island and seven thousand mile railway in Manchuria. England, Germany and Russia moved to contain Japan so that it would not occupy China. Besides, the Meigy rule in Japan was no better than that of the Tsar in Russia and was equally oppressive. Army was systematically given prominence and civil liberties had no place in the scheme of things. Press was suppressed. Japan also aspired to bring Asia under its sphere of influence.

Japan's victory had given cause to some British newspapers and periodicals to press for re-examination of England's policy towards Russia, India and Afghanistan. England by then had a treaty with Japan, which had accepted England's right to defend India. Mr. Leonard Courtney in a letter to 'The Times' had described the treaty as humiliating. 'The Westminster Review' of November 1905 disapproving of this criticism said, the questions asked by Courtney were the same which this so Imperial Government was driving all the thinking people all over the world and also in India to ask themselves. The effect in India itself cannot but be most damaging to our prestige. Upon that prestige and upon the loyal attachment of the native population our rule in India depends. If once the native races are alienated from us, our rule is at an end. We cannot hold India by force of arms alone. Yet that seems to be the aim of Tory Imperialism. For that they would subject this country to the manifold evils of conscription, and call in 'the yellow man' to aid John Bull in bearing the 'the White man's burden'. Happily the present Tory Government is 'under sentence of death'. Its chequered career may soon close; and then we should see once more as Viceroy a sane Imperialist, a Liberal of the type of Lord Ripon, who won such affection and such honour in that role. We should see the 'forward' party brought to heel, the extravagant military expenditure ruthlessly cut down, the crushing burdens on the ryots materially lightened, and the native races trained in that self-government for which, as in the case of Bengal, they have proved themselves so well—in the eyes of a Tory Government too well-fitted. Thus and thus alone, may the evil wrought by Tory Imperialism be undone".

Four months before the Benares Congress, Lord Curzon had resigned and

Lord Minto had taken over. At Benares, when Gokhale as the president-elect of the Congress was taken in a procession, Lala Lajpat Rai accompanied him. Lajpat Rai who had distinct memory of that event said that Gokhale was overwhelmed by the grand reception and tears of joy and gratefulness were in his eyes. It was inevitable that Gokhale should have reviewed Lord Curzon's regime in his address. Gokhale, of course, praised the qualities of the former viceroy, but he also described how Curzon's regime alienated the people of India from the administration. He compared Curzon with Aurangzeb. "There we find the same attempt at a rule excessively centralized and intensely personal, the same strenuous purpose, the same overpowering consciousness of duty, the same persistence in a policy of distrust and repression, resulting in bitter exasperation all round". Gokhale said that Lord Curzon did not understand India, he thought India was a country where Englishmen were to monopolise all power. Curzon, in his farewell speech as the Viceroy, enumerated his achievements. He tried to show the reduction of salt duty, more grants for education and irrigation etc., all these, he did in spite of the opposition of the educated classes. But Gokhale pointed out that it was Congress, which was demanding all these for a long time.

Gokhale then referred to the partition of Bengal and severely criticised Lord Curzon and his administration. He said, Curzon and his advisors had all the means to know the intense feeling of resentment of the people, but they deliberately ignored them. When it was known that some sort of a scheme of partition of Bengal was under the active consideration of the government, about 500 meetings were held in the province. But the government did not relent. The most natural course according to Gokhale was to take away Bihar, Orissa and Chota Nagpur from Bengal and form a separate province. Gokhale then dealt with the partition scheme and showed how harmful it was. He was ready to give the new viceroy, Lord Minto, some time to reconsider the scheme and make proper amends. Gokhale described the mass agitation in Bengal as a great landmark in the history of the Congress. He welcomed the great tidal wave of true national consciousness. The boycott movement against the British goods, in Bengal, was the expression of frustration because of the apathy of the government. Gokhale said that the movement was a political weapon and the people of Bengal were justified in taking that step. But Gokhale advised that the weapon like that had to be reserved for extreme occasions. He, then, discussed the practical aspect of the boycott movement. His contention was that it was impractical and suicidal to spread the movement all over the country. He gave the details of overall capacity of our spinning mills and showed how they would not be able to satisfy the demand for cloth in the country. He, therefore, advised that the movement should be confined to Bengal where the grievance was genuine and the attitude of the government reprehensible. This latter part of Gokhale's speech, though practical, was out of tune with the sentiments of the majority of delegates.

In England, on leave before returning to India, Curzon felt that urgent attention must be given to the Afghanistan problem. In his stay in England Curzon had discussions with the prime minister and the Secretary of State. The consensus was that this problem had to be solved without giving the impression to the Amir that England had retreated and cowed down. In England it was urged by some that the time was opportune to strike at Russia when she was engaged in fighting with Japan. But nobody trusted Amir who had demanded a large amount as aid. Curzon thought it was dangerous to give such aid, as Amir might use it against the British. The C-in-C, Lord Kitchener, suggested that Britain should take the responsibility of defending Afghanistan, to which Curzon had strong objections. He feared in case Afghans did not fight, England's prestige would suffer. So a representative of the Government of India was sent to Kabul to negotiate with the Amir, who was not playing ball and Curzon was also taking a stiff stand.

The British government, initially supported Curzon, but the Secretary of State, Brodrick realised that it would lead to a blind alley. Brodrick, in a letter to the Governor of Bombay, expressed doubts about the policy pursued by Curzon, which might create a stalemate, and Amir would be completely alienated. Curzon wanted the draft of the treaty, which the Amir had proposed, rejected; but the British government after careful thought decided to accept it in spite of the strong protest by Curzon. Earl of Middleton, who was the war Minister in the Balfour cabinet said, "For some time previously Curzon's private letters, including the official letter written every week to the Secretary of State, had shown symptoms of increasing unrest, and were full of threats as to the course he might feel it necessary to take. The two Governments were, in fact, running on lines which could only end in a collision, the Cabinet regarding with increasing apprehension the high-handed policy of the Viceroy, and Curzon claiming for the opinion of the Indian Government a predominance, which as Balfour remarked at the time, would rise India to the position of an independent and not always friendly power."[20] Balfour, as a personal friend of Curzon, tried always to assuage the ruffled feelings of Curzon and in one of the letters advised him that no minister including the prime minister could get everything done according to his wishes. If some suggestions were not accepted by the Cabinet or the Secretary of State, Balfour asked Curzon not to take that as a personal slight.

The second point of differences between the viceroy and the Cabinet was how to deal with Tibet. Curzon could not tolerate the intrusion by Tibet in the Indian territory which the Tibetan government was often making. He also apprehended that Russia might bring Tibet under its wings. For three years Curzon wrote several letters to the Dalai Lama, which the Tibetan ruler sent back to Curzon without opening them. Blanche Dugdale, a niece of Arthur Balfour, writing about the differences between Curzon and the Cabinet on the question of Tibet, says, "Between the time of taking the decision in June 1903, and Lord Curzon's visit to England in the summer of 1904, he had to a certain extent forced his own policy upon the Cabinet with regard to Tibet. In this case as in that of Afghanistan, Lord Curzon worked for closer contact, penetration, establishment of permanent influence, at almost any cost, as the only means, in his view, of countering the intrigues of Russia. A British Mission, under Colonel Younghusband, advanced upon Lhasa, where it did not penetrate without the use of force. It ended by demanding conditions from the Tibetans, which would have committed Great Britain to keeping a control over the country for seventy-five years. These terms, imposed by Colonel Younghusband, were promptly repudiated by the Cabinet, to the intense mortification of Lord Curzon, who was in London at that time".[21]

Lord Curzon also resented the demand by the Secretary of State, Brodrick, to send twenty thousand coolies to Transvaal for railway work. Curzon wrote, "The name of South Africa stinks in the nostrils of India. The most bitter feelings exist over the treatment meted out to Indians in the Transvaal and Natal. Any attempt to ignore or override this feeling would produce a commotion greater even than that over the South African garrison, while the recollection of the latter would tend to inflame it. We are not in the least anxious to send Indian coolies to work upon the railways in the Transvaal or anywhere else. Already tens of thousands of Indians live in South Africa, subject to invidious and sometimes odious disabilities. Surely you do not mean to order Government of India to send coolies to the Transvaal whether they like it or not? I cannot without a good deal of thought and study swallow the proposition that, having saved South Africa at the outbreak of the war, it is now the duty of India to develop it". Dilating upon the importance of Indian opinion, Curzon pointedly repeated that there were some things, which the Home Governments, could no longer do at India's expense. For five years he had been preaching the doctrine of Empire, but Indians were disposed to treat it as a farce.[22]

Curzon and the Cabinet had another serious difference of opinion. At the insistence of Lord Curzon, Lord Kitchener was appointed as the C-in-C of India. War minister Middleton argued with Curzon how Kitchener was required in England, but Curzon refused to budge. Middleton correctly anticipated that the two being intensely self-centered, would not be able to work together. Within three months of his arrival in India, Kitchener came to the conclusion that the administration of the army in India was inefficient. He also believed that there was dual control of the army, as besides C-in-C, there was a Member for Defence in the Viceroy's Advisory Council. This arrangement to him was not conducive to the efficiency of the army. So he suggested the abolition of the post of the Member for Defence in the Viceroy's Advisory Council and appoint the C-in-C to the Council. Curzon thought that if Kitchener's demand were accepted, the

C-in-C would have much more powers, which politically would not augur well. Both Curzon and the Advisory Council of the Secretary of State agreed that the dual control of the army was not advisable; but Curzon was opposed to give C-in-C a seat on the Viceroy's Advisory Council. Prime Minister Balfour did his best to persuade Curzon, but it was of no avail. So Curzon resigned. His resignation was hailed in India; but in England, the opinion was divided.

'The Times' wrote on August 21, 1905. "While we think that Lord Curzon made a mistake in withdrawing his first resignation and another mistake in choosing the occasion of his second resignation, we are satisfied that other persons involved in the discussion have been seriously at fault. The tone of Mr. Brodrick's dispatches has not been calculated to bring about an amicable settlement of the issues in dispute. He was justified, no doubt, in vindicating the rights of his office, but this object might have been effectively achieved without asserting them with a crudity which could hardly fail to give offence, even to a man less sensitive than Lord Curzon on questions of personal and official dignity. Lord Curzon has proved himself to be the greatest Viceroy of our times, as Lord Kitchener is the greatest of our younger soldiers. They are both men whom the Empire can ill spare". 'The Westminster Review', in the October 1905 issue said, "The danger to our rule in India comes not from without, but from within, and chiefly from the heavy military expenditure; a drain likely to be heavier still, now that Lord Kitchener has, at the cost of Lord Curzon's resignation, won for himself a free hand. In the whole of Lord Curzon's rule, nothing became him so well as the leaving of it; for by the gross extravagance of the Delhi Durbar, held at a time when plague and famine were ravaging the country; by the 'peaceful' mission to Tibet, by his breaking down of local self-government and of the education system; and by such insensate schemes as that of the partition of Bengal, Lord Curzon has done much to alienate our fellow-subjects in India. He stood staunch, however, for Free Trade and for supremacy of the civil over military power; and this must be accounted unto him for righteousness".

Lord Curzon, speaking in the House of Lords, asserted that behind his resignation there was some principle involved. Two years after, in a speech in Birmingham, he spoke on 'True Imperialism'. Curzon had romantic notions about the British Empire and his speech was in keeping with it. He defended Clive and Hastings and said, if their career was taken into account, it could not be said that there were some intrinsic defects or shortcomings in the Empire. Curzon compared the British Empire to Saturn.

He said as with the Saturn there were many rings around the British Empire also. Curzon said that even if Canada and some other colonies became independent, England would not be adversely affected. But if India became free, what would happen? Curzon had no doubt that immediately after achieving independence, India would fall a prey to some conqueror. If this did not happen, then it would be a victim of the competition among some powers and would fall apart. With the loss of colonies and India, England's trade would be affected and army would have to be reduced. Coal mines and docks might come to a standstill and England would be slightly better than Belgium. Empire had brought glory to England, but it brought a key to duty and service to the mankind. England's strength was not dependent on the military might, but on the moral authority. But in no case the civil authority should be subordinated; otherwise military authority would become superior. Curzon reminded his audience that it was difficult to rule India, as Indians were racially different and its customs and religion were different from those of Englishmen. There, the society was steeped in old tradition and customs. Nationalism was taking roots, but it would be a mistake to give autonomy to India which would ruin the country and that would be a betrayal of the trust. Curzon's speech naturally came under criticism in India and also in England.

Bengal was partitioned under the rule of Curzon, which infuriated the people and created problems for the British Government; but Congress also entered into a difficult period. Pherozeshah Mehta, Surendranath Banerjea and some others were facing opposition within the organization. The new subject of controversy was about the nature and direction of the Congress work. Gokhale could not attend the Madras session of the Congress in 1903. Most of the delegates were bored by the presidential address and also many other speeches. Gokhale's friend and novelist from Maharashtra, H.N. Apte, who attended it, conveyed his impressions to Gokhale. He wrote, "the younger was not satisfied with the working of the Congress and there was the hankering for something new—although nobody could say what it was that was wanted".

Sir Ramesh Chandra Dutt was one of those earnest enough to set the house of the Congress in order. On February 1903, he wrote to Gokhale, "You have pointed out to me a new path of usefulness and fired in me a new ambition. And the last years of my life shall not be lived in vain if I succeed in organizing our work in India and leading all the patriotic aspirations. Let us suppose the next Congress creates an Executive Committee consisting of Mehta, Charlu and myself for organizing and conducting Congress work in India. I was even thinking adding the names of Malviya of Northern India and Mudholkar of C.P. and Berar to make a Committee of five members; a central place of a permanent office (Bombay, Amraoti and Allahabad). I will in the course of three winter months visit all the provinces, create 50 affiliated Congress Associations, frame rules for them, explain their work to them—and inspire in them a new life. More than this we will train these Associations to work along the same channel. We will focus all the forces of the country in the same centre, and we will work and speak on every question with a united voice of a nation. We will create a moral power which the administration will soon enlist in the cause of good government".[23]

Dutt in another letter to Gokhale on November 12, 1903, suggested that Pherozeshah and Dutt himself should work jointly as Executive Committee, which would work throughout the year. He was confident that Mehta and he himself would work closely and the decisions would be joint ones. He suggested that Gokhale should be the paid Secretary. Though Dutt had written all this with good intentions and with a view to galvanize the Congress into a live force, it was far from reality. First, his belief that he would be able to work with Pherozeshah and take joint decisions was a daydream. Pherozeshah would not have allowed Dutt to be his associate on equal footing. Second, Wacha, without naming Pherozeshah, had already complained to Dadabhai that leaders like Mehta were not giving enough time for Congress. Dutt also wanted to create a moral force. But the new generation of Congressmen and especially the atmosphere created by the partition of Bengal had challenged the moral authority of the old leaders like Mehta.

Congress leaders had to face the test of this changed mood of the congressmen at the Benares session. When a resolution welcoming the Prince of Wales, later George the fifth, came before the session, Lala Lajpat Rai moved that it was unnecessary and unwarranted. He was supported by Tilak. Lajpat Rai said that the country had recently gone through the ravages of famine, and because of the partition of Bengal and general repressive policy of Lord Curzon, there was dissatisfaction all round. Sensing this the bureaucracy had planned this visit of the Prince. Old leaders of the Congress naturally disliked this amendment by Lajpat Rai, while many Congressmen from Bengal, Punjab and Maharashtra supported it. Lajpat Rai writes, "At last the resolution (welcoming the Prince) was carried by a majority, but we announced immediately that we would oppose it again in the general meeting of the National Congress. This enraged the old leaders, and the UP leaders were frightened. Information was sent the same night to the Commissioner, the Officer Commanding and the Police Superintendent of Benares. Next morning Munshi Madho Lal of Benares brought the Deputy Commissioner to the pandal. They had begun to fear that there might be some rioting, and were making preparations accordingly. We were dubbed as sedition-monger and 'badmashes'. The whole of that night and the next morning this situation remained the topic of discussion. Threats were held out to us in the morning. Some said we were bringing the province into disgrace, others feared that the Congress would be dead. So on and so forth. But our resolve remained unaffected. At last Gokhale arrived, but instead of going to the Congress pandal, he began to persuade me. When he found me inexorable, he made a personal appeal to me and asked me to waive opposition for his sake. To this I agreed and gave him a promise that we would abstain from attending the sitting whilst this resolution was being dealt with, so that we might not have to oppose it; the understanding was that in the record it would not be said that the resolution was accepted unanimously. I got Tilak to agree to this understanding."[24]

Later, Srinivas Sastri in his lectures on Pherozeshah Mehta narrated how Gokhale tried his level best to persuade Pherozeshah to attend the Benares session of the Congress, but Mehta, did not relent. Sastri also said that the speech delivered by Lajpat Rai in the Subjects Committee of the Congress was "impetuous and the strongest." Both Gokhale and V. Krishnaswami Iyer took fright. C.V. Munnuswami was a Congress reporter at the time. Krishnaswai Iyer told him to omit all those passages from Lajpat Rai's speech. Gokhale also repeated this appeal. They might have thought that by this they would succeed in shutting out the speech from the government. But as Sastri said, there were many CID men and informants present in the session.

Thus when Dutt was thinking of regeneration of the Congress organization, seeds of discord were sown not only in the Benares Congress, but even before. Benares Congress signalled that the storm would break out any day. That day came after two years and the Congress was split.

REFERENCES

1. V.S. Srinivas Sastri, *My Master Gokhale*, Model Publications, Madras, 1946, pp. 246-247.
2. Sir Bipin Krishna Bose, *Stray Thoughts of Some Incidents in My Life,* G.A. Natesan and Co., Madras, 1923, p. 192.
3. D.A. Washbrook, *The Emergence of Provincial Politics: the Madras Presidency 1870-1920*, CUP, Cambridge, 1976, pp. 29-31.
4. Wilfrid Blunt, *My Diaries*, Single Volume Edition, Markin Secker, London, 1932, p. 676.
5. C.J. O'Donnell, *The Failure of Lord Curzon: a Study in Imperialism,* Shree Publishing House, Delhi, 1982, pp. 17-18.
6. Nash Vaughan, *The Great Famines and its causes*, Longmans, NY, 1900, pp. 5-10.
7. V.S. Srinivas Sastri, *My Master Gokhale*, Model Publications, Madras, 1946, pp. 248-249.
8. R.P. Patwardhan *Dadabhai Naoroji Correspondence*, Vol. 2, Part 2, Allied Publishers, Bombay, 1977, pp. 789-790, 825-826.
9. John R. McLane, *Indian Nationalism and Early Congress*, Princeton Uni. Press, Princeton, 1977, p. 174.
10. Lokmanya Tilak, *Samagra Lokmanya Tilak*, Vol. 7, Kesari Prakashan, Pune, 1969, pp. 676-677.
11. Pal Bipin Chandra, *Memories of My Life and Times,* Bipin Chandra Pal Institute, Calcutta, 1973, pp. 435-438.
12. V.S. Srinivas Sastri, *The Life and Times of Pherozeshah Mehta*, Bharatiya Vidya Bhavan, Bombay 1975, pp. 100-101.
13. Gokhale Papers.
14. B.R. Nanda. *Gokhale, the Indian Moderates and the British Raj,* OUP, Delhi, 1977, pp.138-139.
15. Gokhale Papers.
16. V.S. Srinivas Sastri, *My Master Gokhale*, Model Publications, Madras, 1946, p. 225.
17. *Gokhale Papers.*
18. William Wedderburn, *Allan Octavian Hume*, Pegasus, New Delhi, 1974, p. 99.
19. Dadabhai Papers.
20. The Earl of Midleton, *Records and Reactions, 1856-1939*, John Murray, London, 1939, p. 198.

21. Blanche E.C. Dugdale, *Arthur James Balfour: First Earl of Balfour, 2 Vols.* G.P. Putnams' Sons, NY, 1937, p 300.
22. David Dilks, *Curzon in India, Vol. 2*. Taplinger Publishing Co., NY., 1969, pp. 129-130.
23. B.R. Nanda, *Gokhale, the Indian Moderates and the British Raj,* OUP, Delhi, 1977, pp 164-165.
24. Vijay Chandra Joshi (Ed.), *Lala Lajpat Rai, Autobiographical Writings,* Uni. Publishers, New Delhi, 1965, pp 110-111.

Chapter Eleven

PARTITION OF BENGAL

After the Benares session of the Congress, the Prince of Wales met Gokhale. Harold Nicolson who accompanied the Prince had noted the following conversation between the Prince and Gokhale. "I have", the Prince said to him (Gokhale), "been reading your speech at Benares, in which you said it would be better for India if the Indians had a much larger part in the administration. I have now been travelling for some months in India, seeing vast crowds of Indians in many parts of the continent, and I have never seen a happier-looking people, and I understand the look in the eyes of the Indians. Would the people of India be happier if you ran the country?" Gokhale replied: "no sir, I do not say they would be happier, but they would have more self-respect." "That may be," the Prince answered, "but I cannot see how there can be real self-respect while the Indians treat their women as they do now". "Yes," said Gokhale, "that is a great blot."[1] Nicolson himself was skeptical about the assertion by the Prince that he saw happiness in the eyes of the Indian masses. He wondered as to when the Prince got the time to look into the eyes of the masses when he was all the time surrounded by officials. Out of politeness, Gokhale did not ask his royal guest that question. However, the Prince had written to his father that the feeling in India was strong against the government because of the partition of Bengal. If he knew that there was a strong feeling against the government, how could the people be happy, as claimed by him?

In the Congress session Surendranath Banerjea voiced discontent generated by the partition of Bengal. Gokhale, in his presidential address, had condemned the partition scheme. There was no dispute that Bengal was then an unwieldy province, as Assam, Orissa and Bihar were also part of it, and it was difficult to manage. In the Eastern part of Bengal and Assam there were very few police, which gave free hand to the decoits and other anti-social elements. Way back in 1866 when famine was raging in Bengal, an official, Sir Stafford Northcote, suggested that Bihar and Orissa should be separated from Bengal. In 1891, in a meeting to consider the problems of security of the Eastern India, Bengal, Orissa, Burma, Bihar and Assam, it was suggested that Bihar, Orissa etc. should be separate provinces so that Bengal would be better governed. Commissioner of Assam, Sir William Ward, proposed in 1896, that Lusahi area as well as Chittgaong and Mymensingh should be incorporated in Assam. But this was opposed by Hindus and had the support of the planters as well as the Muslims in that area. Ward was succeeded by Sir Henry Cotton who thought the scheme suggested by Ward was impractical. W.B. Oldham who was the Commissioner of the Chittgaong area, thought the Eastern parts of Bengal, which were mostly Muslim populated, should be separated from Bengal, which according to him would be politically more viable. After assuming the office of the lieutenant-Governor he revived the scheme, which was proposed by Ward.

Lord Curzon accepted the proposal of partition of Bengal in 1903. Herbert Risley, who was the secretary to the Government of India, wrote a letter to the government of Bengal on December 3, 1903. In this detailed letter Risley traced the history of the partition scheme and also emphasised the need for partition. One of the reasons given by Risley was the increase in the population and trade. He said, the scheme was necessary for administrative efficiency. He noted that the scheme envisaged the separate state of the Udia-speaking areas in Orissa province; Dacca and Mymensingh to be incorporated in Assam; and Chota Nagpur in the Central Province. The Bengalis, including landlords and Maharajas, vehemently opposed this scheme. Numerous memorandas were sent to the government against the scheme. Curzon pushed hard. It seemed that the government had finally decided on a partition scheme, which was officially announced on July 7, 1905. Chittgaong, Dacca, Rajshai and Malda were to be given to Assam, and Dacca was to be the capital of the new province of Assam. The government claimed that this would make Assam viable and self-sufficient. The demographic division of the province was to have eighteen million Muslims and twelve million Hindus. But Lieutenant Governor Sir Andrew Fraser revealed the real motive of the government. He said that East Bengal dominated the politics of Bengal, while the Biharis were relegated to the background. He thought partition of Bengal would diminish this dominance.

'The Statesman' of July 21, 1905 came out with a strong criticism of the partition plan. It said: "Our objections and we believe the objections of all reasonable opponents of the scheme (partition of Bengal) are directed against the way in which the scheme has been formulated and put through, and against the objects of the Government which do not get stated, in speeches and resolutions. These objects are briefly: first, to destroy the collective power of the Bengali people; secondly, to overthrow the political ascendancy of Calcutta; and thirdly, to foster in East Bengal the growth of a Mahomedan power which it is hoped, will have the effect of keeping in check the rapidly growing strength of the educated Hindu community. It may be thought if these are the real, though not the usually avowed objects of the present administration, the scheme of partition now proclaimed has been devised with uncommon cleverness and foresight". The government resolution asserted that when the partition scheme was implemented and new province fully developed, it would evoke the loyalty of the people. 'The Statesman', however, cautioned the government that there was a possibility of its hope being belied.

Fraser did not think that Lord Curzon had any evil design in sponsoring the partition scheme. He cites some official notes published by 'The Statesman', which revealed that the officials were probing the problem for some years and did not have any set ideas. Fraser then refers to a note by Lord Curzon in which he wrote: "It seems to me most extraordinary thing that this discussion should have been going on for more than a year without any mention of the matter ever being made to the head of the Government. Had not Mr. Fraser casually alluded to it, when he was staying with me last summer, and in private correspondence, I should have had no inkling that the subject had ever being mooted. And yet during this period secretaries and deputy secretaries have been carving about and rearranging provinces on paper, colouring and recolouring the map of India accordingly. And now at the close, I am invited to give my assent to a document, without the smallest previous reference to me, or attempt to ascertain my opinion".[2] But Curzon had no hesitation in accepting the scheme which was suggested. He even undertook a tour of East Bengal and in his speeches appealed the Muslims to support the scheme, which would restore the lost glory of Dacca, and Muslims would regain their power and importance. He emphasised that the partition was beneficial to Muslims.

R.C. Majumdar has published some of the notes by Curzon revealing his political intentions. Sir Andrew Fraser in his note had stated that the partition would reduce the power of the Hindus from Bengal. Curzon did not approve of this argument as he was more concerned about the political fall out after its revelation. Curzon in his minute on November 10, 1903 said, "I regret to say that in my view, if the letter to Bengal were published in its present form, it would create absolute consternation. When I wrote my minute for the confidential information of my colleagues, it never occurred to me for a moment that its content could be or would be practically reproduced to be dissected by every newspaper scribe. Neither do I propose to send a copy of my minute home. It will be sufficient if I send a copy privately to the Secretary of State to explain the inner meaning of that which it has not been found altogether advisable to say in the letter to Bengal". Another dispatch did not mince words when it referred to apprehension that the partition of Bengal would weaken the power of Bengalis and said, "Their apprehensions are perfectly correct and they form one of the merits of the great scheme. It is not altogether easy to reply in a dispatch which is sure to be published without disclosing the fact that in this scheme, as in the amalgamation of Berar to the Central Provinces, one of our main objects is to split up and thereby weaken a solid body of opponents to our rule".

Curzon wrote to Secretary of State Brodrick on February 17, 1904 saying: "The Bengalis, who like to think themselves a nation, and who dream of a future, when the English will have been turned out, and a Bengali Babu will be installed in Government House, Calcutta, of course, bitterly resent any disruption that will be likely to interfere with the realization of this dream. If we are weak enough to yield to their clamour now, we shall not be able to dismember or reduce Bengal again; and you will be cementing and solidifying, on the eastern flank of India, a force almost formidable, and certain to be a source of increasing trouble in the future". Curzon had similar apprehensions about the Marathas. On March 6, 1903, he wrote, "I cannot contemplate any proposal which would add strength or solidarity of the Maratha community with anything but dismay". Fraser endorsing this view said, "That the transfer of Berar to Bombay would mean tremendous political blunder of consolidating the whole Maratha community of India under the influence and guidance of Poona".[3] Fraser disclosed the political motives behind the partition scheme. Lord Curzon then wrote on 24 July, 1904: "In face of the chief offender, you seem to have got off very lightly about partition. But had the whole correspondence been published, which the Secretary of State actually proposed to do—I expect you would have been crucified at my side".[4]

Herbert Risley played a crucial role in bringing the partition scheme and pushing it to the logical conclusion. Under Curzon he was the home secretary. As a Census Commissioner he had an opportunity to study the caste system in whole of the country and made use of this study by writing a book, which was commended by many. He firmly believed that the English were the trustees of India and so he wanted to move slowly in matters of political rights and reforms. Like many of his countrymen, Risley thought very little about the political demands of the educated Indians, who to him did not represent the interests of the vast masses of India. It was, therefore, natural for him to play a vital role in designing the partition scheme.

In the British Parliament, C.J. O'Donnell, criticising the partition of Bengal, charged that it was prepared in secrecy by Lord Curzon, and the Secretary of State approved it in secrecy, bypassing the Parliament. Moving an adjournment, Herbert Roberts alluded to the suggestion made by Henry Cotton, in 1903, to appoint a governor for Bengal instead of a lieutenant governor, assisted by a Legislative Council. Bhownaggree supported the partition of Bengal. He said that the scheme was prepared by Curzon with great deal of thought and for administrative convenience. He also defended it as a measure of decentralization. Curzon ignored the storm of protest, which the partition generated, not only in Bengal, but in India. This time he conveniently forgot what he had written to

Sir Arthur Goodley, permanent under secretary to the Advisory Council of the Secretary of State, on January 27, 1904. Curzon had told him that it was unwise to suppose that there was no public opinion or it was not developed in India. To think so would be to ignore the transformation for which he claimed he had laboured. He also reminded Goodley that India would progress and one day would be an equal partner in the British Empire. Strangely, he refused to heed to the popular opinion against the partition.

In England, Tories were defeated in the elections and the Liberal Party had come to power. But before giving up the reins, Tory government had appointed Lord Minto to replace Lord Curzon as viceroy. Minto after assuming the reins of office found that the public opinion was against the partition of Bengal. When the British government put its imprimatur on the partition scheme in May 1905, a massive movement to collect signatures started all over Bengal. By July, seventy thousand signatures were collected from East Bengal. Between December 1903 and October 1905 two thousand protest meetings were held. In a meeting in Calcutta it was resolved to boycott the British goods as long as the partition was not annulled. The resolution said, "That this meeting fully sympathizes with the resolutions adopted at many meetings held in mofussil to abstain from the purchase of British manufactures so long as the Partition Resolution is not withdrawn and as a protest against the indifference of the British public in regard to Indian affairs and consequent disregard of Indian public opinion by the present Government". Surendranath Banerjea gave much importance to the wording of the resolution. He said that the boycott was a temporary measure and was to be called off as soon as the partition was annulled or modified.[5] Leaders of Bengal were facing a dilemma as they thought that it was dichotomy to appeal to the British Parliament against partition and at the same time boycott the British goods. Hence the resolution was so worded as to make the boycott temporary. However, opinion in the Congress was divided, which became evident in the Benares session. It could be seen from the diary of B.G. Khaparde that when he moved a resolution about swadeshi, not only the delegates from Madras opposed it, but even those from Bengal stood by the Madras delegates. Opposition from Bengal to the swadeshi was unexpected according to Khaparde. He later succeeded in persuading the delegates from Bengal to change their position.

Partition had also unleashed suppressed emotions of the youths of Bengal, some of whom turned to revolutionary activities. Government used aggressive measures to put them down. 'Sudharak', whose English section was edited by Gokhale for a couple of years, was taken over by the Servants of India Society. In its May 11, 1905 issue, it dealt with the happenings in Bengal. It said that the people of Bengal were agitated because of the partition. It would be wrong to assume, as the Secretary of State had done, that the agitation was a temporary phase, which would soon die down. The Secretary of State's statement had angered the people and the agitation had become much more intense and widespread. If no steps were taken to assuage the feelings of the people, then many untoward incidents might occur. Those young people who had come into limelight by their irrational activities were the victims of the present situation and deserved sympathy. Others were also to be blamed for the present situation, and the government could not be absolved of any blame. It was not just newspapers owned by the Indians that lent support to the agitation and were critical of partition; some newspapers owned by Anglo-Indians also were critical. 'The Daily News', in England, called for review of the partition scheme and to postpone its implementation. But the government was least inclined to do so. On January 12, 1906, the Indian Association sent a memorandum to Lord Minto against partition, which was turned down. He declared that nobody should think that the partition would be revoked. He clarified that he was an administrator whose duty was to implement the government policy. He pointed out that there were many who could not agree with the arguments advanced against partition. Lord Minto said that though he was not against swadeshi, he had objection to the use of the word in a wrong way. Minto's reply angered people. Many in India had hoped that as Morley was appointed as Secretary of State he would respect the feelings against partition. They were admirers of his biography of Gladstone and his book *On Compromise,* which they thought was a testament of liberalism. In fact, there was no cause for such hopes. When he was editing 'Pall Mall Gazette' in 1880, he had published an anonymous article in June of that year, which said that "Bengalis have the skill to get through examinations and dreamt that they could govern India. They also thought that India would have a parliament, which they would dominate by their eloquence. But it would be a gross mistake to grant such demand". The same article made it clear that though Tories and the Liberals differed on many subjects, their views about the internal situation in India were almost identical. 'The Times of India' reproducing this extract advised Lal Mohan Ghose who was then addressing meetings in England, that he should take note of this article published in a daily, which was edited by a Liberal leader (Morley) from whom Indians had high expectations. Morley had no special sympathy for or knowledge of India. Besides, he was averse to introduce any sudden or fundamental changes.

Gokhale was one of those who had hoped that Morley would undertake political reforms and give justice to Bengal. The British Committee and also a committee of Parliamentarians sympathetic to India urged Gokhale to visit England, as Liberals had come to power. Gokhale then went to England in April 1905. He stayed there till October and was fully engaged in giving speeches and interviews and meeting people who mattered. He addressed meetings in London, Cambridge, Liverpool etc. Most of his letters to his colleague in the Servants of India Society, Mr. Dravid, give the idea of Gokhale's preoccupation, without any consideration for his health, which was delicate. One of his letters described how in a Cambridge meeting a retiree from the Government of India's service made a critical speech and how he (Gokhale) politely but firmly countered disagreement. Gokhale also participated in a peace meeting and jointly addressed a meeting arranged by Mohammedan Association.

But Gokhale's most important engagement was with Morley. After his first meeting with Morley on May 10, 1905, Gokhale wrote to Dravid, that his meeting with Morley was 'cordial and satisfactory'. He, then, said, "I may tell for your own information that I made a passionate appeal to Mr. Morley, yesterday, to realize the great responsibility of his teachings in his present office, and he was much moved, and he spoke very freely of his difficulties and his intentions. You will be able to judge how cordial and satisfactory the interview was from the fact that when I expressed the hope before parting that if Bengal affairs took most of my time at the next interview, and I was not able to lay before Mr. Morley the proposals of reform that I have come here to press on his attention, he would give me the third chance of seeing him, he said, it is not a question, Mr. Gokhale, of how many interviews, I would grant you, but how many you would give me. And if you are equal to ten interviews I would like to have all ten of them". Gokhale had discussions with Morley on Bengal affairs. On June 8, he wrote to Dravid, "I may tell you privately that Mr. Morley has discussed very fully Mr. B. Fuller's doings with me and I have pressed my views of the situation with all the force I could command. Of course, this is a confidential matter".

Gokhale's July 6 letter was much more detailed. He said, "I expect Mr. Morley to make a statement about East Bengal affairs and I shall be really disappointed if Fuller's transfer from that province is not announced. Such an announcement has been virtually promised to me and was to have been made on Tuesday last, but the India office people seem to have again prevailed so far as to secure postponement of the announcement. I had so far five interviews with Mr. Morley and three with Under-Secretary. I told Mr. Morley that as his position was most difficult between two sets of conflicting representations, the best way out of the difficulty was to appoint a Royal Commission consisting, say, of seven men, to go out to India to inquire whether present association of the people with the administration of their own affairs was adequate, considering the spread of education within the country, and if not, what measures might be adopted to make it adequate. There should be two Anglo-Indian officials on this Commission, two men from our side, (one of them should be Sir William Wedderburn and other an Indian) and three independent English politicians (one being himself and the other two good liberals, to give the Commission a slightly predominant liberal character, as it was the Liberal government that would be appointing him). The proposal has been very formally received by Mr. Morley and he is considering it at present. He wants to make an announcement on this subject on 20 July. If he does that, and if he moves Fuller and Emerson from their present positions before this, and if he appoints Mr. Dutt to his Council at an early date, public feeling in India will, I think, be conciliated to some extent. While Commission is holding an inquiry, Mr. Morley will have time to study different questions, for himself. The Commission will give him two things that he wants at the present moment—time and a definite lead". In another letter on July 13 Gokhale told Dravid, "The present difficulty of Mr. Morley is that he is surrounded by men who are antagonistic to Indian aspirations. And he, therefore, finds it difficult to face what is naturally regarded as expert advice. Moreover, he has not yet time to look into Indian question for himself, and our countrymen meanwhile are being impatient".

Morley did not make any statement, which would have satisfied the Indians. However, Gokhale was optimistic. Before his departure from London to India, he wrote to Dravid on 27 July, "I am on the whole not dissatisfied. Only those who have any knowledge of the tremendous difficulties under which Mr. Morley had to make up his mind as to what he would say or do can realize adequately the significance of that part of his speech, which deals with the immediate future. His presentation of the economic situation need not perturb us, because he was speaking to his official brief. So too his deprecation of our aspiration to attain one day the position of a self-governing colony is of academic interest as that question does not arise in connection with the immediate future, in regard to which alone Mr. Morley is all powerful and about which he has on the whole, announced a liberal policy. A further reform of the Legislative Councils has been definitely promised. The Queen's Proclamation has been reinstated and we may soon expect definite action to be taken under it. The salt tax is now doomed; military expenditure will be kept under control, if not at once reduced. In addition to these I happen to know that expenditure on elementary education is to be substantially increased and judicial and executive functions will soon be separated. I think Mr. Dutt's appointment to the India Council will soon come, so also the removal of B. Fuller to another province".

Gokhale had his last meeting with Morley and he said he was satisfied to the highest degree. Gokhale in his letter to Dravid on August 3, said, "Mr. Morley spoke without reserve and spoke with much feeling and he indicated to me what he proposes to do during the next few months. I can tell you that we never had so true a friend of our aspirations in a responsible position since Lord Ripon's days. Every fresh day he spends at India Office, our cause gains and the official side loses and if only our countrymen will have a little more patience, for say six months more, they will have no cause to regret their confidence in the present Secretary of State. And now I want you to do what you can to prevent unnecessary criticism of Mr. Morley in the Press". Gokhale wanted the Indian leaders and press to remember constantly that if they wanted to criticize some of Morley's announcements, they should do so with an understanding that Morley was a friend of India. Gokhale was pleased that the Madras newspapers were not harsh about Morley. Morley himself had urged Gokhale to ask his countrymen to show some patience to him.[6]

Morley's speech, which Gokhale feared would not be liked by Indians, was delivered in the House of Commons on July 4, 1905. He made some conciliatory remarks at the outset, but warned the Commons that he did not mean to bring in the British parliamentary system to India. That would be a dream and a farcical one. Such a system would not be in the interest of India. The English should not impose their institutions on any country without ascertaining whether its tradition was conducive to their growth. It would not be possible to plant English Oak trees in India; but it was possible to follow the principles of English constitution. Not only adult franchise could not be introduced in India but she could not also be elevated to the level of Canada. Some members of the Commons disapproved Morley's speech, which they thought was not strong enough. Henicker Hutton was one of them who said the opinion in Bengal should not be taken as that of the whole country. He reminded the House that there were many castes and races who were against the Bengalis. The question, according to him, was whether the government should give importance to pen-pushers or to the marshal races. India was not a nation and if an elective principle were to be adopted, then that government would be of some classes and not of the people. Hutton referring to speeches made by Gokhale and Ramesh Chandra Dutt said, that though they might be moderate, the speeches made in India by others were more significant than of these two. He objected to those who after retiring from the government service in India were 'instigating' Indians and supporting the movements against the administration.

While Gokhale was in London, Fuller had resigned as the lieutenant governor of Bengal and his resignation was accepted. Fuller had punished a school at Shirajganj in the Pabna district of Bengal, which Lord Minto did not approve. He was asked to withdraw his order, which Fuller refused. Lord Minto then asked him to resign. Speeches and actions of Fuller had already embarrassed the government. He blatantly displayed his partiality to the Muslims and publicly said that the Muslims were like the most favourite wife. At Barisal, a meeting, which was to be held under the presidentship of Surendranath Banerjea to protest against partition, was banned by Fuller; and Banerjea and some other leaders were arrested. Both Morley and Minto disapproved of this action and Morley informed Minto that it would be extremely difficult for him to justify this action in the Parliament. Though Morley was dissatisfied with Fuller, he was thinking of transferring him to some other province. Morley's exasperation with Fuller could be seen from one of his letters to Minto. He wrote, "If the agitation subsides, so be it. If not, I must say frankly that it will be impossible for me to carry both partition and Fuller on my back".[7]

Fuller had his supporters in the viceroy's Executive Council. One was Denzil Ibbetson who told Lord Minto that it would be a political madness to throw out Fuller without giving him any opportunity to defend himself. If Morley had any complaints against Fuller, he should convey them to the Government of India and Fuller be asked to reply. Ibbetson felt that if this course was not followed, then it would be construed that the Bengal agitators and not the Government of India were ruling the country. But Fuller was so impetuous that he did not wait for his friends and supporters to bring about some amicable settlement. When Minto asked him to rescind the punishment order served on a school in the Pabna district, he sent in his resignation. At Barisal, police officer Kemp and magistrate Emerson cast aside all caution. Emerson, going against the law, sentenced Surendranath. It then became difficult for Morley to defend Fuller in the House of Commons. Returning to England, Fuller continued with his antics. He made several speeches and wrote articles sometimes contradicting himself. In one of his speeches he criticized Partition scheme and then declared that Muslims could not rely on the fairness of the Government of India.

Lord Minto, after studying reports about the Congress politics, wrote three letters to Morley between April 3 and May 9, 1905. He wrote, "I think myself it is a mistake to ignore the existence of the Congress. The section of the population which it represents will never, I am convinced, possess the grit to play a leading part in the Government of India as a whole, but it does represent Indian advanced thought on many subjects which must affect the future administration of this country, and it will be a greatest mistake to attempt to set the Congress aside and to refuse to have anything to do with it as a factor in the present history of India". Minto also wrote that if Congress selected good representatives, he had no objection meeting such a delegation. He thought, Gokhale represented the best elements in the Congress and was confident that it was worthwhile to keep in touch with Surendranath and Moti Lal Ghose. But Minto said that Congress had many bad elements and general tone of the Indian press was becoming increasingly seditious. Minto said Gokhale might not agree with the inflammatory material circulated by the Congress, but he was playing with fire. The viceroy was opposed to introducing representative government in India as he thought that many marshal races would not tolerate the Bengali dominance. Minto was prepared to appoint Gokhale to his Advisory Council and nobody else. He thought, as the English constitution was evolved over some centuries, Bengalis should not venture to emulate it. Morley in his reply generally agreed with the Viceroy. He thought that it was advisable to understand the ideas of the Congress leaders. Morley supported the idea of meeting a Congress delegation, but he told the viceroy to be cautious and to go slow. Morley referred to Duke of Connaught who believed that Congress was rapidly turning into an evil force. But Morley believed that whether Congress would be an evil force or not would depend entirely on the English.

Minto was also thinking of creating a council of the Princes and landlords as a counterfoil to the Congress. This Council was to meet for a week in a year with a carefully chosen agenda. But Morley was not very enthusiastic about this proposal and raised many queries. Minto, analyzing the causes of discontent in India, concluded that one of them was the treatment meted out to the Indians by the Englishmen and women. At first the viceroy did not admit that it was the racist attitude of the English, which had created such resentment and animosity. But eventually he realized that the racial superiority displayed by the English had its reaction. Minto himself one day was shocked to see the usual Sikh security guards posted in the Viceregal House removed on the day of a ball. When Minto made inquires, he came to know that the change was made temporarily, as those Englishmen and especially English women who would attend the ball, would not like the Indians to be around.

Immediate problem before Lord Minto was of the agitation against the partition of Bengal. As the government did not budge from its resolve to go ahead with the partition plan, boycott of the British goods was announced which gained momentum. When Gokhale was in England he had to deal with this movement, especially in meetings in the cotton-mill areas like Manchester. Addressing a meeting in Manchester, Gokhale admitted that the boycott movement would affect the cotton-mills in England, but asked what else the Bengalis could do? Numerous petitions were sent to the government and hundreds of protest meetings held but the government refused to change its policy. So the Bengalis decided to attack the vital interests of the government. Gokhale appealed to the Manchester workers that they should not be angry with the Indians, but with those officials of the Government of India who had brought this partition. In his presidential address to the Benares session of the Congress, in December 1905, Gokhale had appealed to strive hard for establishing industries in India. Lokmanya Tilak in an editorial had enumerated which industries could be started without much capital expenditure. Bombay's cotton industry benefited by the swadeshi movement, but Bombay leaders like Pherozeshah were not the supporters of the swadeshi movement. They even saw to it that the movement did not spread to the other provinces. On the other hand, Bengal where the boycott movement had taken roots, did not see any significant industrial growth.

Outside Bengal, Lokmanya Tilak was a strong supporter of swadeshi. Arvindbabu Ghose in various articles not only supported the agitation against partition, but also denounced the Western education and civilization all together. Surendranath Banerjea had said that the idea of boycott was in the public mind for some time. "It first found expression at a public meeting in the district of

Pabna, and it was repeated at public meetings held in other mofussil towns. And the successful boycott of American goods by the Chinese was proclaimed throughout Asia and reproduced in the Indian newspapers".[8] Swadeshi spirit was aboard. Thus in 1906 when a session of the Industrial Conference was held in Calcutta, Maharaja of Baroda, Sayajirao Gaikwad, in his inaugural speech supported swadeshi. He said that steam power had made revolutionary changes the world over. At the same time powerlooms were taking the place of handlooms and in the course of a decade the number of weavers in the mills had to be reduced by twenty-three per cent. As electricity was used for jining operations, eighty-six per cent of the workers had lost their jobs. However, the cotton mills had made rapid strides in the country. Forty years earlier there were 13 cotton mills, but by 1904 this number had gone up to 203. Bombay mills were providing employment to hundred and seventy thousand workers and jining factories to another thirty thousand. In 1904 the number of powerlooms were forty-seven thousand. Sayajirao also said that because of the swadeshi spirit, some new cotton mills had come up in Bombay as well as in Ahmedabad. The state of Baroda was running one mill for two decades, but it was soon to be privatized. He said that India should produce fine cloth and also go in for iron and steel production. Compared to England, India was producing very little coal and had to increase the production.

Achievements of the Swadeshi movement are noted by Sumit Sarkar. He says, "Country cloth, admittedly more lasting than imported piecegoods, was still more than twice as expensive, and there was also a factor of middlemen-cum, moneylenders domination—quite 75 per cent of the weavers are dependent on mahajans and their earnings averaged less than Rs.8 a month". G.N. Gupta found little or no marked improvement in the material conditions of the weavers. It is interesting and significant that Swadeshi made no attempt at all to break this stranglehold on the artisans—we never hear of efforts to organize artisans cooperatives, for instance".[9] The boycott movement had effect on mainly cloth trade. 'The Statesman' published a report that between September 1904 and September 1905, in the eight districts outside Calcutta, British cloth had come down from rupees seventy-seven thousand to nine thousand. R.C. Majumdar cites some official reports. According to him the collector of Customs had calculated on September 1906 that within a year, "The boycott has been chiefly directed against salt, cotton, piecegoods and possibly yarn, boots, shoes and cigarettes. The annexed statement shows a decrease in the import of foreign salt by 1,40,000 *maunds* and an increase in the Indian (Aden) salt from 48 to 77 thousand *maunds.* The imported cotton piecegoods decreased by three crores of yards and the value of imported cotton twists and yarn fell by nearly a crore of rupees. The import of foreign shoes fell by 75 per cent and cigarettes by nearly 50 per cent. One of the European firms in Bengal cabled as follows to England,

'Boycott results are disastrous. Boots are not saleable; the busy season is closed; hosiery, hats and waist-bangles are also affected. A distinction is being made between English and continental goods. Japanese imports are doing very well at low prices. One firm has marked their English goods 'Made in Germany'; and succeeded in selling them".[10]

However, the success could not be said as spectacular. Sumit Sarkar says, "The famous telegram of September 1, 1905, from the Marwari Chamber of Commerce in Calcutta to Manchester Chamber calling for the withdrawal of the partition, "as otherwise, we shall be ruined and shall not be able to make future contracts", and the spectacular drop in 'Laxmi' or lucky day contracts (the auspicious day in the pujas on which business agreements for the coming year were customarily signed) from 32000 packages in 1904 to only 2500 in 1905, were thus not due to patriotic motives alone. Once the trade dispute had blown over, the Marwari traders began renewing their bideshi contracts, and on May 21, 1906, the 'Bengalee' denounced them as the greatest enemies of the Swadeshi movement. The Bengal nationalists attempted to woo the Marwaris through the Maharashtrian leaders, Tilak and Khaparde, but despite the latter's complacent diary entry, compradore ties proved stronger than patriotism".[11] Though Sumit Sarkar did not find any marked improvement in the income of the weavers, 'The Manchester Guardian' representative, Henry Nevinson, had other views. "It (swadeshi movement) spread like a gospel through both provinces of Bengal. Within a few months the reports of our Commissioners were full of it: 'The Swadeshi movement has contributed largely to the development of cotton cloth industry in all districts of this division' writes the Commissioner of Burdwan in Western Bengal, 'except Bankura where the inclination of the people to use country-made things is not pronounced and consequently the sale of the Manchester goods has not much decreased". In the Indian Trade Journal (July 1907) published by the government, the magistrate of Hoogly is quoted as saying, "It appears that while formally the weaver had to make advances from the middlemen, they are now very much better off, and, if anything, the middlemen are sometimes indebted to them. There cannot be any doubt that on account of the Swadeshi movement, the weavers as a class, who are a stay-at-home people, have distinctly advanced. Fly-shuttle looms are being largely used, and the people are said to appreciate them". In the report on the Land Revenue Administration of the Lower Provinces (1906-7), we read: "It is reported that on account of the demand for country-made cloth, weavers working with fly-shuttle can make as much as Rs. 20, a month (about double the average earnings of the class) and that the demand for their services is daily increasing—some prospect of improvement in their material condition is held out by the present Swadeshi movement, in as far as it may induce the younger generation to devote themselves to a technical rather than a literary profession".[12]

Among the British officials Lord Minto had by and large taken a near realistic view. He wrote to Morley, on December 1, 1905, "There is no doubt that the agitation has been unscrupulously fostered, and that influence has been brought to bear on the student class and the Universities to join in the movement. But at the same time I cannot but think that there is much more genuine feeling in the movement than the official mind is prepared to admit. It would be perhaps unfair for me to express myself too strongly as to a piece of legislation, the necessity of which it would only be possible thoroughly to understand after a detailed analysis of many considerations and an intimate knowledge of local feeling, but I cannot help suspecting that local feeling has been treated with some want of sympathy in aiming at what in the official mind is considered necessary for administrative machinery. The population of Bengal has no doubt bitterly resented the action which has taken so large a slice from the province". Lord Minto was more forthcoming in his letter to Morley on December 20. He criticized Lord Curzon for his provocative speeches about the partition of Bengal when he was the viceroy. Minto said that the partition scheme was hatched in secrecy without consulting those who ought to have been consulted. Morley had also realized the folly of the manner in which the scheme was implemented. Participating in the House of Commons debate he expressed his disapproval that the Indian people were not taken into confidence, but at the same time he said the scheme must be given some time.

After the arrests of Surendranath at Barisal some officials acted in such a way as to instigate communal riots. Gokhale came to know of the arrests and the communal riots when he was in London. He appraised Morley about the situation in Bengal and requested him to take adequate measures. Nevinson, who had visited some places in East Bengal, writes: "In Commila, Jamalpur, and a few other places, rather serious riots occurred. A few lives were lost, temples were desecrated, images broken, shops plundered and many Hindu widows carried off. Some of the towns were deserted, the Hindu population took refuge in any 'pukka' house (house with bricks or stone walls), women spent nights hidden in tanks, the crime known as 'group rape' increased, and throughout the country districts there reigned a general terror, which still prevailed at the time of my visit. Thus a new religious feud was established in Eastern Bengal, and when Mr. Morley said in the House of Commons that the disturbance was due to the refusal of Hindus to sell British goods to Mohammedans, it was grotesque instance of the power that officials have of misleading their Chief. I have almost invariably found English officers and officials on the side of the Mohammedans where there is rivalry of races or religion at all.—It was against the Hindus only that all the petty persecution of officialdom was directed. It was they who were excluded from Government posts; it was Hindu schools from which Government patronage was withdrawn. When Mohammedans rioted, the punitive police ransacked

Hindu houses, and companies of little Gurkhas were quartered on Hindu population. Priestly Mullahs went through the country preaching the revival of Islam and proclaiming to the villagers that the British Government was on the Mohammedan side, that the Law Courts had been specially suspended for three months, and no penalty would be exacted for violence done to Hindus or for the loot of Hindu shops, or the abduction of Hindu widows".[13]

Riots in 1907 were more serious. According to some Muslim historians, the riots were instigated by some Hindu landlords against the Mohammedan tenants. They also say that Mohammedan tenants who deposed against the Hindu landlords were the victims of their wrath. Alexander Lipski, a historian, refers to the allegations that Hindus were pressurizing the Muslims to take part in the anti-partition agitation and the Hindu moneylenders were refusing to lend money unless such support was promised. However, he holds British government mainly responsible for fostering division and feud between the two communities. He says, "An appreciation of the political motive behind the partition clarifies subsequent British behaviour and policy. There is no doubt that the effect of partition was a rise in communal tension. A close analysis of British comments upon Hindu-Muslim trouble indicates that this effect was not an accidental or unwanted product but rather that the purpose of official policy was to create an atmosphere of Hindu-Muslim rivalry". Some British rulers apprehended the possibility of the Muslims participation in the national struggle and so advocated the policy much favourable to the Muslims according to Lipski. He cites a letter by Minto to Morley, on August 22, 1906, which said that as long as the Muslim's agitation against the Fuller's dismissal did not go out of control, it would be useful to the Government.[14]

At this time the Nawab Salimullah, who was bankrupt, was rescued by the generous loan of one hundred thousand pounds by the government with considerably low rate of interest. Salimullah had eight sons and the family was divided. Salimullah's sons were supporters of the agitation against partition and in order to placate the Nawab, the government advanced this loan on easy terms. Morley found it difficult to justify this unusual display of generosity. This same Nawab took lead in establishing the Muslim league in 1906. The partition of Bengal served its purpose to alienate the Muslims from the mainstream politics and their leaders were keen to make the partition permanent. Partition had given feudal elements and the Mullahs an opportunity to reestablish their dominance over the Muslim masses. Those Muslims who opposed partition were eventually relegated to the background. Some Muslim advocates in the Calcutta High Court were against the partition but they could not provide leadership. It was Sir Antony MacDonnell, governor of UP, whose policies helped the efforts of the Muslims in organizing themselves. Sir Antony issued a circular replacing Urdu by Hindustani with Nagari script. He gave no patient hearing to the Muslim delegation, which urged to maintain the status quo. This shocked Muslims who were all the while confident that the British government was their true supporter. Students of Aligarh who for some time kept themselves aloof from politics, began to think that they had to give a lead to the Muslims. One of the graduates of Aligarh, Gulam Urs Saklen, through his weekly, appealed to the Muslims to have their own organization. He did not see any advantage to the Muslims in joining the Congress. Muslim representation in municipalities and local boards, abolition of the course in Persian in UP and the newly started controversy of Hindi versus Urdu, all these were grist to the propaganda machine of Saklen. He was opposed to the dominance of the landlords in the proposed organization of the Muslims. But meanwhile La Touche, who replaced MacDonnell as governor of UP, restored Urdu and rescinded the order of his predecessor. With this the enthusiasm of the landlord class for the new Muslim organization waned. But the partition of Bengal awakened the Muslims who felt that renewed efforts must be made to establish a political organization.

Aga Khan had claimed that he tried hard to persuade Pherozeshah Mehta and some Congress leaders to do something to bring in Muslims in the main political stream, but failed in his efforts. Pherozeshah and other Congress leaders were bound to fail even if they had tried, as the leaders of the Muslims and the Congress were working at cross-purposes. So Moshin-ul Mulk wrote to Theodore Archibald, the new principal of the Aligarh College, and asked his advice whether a memorandum could be submitted to the viceroy as he had received numerous letters from many parts of the country urging the necessity to establish a Muslim political organization. Mulk had said in his letter that Liberal government in England had created unrest among the Muslims and there was every danger that Muslim youths might join the Congress; and if that had to be avoided, Muslim organization must be established. Mulk believed that the future of India in the hands of Morley would not be bright. He deplored that the Muslims stood behind the Government but felt betrayed and asked whether they should follow the path of agitation like Congress to get their demands satisfied. Archibald sent the copies of the correspondence of Mulk to the Viceroy and the Secretary of State. After receiving a letter from Mulk, Sir James Dunlop-Smith, secretary to the viceroy, noted in his diary on September 10, 1905: "What I want to stop is these young Mohammedans forming small societies all over India. Once they start that game they can make us really anxious. Bengalis are a low-lying people in a low-lying land with the intellect of a Greek and the grit of a rabbit. It is the Mussulmans with green flag calling for blood and the Mahratta Brahmin—not the Mahratta but the Brahmin, whom we have to watch".[15]

When Mulk received the signal that the viceroy would meet a Muslim delegation, Mulk and Sayyad Hussaien Bilgrami drafted a memorandum and a meeting was called on September 15-16, 1906 at Lucknow, which with some changes endorsed it. However, Muslims were not united on partition of Bengal. Those from Aligarh and from other places were not as keen as Nawab of Dacca and the Muslims from East Bengal to retain the partition scheme. That was why the demand put forth by the Nawab of Dacca to retain the partition at any cost did not find place in the memorandum. Leaders from Aligarh and other parts of India were more concerned about securing more and adequate representation to the Muslims in the reforms, which would be introduced in the near future, and this was upheld by the Lucknow meeting.

Meanwhile Lord Minto heard that some Muslims were supporting the agitation against partition. However, lieutenant governor conveyed that Hindu landlords were coercing the Muslim tenants to support the agitation. At the same time it was 'The Times' (London) which took it upon itself to create a congenial atmosphere for the proposed Muslim delegation. In an editorial, on September 26, 1906 'The Times' wrote: "But there is no political force favourable to British rule of anything like the importance of the Musalman community. Englishmen who know of India only what they can learn in the Statistical Abstracts, are sometimes inclined to undervalue the importance of the Mohammedans because they number only 53 millions out of a total of 231 millions in British India. The wealth and social consideration, which they have inherited from the days when they were the ruling people in India are not by any means the only reasons of the political importance of the Mohammedans. They are a martial people, and pride themselves as much as the Rajputs and Sikhs on the fact that 'their ancestors always wore the sword which though taken from their belts, still remains in their hearts'. Although they live in many different provinces of India they all claim to speak the same language; Urdu (or Hindustani) is, they assert, the national speech of the Indian Moslems".

Muslim delegation met Lord Minto on October 1, 1906. Minto had informed Morley about this meeting who asked Minto to be cautious. The memorandum presented to the viceroy at Simla conveyed that the government should consider the social standing of the Muslims who were the rulers of India a century ago. Muslims also had special relations with the British government. However, this relationship was endangered by some recent happenings, which had made the Muslim youths impatient and oblivious to the advice to have patience. Muslims were denied the posts in the government service because of the principle of competition. When the reforms scheme would be drawn, care should be taken to give the Muslims adequate representation. Lord Minto thanked the Muslims for the trust they had in the British rule. He admitted that there was dissatisfaction; but explained that it was found in a class which had received English education and not because of the mal-administration. Minto made it clear that the Western institutions could not be introduced in India. He promised to see that the Muslims would have adequate representation irrespective of their numbers. He also assured the delegation that if any changes were made without giving due consideration to the tradition and faith, they would defeat their purpose. The changes would be made with a view to safeguarding the interests of the Muslims.

'The Economist' slightly differed with 'The Times' on the question of Muslim representation. In an editorial on October 6, 1906, it admitted the importance of the Muslim community in India but said: "Whatever may be the political atom in India, it is assuredly not the individual of Western democratic theory, but the community of some sort. Mohammedan body is, at any rate, solid, well-organized, as well as loyal—even against the pan-Islamic attractions. It is, morally, at least the equal of Hindus, and, in the qualities most required for government, is probably superior. Mr. Gokhale proposed last year at the National Congress that the number (members of the Viceroy's Council) should be raised from five to twelve. There may be room among the additions for one or two Mohamedan members, but it is little difficult to justify a two-fold representation, local and corporate, unless a similar principle is applied to other communities, which are primarily religious and racial. We must not, of course, overlook the possibility that the Mohammedan agitation and sympathetic reception of its aims by Englishmen may stimulate Hindu Nationalism. That danger, however, is not so serious as it appears. Agitation may be tempered, as well as stimulated, by counter-agitation, and the Swadeshi movement seems to be already on the wane. At any rate, the Moderate party in the Congress has taken alarm. It is significant that the Committee, which has to nominate the President has hastily selected, not an extremist like Mr. Tilak, but a well-known Liberal Mr. Dadabhai Naoroji. It remains to be seen if the Mohammedans will now attend the Congress. For their own sakes and India's it would be well if they did. They cannot amalgamate with the Hindus, but they might at least discuss new subjects well worth ventilating, and show that they, too, are profiting by the unrest which the education has brought to India". Morley was pleased with the achievement of Lord Minto and wrote that Lord Minto had established his authority. He thought that his critics who were all the while harping that the bureaucracy was at the loggerheads with the people of India, had a fitting reply and all their plans would be defeated.

'The Times' was pleased with the memorandum by the Muslim delegation and wrote on October 1, 1906, "For another reason the Mohammedan memorial is a remarkable document; it is almost the only piece of original political thought which had emanated from modern India. All the proposals, which had put forward from time to time by the Congress are unimaginative reproductions of the ideas, which form the stock-in-trade of English politicians. Nothing has made the average Englishman so skeptical of the wisdom of the Congress as this absence of Indian colouring in its political programme. The Hindu politicians have made no attempt to develop Indian institutions so as to satisfy the modern needs; they have not based their reforms upon any political instinct or proclivity manifested by the people of India in the past. They have imported their political programme ready-made from England, and warm as is an Englishman's regard for his own Constitution, he has a shrewd suspicion that it cannot be grafted on to an Indian stem. Mr. Morley gave expression to the instinctive feeling of us all, when he said that the idea of transplanting British institutions wholesale into India was a fantastic and ludicrous dream. This is what the Mahomedans have realized; their memorial contains the first practical suggestion that has been made by any considerable Indian party for adapting British institutions to the conditions of India".

After the Muslim delegation waited upon the viceroy, Aga Khan wrote to Dunlop-Smith that he had advised Moshin-ul Mulk, that he henceforth should take step only with the consultation with the government. This letter of Aga Khan could explain why the Muslim League politics remained pro-government in the coming years. In the meeting of the Muslims, Vikar-ul Mulk was nominated as president and afterwards he and Moshin-ul Mulk were the joint secretaries of Muslim League, which till then was not a political organization. It was seen that the Aligarh and UP would have controlling authority in the organization. Membership was restricted and not open. Four hundred members for the All India Muslim League were nominated for five years, out of which seventy were from UP. The yearly subscription was rupees twenty five and condition for the membership was to have annual income of at least five hundred rupees. With the success of the delegation which waited upon the viceroy at Simla, Nawab of Dacca feared that the Aligarh group would dominate the Muslims. He, therefore, moved to make the League a political organization. As the Nawab received good support, the Aligarh group had to have some understanding with the Nawab. Thus, the formation of the Muslim League as a political party was announced on December 30, 1906.

The hands of the British government were strengthened by the support of the Muslim leaders, and the Muslim leaders in turn were satisfied by the promise, which Lord Minto had given to them.

REFERENCES

1. Harold Nicolson, *King George The Fifth*, Constable and Co., London, 1952, p. 86.
2. Lovat Fraser, *India Under Curzon and After*, Sagar Publications, London, 1911, pp. 877-879.
3. R.C. Majumdar, *The History and Culture of the Indian People: Struggle for the Freedom*, Part 2, Vol. 11, Bharatiya Vidya Bhavan, Bombay, 1969, pp. 21-23.
4. Sumit Sarkar, *Swadeshi Movement in Bengal, 1903-1908*, People's Publishing House, New Delhi, 1973, p. 16.
5. Surendranath Banerjea, *A Nation in Making*, OUP, Bombay, 1963, p.178.

6. Gokhale Papers.
7. M.N. Das, *India under Morley and Minto*, George Allen and Unwin Ltd., London, 1964, p. 39.
8. Surendranath Banerjea, *A Nation in Making*, OUP, Bombay, 1963, p.176.
9. Sumit Sarkar, *The Swadeshi Movement in Bengal, 1903-1908*, People's Publishing House, New Delhi, 1973, pp.122-123.
10. R.C. Majumdar, *The History and Culture of the Indian People: Struggle for the Freedom*, Part 2, Vol. 11, Bharatiya Vidya Bhavan, Bombay, 1969, p. 42.
11. Sumit Sarkar, *The Swadeshi Movement In Bengal 1903-1908*, People's Publishing House, New Delhi, 1973, pp.142-43.
12. Nevinson Henry W., *The New Spirit in India,* Metropolitan Book. Co., Delhi, 1975, pp.179-180.
13. Nevinson Henry W., *The New Spirit in India,* Metropolitan Book. Co., Delhi, 1975, pp.192-193.
14. Alexander Lipski (Ed.), *Bengal East and West,* Asian Studies Center, Michigan State Uni., East Lansing, 1969, pp. 50, 62, 66-68.
15. Martin Gilbert (Ed.), *Servant of India*, Longmans, London, 1966, p. 56.

Chapter Twelve

WARRING CAMPS IN THE CONGRESS

In the Congress, on the contrary, controversy between the radicals and the moderates became intense and acrimonious. Partition of Bengal had given rise to the radical ideas and anti-government feelings were widespread. The new elements in the Congress were demanding a change in the Congress policy, which they thought to be too soft towards the government. They insisted that the party should support the swadeshi movement vigorously and do whatever was possible to embarrass the government. But the old Congress leaders were not prepared to change their policy. Gokhale had understood the depth of the feelings of the Bengalis against partition, but he did not favour the demand to enlarge the scope of the boycott movement to all India level. He had confidence in Morley and did not want to add to his difficulties by intensifying the boycott movement and creating an anti-English atmosphere. Even Surendranath Banerjea did not differ. He was radical in Bengal and moderate outside. Leaders like Bipin Chandra Pal and Arvindbabu led the radical wing.

Even with the internal division in the organization, it was decided to hold the annual session of the Congress in Calcutta in 1906 winter. Gopalrao Deodhar, a colleague of Gokhale, found the Congress work in Calcutta at standstill. Deodhar wrote to Gokhale, on August 9, "The differences are so bitter and sharp and the attitude so irreconcilable that to me the chances are the Pal Party would have an upper hand. There is no possibility that any large liberal and commonsense view be taken by the destructionists and obstructionists in any way, and on this account the minds of the Congress leaders are full of anxiety regarding the fate of the Congress". Deodhar called this group as anti-Congress, which did not want the session of the Congress. He believed that if this group did not succeed, then it would create difficulties in the session. Deodhar accused this group of maneuvering to capture the Congress organization. Surendranath Banerjea was sanguine about the situation and informed Dadabhai that the constitutionalists in India had lost ground and were weakened and the agitationists had become strong; that was because of the failure of the Liberal government in England and Morley's reluctance to modify the partition scheme.

Gokhale was alarmed by the reports, which he had received from Deodhar and others about the Congress affairs in Calcutta. He revealed his mind in a lengthy letter to his friend in Madras, V. Krishnaswami Iyer, on September 29, 1906. Gokhale said, "Calcutta has been for some time past a regular pandemonium. Surendranath's inexcusable excesses, the 'Patrika's' vindictive pursuit of Mr. Surendranath, the fierce quarrel between Surendranath and Bipin Chandra Pal and the latter's unscrupulous ambition to play at all cost the role of a new leader, Anglo-Indian ferocity let loose against the Indians, Mahommedan ill-will stirred up against Hindus, and last, the offense given by the Hindu-Mahommedan to orthodox Hindus—all of these have created in Calcutta a situation from which the Congress cannot hope to escape without serious injury. The only man who seems to retain his head on his shoulders is Mr. Bhupendranath Bose. But for the past two or three years his influence has been rapidly on the wane, and his position is a most difficult one; Bipin Chandra Pal unscrupulously assailing him on one side and Surendranath resenting the curbs which he puts on the other. The preparations for the Congress have not yet been taken in hand, though we are now at the end of September. A huge unwieldy reception Committee consisting of anybody and everybody was no doubt formed two months ago, but no care was taken in regard to the men that were put on it, any name that was handed in being accepted. The result is that neither Surendranath nor Bipin Chandra knows which side has a majority on the reception committee and they are both postponing the election of an executive or working committee out of this body, as that means the first open trial of strength between the two parties". Gokhale then narrated how the new party of Bengal under Bipin Chandra Pal wanted to sweep away the programme of the Congress replacing it by a radical one which would call for boycott of not only of English goods, but also of all the schools, colleges and Government services and honours. Gokhale concludes, "It is sad, inexpressibly sad that all this should occur at the very moment when the viceroy and the Secretary of State are contemplating an important step forward. It may be that we are after all, as an ancient writer says, 'mere sport of aimless destiny'."

In a letter to Natesan, (October 2, 1906) the publisher friend, Gokhale said that Pal had never worked for the Congress in the past. He called him unscrupulous and inordinately ambitious. Gokhale then said, "He (Pal) uses brave words, but behind those words, there is neither courage nor character, and of course, there is no judgement, and I have little doubt that in a year or two we shall see this man's collapse, whatever noise he may succeed in making temporarily. Mr. Tilak is, of course, a different kind of man, but he too, I am sorry to say, is afflicted with an ambition to which there are no limits. Mr. Tilak has a matchless capacity for intrigue, and he is not burdened with exacting conscience. As a result, he is often able to play for his own hand when to all appearances he is fighting for principles only. His great talent, his simple habits, his sturdy and dauntless spirit and above all the cruel persecution which he has had to bear at the hands of the government have won for him the hearts of the millions in all parts of the country. And this general affection and admiration make it comparatively easy for him to play his game. Sir P.M. Mehta's unyielding and somewhat dictatorial attitude may be justly deplored. I do not think that a greater conciliation on his part would have made any difference as regards Mr. Tilak's ambition and his methods. Lala Lajpat Rai as a public worker is, I think, more selfless than either Mr. Tilak or Mr. Pal. I am sure that though his name is being freely used by Mr. Pal and his party, he is not with them in their views or methods, and he perhaps would have been more actively on our side today if greater tact had been displayed in the past in meeting the wishes of men like him".[1]

Lokmanya Tilak had his own views about the malady afflicting the Congress. In an editorial in 'Kesari' of July 10, 1906, he said, "the Congress, though only twenty one years old, had adopted a course of action which was eighty years old. Indians would do better by studying the experience of the Irish. It was obvious that even though the British empire had white and brown or black population, it was run only for the benefit of the whites. Those who were confident that constitutional agitation would alone succeed, had received a slap by Mr. Morley. Even after this if somebody wanted to continue to beg, then he would be regarded as a fool or shameless. Rulers do not want to part even with little power and so the Congress had to change its course". He again advocated boycott.

With the mess created in the Congress in Bengal, question of selecting a president became all the more important. Sensing that the nomination of Tilak would invite stiff opposition, his friend Khaparde, publicly sponsored Lala Lajpat Rai. This had the support of both Tilak and Pal. But Pherozeshah, Surendranath and even Gokhale did not approve of Lajpat Rai's nomination. Lajpat Rai would not have taken the Congress to an extreme radical course and might have been the best person to bring about some reconciliation in the Congress. But Pherozeshah, Surendranath and Gokhale were not in a mood to compromise. They feared that Lajpat Rai would play into the hands of the radical leaders. Wedderburn, however, was ready to accept Lajpat Rai. But his advice was not heeded. So Surendranath after consulting Bombay leaders decided to put up Dadabhai Naoroji's name and sent a telegram to Dadabhai requesting him to accept the invitation and save the Congress. This had the desired effect and Dadabhai accepted the invitation. Correspondence, which followed this acceptance with Dadabhai, brings forth the sorry state of affairs of the Congress and the animosity between the two groups of leaders. In a letter following his telegram, Surendranath told Dadabhai that Tilak's name was put forward by Pal and some others, but that would be vehemently opposed and Congress would split if Tilak got elected.

Earlier, Dadabhai, aware of the controversy in the Congress had written to Lokmanya Tilak impressing upon the latter not to do anything, which would in any way harm the Congress. Tilak replying to him on September 21, 1906 said that Dadabhai was the guru of them all in political matters and he himself highly valued receiving a letter from him. He assured Dadabhai that he was not involved in the quarrel and had nothing to do with it. Tilak also assured that he would not allow the Congress to be split on his account. He added, "The present controversy is one of the methods. Many of us honestly think that Congress may do some real good by organizing the methods of self-help in this country. We are not going to charge Mr. Morley or any of our friends with dishonesty. What we say is that they are helpless under the circumstances, and that we must help ourselves before they help us. Swadeshi, boycott, strikes, national education are pointed out as instances or directions in which the Congress may do useful work. No one has the least intention of taking up the revolutionary methods. The Liberal government cannot be expected to be always in power and what is granted now may be withdrawn tomorrow by the Conservative party. We must learn self-reliance, and that is exactly what the new party, if it can be so called, proposes to do. They wanted to begin with the choice of the president, but as you have consented to come down, no one will dispute the choice. But the question of methods still remains to be settled and I for one shall be glad to have it settled under your presidentship".[2]

Surendranath, Wacha etc. took Dadabhai's consent as their triumph. Surendranath could not suppress this feeling while writing to Dadabhai. He said on October 11 that the new party had no standing in the country. He also informed that his group was considering to send a memorandum to Morley to modify the partition of Bengal, but the new party was opposed to it. Surendranath alleged that the new party did not want the government to modify the partition scheme. This would ensure that the people would remain angry and discontented and give strength to the new party. Wacha thought that with Dadabhai's consent to preside over the Congress session, the wind was taken out of the sails of the Radicals. "But they were a set of drowning men who were trying to catch a straw". However, Dr. Sarat Mullik of Calcutta informed Dadabhai on October 17 that some Congress leaders had proposed his (Dadabhai's) name as they were opposed to Tilak; but that had created a feeling of greater resentment. The letter proceeds, "This feeling is not directed against you personally, but against the underhand manner in which the offer was made to you. It was done without taking the Calcutta Congress Committee or any other Congress Committee into their confidence. The question now arises, what are we to do? It is for you to cut the Gordian knot by directing our people to elect a Mahomedan president this year".

Motilal Ghose wired Dadabhai not to accept the presidentship, as his name did not come up for consideration before any meeting. But when Dadabhai gave his consent to be the president, Ghose welcomed him. He told Dadabhai that the Congress must change and must have a programme which would bring Zamindars, middle classes and masses together, When Parnell took up the question of land, Irish people rallied round him. Swadeshi was such a programme, which would have support of all the classes. Motilal appealed Dadabhai to steer the Congress to such a course.

But according to Srinivas Sastri, irrepressible Bipin Chandra Pal wrote to Dadabhai threatening him with an exposure of "all the frauds, which he (Dadabhai) committed when he was connected with Mercantile House". Sastri said that Dadabhai showed that telegram to Gokhale and told him that he should not be worried as it had absolutely no basis. The Grand Old Man also told Gokhale, that that telegram by Pal had convinced him that the Congress had to be saved from such idol-breakers like Pal and he must preside over the Calcutta session of the Congress. Lala Lajpat Rai, whose name was suggested by Pal and others for the presidentship, refused to oblige them. In his autobiographical writings he has criticised the emotional politics of both Pal and Arvindbabu. He was of the opinion that when the enemy was very strong, it was suicidal to waste one's energy in petty quarrels.

'The Times' took note of the controversy in the Congress in its editorial column as well as in the 'Indian Affairs' column. The writer reminded the Congress leaders that they could not play the part of a properly constituted opposition party, as they had no power to overthrow the government by showing the majority. The writer, therefore, wanted Congress to desist from constant criticism of the administration. 'The Times' on October 16, 1906 said, "The two parties (in the Congress) are the Moderates, whose professed object is the gradual and progressive development of India, until India attains the same place in the British Empire as the great self-governing colonies; and the Extremists, who avow their desire to get rid of the British connection at the shortest notice. The first is in principle compatible with devoted loyalty to the Crown and to the Empire, and may to some extent command the sympathy of many Englishmen, both in India and at home. The second is openly and flagrantly seditious. They believe that they can make the British Government impossible in India within a generation or two by judicious abuse of the rights which they enjoy under the shelter of law". An article in 'The Times' published the same day, referred to a private and confidential letter written by Pal to Banerjea when they were friends and afterwards released by Pal. In that letter Pal informed Banerjea that a great friend of Bengal in London urged Banerjea to continue the agitation as he had 'conferences' with some persons in London. Pal insinuated that conferences were with some minister. The same person had advised Banerjea that there should not be let up in the meetings and propaganda campaign, which would bring the British government round. An anonymous writer of the article took exception to such propaganda. In the end he appealed to the moderates and said, "If the Extremists can carry the election of Mr. Tilak, the Congress will be definitely committed to a policy of sedition, and those who are against such a policy must either secede from it altogether or at least form themselves in irreconcilable opposition". The writer of the article, was blissfully unaware of what was actually going on in the Congress, as Dadabhai was nominated as the president and Tilak had no intention to defy him. The writer in 'The Times' had also advised the Moderates to part company with the 'Extremists', a step, according to the writer, would be hailed by the Muslims. It would also be welcomed by the British and would pave the way to satisfy most of the demands of the Congress. But when after a year Congress was split and came under the control of the moderates, neither the Muslims hailed it, nor did the government come forward with any scheme to satisfy the main demands of the Congress. On the contrary, reforms that were proposed created more controversy.

It was hoped that with Dadabhai's presence, Calcutta session of the Congress would face no difficulty. But this was not to be. The chairman of the Reception Committee, Rash Bihari Ghose in his address of welcome in the session criticised the policy of repression against those participating in the agitation against the partition. He characterized it as Russian method. Ghose declared that though they were loyal, they could not forget their miserable position. He said, being believers in constitutional methods, they were not retaliating against the oppressive policies of the government. He objected to regard Swadeshi movement as seditious. In his speech Dadabhai said that Indians should enjoy the same rights as the Englishmen enjoy in their country. Swaraj was the only word, which correctly expressed the sentiments of the Indian people. He supported swadeshi movement and called for the interventionist policy to make economic progress in the country. Dadabhai declared his faith in the sense of justice of the British people. He said, if the Indians did not get their demands satisfied, then it would mean that their efforts fell short. Supporting swadeshi, Dadabhai was reticent about boycott. Tilak moved an amendment in the resolution about swadeshi which would have appealed people to adopt Swadeshi even at some sacrifice. As Dadabhai accepted this amendment, Moderates could not object to the amendment.

Two versions of the proceedings throw light on what actually happened. Khaparde noted in his diary that to find out some way to avert any controversy, Dadabhai called a meeting of some leaders and invited those present to state their views about the boycott. Khaparde put forth his views. After him Malviya and Pherozeshah started haranguing the meeting. Khaparde intervened and stopped them. Tilak also lent support to Khaparde. Pherozeshah then played all the tricks and used his charm to pacify opponents. However, Khaparde found out that except Bengal and Maharashtra very few leaders from other provinces supported the boycott. Bombay was divided. To Khaparde, presidential speech was unsatisfactory. Meeting of the Subjects Committee was stormy. Pherozeshah was given a seat next to Dadabhai, which evoked opposition. He was also heckled when he spoke. Even Dadabhai stopped Mehta when he tried to breach the rule. Malviya made himself ridiculous. Gokhale was moving from one place to another making noises like a grudging lady. Resolutions about partition and the constitution of the Congress generated much heat. When Khaparde demanded poll on a resolution, Dadabhai rejected the demand, and Khaparde along with some delegates walked out in protest. Khaparde, however, admits that Dadabhai's concluding speech was inspiring. He says that Pherozeshah was very much angry because of the treatment he received. He told Tilak that Bombay would not have gone the Calcutta way; but Tilak accepting the challenge told Pherozeshah that if he behaved as he did in Calcutta, Bombay would not be different.

Srinivas Sastri in his lecture on Pherozeshah admitted that Pherozeshah was heckled and abused but he commended Pherozeshah for being stoic in the face of furious opposition. Sastri criticized Pal for giving a wider interpretation to the resolution on the boycott. Pal maintained that boycott was to be adopted all over India. It was left to Gokhale to remind the delegates that the resolution was restrictive and as Bengal had been unjustly treated, boycott had to be confined to that province. Congress thus did not split at Calcutta but both factions left the session unreconciled and went on with separate agenda. After the session Tilak and Khaparde went to Allahabad and some other places to address meetings. Gokhale after the winter session of the Central Legislative Council also visited several places in North India to counter the campaign of the radicals.

'The Times' editorial on January 2, 1907, said: "The threatened split between the Extremists—the professed enemies of British rule—and the Moderates has been averted, but averted by the adoption on the part of the moderates of no small part of Extremist policy. It is, of course, disguised, but the disguise is too transparent to deceive anybody who does not desire to be deceived. The speech with which Mr. Naoroji opened the proceedings is as mischievous as they could desire, and it is probably better calculated than anything they could have said themselves to promote the objects they have in view. Mr. Naoroji contends that, because the inhabitants of India are British citizens, they are entitled to all the political rights and privileges, and franchises, which the inhabitants of England enjoy. But the contention has no more root in history or in law than it has in common sense. We have won India by the sword. We hold it by sword. It is well for the small highly-educated classes, which are alone represented at the Congress, that the British sword stands between them and their native enemies. That is the fundamental fact in the whole situation which makes all the claims for full self-government in India absurd". Referring to the formation of the Muslim League 'The Times' remarked, "At all events its formation exposes the hollowness of the Congress to speak for the 'people of India', and it may perhaps remind more cautious members of the body that agitation is a game which provokes counter-agitation, and that in India the counter-agitation may be conducted by the most warlike races of the peninsula."

'The Economist' was no less critical of Dadabhai's speech and resolutions passed in the Calcutta session of Congress. On December 29, 1906, it wrote: "Apart from the familiar economic caricature which closes the address, there are two or three specific suggestions in it to which exception may be taken on practical grounds. England, for example, does not send civil servants or British regiments to India to provide for them at the cost of the native population, but to do necessary work for its benefit; and the introduction of absolutely open competition for the public service would ensure class government of a kind which a large minority of the population would heartily resent. The educated Bengali babu can pass any intellectual test with flying colours; his physical strength, with the special qualifications for the art of government which such strength implies, is notoriously far below that of other people of India. Perfectly open competition would mean Bengali rule. Indeed, the desire to recognize Mohammedan rights was one motive for the partition of Bengal and the Bengali agitation that followed, whatever the degree of sedition that characterised it, was an object-lesson in the incompetence of the Indian agitators and in the dangers of internecine conflict that a purely sectional agitation must set up. Further progress may, as the Mohammedans ask, take its course through proportionate and communal rather than direct individual representation".

Thus both 'The Times' and 'The Economist' adopted the policy which was more inclined to give Muslims weightage, not for any love for them, but to checkmate the Hindus. Some other periodicals took different position. 'The Westminster Review' for example, in its February 1907 issue endorsed Dadabhai's plea for more participation of Indians in the administration and the beginning to be made immediately. "The obvious first steps towards this ideal are (1) the rescinding of the partition of Bengal, emphatically condemned not only by the Congress but also upwards of two hundred and fifty meetings, attended by nearly a million people; (2) the restoration and extension of the rights of self-government abrogated by Lord Curzon; and (3) the restoration of competition for the services in which admission is made directly in India. Mr. Morley has so far neglected the great opportunity of righting these wrongs inflicted by the late reactionary Government, but it is to be hoped that he will soon bestir himself in the matter".

Lala Lajpat Rai had correctly observed that Tilak, though a radical, was not an extremist and did not want a split in the congress. Arvindbabu and Bipin Chandra Pal, on the contrary, had mounted a vicious attack on the old leadership.

That was why Arvindbabu said that Dadabhai was a leader of the past while Tilak was that of the future. He called Gokhale as Bibhishan and questioned his patriotism. But in few years time Arvindbabu renounced politics and became a 'sanyasi', while Bipin Chandra Pal stayed a long time in London, giving up radical politics to become a moderate. Tilak in his editorial in 'Kesari' on January 8, 1907, clearly stated that he intended to keep the unity of the Congress. He stated that a compromise was reached at Calcutta not because the old party was weak. It was reached because an ideal of swaraj was proclaimed and the session deliberated on the ways to be adopted to achieve it. Tilak quoted Dadabhai who said in his speech that he spent a lifetime in persuading the British public to redress the grievances of the Indians and thereby pave the way for self-government. But he had lost hope; and any other person in his place might have revolted. Tilak then impressed upon the readers that under such circumstances boycott and swadeshi was the only course left.

Gokhale, on the other hand, explained his views about the course to be followed by India in meetings in Allahabad, Lucknow and other places. On February 4, 1907, Gokhale addressed a public meeting at Allahabad, which was presided over by Motilal Nehru. Gokhale's theme was how the constitutional means were the only practical way to be followed and would help India to make progress. Gokhale said, "let me say at the outset that I recognize no limits to my aspiration for our motherland. I want our people to be in their own country what other people are in their own. I want India to take her proper place among the great nations of the World. The question was one not of what was theoretically perfect, but what was practically attainable. The only practical goal is self-government within the empire, and reliance must be placed on the constitutional agitation. What is constitutional agitation? It is the agitation by methods, which they were entitled to adopt to bring about the changes they desired through the action of the constituted authority. But there are two essential conditions; one that the methods adopted are such as they are entitled to employ, and secondly, the changes desired must be obtained only through the action of the constituted authorities by bringing to bear on them the pressures of public opinion". Gokhale then discussed the question of boycott. He said the swadeshi means concerted efforts to industrialize the country. This was the positive concept, while boycott implied vindictive desire to injure another. He then went into details of the total demand of various goods and the capacity to produce them in India. He pointed out that with the available production capacity, it would take considerable time to achieve self-sufficiency.

Gokhale addressed another meeting in Lucknow on February 9 in which he mainly dealt with the swadeshi movement. He said that the movement had come to stay and believed that the true salvation of the country lay in the movement. Gokhale then discussed the problems of capital formation without which industrialization was not possible. Gokhale's arguments were cogent and down to earth. But the atmosphere in some parts of the country was surcharged with emotion and so Gokhale's practical advice did not make impact on the general public. The partition of Bengal had hurt the feelings of the people and they were angry at the injustice done. Therefore, Gokhale's speeches about boycott and swadeshi were construed as an advocacy of the government and anti-boycott, which his critics never failed to drive home.

Several British newspapers and periodicals at the time were discussing the Hindu-Muslim problem and 'The New York Times' also participated. On June 18, 1907 the paper warned that in case of British withdrawal from India, there would be chaos. It said: "It is the opinion of all the observers that if the natives should rid themselves of the British, there would straightaway be a war of races and religions which would end in the Mohammedan rule, of which the little finger would be heavier upon the Hindus than the loins of the British domination".

While Bengal was in turmoil due to partition, there was unrest in Punjab because of the mistaken policy of the government about the settlement land. A large tract of wasteland came under cultivation, as a dam was built on the river Chinab in 1849. The government then distributed land and established colonies. Some special and tenancy laws came into force. For some decades this experiment was successful, but problems developed eventually. Because of water charges, the government was receiving revenue, which paid for the cost of the canals. But with the increase in population, the land was fragmented and the laws enforced earlier were found to be inequitable. They favoured landlords at the cost of tenants. Only landlords could purchase land on easy terms, others could not; which gave rise to litigation. In 1906 water cess was increased which was resented by the landlords. Several protest meetings followed and a new magazine, 'Zamindar', was started which launched a campaign against the government laws and rules. The government then abolished or modified some of the more objectionable provisions of the new law and got the amended bill passed by the Legislative Council in-spite of the opposition by the Indian members. In fact, the amended act was not harmful to the tenants. But the original act had created an atmosphere of mistrust and people had lost faith in the Englishmen as such.

Canals and the colonies were important factors in the Punjab economy. About three million acres of land was irrigated and two million people were settled in the new colonies. As the people had lost faith in the administration, the economy of Punjab was threatened. Government officials were oblivious of the public opinion and wrote dispatches and reports that were far from reality. They were convinced that the rural population was provoked by the urban leaders. Punjab Lieutenant-Governor Sir Denzil Ibbetson completely relied on these reports. Besides, land revenue in Punjab was increased after fresh assessment. Land near

Rawalpindi was fertile and belonged to the landlords and money-lenders who were agitated by the increase in assessment. This resulted in disturbances. Ibbetson then deported Lala Lajpat Rai to Mandalay on May 9, 1907 without giving him any opportunity to defend himself in the court. Another leader, Ajit Singh, was also arrested and deported. Ajit Singh was very much virulent in his criticism of the government unlike Lajpat Rai. But the government did not discriminate between the two. The deportation of Lajpat Rai was condemned all over India and the agriculturists in Punjab received wider support. The Government of India went by the reports of Ibbetson. Morley based his reply in the Commons on the dispatches of the Government of India. He defended the measures adopted in Punjab, as he said the whole atmosphere in the province was volatile.

The House of Commons discussed the Punjab situation on June 6, 1907 when Dr. Rutherford drew attention of the House to the fact that it was the rule of ordinances. If the accused were proceeded against in the court of law, it would have generated publicity, which the government wanted to avoid. Therefore, the government used special powers under the ordinance. Rutherford believed that the publicity was essential in such cases. Rutherford termed the deportation of Lala Lajpat Rai and Ajit Singh as unjustified and said that the Indian press was threatened while Tory press in England go scot-free even though they were writing viciously against the Indians. Rutherford regretted that one of the great liberals (Morley) had connived at the Indian rulers in resorting to Russian methods. If this had to be continued then, Rutherford said, it would be better to discontinue teaching British history in India. He then read out some of the excerpts from Morley's speeches on Ireland. C.J. O'Donnell, following Rutherford, criticised the advance of a large loan on easy terms to the bankrupt Nawab and called for the annulment of the partition of Bengal.

Morley defended the action of the Punjab government as well as that of the Government of India. He assured the members that he had not discarded his liberalism. He described the Punjab agitation more as political than about the land. Giving statistics he pointed out the majority of the public meetings in Punjab were political and few of them were devoted to the problems of landlords or tenants. Morley cited a report by Ibbetson who in his report accused Lala Lajpat Rai of instigating and provoking the agriculturists against the government. Some pamphlets were distributed among the soldiers in order to create dissatisfaction among them. Morley admitted that the gap between the people and the officials had widened. According to him that was due to the policy adopted for the last six years, which gave emphasis on efficiency and not on sympathy. Morley reminded the House that the measures adopted by the Government of India had been approved by the Parliament and thereby by the people of England. He, however, informed the House that some new measures were under the consideration of the government and some steps would be taken to bring in political reforms. But it was found that the whole foundation on which Morley based his reply was far from reality. Depending solely on the unfounded reports of Ibbetson, Lord Minto raised a scare when he informed Morley that there was widespread belief that at the time of the fiftieth anniversary of the 1857 revolt there would be a similar uprising. Because of this widespread belief Englishmen kept their arms with them and English soldiers slept with guns by their side. The Sikhs were told that in 1857 they saved the English people, but now they had gone against them. To Minto Lala Lajpat Rai was rabidly anti-British and Ajit Singh was supposed to be a henchman of a Russian spy.

He wrote to Morley: "The head and centre of the entire movement is Lala Lajpat Rai, a Khatri pleader, who has visited England as the Congress representative of the Punjab. He is a revolutionary and a political enthusiast who is inspired by the most intense hatred of the British Government. He keeps himself in the background, but the lieutenant-governor has been assured by nearly every native gentleman who has spoken to him on the subject that he is organizer-in chief." Some Anglo-Indian as well as the British papers published scary news and poured oil on fire. King Edward was alarmed and advised Morley to look at the Punjab situation more seriously without any loss of time. In fact, the discontent was mainly due to the thirty per cent rise in the land revenue. The Sikh soldiers who came home on leave were disturbed by such rise. Their discontent was not because of any pamphlets. Hauns Raj, who was arrested in Rawalpindi, told the court that the meeting, which he addressed was to ventilate the grievances of the agriculturists against the rise in land revenue. The mass of evidence that came before the court of the district judge told the same story. The district magistrate in his judgement called the prosecution evidence as cooked up, and freed many accused. But Minto failed to inform Morley about this turn of events and when all this came out, Morley had to face an angry House. Minto realizing his blunder quietly changed the course, and Ibbetson was transferred.

The Punjab agitation was discussed in some British newspapers for some time. 'The Times' in its issue of May 22, 1907, published a newsletter from its correspondent, which said that Punjab was witnessing racial hatred between the Indians and the English. He then asked whether it would lead to the repetition of the 1857 revolt. But even before the Punjab agitation, it was left to an anonymous American writer to voice the same feeling in the October 1906 issue of the American monthly, 'Review of Reviews'. He endorsed the views expressed in an article in the English 'Blackwood' magazine which said: "The scattered here and there throughout the continent, under normal conditions, are a few single sentries from the quarter guard of each battalion. There are no bright lights in barracks during the night. In every barrack-room containing, say, from sixteen to twenty men, there are usually two flickering oil lamps easily reached and extinguished. By means of concerted, silent movement, not necessarily involving more than a small section of a city's native population, the single sentries, approached stealthily from behind, could quickly and easily be stricken down". The writer of the 'Review of Reviews', said: "Even without the connivance or moral support of native troops, or of native servants, every white man, woman and child, within and beyond the cantonment limits could—and doubtless would—be sacrificed before the lapse of an hour". 'The Economist' discounted such fears in its May 25 issue. It said: "Probably the dangers have been exaggerated alike in Lahore and in the Punjab. The army has not been affected; the Mohammedans have not let their resentment against the Bengalis take shape in violence; and the student 'agitators' have received fair warning that if the Universities do not check their imitation of the Russian students, the Government will intervene to shut them off from a University career, and, therefore, from professional or official life. The approach of the fiftieth anniversary of the Indian Mutiny has, no doubt, set up some apprehensions. But there has been none of the slackness in important quarters in India which facilitated the outbreak in 1857. But we have to face the abiding fact, attested by a consensus of competent testimony, of a new racial hatred of English in India. There is far less excuse for it, happily, than there was in the last days of the Company rule. We have to face the rise of the racial consciousness, which extends itself illogically from one race to its rivals and claims to set the heterogeneous 'people' of India against their British rulers. We must persevere with our burden, maintain order, providing as many safety valves for discontent as is consistent with that aim, and raise the standard of life".

Gokhale, who stayed with Lala Lajpat Rai in Lahore in February, was very much disturbed by the deportation of the Punjab leader. He wrote a letter to 'The Times of India', on May 21, 1907 in which he said that the government had taken harsh measures due to panic. He expressed confidence in Lajpat Rai's motives who would not, according to Gokhale, resort to violent agitation and would not induce others to do so. Gokhale blamed the government for not listening to the grievances of the people of Punjab and for not taking adequate steps accordingly. He discounted the fears that there would be a repetition of the 1857 revolt. Gokhale had sent a copy of his letter to 'The Times of India' to Lord Minto. He was also considering to send a delegation to the Viceroy and if he did not properly respond, to follow it with delegation to Morley. Gokhale's letter and his intervention in Punjab were disapproved by Lord Minto who wrote to Morley on June 10: "Gokhale has, in my opinion, lost much valuable ground in the last few weeks. Many people believed in the honesty of his political intentions. If he had come forward in our recent difficulties as an advocate of constitutional reforms and had spoken out boldly against preaching of sedition, he might have played a great part. He has done nothing of the sort". The letters and reports he had received also disturbed Morley. Gokhale also wrote to

Wedderburn that the Liberal Government was not doing anything to check the Government of India, which was using repressive measures. Gokhale also took exception to Morley's budget speech which he thought insulting to Indians. Wedderburn as usual sent a copy of this letter to Morley, who thought that it would be better if Gokhale did not visit England, as he feared that the members of Parliament who were sympathetic to India would be influenced by the advocacy of Gokhale. Herbert Risley who was in England at that time met Morley who asked the visitor if Gokhale was extremely simple or extremely crooked? Risley told Morley what he had already conveyed to Lord Minto, "that facts did not point to simplicity or good faith".[3]

Minto continued to be angry with Gokhale, so he wrote to the Secretary of State again on August 7: "I can only say that if he (Gokhale) chooses to play with fire, he must be prepared to face the consequences. We can't afford to allow him to tamper with the army....I am thoroughly disappointed with Gokhale". Minto did not elaborate as to how Gokhale was tampering with the army and Morley also did not ask for any elucidation. Gokhale being frustrated by the attitude of the government, apprehended that the unrest in Punjab would be used by the officials as an excuse to stall the reforms which Morley intended to introduce. He, therefore, thought it advisable to send a memorandum to Lord Minto. But Pherozeshah refused to sign such a memorandum. So Gokhale issued a statement on June 14, 1907 that said: "Of course it is open to the Government to say that the tranquillity prevailing at present is due to the drastic measures adopted by them. But the people of this country believe, and will continue to believe, that there was never any real chance of a second mutiny and that Lajpat Rai has been sacrificed to the nervous apprehension that suddenly seized the authorities. It is possible that Mr. Morley may throw some light on the case of Lajpat Rai. He certainly owes this to himself, not less than to the people of this country, over whose destiny for the time he presides. I think that public agitation must now be directed for some time to securing Lajpat Rai's restoration to liberty, or at any rate to securing for him an opportunity to meet the charges on which the action of the Government has been based. Mr. Morley spoke the other day of interest which the Indian party who are anxious for changes in the administration of the country undoubtedly have in the prevention of disorders. We certainly do not want any disorders in the land. But the reforms contemplated will lose their meaning if they cannot be had without the deportation of such earnest and high-minded workers in the country's cause as Lajpat Rai".

Both Gokhale and Morley were facing difficult situation and struggling to find some solution. Gokhale had great faith in Morley, but was disappointed by his inability to take any steps towards political reforms and also persuading Minto to give up repressive measures, which had created intense anti-government feelings in India. Some of his own moderate colleagues were alarmed by the rising tide of radicalism and by the cult of the bomb followed by some young men. Gokhale's friend, Krishnaswami was urging him to stick to the path of moderation. He even blamed Bengali leaders for alienating the Muslims by their agitation against partition. Krishnaswami thought Lala Lajpat Rai was good at heart but a thoughtless person. He wanted Gokhale and Pherozeshah to wage a vigorous campaign against the radicals. Krishnaswami was unaware of the public mood and did not know that such a campaign would be a damped squib. Morley, refusing to accept his inability to rein in the Government of India and motivate his Council to begin thinking about some political reform measures, was expecting Gokhale and other moderates to denounce the radicals and have some understanding with the Government of India. The radical members of Parliament as well as Liberals sympathetic to India were pressurizing Morley to rid himself of his inactivity. Keir Hardie, a firebrand MP, went to the length of moving a resolution to empower the Parliament to vote on the salary of the Secretary of State when the Indian budget was to be debated. Though this resolution was defeated, the margin was not large and the manner and tone of the speeches made Morley sad. Hardie asked Morley whether he had bade goodbye to liberalism. 'The Economist' at this time came to the rescue of Morley. It said that criticism against Morley was futile as Morley had not given up his liberalism. It asked the critics to go through Morley's famous book *On Compromise*, in which Morley had expressly stated that one could hold some views, but it was difficult to implement the same; one had to consider what was desirable and what was possible. Morley could be right, but because of his dilemma, he found himself deserted by his liberal friends. He, therefore, became more demanding from people like Gokhale. But Gokhale had his own compulsions.

REFERENCES

1. Gokhale Papers.
2. Dadabhai Papers.
3. M.N. Das, *India Under Morley and Minto*, George Allen and Unwin Ltd., London, 1964, p. 97.

Chapter Thirteen

CONGRESS SPLIT

Gokhale felt disheartened by the repressive measures of the government and the increasing pressure from the radicals in the Congress. He feared that the Congress was hastening towards a split, which would be harmful to India. He wrote to Wedderburn on October 1, 1907, pouring his heart to him: "the outlook seems to be as dark as could be". He again wrote to Wedderburn on 17 October. This letter was given to Morley by Wedderburn who conveyed the contents to Lord Minto. Morley said: "One of the most interesting Indian things that have come my way is a letter from (Gokhale) dated 17th October. The one absorbing thing is how to avoid the split in the Congress. 'The outlook at this moment is as dark as dark could be'. He had no hope that any solution can be found, short of removing the sittings of the Congress from Nagpur. But this 'means a split, as the New party in that case would probably insist on holding their own separate Congress at Nagpur'. If split does come, it means a disaster, for the bureaucracy will then put down both sections without much difficulty. They will brush Gokhale and his friends aside on the ground that they have no large following in the country, and will put the New Party down on the plea that most thoughtful people are against them. Morley then gave his assessment, "I have often thought during the last twelve months that Gokhale, as a party-manager is a baby. A party-manager, or for that matter any politician aspiring to be a leader, should never whine. Gokhale is always whining, just like a second rate Irishman between Dan O'Connell and Parnell. Now if I were in Gokhale's shoes, if he wears shoes, I forget, I should insist on quietly making terms with the bureaucracy on the basis of 'Order plus Reforms'. If he would have the sense to see what is to be gained by this line, the 'split' when it comes should do him no harm, because it would set him free to fix his aims on reasonable things, where he might get out of us sixty or seventy per cent of what he might ask for". Morley had quoted further from Gokhale's letter which told Wedderburn: "The feeling against Mr. Morley in the country is so strong at present, that no one who puts in a word for him has a chance of being listened to. In fact, it is no longer mere 'regret' or 'disappointment', or even 'dislike' or 'distrust': it is, I grieve to say, *disgust and detestation* and God knows if it ever will improve".[1]

Gokhale in his letter to Wedderburn dilated upon his expectation from the government to improve the atmosphere of distrust and hostility. His suggestions were: release of Lala Lajpat Rai; annulment of partition, without taking away any of their recent gains of the Muslims; recasting of the proposed reforms, appointment of at least two Indian members to the Executive Council of the viceroy; extension of local self government; separation of executive and judiciary; free primary education. It took the government sometime to move in the matter; but even then the reforms were below the expectations of the people.

Morley by his speech in the Commons in June 1907 had given offence to even moderate Congress leaders. Wacha's letter to Dadabhai, on June 29, is indicative of the feeling of anger and frustration among the Congressmen. Wacha said, "Mr. Morley has gone one worse than Lord Curzon, when he sweepingly alleges that all educated classes are enemy of Great Britain. This shows how far his weak mind has been gained over by the India Office conspirators. And to say that we are hankering after official emoluments is another sweeping allegation, unjust and unfounded. Mr. Morley is in his dotage and has undone his reputation. The India Office has proved to be his grave and the India Council members his grave-diggers. Another Liberal or Radical idol is broken. Mr. Morley seems to have forgotten all past political history. Pity".[2]

Morley was in two minds. He was supporting measures which Lord Minto was adopting; but at the same time he was asking Minto to show sympathy to the Indians. Minto was not impressed by this plea. He reminded Morley that the British in India were in a way a small garrison surrounded by millions of people who were not used to western political methods. If the government did not now use its strength, then it would be doomed. Minto, sometimes used to be annoyed by the discussions in the British Parliament. He used to tell Morley that it was he who was dealing with the situation in India and was much more aware of the reality than the members of Parliament who were five thousand miles away; and therefore, was entitled to have more freedom of action. Morley could see the point in this argument and was wary of some new democratic elements whom he could not welcome. Churchill had rightly observed that Morley was a representative of the Victorian era who wondered why it did not begin early and why it ended. In one letter Morley confessed that he was disturbed by the new trend in the Parliament. He was equally critical of the Tory Party as that of the Liberal. Morley said the majority of the members of Parliament were shallow, and unfortunately their opinions and actions did influence the policy of the government. The shortcomings of the members reflected those of the country. These were revealed sometime by the Tories and other times by the

Liberals. He did not give much importance to the newly formed Labour Party. He wrote to Minto that he had been elected from Newcastle for twelve years which was dominated by workers. He knew that the British labour was middle class and individualistic unlike the French. Though Morley desired that political reforms were overdue in India, he was very particular to see that they should be of limited nature and not very wide. The Tory party, the viceroy and the bureaucracy were bound to limit the scope of such reforms. One of the reforms was to expand the Viceroy's Council and include an Indian member. But it was thought that Muslims should also be represented and so it was decided that two Indian members be appointed on the Council. This was under consideration since 1906. But Lord Kitchener, who was a member of the Council, opposed it. Some members suggested that the Secretary of State's Council could have two Indian members. Ultimately it was decided that Secretary of State's Council should have two, while the Viceroy's Council should have one Indian member. Accordingly, Morley sent two names to King Edward on August 26, 1907 for approval. One was that of Krishna Govind Gupta who was a well known lawyer and a member of the Revenue Board of Bengal, and other was that of Syed Hussain Bilgrami, who was for a while a member of the Central Legislative Council and afterwards an advisor to the Nizam.

As the government was not moving to satisfy the main demands of the Congress, the discontent continued. Bengalis could not be satisfied unless the partition was abrogated or modified in such a way as to bring all the Bengali speaking population in one province. Agitation was widespread and some of the speakers like Bipin Chandra Pal and Arvindbabu were inclined to use emotional and extreme language. Revolt of 1857 was mentioned very often. Pal used to say that with the establishment of the Congress it was hoped that the way for political reforms would be paved. But instead, repression was let lose, culminating in the partition of Bengal. Though public opinion had been expressed against the partition, the government remained totally indifferent. People, therefore, had lost all faith in the British government and they didn't think that justice would be done. Some people advised the constitutional methods, but as the country had no constitution, there could not be constitutional agitation. Even then agitators did not want to break the established laws. It was said that the British had conquered India by sword, but that sword was that of the Indian soldiers. In 1857 the same sword was used against the British. British were very few in whole of India and how many of them were armed? Even Russia and Germany could not keep armed soldiers in every village. It was the Indians who were running the administration. British officers, judges etc. were dependent on the subordinate staff, which was all Indian. If this staff refused to work, the administration would come to a standstill. After being independent by such methods, Swadeshi would be the adopted policy of the new government and all import of the British goods would stop. India would be industrialized and the Little England would be unable to compete with a huge India.

The government was angry with the writings in Arvindbabu's 'Yugantar' and 'Bande Mataram'. Both periodicals were appealing the Indians to prepare for ultimate sacrifice. They said that if one could not live as a man, one could die like one. Arvindbabu did not think that swadeshi should be confined to some British goods. He wanted to discard the Western education and culture and revert to Indian culture. Arvindbabu did not openly go against the Muslims, but his appeal to follow ancient—Sanatan—religion could not be acceptable to the Muslims. Lokmanya Tilak differed from Arvindbabu. He was all for swadeshi, but did not emphasize the revival of the ancient Hindu culture and knowledge. Rabindranath's contribution to the agitation is very aptly described by R.C. Majumdar. He writes: "The idea which inspired Bankim Chandra to write the Bande Mataram hymn, was expressed through charming poems and songs by Rabindranath. But the poet did great deal more. He sang the glories of ancient India and its culture and held vividly before the people the portraits of Shivaji and Guru Govind Singh as nation builders, and of Banda as a symbol of stoic heroism and spirit of sacrifice displayed by the Sikhs. Many of his ballads touch upon the patriotism, chivalry and heroism of the Rajputs and the struggle of the Marathas and Sikhs for freedom".[3]

Reviewing the volatile situation in India, Thomas Millard, who spent few months in India, wrote an article in May 19, 1907 issue of 'The New York Times'. He attributed the resurgence in India to the rise of new spirit generated by the Japanese victory over Russia. He then says: "While the present disorder in India can hardly be taken seriously presaging another mutiny, the Government regards the situation as one calling for tact coupled with firmness. Prominent British officials in India have not felt at ease for several months past, nor will they until the agitation entirely subsides. Thus we may confidently expect to see the present disorders pass, at least for a time. But the kernel of unrest will remain untouched, and its underlying sentiment will continue to smother. The more enlightened and, perhaps the most aggressive native leaders do not think that time for even a partial recovery of national autonomy is ripe. But with all Asia in ferment of new ambitions, India is not the least of the various danger spots".

Some prominent Indians, however, were opposing not only the agitation but also the political reforms in general. The Maharaja of Benares was one of them, whose official wrote a letter on behalf of the Maharaja to 'The Pioneer' expressing concern about the growing seditious atmosphere in the country. The letter reminded the Englishmen that India was not England and never would be. The reforms which India needed must be natural and should not be revolutionary. Not those who shout 'Bande Mataram' would bring the political reforms, but only Rajas and Maharajas would. The letter criticized the Indian language newspapers, which it said were treated with disgust by the reasonable people. Most of the editors of Indian language papers were young and published false news and induced the emotional young people to seditious activities. Those students who indulged in unlawful activities should be flogged and if they continued with such activities, must be rusticated from the educational institutions. The letter at the end declared that people with estates alone were the true leaders and not those who were indulged in speech-making. Shapurji Bharucha, president of the Bombay Share Market, was much more nasty in his criticism of the political trends in India in general and agitation in Bengal in particular. He disapproved the turn which the politics had taken; which he said was much more aggressive, and the language of the material published by Congress was extremist. Bharucha asked what happened to the large amount of money, which the Bengalis received in the last fifty years by sales of land, the prices of which had considerably increased. He described Bengalis as emotional and unrealistic. He said even if they talked of revolution they were not the people to fight as they were even afraid of blood. Shapurji's criticism was another indication how by that time Parsi community was drifting away from the Congress. Wacha had warned Dadabhai about this development which he regretted. Shapurji's criticism was not only unwarranted but also totally oblivious of reality. Many Bengali youths, including some young women, had joined revolutionary societies and had suffered. Several of them were sent to Andamans and also went to the gallows. They were not afraid of taking blood of the officials nor were they afraid to shed their blood and lay down their lives.

K.C. Dali, who was one of the high officials in the Intelligence Department of the Government of India, in his report, described how from the last decade of the nineteenth century, secret societies sprang up in Bengal. According to him, this trend started in 1897. Some people from Maharashtra had moved to Benaras and other places in north India and they started schools, and some of them had established Chapekar society. Chapekar was one of the assassins of Rand in Poona. In addition, in 1902 Bengal saw the rise of Shivaji cult, which had reached different parts of Bengal at the time of Partition. Later, Seditious Committee came to the conclusion that it was this Shivaji Cult, which was responsible for the spread of seditious activities in many parts of country including Bengal. In the initial period secret societies in Bengal did not have political objectives. But after the assassination of Rand in Poona, they started thinking on political lines. They then decided to distribute arms to their members. According to Dali, a young man sang a patriotic song in a public meeting at Savarganj, in Bengal, on July 26, 1905 that electrified the atmosphere and from then onwards the idea of an armed revolution to overthrow the British rule gained ground. In 1903 Sarladevi Ghosal and P. Mitra established a secret society. Okasura, a Japanese, joined them. As the secret societies were springing up in Bengal and in other parts of India, so also there was no dearth of informers. One such informer conveyed to the government that a mine-owner and a judge of the High Court, Charu Chandra Dutt, were giving monetary help to the revolutionaries.

In 1905 a society by name Anushilan was established in Bengal which had branches at several places in the province and was presided over by P. Mitra. Though its open activity was giving lessons in physical exercise, it had a secret committee which was for armed rebellion. The society had two factions; one of which stood for educating and inspiring the Indian Army for revolution and the other preferred to resort to the assassination of the government officials. The Anushilan had a significant influence on the social life of Bengal. For some time the Society depended on the voluntary contribution from the public, but as work increased, its demand for money also increased proportionately. Society members then started looting government treasuries. Arvindbabu, who was in the service of the Baroda government, came to stay in Calcutta after retiring from the service. He joined his brother Barindra Kumar who was already involved in revolutionary activities. Arvindbabu took over 'Yugantar', a weekly started by his brother. By this time he became a devotee of Bhavani, a goddess of power and he started preaching this cult. Barindra Kumar, Hem Chandra Das and Ulhaskar Dutt had collected some arms and bombs. They had a plan to assassinate the then lieutenant-governor, Sir Bampfylde Fuller, but did not succeed. Hem Chandra Das went to Paris where he met P.M. Bapat from Maharashtra and both of them saw a Russian lady who gave them lessons in making bombs. French police who were aware of these activities conveyed the information through their government to the British authorities. Morley appraised Minto of these activities.

Vinayak Damodar Savarkar reached London in 1906. Before going to London, Savarkar had started a society, the Mitra Mela, which afterwards was named as Abhinav Bharat. Savarkar as a student of the Fergusson College in Poona was rusticated for participating in the public bonfire of foreign clothes. In Paris, one of the rich Indians, S. Rana, had established a fund to award fellowships to the Indian students. Lokmanya Tilak recommended Savarkar for the fellowship, which enabled Savarkar to go to London. After a while he started sending pistols to India, secretly. As 1907 was the fiftieth anniversary of 1857 revolt, Savarakar wrote a book, which was banned by the Government of India, but several copies could reach India, clandestinely. Thus, Maharashtra, Bengal and Punjab were the three provinces where the revolutionary activities were intense and partition of Bengal strengthened them. In London, the main centre of the revolutionary activities was the India House, started by Shamji Krishna Verma. He came from Kathiawad and was a Sanskrit scholar. Monier Williams, who too was a Sanskrit scholar, recommended Verma for a scholarship to Oxford University. After his graduation he started a periodical, 'Indian Sociologist'. Verma used to stay in Paris, but he purchased a house in London, used mainly as a residence for Indian students.

Revolutionary activities in India, coupled with the politics of the Radicals in the Congress, alarmed the government. Annulling the partition of Bengal or modifying it, was the effective way to bring peace in the country; but government resorted to repression. In 1907 a ban was imposed on the seditious meetings in Bengal and Punjab. It was left to local authorities to decide which meeting was seditious. Morley, anticipating restrictions on the newspapers, wrote to Lord Minto on May 3, 1907: "You may be sure of my firm support, even if the sternest things should unluckily be needed. It may turn out that you will want that support not only against sedition-mongers, but against your law-and-order people, who are responsible for at least as many fooleries of history as revolutionists are. I only hope that plenty of deliberation, and comprehensive balancing of pros and cons, may precede any strong measure. I hope further where time permits you will acquaint me with your intentions well beforehand, more especially where the Press is concerned. It won't surprise me if you desire to take some steps in Press matters, but you should know that people here are very sensitive about this, not merely ultra-radicals, but the papers like 'The Spectator', from which I enclose an extract as a specimen. Much attention has naturally been paid to Lord Cromer's resolute refusal, in his last report, to muzzle the Press in Egypt. If there be a scintilla of real evidence that seditious rags are infecting the Native army, nobody would refuse suppression. Only you won't forget that in moments of excitement, such as this may become, people are uncommonly liable to confuse suspicion and possibilities with certainty and reality".[4]

Morley came under increased criticism inside and outside the Parliament, because of the policy of the Government of India. He tried to reply to his critics and again refuted the charge that he had given up his liberalism. On August 21, 1907 he addressed a public meeting in his constituency—Arbroth. Morley said, "It was alleged to have been said by a British Member of Parliament, that whatever is good by way of self-government for Canada, must be good for India. In my view that is the most concise statement that I can imagine, of the grossest fallacy in all politics. First of all, I hope that the Government of India, so long as I am connected with it and responsible for it to Parliament and to the country, will not be hurried by the anger of the impatient idealist. How many of the tragic miscarriages in human history have been due to the impatient idealist? The Governments have been obliged to take measures of repression; they may be obliged to take more. Those of you who have followed Indian matters at all during the last two or three months are aware that there is a reform scheme, a scheme to give the Indians chance of coming more closely and responsibly into a share of the Government of their country. The root of the matter (discontent) is racial and social and not political".[5] Morley made it clear that the first duty of the Government of India was to keep law and order. He even defended the restrictions on press in exceptional circumstances.

The Government of India might have been emboldened by the speeches of Morley, and in order to make the powers under the ordinance permanent, it brought a bill which was opposed vigorously by Gokhale in the Central Legislative Council in November 1907. He said the Seditious Meetings Bill was unwarranted, as there was no serious threat to the regime. Alluding to the situation in Punjab, Gokhale said there was only one meeting after the promulgation of the ordinance. It was held in Delhi and attended by Hindus and Muslims. The meeting was held to demand the release of Lala Lajpat Rai and there was no disturbance after the meeting. In East Bengal also there was no disturbance of public peace. Gokhale then said, "The bulk of the educated classes in India feel, and feel keenly, that during the last six months, their aims and their activities have been most cruelly misrepresented before the British public, and that they have not had fair-play during the time. Exaggerated importance has been attached to the utterances of a few visionaries, and advantage has been taken of every accidental circumstance to represent an agitation for reform and for the removal of specific grievances as a moment for revolt. The saddest part of the whole thing is that the Secretary of State for India has fallen a victim to these grievous misrepresentations. Possessing no personal knowledge of the people of this country, and overwhelmed with a sense of vast responsibilities of his office, he has allowed his vision to be obscured and his proportion to be warped. From time to time he has let fall ominous hints in the House of Commons, and more than once he has spoken as though some great trouble was brewing in India and the country was on the eve of a dark disaster. I think the Government are repeating in this matter the great mistake they made when they partitioned Bengal. A few men in Bengal have taken to practicing a new gospel and here and there in the country one occasionally hears a faint echo of their teaching. But their power to influence the people—to the extent to which they are able to influence them—is derived mainly from the sense of helplessness. Your Lordship has already taken a most important step in the direction of such conciliation in so far as Punjab has been concerned by vetoing the Colonisation act. Let the work of conciliation be carried further and let the deported prisoners be brought back. As in the Punjab the Colonisation Act has been vetoed, so in Bengal let Partition be modified in some manner acceptable to the Bengalis". After the Select Committee made some minor changes in the Bill, Gokhale speaking on the amended Bill said, "As regard the Moderates denouncing the Extremists, it is not such an easy matter. Such denunciation is largely a matter of temperament. All people do not always denounce whatever they disapprove. There are certain Anglo-Indian newspapers which constantly revile Indians. Has the Honourable Member (who demanded such denunciation) ever denounced anything that has appeared in their columns"?

When the government was resorting to harsh measures, Congress was embroiled in internecine controversy and struggle. Nagpur was to be the venue for the Congress Session in 1907. But the radicals and the moderates were constantly at loggerheads. Each of them was striving hard to secure majority in the Reception Committee. It was obvious that the majority would have the upper hand in getting the president of its choice. Radicals wanted Tilak as president. If the radicals had the majority, they could certainly bring resolutions favouring boycott, Swadeshi and indigenous education system, which were an anathema to the moderates. News from Nagpur was not palatable to the moderates. Krishnaswami Iyer suggested to Gokhale that Pherozeshah and Gokhale should issue a joint statement declaring that they disapprove of the position taken by the radicals. Gokhale rejected this suggestion telling Krishnaswami that as the Anglo-Indian papers were asking the moderates to denounce the radicals, such a joint declaration would be inappropriate. In his opinion only when the Government policy regarding the political reforms was clear, then the moderates should decide whatever had to be done about the radicals. Gokhale also told his friend that they should wait to see how the Radicals would face the repressive measures of the government. He believed that Radicals like Pal would be cowed down and then their followers would be disillusioned about the leadership realizing that the moderates were on the right path. Pherozeshah agreed with Gokhale and suggested Nawab Syed Mohammed Bahadur as the president, while Gokhale wanted Dr. Rash Bihari Ghose.

On September 22, 1907, the Reception Committee of the Congress met at Nagpur Town Hall. The Moderates had a clear majority but they were bullied by a minority of the members who were mostly students, and some of whom were enrolled without proper credentials. Chitnavis, who was the chairman of the Reception Committee was very weak and could not control the rowdy crowd. The people came to blows with each other and the meeting ended in confusion. R.N. Mudholakar, a prominent moderate, wrote to Pherozeshah on October 2, about the fiasco. He said, "The extremists, though there are only few of them on the Reception Committee, are active, energetic, bold and unscrupulous. They have captured the executive committee, because the Moderates were most of the pusillanimous, inactive and indolent. Though the Moderates had about 500 present at the meeting of September 22, they were thoroughly cowed down by the rowdyism of about two to three dozen extremists. The Nagpur Koshtis have long been known to be a turbulent lot and the Nagpur school boys and college boys have been for years more or less unruly. These mischievous elements have been set in motion against the Moderates, and excepting the few of these, the majority are afraid of attending any meeting. Under these circumstances the only course open to us is to change the venue of this year's Congress".

It seems Gokhale was hopeful that some solution would be found and the session would be held in Nagpur. He had, as secretary of the All India Congress Committee, instructed the Nagpur leaders that in view of the rowdyism already displayed, the spectators should only be permitted in the pandal at the time when president addressed the session and not when the Subjects Committee met. But that eventuality did not occur. Moderates might have lost at Nagpur, but the Radicals failed to prevail. Pherozeshah called a meeting of the Central Congress Committee at his home, which was attended by Tilak and Khaparde from the radical wing. A compromise solution was suggested that both groups would have equal number of members on the executive committee of the Reception Committee and some additional members to be nominated by the Central Standing Committee of the Congress; money collected to be handed over to the new committee. This was foolishly opposed by Khaparde, and he played into the hands of Pherozeshah, who immediately invited some Congressmen from Surat who expressed their readiness to call the Congress session at Surat. In fact, Madras had invited the Congress session, but Pherozeshah took it to Surat. The next day Tilak offered to accept the compromise formula, which Pherozeshah rejected and the Radicals had to beat a retreat. Tilak later wrote that Surat was a street owned by Pherozeshah. But Pherozeshah could take the Congress session to his street because Khaparde played his cards badly and Tilak did not control him.

Tilak wanted Lala Lajpat Rai to preside over the session of the Congress at Surat. In an editorial on December 10, 1907, Tilak said that, for the sacrifice and suffering for the cause of India, Lalaji deserved this honour more than Dr. Ghose who should withdraw and make room for Lala Lajpat Rai. He castigated Gokhale for canvassing for Ghose. Tilak also denounced the position of the Moderates who were insisting that the agitation should be constitutional. He asked where was the Indian constitution? Tilak said it was high time that the Moderates give up their belief that by persuading the English public they would achieve the Congress objective. He then declared that if the Moderates wanted to so conduct the Congress affairs, which would not offend the government officials, then it was better to wind up the whole show. He reminded the Moderates that the Congress was established with a view to geting its objectives realized by lawful means. There could be two or more view-points about the way the Congress affairs should be managed. Like the British Parliament, Congress also could have two parties. The majority should not assume that Congress was their private estate; and should be ready to make way for the other party if it secured majority. Tilak characterized the Surat session as that of the Mehta and Company. Moderates did everything to fortify their position.

Prior to the Congress session at Surat, the Bombay Provincial Conference had its session in the same city. Sir Bhalchandra Bhatvadekar presided and Pherozeshah appealed to the delegates not to move a resolution advocating swadeshi and national education. Bhatvadekar ruled that the swadeshi resolution should be moved in the Industrial Conference, and debarred it. He also ruled out the boycott resolution. Moderates maintained that in Calcutta it was accepted that boycott was confined only to Bengal; and therefore it was unnecessary to pass such a resolution by any other province. Provincial Conference accepted this position. Pherozeshah opposed all efforts to move any resolution about the national education even in the open session of the Provincial Conference. The Provincial Conference of the Central Provinces and Berar was held at Raipur, which also rejected any resolutions on the subject of swadeshi as well as National Education. United Province had its conference at Allahabad where Madan Mohan Malviya behaved high handedly by disallowing those who were supporters of the boycott. So Lala Lajpat Rai had to satisfy himself with a speech on the subject at a public meeting.

Thus both the Moderates and the Radicals gathered at Surat with a view to fight it out. Khaparde went to Surat before Tilak's arrival and addressed some meetings, making fun of the Moderates. He could speak Gujrati well and with his humourous and sarcastic speeches he regaled the audience. Much has been written on the Surat session of the Congress, which was expected to be one-sided. It is, therefore, better to rely on the report of Nevinson, a 'Manchester Guardian' representative, who was present at the session and covered it extensively. Nevinson said that the journey for Ghose from Calcutta was all roses as he was greeted everywhere and made small speeches at some railway stations. The atmosphere in Surat was full of suspicion and rumours were rife in the Radical camp. Nevinson then says: "In the afternoon of Christmas Day, just before the President-elect arrived in insecure triumph, Lala Lajpat Rai himself went to the Nationalist camp. Lajpat Rai, the quiet, fearless man, with all the honour of dishonour still upon him; a moderate, a close friend of Gokhale, but a patriot above suspicion, a man put forward as President by the Nationalists themselves, had he not refused to stand rather than hasten the dangerous breach. Surely he, if anyone, might serve as peacemaker. He proposed a conference between the parties, five leaders a side. The Nationalists appointed their representatives. On the bare hope of peace, Lajpat Rai sought Mr. Gokhale at the station as the president-elect steamed in. What a moment to arrange a conference! How could even Gokhale appoint five leaders to represent sixteen hundred delegates?"

"That night few slept. Backwards and forwards, from tent to tent and house to house, the leaders passed, discussing, consulting, deliberating, full of uncertainty and apprehension. Morning found them still apprehensive and uncertain. In a last effort to secure Mr. Surendranath Banerjea, if not peace, Mr. Tilak, Arvindo Ghose, and Mr. Khaparde went to his house with proposals. To Surendranath they proposed two conditions under which they would refrain from opposing the President's election—the four Calcutta resolutions on self-government, Swadeshi, Boycott and National Education must be repeated in the same form as last year; and some 'graceful allusion' must be made by one of the speakers on the election of the President, 'to the desire of the public to have Lala Lajpat Rai in the chair'. He advised the Nationalists to seek an interview with Mr. Gokhale or Mr. Tribhovandas Malvi, a Surat gentleman, Chairman of the Reception Committee. They did not attempt to see Mr. Gokhale. Mr. Malvi could not see them, because he was engaged in a prayer."

"The meeting was to have begun at one, but to allow time to burn the body of a Scinde delegate who had died, it was put off till half-past two. The delegates number perhaps sixteen hundred, of whom five hundred might be called Extremists of one kind or other. On the platform sat some thirty or forty Indian ladies, Parsis for the most part, but Hindus and Mohammedans as well, significant of a deeper change than politics. The other thousands were the indistinguishable audience who had come to listen or perhaps do more than listen. The platform people began to arrive. Then a quiet, a white turbaned figure, with sad determination in his look, entered from the side. Like one man, the ten thousand sprang to their feet, cheer followed cheer; it seemed as though the cheering would never cease. Who does not love the man that has suffered for a cause? It was Lala Lajpat Rai."

"A few minuets afterwards the Volunteers were seen lining the central passage again, and up the midst in a solid body came Dr. Rash Bihari Ghose, the President-elect; Sir Pherozeshah Mehta, the mitred Parsi, Mr. Wacha, Mr. Surendranath Banerjea the orator of Bengal, Mr. Gokhale whom some were tired of hearing called the Just; and other leaders of the Congress. At the site, the opposition shut its voice. Mr. Tribhovandas Malvi, Chairman of the Reception Committee, rose to welcome the Congress in the name of his native Surat, and there was silence. The Address ended. Dewan Bahadur Ambalal S. Desai rose formally to propose that Dr. Ghose, already designated President, should now take the Presidential chair. At the name of Dr. Ghose, deep murmur of dissent was heard again, and one shrill voice cried, 'Never'! But the moment Diwan sat down, Mr. Banerjea was standing in his place beside the table. He was to second the proposal that Dr. Ghose should take the Chair. Hardly had his immense voice uttered ten words when, like the cracking of thunder that begins before lightening ceases, the tumult burst, and no word more was heard."

"Waving their arms, their sticks and umbrellas, a solid mass of delegates and spectators on the right of the Chair sprang to their feet and shouted without a moment's pause. Over their heads was the label, 'Central Provinces'.—'Remember Nagpur', they cried, 'Remember Midnapur!' The whole ten thousand were on their feet. Mr. Malvi, still half in the chair, rang his Benaras bell, and rang in vain. Surendranath sprang upon the very table itself. Again and again he shouted, unheard as silence. He sat down, and for a moment the storm was lulled. The voices of the leaders were audible, consulting in agitated tones. Dr. Ghose shrill, impatient and perturbed with anger. Again Surendranath sprang on the table, and again the assembly roared with clamour. Again the Chairman rang his Benaras bell, and rang in vain. In an inaudible voice like a sob, he declared the sitting suspended."

"After twenty-two years of steady and regular procedure the Congress had broken up in less than an hour. To the excited groups into which the great assembly split, it seemed incredible. I conversed with Mr. Kelkar of Poona, editor of 'Maratha', as Mr. Tilak's lieutenant. The outbreak, he said, was accidental and unexpected. They had determined to oppose Dr. Ghose's election, but not by tumult; they would not even have opposed it had not the Moderate offer of compromise come too late. I visited the Nationalist camp far across the town, and found Mr. Tilak himself, just returned from his dubious triumph, sitting naked in his cloth. He gave me the same assurance. The whole thing had been a mistake; it had all happened because the undertaking to renew the Calcutta resolutions had reached him too late—not till the Chairman had begun his speech. The resolutions had then been handed to him by Mr. Gokhale, and he had admitted he would himself have been satisfied if certain changes in their wording had been removed and the original form restored. But by that time it was too late to reassure his followers."

"The morning of December 27th again found them at variance, still uncertain, their mood more fretted by sleeplessness and anxiety. By noon the pandal was again full to over-flowing. At one o'clock the presidential procession entered. Again Dr. Rash Bihari Ghose bore with him the printed copy of his Presidential address, which ought to have been delivered the afternoon before, and had, unhappily, appeared that morning in some of the Calcutta papers, with an attack upon the Extremists, still unaltered."

"In the front row of the delegates, not in the place reserved for him on the platform, Mr. Tilak was seated. As the procession entered, he sent a note to the chairman by one of the boy volunteers to say he wished to speak on the election of the President, after the seconder had spoken. Mr. Malvi called upon Mr. Banerjea to take up his speech, seconding the appointment of Dr. Ghose as a President. In inaudible words Mr. Malvi proposed that Dr. Ghose should take the Chair as President, and amid various shouting he declared the motion carried. Dr. Ghose rose at once to deliver that thoughtfully prepared address. As when lightening flashes in air surcharged with storm, Mr. Tilak was seen standing straight, in front of the Presidential Chair itself, expostulating, protesting, all in that calm, decisive voice of his, the voice of a man indifferent to fate. He had given notice of an amendment, he was there to move it, and there he would remain. 'You cannot move for the adjournment of the Congress', cried Mr. Malvi; 'I declare you out of order'. 'I wish to move an amendment, to the election of President, and you are not in the Chair', Mr. Tilak replied. 'I declare you out of order'! cried Dr. Ghose. 'You have not been elected', answered Mr. Tilak, 'I appeal to the delegates'."

"Uproar drowned the rest. With folded arms Mr. Tilak faced the audience. On the other side of him young Moderates sprang to their feet, wildly gesticulating vengeance. Shaking their fists and yelling to the air, they clamoured to hurl him down the steep of the platform. Mr. Gokhale sweet natured even in extremes, stood beside his old opponent, flinging out both arms to protect him from the threatened onset. But Mr. Tilak asked for no protection. He stood there with folded arms, defiant, calling on violence to do its worst, calling on violence to move him, for he would move for nothing else in hell or heaven. In front, the white-clad audience roared like a tumultuous sea."

"Suddenly something flew through the air, a shoe! A Maratha shoe! Reddish leather, pointed toe, sole studded with lead. It struck Surendranath Banerjea on the cheek; it cannoned off upon Sir Pherozeshah Mehta. It flew, it fell, and, as at a given signal, white waves of turbaned men surged up the escarpment of the platform. Leaping, climbing, hissing the breath of fury, brandishing long sticks, they came, striking at any head that looked to them Moderate, and in another moment, between brown legs standing upon the green-baize table, I caught the glimpses of the Indian National Congress dissolving in chaos".[6]

The pandal was strewn with broken chairs and sticks. Police came and the order was restored. Nevinson has dwelt on the changes made in the Calcutta resolutions about boycott, Swadeshi and National Education. Most of the changes were minor, but as suspicion bordering on hatred had taken hold of the minds of the leaders of the two groups, much was made of those changes and no one was prepared to compromise. At the same time it must be noted that even if there had been no pandemonium, some portions of the Presidential address would have infuriated the Radicals. Dr. Ghose had said that boycott of educational institutions, courts etc.was indicative of frustration and martyrdom was not always taken as judicious. He declared that self-government would not be achieved unless Indians had shown their worth. He castigated the Radicals and their movement.

After the fiasco of the Surat Congress, Radicals had a meeting presided over by Arvindbabu. Tilak spoke for two hours and told the audience how the Moderates made mistakes. But he had kept the door for reconciliation open. Moderates, on the other hand, called a national convention next day at Surat, presided over by Dr. Ghose. Those who desired to attend the convention had to sign a pledge, which affirmed that attaining the self-government as other British colonies was the aim of the Congress; and its faith in the constitutional means to attain this objective. This insistence on the declaration of faith in the constitutional means meant to show that those who did not sign it were not willing to follow the constitutional path. Even some of the people who were prepared to sign the pledge were refused entry to the convention. After some business was transacted, Gokhale moved to form a committee to draft a constitution. This was long stalled by Pherozeshah. But under the exigencies he accepted the resolution.

Thus Congress after its existence for twenty-one years was split. Some British officials were apprehensive that partition of Bengal would strengthen the Congress, which would become a formidable force. But the partition split the Congress and also paralyzed it.

The convention after the Surat Congress was totally a Moderate show, which decided to admit those who would sign the prescribed pledge. Pherozeshah Mehta in an interview to 'The Times of India' on December 29, 1907 stated that he had already predicted that the Congress had to split if it were not to be controlled by the Radicals. He characterized the aspirations of the Radicals as impractical and hence could not be achieved. That was why, he said, a majority of the Congressmen were not inclined to go with them. Pherozeshah made it clear that the aim of his colleagues and himself was to achieve self-government, but it was to be a remote one. Their immediate objective was to bring some improvement in the administration and its working. Pherozeshah warned that the boycott would be self-defeating, as the rival party was that of the rulers and it would retaliate in the same way, which would be harmful. He maintained that Swadeshi implied economic progress. Pherozeshah said that Tilak had no following in the Bombay province and whatever influence he had outside, was due to his being a member of the Congress. But now that the Congress was split, people would know his real character. He held Tilak and the Radicals entirely responsible for the split in the Congress.

Debate about the Congress split spilled over for a long time. Both groups were assertive about their righteousness. The editor of the 'Amrit Bazar Patrika', Moti Lal Ghose, in a foreword to his book *A Step in the Steamer* has given an interesting account about what happened at Surat. He writes: "The blame of the break-up of the Congress at Surat in December, 1907 has been sought to be fastened on Mr. Tilak by his political opponents. But in this matter he did not take one step without consulting me. He dragged me to Surat though I was then ill, and he and I and some other friends settled our plan of work. I remained in the background and Tilak as the leader had to come to the front. All that the Nationalists wanted the Moderate leaders to do was either to withdraw some offensive expressions which the President-elect had used towards them in one of his speeches at a meeting of the Viceregal Council or to permit them to enter a protest against the same in the Congress. When this was proposed, the Moderate leaders were furious. Sir Pherozeshah Mehta was specially intolerant in his tone and behaviour, when we made an attempt to compromise the matter; and later on he refused to see Mr. Tilak, when by appointment he went over to his place to have further talk in this connection. The only course now left to the Nationalists was to record a formal protest against the election of a President who was not friendly to them at the time when he would be proposed to be elected."

"If this legitimate request of the Nationalists were acceded to, everything would have passed peacefully, for they were in a minority and the motion was bound to be defeated. But both the parties had then lost the balance of their minds. Mr. Tilak was not permitted to move the resolution and he on his part was determined to do it and refused to leave the platform unless he was permitted to speak or removed by physical force." No Indian can contemplate this deplorable affair without a sense of shame and humiliation. Accompanied by Ray Yatindra Nath Choudhari I approached him with the following proposal:

> "I told him, 'Look here', Tilak, you alone can save the situation. But it means tremendous sacrifice on your part self-condemnation. Knowing you as I do, I am confident you are prepared for it.—They want your blood. Why not give it to them for the sake of the Congress?—Will you give me a written undertaking saying that you are willing to take the whole odium on your shoulders and make a public declaration to that effect, if thereby the death of the Congress is averted? It would be a noble sacrifice on your part."
>
> "Mr. Tilak was moved. Most of his adherents vehemently opposed the proposal.—Tilak reflected for a while and then arrived at his decision. There was a sad smile on his face and he said, ' Here is the undertaking. And he wrote a few lines to the effect—'I undertake to take the responsibility of this unfortunate incident upon myself if the other party would agree to continue the Congress.'—Ponder on the magnitude of the magnanimity and self-abnegation of the man.—With this written undertaking in our possession I, Ray Yatindra Nath Choudhari and a few other friends ran to the Moderate Camp with a view to bring about a reconciliation, if possible, but we were simply howled out by the Moderate leaders headed by Sir Pherozeshah Mehta."[7]

Tilak also wrote to the chairman of the Reception Committee that according to their talks he was willing to withdraw his opposition and also that of his party to the election of Dr. Rash Bihari Ghose as the president of Congress. They were ready to behave with the spirit of forget and forgive. But he and his colleagues expected that the resolutions passed at the Calcutta session should be reaffirmed and Dr. Ghose should omit the parts of his presidential speech, which were critical of the Radicals. But the Moderates who differed on the meaning and the scope of the Calcutta resolutions did not want to reconsider their position and the Radicals could not forget the interpretation put on the Calcutta resolutions by the Moderates. Gokhale as the secretary of the Congress came out with a detailed refutation of the objections of the radicals. He gave the texts of the Calcutta resolutions and the changes made in those which came before the Surat session.

Gokhale emphasized that the changes were not significant and some of them were only of technical nature. Gokhale criticized Tilak for changing his position about the ultimate objective of the Congress. He cited some of the writings of Tilak. The resolution about swadeshi as passed at Calcutta said that swadeshi was to be accepted even with sacrifice. Gokhale said that this was not mentioned in the Surat resolution because he went by the text in the Congress periodical the 'India', published from London. Gokhale accused Tilak of having his own interpretation of the resolution about the boycott, because even at Calcutta it was stated that the boycott was to be limited to Bengal. Gokhale explained that he could not give any assurance that there would not be any change in the resolutions, as he had no authority to do so, it was the privilege of the Subjects Committee.

According to N.C. Kelkar, Tilak's biographer, Tilak was prepared to attend the convention at Surat, called by the Moderates and sign the pledge, which was to be the condition for the membership of the Congress. He wanted to do this as he believed that Indians should make demands with one voice. He also believed that he would be able to establish his dominance and bring the Moderates to his side. But it was Arvindbabu, who vehemently opposed the idea of attending the convention at Surat. Arvindbabu later described how the scuffle broke out at the Surat session of the Congress. He made it clear that he and some of his friends kept Tilak in the dark and decided to precipitate the quarrel and even start a pandemonium. After the break-up of the session Tilak did not denounce the pandemonium, as he thought it would not befit him to forsake those who stood by him. Later in 1912, R.N. Mudholkar, a Moderate from Amravati, blamed the Radicals for the Congress split. According to him some young men from Berar were to use long sticks to beat Pherozeshah. Some of the 'delegates' from Nagpur were barbers. Mudholkar also said that Khaparde and his friends addressed several meetings in Nagpur, viciously attacking Moderates and more particularly Gokhale, and that the old leaders of Nagpur were intimidated.

Lokamanya Tilak explained his position and refuted the criticism by Pherozeshah and Gokhale in his editorials and editorial notes. Burden of his criticism was that the Moderates were keen to change the resolutions passed by the Calcutta Congress presided over by Dadabhai. He wrote that Dadabhai had changed the tone of the Congress, but the 'King of Bombay' (Pherozeshah) was directing his efforts to concentrate on getting some petty demands accepted by the government as he thought the objective of the self-government was a remote one. He took Gokhale to task for toeing Pherozeshah's line. Tilak then dwelt with the election of Dr. Ghose as the president of the Congress and his challenge to this election. He said that legally it was open to Dr. Ghose or Mr. Malvi to put his (Tilak's) motion of adjournment before the delegates and take the vote. Tilak also quoted the 'Hindu', which had held the same view. Historian R.C.

Mujumdar has observed, "As regards the standpoint of Tilak that he had a right to speak before the President delivered his Address, the legal position is not after all so clearly against him as it was supposed at the time. He had sent a notice of a resolution, and if the Chairman of the Reception Committee thought it was out of order, it was his plain duty to inform him beforehand or to announce it openly in the meeting that a notice was given by Tilak for a motion of adjournment, but he had ruled it out of order. It may be pointed out that Tilak and his party felt that retrogression of the Calcutta resolutions was so vital a matter that they were justified in opposing it in any constitutional manner. This they had openly said and intimated to the authorities. Their conduct is not therefore so reprehensible, after all, as it might otherwise appear. In the light of the later events it is not difficult to make a reasonable guess of the motive which actuated the Moderates. Large installments of reforms were promised by Morley, and the Moderates believed, perhaps rightly, that these would be withheld if the Moderates could not prove the bonafides of their moderation and loyalty to the British by disassociating themselves from the Extremists. The Moderate leaders, who regarded the reforms as their life's work, had honestly believed that these would regenerate the country, were not prepared to sacrifice them for the sake of the Extremists, an upstart body who, they thought, would lead the country to rack and ruin, if allowed to grow in power".[8]

All over the country Moderates and the Radicals were engaged in controversy. Moderates everywhere maintained that there was no intention to change the Calcutta resolutions so as to nullify them. However, their leader Pherozeshah Mehta in an interview to 'The Times of India' had expressed his opposition to every resolution passed at Calcutta. His position was totally contradictory to the views of Dadabhai. Srinivas Sastri, in one of his speeches on Pherozeshah Mehta, had confessed that, "Why the Moderates should have been at great pains as they suspected, to drop these resolutions, it was not clear, but when it was said that they would drop them, they started a movement of defence. They abused people right and left for a thing which they did not intend to do".[9]

The happenings at Surat were discussed by several newspapers in India and abroad. 'The Statesman' on January 4, 1908, said: "It is natural that those who support the national movement in India should be deeply disappointed by the proceedings at the Surat Congress". It suggested that to develop a spirit of responsibility in the Indians, they should also be given a share in exercising it. The editor of 'The Hindu' of Madras, had sympathy for Tilak's politics, but said that nobody knew what perversion had taken hold of the Radicals at Surat. The paper observed that Tilak and his friends could not absolve themselves of the responsibility of breaking the Congress by rowdyism. The campaign to compel Dr. Ghose to give up the presidentship was improper and wrong. Surat had shown that the Radicals were prepared to give up civility and constitutional methods and go to any length. No educated person with commonsense could justify their action. 'The Hindu' then asked whether the Radicals thought that it was wise to muzzle a person like Surendranath Banerjea, who had devoted his whole life to the service of the country?

'The Times', in some editorials and newsletters, had criticized the Bengal agitation and fiery speeches of Bipin Chandra Pal. It justified the deportation of Lala Lajpat Rai which according to 'The Times' helped in bringing the peace in Punjab. It said that Morley was finding it difficult to bring round the reasonable Indian opinion to his side, as the Moderates had no courage to come out openly against the Bengali agitators. So the stand taken by 'The Times' about Surat split could be anticipated. On December 14, 1907, i.e. before the Surat session, 'The Times' wrote: "While we are not without some sympathy for the genuine Moderates in their present plight, it is necessary to add that they have largely brought it on themselves. Their lack of moral courage and their silent countenance of the dissemination of sedition are primarily responsible for what has occurred. The Bombay leaders, appear to be now honestly trying to save the Congress from suicide, were careful enough to prevent the introduction of boycott, with its incitement to disorder, into their own province; but they never raised their voice in protest against the scenes that distracted Bengal. Mr. Banergee now finds it necessary to call the extremists 'traitors'; but at an earlier period he did not hesitate to appear on the same platform with them, or to encourage and defend the preposterous 'National Volunteers' who now repudiate him.—The only remedy is for the Moderates boldly to recognize that the Extremists are hopelessly irreconcilable and that their real purpose is to destroy the Congress, if they cannot, by capturing it, produce anarchy in Indian public life. Properly and reasonably constituted, the Congress might still, at any rate, be a useful outlet for public opinion in India. As it exists today, it is, quite apart from the question of the Extremists, an abiding mockery of its own aspirations. It pleads for a greater measure of self-control in India, but it cannot even control itself. It asks for a better system of representation, but its own methods are a direct negation of all recognized principles of representation. It clamours for an elective form of government, but it dares not introduce a proper system of election into its own organization, because its controllers know that if they did, the result would instantly be that they would be swept away by an inrush of apostles of disorder."

'The Times' commented on the Surat session of the Congress on December 30 and January 27, 1908. On December 30th it came down heavily against the Moderates and also on Tilak. The Moderates were accused of double talk and of lack of courage to oppose the radical elements. They cannot be moderates inside and Extremists outside said the paper. 'The Times' said: "They did not represent even their own unanimous views, for in their secret enclaves, bickering has been incessant. They did not represent the views of the sixty million Mohammedans, who have steadily held aloof from the Congress, or of the Rajputs or a large proportion of the Sikhs, or a bulk of subjects of the native Princes. Parsees apart, the organization is almost entirely Hindu; among Hindus it is largely Brahmin; among Brahmins it illustrates that singular tendency by which lawyers and politics seem inseparably associated". About Lokmanya Tilak, 'The Times' was particularly nasty and also ignorant. It said: "Mr. Tilak is a political enigma, even in a country where politics are often the queerest jumble of ideas. He is feared and distrusted by nearly all sections of Indian political opinion, yet he contrives to hold his own, to enlist the aid of large number of followers, and to foment agitation. He seems to have no political principles, but to aim at destruction pure and simple".

At Surat a long delayed committee was formed to draft the constitution. This was discussed at Allahabad in a convention on April 18 and 19 and the draft was endorsed. The Constitution declared that objective of the Congress was to achieve the same status for India, which other colonies of the empire enjoyed. It was also affirmed that this objective was to be achieved by constitutional means. The convention was attended by the delegates of Bengal, Bombay, Punjab etc. It was enjoined on those who attended the convention to sign a creed, which declared faith in the constitutional means. This came under fire from the delegates of Bengal and Punjab. Wacha threatened that if such a pledge was rejected, he would wash his hands off the organization. In the end delegates from Bombay and the United Provinces having a majority could get the pledge approved. Thus, a constitution as well as the pledge were adopted, but the members of the Congress had to accept some restrictions and the doors of the Congress were closed for the leaders like Lokmanya Tilak. The All India Congress Committee henceforth was authorized to admit members and decide on the programme of the Congress session. One of the prominent Congress leaders was Motilal Nehru who after the convention wrote to his son that he was satisfied with the achievements of the convention and that the Radicals would be admitted to the Congress only after signing the pledge. Jawaharlal Nehru, who was studying in England, wrote back to say that he did not approve of the politics of the Moderates and favoured the stand taken by Tilak. Bombay Moderate leaders were displeased with the position taken by Surendranath Banerjea at Allahabad convention. Banerjea had to have some understanding with the Radicals in his province, as Bengal was seething with discontent and the agitation against partition had become intense and sometime violent. If he had toed the Moderate line, his leadership would have come to an end. That was why both Surendranath and Arvindbabu came on the same platform of the Bengal Provincial Conference, which met after the Surat split. 'The Hindu' welcomed this, hoping that Congress would eventually be united. Bombay and Maharashtra did not follow Bengal. On the contrary, dispute between the Moderates and the Radicals became bitter. Both factions were claming that they controlled the Congress organization.

Lokmanya Tilak moved to organize conventions on district and even on the Taluk level. Though Tilak had taken this aggressive posture and unleashed a barrage of criticism against Pherozeshah and Gokhale, he kept the door open for compromise. He said that Congress should be open to different viewpoints. In the annual session both parties should place their views before the delegates and those who get the majority should lead, while the other group should act as an opposition. But the Moderates were not in a mood for reconciliation. Bombay leaders decided not to convene a provincial conference, so Tilak called one convention at Bombay and the other at Dhulia. He again appealed to all Congressmen to work together. He said the Congress did not belong to one caste and it also did not belong to one group. It should not be an exclusive preserve of one faction, but should be inclusive and people with different viewpoints must have free access. But the Moderates had lost all patience with him. A statement by Pherozeshah Mehta was a clear indication of how reconciliation was not possible. Mehta, rejecting the demand of the Radicals to reaffirm the Calcutta resolutions about boycott and swadeshi in subsequent sessions of the Congress, said it was impertinence on the part of the Radicals to make such a demand. Every session must be given freedom to pass resolutions. He said that an appeal to unite the Congress at any cost was emotional. Unity would not reveal the real depth of the differences and so let the two groups go by the separate ways and have separate sessions. He said the emotional appeals should be stopped once and for all. As expected Pherozeshah came under attack by the Radicals. 'Amrit Bazar Patrika' wrote that those who were out of the Congress could sign the pledge and join the Congress again; Pherozeshah wanted to bar them altogether, which was unjustified. It said, Pherozeshah was adopting a posture same as the Government of India.

The government was well aware of the main points of disagreement between the two factions in the Congress. Besides, whenever Gokhale as well as Dr. Ghose met Sir James Dunlop-Smith, secretary to the viceroy, he came to know the line of thinking of the Moderate leaders. Dunlop-Smith had prepared a note for the viceroy on the basis of his conversations with Gokhale. He wrote: "Mr. Gokhale proposed that few representative men from Eastern Bengal should have an interview with your Excellency. They would state their case and need be promised nothing. I gathered that Mr. Gokhale is somewhat tired of the Bengalis. He says that Mr. Moti Lal Ghose is not straight; is a 'sneak'; that Surendranath Banerjea is incapable of organization, that he never does any real work and habitually mistakes form for substance. The only non-official Bengali with any real purpose and any capacity for self-sacrificing work in a national cause is Babu Ashwini Kumar Dutt. Mr. Gokhale spoke quite impressively of the belief the educated classes have in your Excellency's sincere wish to meet their aspirations, wherever possible and play them fair". C.F. Andrews, who was working in the Indian community in South Africa, had come to India and wrote to Dunlop-Smith on January 28, 1908: "The temper of the Moderates is this: Surat has been a great gain, but at a great cost. Government does not realize how much we have had to suffer in making the split. We are very, very sore about it—sore with Tilak party for the insults we have received from them, and sore with the Government for not holding out the hand of friendship to us and making some generous concessions—above all for playing into the hands of Tilak on Transvaal question. Now I watched carefully the effect of the Viceroy's words at Simla on the Sedition Act. Lord Minto's words had a very marked effect indeed. They did more to stiffen the backs of the Moderates against the Extremists than anything last year. What I long for is, a renewed request for suggestions as to the reform proposals".[10] Lord Minto was satisfied that Congress had split and conveyed his feelings to Morley. But Morley replied that it was expected that congress would be flat, but it had split; however, after sometime the Radicals would succeed in establishing their dominance on the organization. He, therefore requested Lord Minto to move in the matter of political reforms.

REFERENCES

1. V.S. Srinivas Sastri, *My Master Gokhale*, Model Publications, Madras, 1946, pp. 171-172.
2. R.P. Patwardhan, *Dadabhai Naoroji Correspondence, Vol. 2, Part 2,* Allied Publishers, Bombay, 1977, p. 639.
3. R.C. Majumdar, *The History and Culture of the Indian People: Struggle for the Freedom Part 2, Vol. 11,* Bharatiya Vidya Bhavan, Bombay, 1969, p. 66.
4. Morley, *Reflections, Recollections, Vol. II,* The Macmillan, NY, 1917, pp. 212.
5. Morley, *Indian Speeches 1907-1909*, Macmillan, London, 1909, pp. 35, 37-43.
6. Nevinson Henry W., *The New Spirit in India*, Metropolitan Book. Co., Delhi, 1975, pp. 242-250.
7. Parmananda Dutt, Ed., *Memoirs of Moti Lal Ghose*, Amrita Bazar Patrika Office, Calcutta, 1935, pp. 171-173.
8. R.C. Mujumdar, *The History and Culture of the Indian People: Struggle for the Freedom,* Part 2, Vol. 11, Bharatiya Vidya Bhavan, Bombay, 1969, pp. 93-94.
9. V. S. Srinivas Sastri, *Life and Times of Sir Pherozeshah Mehta*, Bharatiya Vidya Bhavan, Bombay, 1975, p. 122.
10. Ed. Martin Gilbert, *Servant of India*, Longmans, London, 1966, pp. 122-123, 127-128

Chapter Fourteen

CHANGED POLITICAL CLIMATE

It took some years for the Radicals to dominate the Congress. But Tilak did not want to lose time. He asked his colleagues in Bengal to form a new party and to visit all parts of the country for the same. Tilak himself was present at a meeting of some prominent Radical leaders in the office of the 'Amrit Bazar Patrika' in Calcutta. But one of the Radical leaders, Bipin Chandra Pal, after his release from jail, went to England and stayed there till 1911, as he believed that a political campaign in England must have a priority. Arvindbabu had taken to revolutionary politics and so he could not participate in the political work, which Tilak thought very important. Arvindbabu along with his brother Barindra Kumar were involved in the revolutionary politics which had a significant following in Bengal and Maharashtra. So even if the government officials were satisfied by the Congress split at Surat, they had no respite and had to face somewhat dangerous situation. The Moderates were wary that the politics of the Radicals would delay the political reforms about which Morley had talked so much. Now the cult of bomb and series of assassinations of the officials had made the situation more complex and more volatile.

This new cult began sometime before the Surat Congress and in 1907 an attempt was made to blow up the train of the lieutenant-governor of Bengal. That was, according to Minto, an individual act and was not an organized one. But a fortnight afterwards a Dacca magistrate was shot at. Then began a series of attacks on European officers and those Indians about whom the revolutionaries had a grudge. Anushilan committee was providing arms and also giving training to use them. In May 1908, armed men missed their target and two English ladies died. Though the press and the government said that the two English ladies fell victim to the attack, one of them was an Indian married to an Englishman. This incident was the retaliation against Kingsford, a district magistrate, who had ordered to flog a person suspected of criminal action, which infuriated Khudiram Basu and Prafulla Chandra Chaki who threw a bomb on Kingsford's carriage.

That missed the target and the two ladies fell victims. Chaki committed suicide in the prison and Khudiram was given a death sentence. Entire Bengal was surcharged with emotion by this martyrdom. Mendicants who went from village to village sang in praise of Khudiram and Chaki. In Calcutta, the police raided Maniktala garden and seized a large quantity of arms. Arvindbabu and his brother were among the thirty-two who were prosecuted for this. The case went on for a year and Arvindbabu was sentenced. After his release he became a changed person. He came to the conclusion that armed rebellion would not succeed, and renouncing everything he settled in Pondechari.

Charles Targart, a police officer in Calcutta, made a speech in London after his retirement, which was published as a booklet. He said that in Bengal not a single educational institution was without a revolutionary group. He also found that common people had great love and respect for those who were prepared to die for the country. Besides 'Yugantar' and 'Bande Mataram', several newspapers and periodicals were publishing literature extolling the virtues and need of the armed revolt. James Campbell, a civil servant, after his retirement wrote a book *Political Trouble In India,* giving extensive extracts from such writings between 1907 to 1917; while Gerald Barrier's book titled *Banned* deals with the controversial literature between 1907 to 1945 giving extracts of such writings which came under government scrutiny and were banned. C.F. Andrews had written to Sir James Dunlop-Smith on March 1, 1908 about the changed political climate in India and particularly in Bengal. He said: "There is a rapid Hinduising of 'national' ideas going on among the younger men. The boycott spirit follows inevitably as a consequence. The religious element mingles with the political. The key to a great deal of what is happening is contained in a sentence in a recent Oxford Mission Report: Keshab Chandra Sen has ceased to be a national hero. Young Bengal is looking now to the ideals of Ram Krishna and Swami Vivekananda. Our students are all reading cheap reprints of the latter's works together with Bipin Chandra Pal's book *The New Spirit* and Swami Abhedananda's *India and her People*. In these a definite Hinduising ideal is set forward and Hindu religious colouring is given to National ideas. This accounts for the extraordinary popularity of Mr. Tilak and the decline of the influence of Mr. Gokhale. We have ourselves been to blame for over-Anglicising, and the reaction in one sense is natural. But it will be very serious if it becomes a religious fanaticism, for that may reach the masses. Here then is one point to be borne in mind in considering the aims and aspirations of the Graduates. They need to be met on that ground; i.e. not merely to be told that they may have *Western* Institutions in the future; but rather that we want to give them back their own great Indian past, not discard it: we want them to develop their own Indian qualities, not to crush them or neglect them".[1]

Nirad C. Chaudhari has also vouchsafed that Hindu thought had swayed the youths of Bengal. He says, "We had to fall back on the patriotic songs composed in the preceding era, many of which were by Tagore and breathed a lyrical love for our country, both India and Bengal. The patriotic lyricism was the second note in the emotion we felt at the coming of the nationalist agitation, and its poignancy lay in the continuous evocation of the beauties of nature. In demagogic politics the less extreme never has any chance against the more extreme...and therefore the liberal form of nationalism began to lose not only support but reputation. We always turned up our noses at the mere mention of the Moderates. As we grew older we read about the wars of the Rajputs, the Marathas and the Sikhs against the Muslims, and of the intolerance and oppression of Aurangzeb. The other and the more dangerous form of aggravation of Hindu-Muslim antagonism of the Swadeshi movement was that this hostility was now brought down from the historical to contemporary plane. The year 1907 was a year of very bad feelings between Hindu and Muslim."[2] There was considerable animosity among the Muslims against Hindus. Sumit Sarkar has given some extracts from newspapers. Some portions of a long poem '*Krishak Bandhu*' show that the Muslims were asked to recite only Koran and act according to the precepts of the Holy Book. It regarded both the Moderate and Radical congressmen as enemies of the Muslims. On the other hand, young Muslim Moulana Azad was appealing the Muslims to join the anti-partition agitation. He even thought it advisable for the Muslims to join the revolutionary groups of the Hindus. But he found that those groups were prejudiced against Muslims as being supporters of partition.

Increased unrest and violence worried many British newspapers and periodicals. 'The Times' on May 7, 1908, was critical of some Members of the Parliament who the paper thought were adding fuel to the fire. It said, "Bipin Chandra Pal, who has received public benedictions of Mr. Surendranath Banergee, stumped the country in support of Mr. Tilak. The Congress camp has sheltered some very strange bedfellows. If it is ever reconstituted, it will have to move far more warily in future. The extenuating circumstance of invincible ignorance may perhaps be pleaded in favour of wandering journalists who have orated at extremists meetings, and peripatetic members of Parliament who have shouted "*Bande Mataram*" and hobnobbed with questionable agitators. Far less excusable has been the conduct of those members of Parliament with Indian experience who, in the House of Commons and out of it, have helped to fan the flames of Indian agitation. We cannot conceive anything more injudicious, for example, than the present attempt to raise afresh in Parliament the close question of the partition of Bengal. But if the great work of reform must be patiently prosecuted, it is imperative that such dastardly plots as that now disclosed shall be crushed with swift and exemplary severity. The lives of thousands of Englishmen and

English women in India depend for their future protection against assassination upon the stern suppression of forces of anarchy now revealed".

Lord Minto and his advisors held that the only remedy to stem the tide of violence in Bengal was to put some restrictions on the newspapers and periodicals, which encouraged seditious writings. So a new legislation was passed by the Viceroy's Council just in two hours in June. Morley who by that time had been made a Member of the Lords, was appraised of this legislation a month earlier. Lord Morley informed Lord Minto on May 28, 1908 that the draft of the Press Act which the viceroy had sent was put up before the Cabinet. "In the Cabinet Ripon was very restive, remembering his own reversal of Lytton's Press policy. I do believe that our introduction of a *judicial* element at every stage is an improvement, apart from general principles of a free Press on the one hand, and maintenance of Law and Order on the other. In the first place, it will tend to reconcile the liberal opinion (not in a party sense) here, and that is something. In the second place, it will make it easier for the Moderates to resist the Extremist attack. Such an attack is sure to come, and it is our business, as I think, not to do anything that will give anything that will give substance to Extremist taunts and reproaches against their Moderate opponents. Of course, our proceeding must be effective, but I do not think that any of the modifications suggested here will at all impair your purpose. In any case, do not forget the vital importance—*from your point of view*—of carrying English opinion with us. If there are any signs in the Press or in the H. of C. that a substantial body of opinion here condemns these new powers as excessive or as superfluous, then the incendiaries in India have something plain to go upon, both in their antagonism to the G. of I. and to their moderate opponents. If I have been able to do any real service during the difficulties of the last eighteen months, it has been this, that I have succeeded in keeping back the formation of any serious group at Westminster whose utterances and tactics in our public life would have provided powder and shots for the revolutionaries in India".[3]

Though the Press Act came into force in 1908, the Government of India had used the powers under the 1818 Act earlier and had already proceeded against many newspapers, their editors and publishers. Many were deported by the courts. It became routine to be sent to gallows or to Andamans. Because of this, Lord Morley became restive and advised Minto to restrain the officials. He said, "Well, I am as much for Vigour as they are, but I am not going to admit that Vigour is the same thing as *Pogroms.* When I read that of the author (or printer) of a 'seditious' pamphlet being punished with seven years of transportation, I feel restive. I have ordered that the pamphlets and proceedings should be sent to me, and it may prove that I have been misinformed. I hope so. Then…is said to have sentenced some political offenders (so called) to be flogged. That, I am advised, is not authorized by the law either as it stood, or it will stand under the flogging provisions as amended. Here also I called for the papers, and we shall see…said to me this morning, 'you see the great executive officers never like or trust lawyers'. 'I will tell you why' I said, 'it's because they don't like or trust law: they in their hearts believe that before all else the virtues of will and arbitrary power'". But when the Press Act came into force, there was substantial increase in the convictions and deportations. Morley was all the while cautioning Minto about the excesses. On July 14, Morley seems to have been exasperated and in that mood wrote, "I cannot on any terms whatever consent to defend such monstrous things. We must keep order, but excess of severity is not the path to order. On the contrary, it is path to the bomb".

Morley was giving warnings against excesses by officials because he had read documents about the court case against Lala Lajpat Rai and was staggered by the injustice of the case. At that time Bishop of Lahore met him who appraised him of the situation in Punjab. The Bishop told him that in Punjab, it was not that the Indians were on trial, but the Englishmen. Lord Morley was so impressed by him that a thought came to him to make him the governor of Punjab. Morley never believed in the wisdom of the bureaucracy. He had his experience as a minister in charge of Ireland. That was why Morley used to suggest to Minto often that he must examine the real worth and efficiency of his Advisory Council. Morley trusted the governor of Bombay—Sir George Clarke—whose letters to the Secretary of State did not give any flattering picture of the administration of Lord Minto. Clarke had been to Simla to get some of the problems facing the Bombay government solved; but he was disappointed. He became convinced that Minto was not the viceroy who would go deep into any problem and was not inclined to consult his officials. According to Clarke, Minto had little grip on the administration or knowledge. Viceroy shunned discussion. The governor also found that Simla was unnecessarily crowded by the officers who had no business to be there.

Many high and low British officials in India firmly believed that India was on the verge of revolt and severe measures were called for. Sir George Clarke was one of those officers. Lokmanya Tilak and his new party stood for boycott, but there was no shred of evidence that either Tilak or his party had any connection with the revolutionaries. But Clarke thought that there were many who could be carried away by the 'irresponsible' propaganda and hence Tilak's writings had to be carefully examined. When the 1908 Press Act authorized the government to proceed against those who indulged in 'seditious writing', Governor Clarke decided to punish such writers in the Bombay province. In fact, six months before, he had called a meeting of the editors from the province and met Tilak who, after the meeting, moved a vote of thanks to the governor. After the meeting Clarke wrote to Morley, "I can't help thinking that long ago he (Tilak) might have been taken in hand; but a high caste Brahmin, I am told, never forgives imprisonment". Morley replied. "I like this high-caste Brahmin of a man, never forgiving the stain of imprisonment, as you say. Quite a man worth trying to get hold of, and I dare say you are right in thinking it might have been possible at an earlier stage. Alas"![4]

'The Economist' of June 20, 1908 had echoed Morley's views about the political situation in India and the methods to be adopted by the government. It said: "In the great towns of Bengal and Bombay and Northern India there is an ever-growing body of trained native opinion, informed and stimulated, often misinformed and prejudiced, by the clever pen and ready tongue of the educated Hindoo. What was needed at this moment is the knowledge, strength, sympathy and imagination of statesmanship, and these qualities by universal consent are united in a singular measure in the person of the Secretary of State. We do not for one moment expect or wish that he should placate the Indian extremists". The weekly then called for political reforms but emphasized that some measures must be taken to remove the poverty of India. Sir Fleetwood Wilson was one time a finance member of the Viceroy's Council. This able official afterwards was appointed to the War Ministry in London. Lord Morley wanted him to go back to India and take up the same responsibility as before and also keep him informed about the administration. Sir Fleetwood came to India in 1909. His letters threw much light on Minto's style of functioning. On July 23, 1909 he wrote to Sir Lawrence Jenkins, a Judge of the Calcutta High Court: "If present practice of acting solely on the advice of Adamson (Home Member) and Risley is to continue, no self-respecting man would remain here. I don't mind so much being ignored, what I will not stand is being pledged without my opinion being recorded. The whole Government is in the hands of the Secretaries. They meet him (Minto) once a week and it seems to me they do just as they like. Which is bad for India". Morley was shocked when he received a copy of this letter. He knew that the viceroy had to act after consulting his Council. Though he had overriding powers, they had to be used occasionally.

On May 3, 1909 the Government of India had sent an important communication to the Secretary of State about how to curtail the rights of the deportees. But Wilson, though a member of the Viceroy's Council, was completely in the dark about it, as it was generally held that the member should be consulted only about his own portfolio. However, Wilson thought that the whole council must be consulted. Wilson then wrote to Lord Morley: "I do not join in the chorus of condemnation of Risley, but I do think that Risley as the mouthpiece of lady Minto (renowned as 'the real viceroy') is a source of danger. I have twice had to pull up Lady Minto for absolutely unauthorized and in my opinion 'illegal' expenditure; the result being that she cordially hates me." Wilson regarded Minto as clever but indolent. He regretted that the administration was in the hands of the Home Department, which was taking policeman's view.[5]

Though Sir George Clarke was not initially inclined to use harsh measures against 'Kesari', many officials in the Presidency had no patience with several newspapers and especially with 'Kesari'. They were of the view that Tilak and his 'Kesari' were responsible for the growing atmosphere of sedition in the Bombay province. So they were pressurising the governor to take action against Tilak, to which the legal advisor to the government concurred. Lokmanya Tilak had anticipated such an action and when S.M. Paranjpe, editor of 'Kal', was prosecuted, Tilak became convinced that an action against him was in the offing. So Tilak along with some of his friends issued a statement on May 22, 1908, which regretted that because of violent activities of some young men from Bengal, some unfortunate murders had occurred. They were not because of some intemperate speeches or writings, as was supposed by some, but because of the indifference of the government and its repression. The statement warned that such repressive methods were bound to be futile and so it asked the government to refrain from it. The only remedy was to adopt a broader view and take steps to redress the grievances of the people and to fulfill their legitimate aspirations. This would also be in the excellent tradition of the British government said the statement. The Bombay government was not taken in by this. When 'Kesari' published some articles about the bomb-throwing incidents in Muzzuffarpur, Governor Sir George Clarke invited the opinion of Mr. Invararity, a legal luminary of Bombay. His opinion was that the government could successfully prosecute Tilak. Clarke had taken precaution to inform Morley that he was taking the legal opinion before taking any action against Tilak. When he received Invararity's opinion, he asked his officials to proceed accordingly.

However, when Morley read the translation of one of the articles published in the 'Kesari', he thought it advisable to ignore them and so advised Clarke not to proceed in the case. But the Governor was not convinced. He explained, "Policy, in the larger sense demanded the prosecution of Tilak as the head of the Extremist party in Western India and a powerful influence for evil. I could not strike at the smaller men and allow it to be said that we were afraid of Tilak." Morley was not impressed by the argument advanced by Clarke. He then wrote to Lord Minto: "I have read the two articles. Bad enough to warrant a prosecution, if you wanted one on general political grounds, but not at all so bad as to make a prosecution inevitable. Of course Clarke might easily have convinced me that the proceedings were wise, if he had shown the state of his presidency made a severe lesson and stern example necessary. But I gather from his letters that he thinks nothing so ill of his people, and he plainly has not weighed all the ulterior consequences of every sort. If his people are in an inflammable state, the trial will inflame them still further; if they are not, he could afford to Tilak's shuffling stuff, with all its vicious innuendoes and mischievous plausibilities, go by".

Tilak was arrested on June 24, 1908 on the charges of sedition and spreading dissatisfaction against the government. The case opened before Justice Davar, in Bombay High Court on July 13. Ironically the verdict was given on Tilak's birthday on July 23. Lokmanya Tilak was sentenced to six years and was deported to Mandalay. Bombay was much disturbed as soon as it was known that Tilak was to be prosecuted. When the case opened, everyday, one or more cotton mills went on strike. The government called military to guard the roads leading to the High Court, but people went as near the High Court as was permissible. On the day of judgement, in spite of the heavy rains, large crowds gathered on the streets, and when it was learnt that Tilak was given six years imprisonment, workers of Bombay went on a strike for six days. People were not deterred by the presence of the army and the European officers; on the contrary they were making fun of them. On July 18, the crowd pelted stones and bricks at the army and the police, who then opened fire. It was said that number of those who died was fifteen, and several were injured. Police took hundreds into the custody.

Sir George Clarke was made a peer later; who as Lord Sydenham wrote his memoirs about his regime as governor of Bombay. He also quoted some of his letters to Morley. Lord Sydenham found Lord Morley to be more conscious of his own intellectual superiority and believed that he knew much more than the people who were actually running the administration in India. The officials in India might not have the capacity to explain the complex situation, but they took the decisions after great deal of deliberation, he said. Letters of Morley were eloquent testimony to the fact that it was difficult to govern thirty-two crore people of India from London. The administrators in India were mainly concerned about the dumb millions. On the contrary the Secretary of State was worried by the disturbance in the Parliament or outside it. Lord Sydenham then referred to Morley's advice that like Cavour, an Italian leader, it was better to wait, as time showed the way in the difficulty. But Sydenham said India was not Europe. In an Asian country those who waited got punished. Lord Sydenham averred that after the arrest of Tilak his (Sydenham's) influence increased significantly; but he himself had noted that after Tilak was convicted, he had called a meeting of some important citizens of Bombay and realized that Tilak had wide sympathy. If that was the mood of the citizens, how did Sydenham think that his influence increased by the incarceration of Lokmanya Tilak?

Srinivas Sastri and his colleague from the Servants of India Society, Mr. Dravid, were present in the court at Tilak's trial. Sastri in a letter to Mr. Krishnaswami Iyer on July 25, 1908 draws a vivid picture. He said, "I was in Bombay during the last three days of the trial. When the catastrophe was reached at the end of an extraordinary night-sitting lasting till 10 o'clock and justice Davar bit out his sentence in slow, solemn tones amid death-like silence, the effect on us was crushing that we—that means Dravid and I—left Bombay precipitately causing no longer delay than was necessary to pick up our things.

Yesterday we had a long letter from Mr. Gokhale. We wrote back promptly—adding a request that he should use his influence with Morley and others to secure for Mr. Tilak something like a considerate treatment accorded to political prisoners. I needn't say that Poona lies prostrate under the blow which is felt in every home. The one thought of everyone is the great gap left in the ranks of public men. No single man can take his place here. 'The Dyan Prakash' forgot old quarrels and paid the fallen hero a generous tribute. Mrs. Tilak's condition, as she has had acute diabetes for some weeks, threatens to add a tragic touch to the situation. Tilak himself manfully bore himself throughout, and clear as his voice ran as he called on higher powers that guided the destinies of nations, looked greatly pull down by age, diabetes and terrible strain of the last fortnight, and few hope to see him alive at the end of exile. In the general depression, however, a clever young lawyer bids us cheer up. The misjoinder of trials under different sections is a rational error, says he; and as he read to us the different sections of the C.P.C. dealing with misjoinders, we thought the matter so patent that we suspected something deeper as we couldn't conceive of a High Court judge making such a mistake. "But you don't know Davar", says he, "and we lawyer generally prepare legal traps in these trials. We could only open our lips in ignorant wonder".[6]

Sastri had mentioned 'Dnyan Prakash' editorial, which said: "The gap which has occurred in Maharashtra by the conviction of Mr. Tilak will be difficult to fill by anybody else till someone of such eminence comes forth". Both 'Indu Prakash' and 'Sudharak' were liberal papers supporting Moderates in the Congress. They also paid generous tributes to Tilak. 'Indu Prakash' said that: "Tilak was not one individual, but a power to be reckoned with. His conviction was a blow to everybody and was a national calamity." 'Sudharak' describing the mood in Maharashtra said that "everybody felt that he has lost someone who was the mainstay of his family". Hyndman's letter to 'The Times' appeared on July 27. He categorically said that there was nothing in the articles of Tilak, which was incriminating and instigating the use of a bomb. Englishmen support those in Turkey or Russia who stood against the tyranny and they generally support the agitation against oppression. Hyndman pointing out the inconsistency asked how then the same Englishmen endorsed the oppressive policies of Morley and Minto in India. He said it was significant that in the Jury there were seven Europeans and two Parsis and the Jury was not unanimous. To Hyndman it was the height of folly to imagine that England's rule over India would be permanent. He wrote in the 'Justice', a London journal: "When the history of the governing classes comes to be written, a few generations hence, we firmly believe the judgement of the posterity will be that a viler set of ruffians never degraded the records of mankind. The conviction of the noble patriot and a martyr, Bal Gangadhar Tilak, was as gross a miscarriage of justice as ever been known, even under our carpetbagger disposition in India. There is no justice for Indians". 'The Morning Leader', a London daily, said: "There are very few people in England in a position to realize what the arrest of Mr. Bal Gangadhar Tilak, a nationalist leader of Poona, actually means in India. His personal power is unapproached by any other politician in the country; he dominates the Deccan, his own country, and is adored with a kind of religious fervour by every extremist from Bombay to the Bay of Bengal. He is a thinker and fighter in one".

'The Times', as expected, came out strongly in support of the conviction. On July 23, 1908: it wrote: "The conviction of Mr. Bal Gangadhar Tilak, in the Bombay High Court yesterday, marks the close of the most important trial for sedition held in India for some years. The sentence may appear somewhat severe, in view of the fact that the articles upon which the charge was based were not frankly of the murderous type which have appeared in other Calcutta and Bombay journals; but it has to be remembered that Mr. Tilak had been previously convicted for a similar offence. Moreover, there is, perhaps, a greater element of danger in the insidious suggestions and the mock moderation of the writings of journalists like Mr. Tilak, than the open and bloodthirsty incitements of journals of the class of the notorious Calcutta publication, the 'Yugantar', whose printer was also sentenced yesterday. Mr. Tilak's articles were very clever examples of the art of disseminating veiled sedition, which is now practiced so extensively in India. Mr. Tilak remained at the moment of his conviction the most conspicuous politician in India, and among large sections of the people he has enjoyed a popularity and wielded an influence that no public man in the Dependency could claim to equal. The Extremist movement, in its open manifestations, both within and outside the Congress, was almost entirely his conception. The wrecking of the Congress last Christmas was solely due to personal intervention, and was the outcome of his desire to capture the organization from the Moderates. There were passages in which Mr. Tilak described bomb-throwing as 'horrible', but the 'excess of patriotism,' and the ease with which bombs might be made and used, seem to be his stronger note. The real importance of Mr. Tilak's conviction lies in the fact that he is the acknowledged and undisputed leader of the Extremist movement in India.—What Mr. Tilak thinks of our military strength in India, despite its increasing cost, was frankly explained in one of the articles for which he is suffering imprisonment. He wrote: 'Compared with the Imperial sway of the Moguls, the English Empire in India is extremely weak and wanting in vigour from the point of military strength. Were the English Army in India to be confronted by the difficulties similar to those which Aurangzeb's forces had to face, then the English rule would not last for a quarter of a century'."

In India, a comment by 'The Mussalman' of Calcutta was typical. After posing the questions like many other Indian newspapers, that why any Hindu or a Muslim juror was not appointed on the panel, it said: "It is unfortunate that the courts in the land are becoming more or less devoid of a sense of proportion in inflicting punishment in case of a political nature". 'The Hindu' was not surprised by the sentence of six years to Tilak, as it said by refusing the bail, the judge had indicated his mind. "Justice Davar has said in his judgement that only a perverted person would think that Tilak had not committed an offence. But those who had read the articles ninety-nine per cent would have wondered how the government under the governor like Sir George Clarke could have found them seditious and worth prosecution." The paper did not find any difference between the ultimate conviction and the government direction. 'The Statesman', however, fully supported the judgement convicting Tilak. It said on July 24, 1908: "No one can question the fairness of the trial. He has been condemned because he has failed to satisfy a jury of his fellow-subjects that he did not use the language which exceeded the bound of lawful criticism of the British Government. The verdict seems to us to be one which must be frankly accepted as rendering a substantial justice to the accused. A point can be reached at which liberty becomes a dangerous license, and every sensible man will agree that at some stage or the other it becomes not merely the right but the duty of the Government to intervene".

Gokhale was in London when Tilak was convicted. His several letters to his colleague, Wamanrao Patwardhan, reveal how he was disturbed by the conviction of Tilak. On July 17 he wrote: "The telegraphic summaries of Tilak's defence have made very good impression on friends of India in this country. This is the real Tilak, as he was and would be, but for the pernicious influence of those around him". On July 23, 1908 he said: "This mornings papers contain telegrams about shocking sentence inflicted on Mr. Tilak. There is, of course, no doubt that he will be brought back and set free after the things quieted down; if and when they quiet down. (Still the conviction and sentence will really be a great blow to our party, for part of the resentment against the Government is likely to be directed against us. However, there is no help in the matter and we must go on with our work as well as we can)". On August 13 Gokhale wrote: "As regards Mr. Tilak I have not the least doubt in my mind that after a little time, he will be treated with every consideration, and that next year, after the proposed reforms have been inaugurated, and things are quiet in India, he will be brought back and let free. You may rest assured that I will do everything that I possibly can in the matter, though I don't like to say so, as it might be misunderstood by our Extremist friends. Nothing can now be done in England...the matter will really rest with Sir George Clarke for whose judgement Lord Morley has the highest respect. I will prepare the ground while I am in England during the autumn session or during my return to India in December. I will follow up with the personal appeals to Sir George Clarke, though everything will ultimately depend upon the state of things in the Bombay Presidency in particular during the next few months".[7]

While Gokhale was doing whatever was possible for him to get the release or at least transfer of Lokmanya Tilak to India, he was viciously attacked by some newspapers like 'Bande Mataram', 'Hindu Punch' etc. They spread canard that it was Gokhale who pressurized Morley to arrest Tilak. Gokhale was very much disturbed by such attacks. He gave vent to his anger to Wamanrao Patwardhan in a letter on September 2. He said, "It is true that such attacks are particularly cowardly and detestable in this instance, because they are made against an absent man, and in the present state of inflamed public feeling in India, they are wickedly suggestive. But the malevolence of these men is not a new thing. It has pursued me for years past with a virulence which I alone know, and which at one time used to cause me great mental distress but now does not affect me much. The truth is that the bulk of our educated countrymen have as yet neither the true sense of justice nor the manliness nor magnanimity. If you think that the libelous statements which these prints have published have really damaged me seriously and that they are clearly actionable, I have no objection to you getting a lawyer to serve them with notices demanding immediate and full retraction of the charges".

Gokhale communicated his consent to Patwardhan to go ahead with libel proceedings against 'Rashtramat', 'Hindu Panch', 'Bande Mataram' and give a notice to 'Kesari' which had reproduced first paragraph of the news from 'Rashtramat'. Gokhale wrote that the limits of his patience were crossed and these offenders must be prosecuted, otherwise canard against him would persist which was harmful not only to him but also to his colleagues. He instructed Patwardhan that in any case a maximum fine demanded should be five hundred Rs. The money should be given to the Depressed Class League and to Dr. Karve's Female Education Society. Gokhale then said, "I never had any talk whatever with Lord Morley before the prosecution. I had a talk with him afterwards and in that I expressed my deep regret at the prosecution and pointed out its great unwisdom, and I knew as a fact that Lord M. was himself greatly disheartened when heard about Mr. T.'s arrest, though, of course, this must be kept confidential. He felt, as we all felt, the chances of his forthcoming reforms conciliating the people in a substantial degree had been largely reduced by this prosecution. I don't mind confessing that I have been feeling somewhat sad since dispatching a telegram on Monday last. During all these years of public life I have often been pursued by similar malevolence but hitherto I have succeeded in ignoring the attacks. Somehow I feel that I have not been quite loyal to the teachings and principles of my departed master in asking you to proceed against the offending journals as I have done. But the heart is sad, the brain tells me that the course I have used is the course now left to me. Our public is so gullible that it follows such stories. And the public mind at present is so inflamed that it is positively dangerous not only for me, but for those who, like the members of the Society who are closely associated with me and to our work, that these odious accusations should be allowed to circulate". Gokhale also informed Patwardhan that there was no truth in the report that a meeting in the India House, London, denounced him, as he did not attend the meeting which was called to protest against the conviction of Lokmanya Tilak. Gokhale said he was never informed by anybody about the meeting and so he did not attend. Besides, the meeting did not criticize Gokhale. Some students of Shamji Krishna Verma gathered after the meeting and they criticized him.[8] R.P. Karandikar, an advocate from Satara, who had been to London to seek some legal redress for Tilak, in his letter home, on December 2, 1908, emphatically vouchsafed that Gokhale had done sterling work in connection with the political reforms and hoped that Gokhale would succeed. About the allegations against Gokhale that he brought Tilak into trouble, Karandikar said that there was absolutely no truth in that rumour and he was dead certain about it.[9]

The malevolence against Gokhale could have cost him his life. Two attempts were made against his life. One was an unsuccessful attempt to attack him in his house in Poona, and the other was during his train journey. Gokhale scrupulously adhered to some norms in public life and was never uncivil in his criticism against his opponents. That was why on January 3, 1908 he took the editor of 'Dnyan Prakash', a Servants of India Society's paper, to task for using intemperate language against Khaparde. So it was quite in keeping with Gokhale that he should later help the editor of a paper against whom he had taken legal action.

Lord Minto differed with Lord Morley about Tilak's trial. He conveyed on August 5 that the conviction of Tilak would have salutary effect. The Viceroy was convinced that Tilak was involved in the seditious activities. He assured Morley that there was enough evidence to establish that Tilak was the leader of the seditious movement in India. Minto said that not only Europeans but many loyal Indians also were waiting for some such stringent measure as they apprehended a danger to their lives. Minto told Morley that if there was public criticism of the harsh measures in England, then the efforts of the Government of India to destroy the evil tendencies would be nullified. Correspondence between Lord Morley and Lord Minto during the next several months was in a way repetitive. Morley trying to impress upon the viceroy that though the situation in India was volatile, it had to be handled with great care and patience. He was asking the viceroy to restrain the officials from acting with unnecessary zeal in curbing the agitation against the partition of Bengal. He also insisted that Lord Minto should give equal priority to the political reforms. To Minto, on the other hand, law and order was an urgent and immediate problem. He was wary of criticism, in the Parliament and outside, against certain measures used against the agitators, as he believed that seditious activities were strong and widespread.

Morley was not convinced and wrote to Lord Minto on August 26: "You warn me against 'disapproval at home of severe sentences'. And you drew me a vivid picture of the electric atmosphere of the daily life around you and the dangerous inflammation of racial antipathies. Vivid—but I am sure not a single shade too vivid for the plane facts. I wish you would in your next letter tell me the story of the young Corporal who in a fit of excitement shot the first native he met. What happened to the Corporal? Was he put on his trial? Was he hanged? If we are not strong enough to prevent murder, then our pharisaic glorification of the stern justice of the British Raj is nonsense. And the fundamental question for you and me today is whether the excited Corporal and the angry Planter are to be the arbiter of our policy. True, we should be fools to leave out of account the deep roots of feeling that the angry Planter represents and stands for. On the other hand, it is not idle for us to pretend to the Natives that we wish to understand their sentiment, and satisfy their demands of 'honest reformers', and the rest of our benighted talk, and yet silently acquiesce in all these violent sentences. You will say to me, 'These legal proceedings are at bottom acts of war against rebels, and locking a rebel up for life is more affable and polite than blowing him from a gun; you must not measure such sentences from the ordinary standards of a law-court; they are the natural and proper penalties for mutiny; and the Judge on the bench is really a Provost-Marshal in disguise'. Well, be it so. But if you push me into a position of this sort—and I don't deny that it is a perfectly tenable position if you like—then I drop reforms. I won't talk any more of the New Spirit of the Times; and I will tell Asquith that I am not the man for the work".[10] Lord Minto, however, persisted and in his letter of November 30, informed Morley that Satyendra Nath Sinha and Ashutosh Mukhergee told him that though the seditious sentiments were limited to the students and some graduates; behind them was some organized force which supplied money. Minto also feared that more acts of violence were in the offing as arms were being collected.

In England, both Morley and Minto had their supporters and detractors. Sir Bampfylde Fuller, who was forced to resign as the lieutenant-governor of Bengal, writing in the July 1908 issue of the 'Nineteenth Century and After' assured the English public and politicians that there was no discontent against the British rule in India. Some Indian leaders and the vernacular Press by their campaign had instigated some students to agitate. His remedy was to put restrictions on the newspapers and usher educational reforms. Fuller said, "Our policy should be to sit tight, do justice and strictly maintain the peace". In the November issue of the same magazine, J. Nisbet, a retired government officer, assured that there was no threat of another revolt in India. "But (there is a threat of) general rising of the population urged on by demagogues. This dangerous agitation can easily be restrained, just as hill torrents can be controlled at their source; but if it is allowed to gather strength, it will sometime or other flood the country and do untold damage". Nisbet then said the most dangerous time would be when another great power invaded India. That was why he urged timely action against the agitation. Nisbet's article was followed by one written by Edward C. Cox. He said the difference between Radicals and Moderates in India was of degree; as Radicals wanted the British to leave the country immediately and the Moderates wanted it at a later date. Cox warned that English rule had more enemies in India than friends and added that peace could be achieved only by those with moral authority.

However, the July issue of the 'Contemporary Review' carried a review of two books on India and the reviewer warned about the growing discontent in the country. He said that Indians did not feel that they were protected, and are fed up by the British rule. He also warned that it was wrong to assume that the discontent was limited to few people. According to him educated classes might have given vent to the discontent, but they had not created hunger. Mere sympathy would also be not enough as it would not satisfy the appetite of the Indians. The reviewer concluded that, "the hunger of the common people and the hauteur of the foreign rule have brought the administration of India to the present crisis." The reviewer then dealt with the split in the Congress and said that it was wrong to suppose that Tilak has lost ground and had become politically weak. In his opinion Moderates could not appeal to the young people. Comparing Tilak and Gokhale, he said Tilak was easily approachable to anybody and his legal knowledge was useful to people. "Brahmin as he is Mr. Tilak commands the people's hearts. He is a man of impulse and enthusiasm. He shares or appears to share their (people's) prejudices and their sufferings. Gokhale and his party appear to be aloof from the people. He may sympathise with their distress; but this sympathy never dominates him. His methods are not the familiar Oriental ones of his rival. They are the methods of the West". The reviewer also criticised Morley for fiddling for long time while India was on fire.

Even though their approaches differed, Morley persuaded Minto to move in the direction of political reforms. Minto then impressed upon Morley that it was imperative that the move should be initiated from India and not from London. He then entrusted Risley to correspond with the Secretary of State and draw out a plan. Accordingly Risley wrote to Lord Morley on April 30, 1908 and emphasized the necessity to maintain the official majority in the Councils of the provinces. He pointed out that in the absence of such official majority, Provincial Governments would not remain under the control of the Government of India, and even the Secretary of State and the Parliament would find it difficult to rein them in. If the members of the Bombay Provincial Council voted against the policy about the custom duties and the legislation about the factory workers and if the government agreed, then it would accept the opinion of the majority and reject the directives of the Parliament. In his second communication, Risley dealt with the rise of the cult of Bomb in India. He held the Congress leaders responsible for it. He said the Congress leaders had brought the young people in politics who were emotional but had no backbone and were without any tradition. In the consequent communications Risley discussed various topics, such as structure of the provincial legislatures, demarcation of the constituencies etc. He was of the opinion that provincial legislatures should have no more than forty-five members and adequate representation should be given to different castes. There should be an Advisory Council to the viceroy of fifteen members, out of which seven should be Princes and one member each from the eight provinces. He wanted to increase the number of members to the Provincial Advisory Council from seven to twelve. Risley was keen to give adequate representation to different castes and interests. However, Minto feared that the Advisory Council might plead for introducing elective principle and the British government might accept it. So he dropped this idea altogether. Congress leaders were insistent about more representation to the people; but Minto and Risley were determined to protect the official majority and the vested interests. They believed that as the agitators came mainly from the educated classes, it was better to give substantial representation to the landed gentry and the property-owners. Morley held a similar view. The government had argued that thirty-six per cent of unofficial members of the Legislatures under the 1893 Act were lawyers and twenty-two percent were landlords. The government also noted that the landlord class thought it was degrading to contest elections. As Morley accepted this argument, the new legislatures were to have, not a unified constituency but fragmented one based on different interests.

Wedderburn impressed upon Gokhale that his presence in London was necessary, as the government was moving in the direction of bringing in a reform bill. So Gokhale reached London at the end April 1908. This visit was on the background of the Congress split and the spread of the cult of the bomb in India. Gokhale was worried that the agitation in India would delay the promised political reforms. But even otherwise Gokhale disapproved of any such agitation. In a letter to Wamanrao Patwardhan from London, on May 15, 1908 Gokhale wrote: "I am extremely sorry that I should be out of India at such a grave juncture. There really is some fatality connected with my visit to this country. Every time I come here, something happens in India to throw the country into the wild excitement. Whatever the shortcomings of the bureaucracy and however intolerable at times the insolence of individual Englishman, they alone stand in the country for order and without continued order, no real progress is possible for our people. It is not difficult at any time to create disorder in our country—which was going on for centuries—but it is not so easy to substitute another form of order for that which has been evolved by Englishmen during the course of a century".

In London, Gokhale met several members of the Parliament. He had meetings with some liberal editors and addressed several public meetings in and out of London. Lala Lajpat Rai and Sir Ramesh Chandra Dutt, the resident of London, accompanied Gokhale to various public engagements. But Gokhale's meetings with Morley were more important. Gokhale was convinced that as Morley was the deciding authority, it was better to try to get as much demands fulfilled through him and not indulge in criticism. After some meetings with Morley, Gokhale wrote to his friend, Krishnaswami Iyer on September 25, 1908, "Forthcoming reforms will be of substantial character and they will be announced before the next Congress meets. For obvious reasons I cannot give you any particulars in this letter, but I know you trust me, and will not hesitate to take it from me that our faith in Lord Morley will be amply vindicated in December.— It is, therefore, of supreme importance that earnest and thoughtful constitutionalists should assemble in Madras in large numbers from all parts of the country next Christmas and the Presidential Chair should be occupied by the foremost constitutionalist, Sir Pherozeshah Mehta. The Presidential address of this year will have to practically restate the basis on which our public life is to rest in the immediate future."

Gokhale was keeping Wamanrao Patwardhan and Krishnaswami informed with the latest developments with regard to the political reforms. Before sailing for India, Gokhale wrote to Patwardhan on October 30, 1908: "I expect the statement (by Morley) will be satisfactory to our side in India. I think we shall in substance get all I asked for in that confidential note of which I sent Nateshwarrao a copy last month. Here and there may be alterations for instance as regards electorates, electoral colleges may be created for each Division, and these colleges may be built up from Taluka boards so as to secure by a system of proportional representation adequate representation of minorities. The whole scheme will take too long to explain in a letter. But it will be a perfectly fair scheme. The most important thing is to have an elected majority in Provincial Councils with the power of passing resolutions on important matters of administration and finance. And this I am now certain we shall get. This means a machinery will be set up in India which will enable us to advance effectively questioning of internal administration such as free and compulsory primary education, technical education, permanent settlement, agricultural indebtedness and so forth. The Governor may veto a resolution of the Council once, twice but he can't veto it every time. And by holding up public opinion behind the Council we shall be able eventually to get our resolutions acted upon. From this to an executive responsibility to the Legislative Council is only one step, though a long and difficult step; but in ten years or so, that question ought to come within the sphere of practical politics".[11]

Though Gokhale wanted Krishnaswami and others to prevail upon

Pherozeshah to accept the Presidentship of the forthcoming Congress session at Madras, it was decided at Surat session that Dr. Rash Bihari Ghose would be the president. In London, Gokhale had a meeting with Wilfrid Blunt who noted in his diary that it seemed Gokhale had great faith in Lord Morley and told Blunt that India's ultimate goal was to achieve the equal status with the other colonies of the British Empire. Blunt noted, "He (Gokhale) disclaimed any appeal to force in any shape. 'What could we do?' he said, 'against Kitchener and the army?' He would not hear even of obstruction. 'it is no use', he said, 'trying to overthrow the present administration until we have something to put in its place.' Language of this sort may be true, as it certainly is prudent, but it is not a language of revolution. I asked him whether he expected to convert English people or the English Government, by appeals to reason and justice? He said he believed that Morley had a scheme of extending the representative character of the Councils, and they would have to be content with that at present. He had been a great believer in Morley, and had read all his writings on liberty, but he feared that Morley was more for personal than national liberty. I had told him that Morley was a broken reed. 'In that', he said, ' my friend here,' pointing to Lajpat Rai, 'will agree with you'."[12]

The Congress was keen to have political reforms, but the British government had in the Muslim League a convenient ploy to restrain the Congress. The Nawab of Dacca had warned the Moderate Congressmen that if they did not drive out the Radicals from their organization, the Muslim League would not have any relations with the Congress. Referring to this condition laid down by the League, one Edward Lang in an article in the 'Contemporary Review' criticized Dadabhai for 'pampering' the Radicals. Lang was, in a way, speaking for the government. As the Muslim leaders were demanding a separate electorate, Gokhale tried hard to find out a way satisfactory to both Hindus and Muslims. The bone of contention was whether the electorate should be decided on the basis of the territory or on the basis of the interests. The Government of India was insistent about the communal basis and a separate electorate. It argued that as the government was not popularly elected, it was necessary that varied castes and religious groups must be represented in the Legislatures. Except Bombay and the Punjab other provincial governments argued that lawyers and professionals had disproportionate representation in the legislatures, while the landlords were not evenly treated. The Punjab government apprehended that the communal cleavage already existed in the province and it would widen by the communal electorate. Chief Secretary, E.D. Maclagan wrote to the Government of India: "a person chosen from a purely religious electorate is likely to be a person who will represent exclusively the pro-Mohammedan and anti-Hindu view of public questions, whereas nomination is likely to secure a legislator who besides being a Mohammedan will have breadth of view and variety of ideas. For this reason the Lt. Governor would deprecate the extension of any electoral system in this province now or in the near future for the selection of candidates to represent the interests of special religions".[13]

The Arundel Committee held the same opinion as the Punjab government. The Bombay Presidency Association had opposed the separate electorates. It said that the government had a grudge against the professional classes. Landlord class, however, welcomed the provision for electorates based on the different interests. Lord Minto had resolved to give adequate representation to the landlords and the Muslims by election and also by nomination. Government of India accordingly sent a note to the Secretary of State, that wherever possible, Muslims could get representation through the Muslim constituencies; but where it was not possible, they should be nominated by the government. Local governments after consulting the Muslims should decide as to which option was to be adopted. Morley felt it was better to have electoral colleges to give adequate representation to the Muslims. When the Parliament debated the issue, Morley expressed his apprehension that if separate electorates were accepted for the Legislative Councils, the same would have to be extended to the Municipalities and District Boards, which he said would be impractical. Gokhale's suggestion was to have electorates on the territorial basis and additional representation to Muslims to make it adequate. Government officials and some Muslim leaders were striving hard to spike all these efforts by Gokhale. Lord Minto not satisfied with the letters and notes sent to the Secretary of State on the question of the separate electorates, sent his secretary, Sir James Dunlop-Smith, to London. He met members of the Advisory Council of the Secretary of State and prominent Tories to lobby for the Government of India. He had kept relations with the newspapers like 'The Times'. Like Lady Minto, Dunlop-Smith was very particular to guard the interests of his master and strengthen his position.

Later when Lord Morley in his memoirs reproduced some of his letters regarding India, Lady Minto was disturbed, as she thought all the credit for political reforms in India would go to Lord Morley. Therefore, she published her own memoirs and reproduced some of the letters of her husband. A letter by Dunlop-Smith to Lee-Warner on February 20 is pertinent. He wrote: "People out here who know the history of the reform scheme which was lately launched by the historical speech of Lord Morley in the House of Lords, have been much exercised how people at home and even some newspapers out here, have given Lord Morley all the credit of these measures. They are called 'Morley reforms' and it never seems to have occurred to anyone that Viceroy has had anything to do with them except to carry out the instructions of the Secretary of State. Perhaps this was inevitable, as the announcement of these reforms was made in St. Stephen's and not in the Council Room at Calcutta. Be these reforms good or bad, wise or unwise, they were initiated entirely by Lord Minto with the help of his Council, and they have been carried through by the Government of India, subject of course to any alterations, amendments, or additions, the Secretary of State in Council thought necessary. As I told you before, Lord Minto is above all selfish considerations, and so long as he thinks any measure good, he really does not care who gets the credit for it if it is only passed. In this he has as usual entirely effaced himself."[14]

Amir Ali, a judge of the Calcutta High Court, had settled in London after retirement. He was a scholarly writer and was very well connected with the London elite society and had established good relations with the editorial staff of 'The Times' as also with the members of the Advisory Council to the Secretary of State. He established a branch of the Muslim League in London. Aga Khan lent support to Amir Ali, but he had not much support of the League leaders in India. They could not grasp the importance of the work done by Amir Ali in London. He firmly believed that Muslims could not go with the Congress and should have their own politics as they were in minority. To safeguard their interests, Muslims must have separate electorates. He also wanted adequate representations to Muslims in municipalities and district boards and government services. He was uncompromising and was wary of the League leaders in India who he thought were wavering. So he did not hesitate to issue statements on behalf of the League without consulting the Central office of the organization. Morley felt uncomfortable with Amir Ali's rigid views. So he appointed Bilgrami on his Advisory Council, which Amir Ali could not accept. Morley's annoyance with Amir Ali was seen when he asked Minto whether Amir Ali's London office was a branch of the Muslim League in India, or it was the Central office.

The London branch of the Muslim League submitted a memorandum to the Deputy Secretary of State on November 16, 1908 without any consultation with its leaders in India. The memorandum said that the British government should never forget, the Muslims stood for stability in India and their tradition must be recognized. The separate electorate would alone give justice to the Muslims. Muslim leaders from several provinces met Lord Minto in June at Simla when Minto tried to impress on them that separate electorates would isolate Muslim politics from the main line. Minto had promised five seats to Muslims on his Council, but the Muslim leaders told Minto that they would withdraw their demand for separate electorate if they were promised six seats. However, when Ali Imam called a special meeting of the League at Lucknow, he failed to persuade the leaders to accept Viceroy's offer and the meeting passed a resolution demanding separate electorates. Morley's dispatch to the Government of India on November 27 did not provide for separate electorates to Muslims. It suggested that in mixed constituencies some seats should be reserved for Muslims and in other constituencies Hindu and Muslims must vote jointly. While creating electorate college if government could not get twenty five qualified Muslims, then the government was to nominate the Muslims and fill the seats. But this scheme was opposed by Muslim League and other Muslim organizations. At the end of December, Muslim League had its annual session at Amritsar. Ali Imam, who presided, declared that under the Morley scheme those Muslims who would go on the Legislative Councils would not be true representatives of the community. The session rejected Morley scheme, which it termed as unjust. It was decided to send delegations to wait upon Viceroy as well as Secretary of State. Ali Imam then saw Lord Minto and after the meeting the idea of delegations was dropped. Ali Imam might have got the information that Viceroy himself favoured separate electorates. Minto by then had conveyed to Morley that League's opposition to the electoral colleges was justified and understandable.

In London, the League branch launched a campaign against the Morley-Minto scheme. In this 'The Times' played a leading role. On January 11, 1909, 'The Times' did not openly oppose the Scheme, but advised Lord Morley to go slow with the changes in the Central Legislative Council and wait to see the results of the changes in the Provincial Legislative Assemblies. 'The Times' then said: "Of all the questions raised by Lord Morley's proposals the gravest undoubtedly is that of its effect upon the interests and feelings of the Mohammedan population. That it has given rise to very great alarm cannot, unfortunately, be disputed. It would be an evil day for both if the Mohammedan community suspects that whilst we trust mainly to them for material safety of our India Empire, we are ready to delegate to those of their fellow-countrymen from whom they are in many vital respects so profoundly separated—in religion more profoundly even than from ourselves—an undue share of the political and administrative power which we hitherto have retained in our own hands". On 14 January Amir Ali in his letter to 'The Times', declared that Muslims were prepared to cooperate with other communities, but would refuse to be slaves of the majority community. Muslims had demanded that the proposals Morley had made should be modified, which would be nothing more than doing justice.

British Press also discussed these proposals, which showed that the Muslim League had substantial support. Gokhale met Morley several times and had meetings with the liberal members of the Parliament as well as with the editors of the liberal newspapers. On the other hand Amir Ali's strategy was to meet members of the Advisory Council of the Secretary of State, most of whom were retirees from the service of the Government of India and were opposed to the Congress. Some members of the Parliament strongly supported Amir Ali. Critics alleged that Morley was much influenced by meetings with Gokhale and accepted Gokhale's proposals for electoral colleges. One of them asked, who was the father of the proposals? Gokhale or Morley? He said, Morley should rely on the advice of his expert advisors in his Advisory Council than a Deccan Brahman. However, Morley had discussions with some Muslim leaders, though they were not publicized. It was true that Gokhale had several meetings with the Secretary of State, but it was a fact that there was no Muslim leader of Gokhale's stature. After all this controversy Morley met a Muslim delegation under the leadership of Amir Ali. The delegation accepted to give up the separate electorates, provided the government decided the actual representation to the Muslim in comparison with the Hindus. Morley could not give any such assurance to the delegation.

At Madras where Congress met in December, President Dr. Rash Bihari Ghose said that the English rulers were wrong to regard educated Indians as their enemies. Real enemies of England were those officials who did not lose any opportunity to spread hatred against the Indians. Dr. Ghose also criticized the Radicals. He declared that the Moderates had accepted the principle of swadeshi, but they were against the boycott movement. He had no doubt that the boycott of the government as preached by the Radicals was wrong. Gokhale's speech on the political reform proposals was more important than his Presidential address. His emphasis was on the positive aspects of the scheme, which he declared would take India forward. Gokhale admitted that the scheme had many defects and shortcomings, but he asked to consider political reality. Before the Madras session, Pherozeshah Mehta in an interview with 'The Times of India', on December 18, had welcomed the reform-scheme. He said, "Lord Morley had dealt with the question of Reforms in a most statesmanlike way. I find it difficult to conceive that any Conservative Government could have designed a scheme of so liberal and genuine a character as that which is contained in this dispatch. The Reforms now proposed are really of substantial character. My only difficulty about the process of election which is proposed is in regard to the Electoral Collages by which it is suggested that the elections may be carried out. That process is sure to fail with regard to the smaller minorities, but after all it is only as a suggestion that the scheme of Electoral College is put forward and I have no doubt that each Presidency will be allowed free scope to deal with the matter as its own particular circumstances may require to do so. The proposal now put forward is that so many Hindus and so many Mohammedans and so on shall be elected. Of course, in all probability, all Hindus would elect Hindus and Mohammedan electorates Mohammedans". Mehta welcomed the provision to appoint an Indian on the Provincial Executive Councils and did not object to the statement by Morley that it would take very long time to introduce Parliamentary system in India, as other Indian leaders did. He said that he had 'for a long time deprecated the fashion of talking of ideals'. He was for taking a practical view. Mehta was also confident that the partition scheme of Bengal might be modified after the Legislative Assembly and the Executive Council started functioning. Dadabhai Naoroji wrote to Lord Morley on April 5, 1909, complimenting him on the Reform scheme.

The Reforms Bill was discussed at great length in both the Houses of

Parliament. Lord Curzon and members like him were critical, but the Bill was passed. Curzon warned the changes made by Morley in the original scheme would be harmful to the people of India. Lord Amphill envisaged that if a Babu rule came to India, there would be nothing but chaos. Sikhs, Rajputs, Gurkhas were not enamoured of the Parliamentary system and they might revolt. In case of anarchy, no British government would be able to send British troops to India. He asked the government to rule India with firm hand or get out. Lord Crew was afraid that the Legislative Councils would be divided between official and non-official members and the administration might be adversely affected. Lord Minto objected to criticism from some members of Parliament that the Reforms were brought in because of the agitation in India and that the government acted under duress. Minto reminded the secretary of state that the consideration of the scheme had started much earlier and the government did not act under duress. Minto had initiated the proposal to appoint an Indian on his Advisory Council, which was later accepted by the British government.

M.H. Butler was the Commissioner of Lucknow and Minto valued his advice. Butler was a forward-looking officer and was practical enough to tell the viceroy that if the reforms were not initiated, then a day would come when they would have to be given as necessity. He had respect for Gokhale and was aware that Gokhale was held in high esteem by the Indians. So he suggested to Minto that Gokhale was the right person to be appointed on the Viceroy's Council and be made Member for education. But Minto confessed to Morley that, "Gokhale is by far the ablest of that school whom I know. I am bound to say that he has always talked good sense to me. I could not trust him. I don't know what there is behind him. His political career is no doubt directly associated with his bread and butter and I am very suspicious of the wires by which he has worked. He is a Maratha Brahmin, which means a great deal". So Gokhale, though 'by far the ablest', was rejected by Lord Minto. Two names then were under the viceroy's consideration. One was that of Ashutosh Mukhergee and the other was that of Satyendra Nath Sinha. Ultimately, he proposed Sinha as a Member for Law. Sinha being a renowned lawyer was most eligible for the post.

When Morley submitted Sinha's name to King Edward for his approval by referring Queen Victoria's proclamation of 1858, the King made some pungent comments in the margin on March 20, 1909. He said, "Why he (Morley) should bring in the name of Queen Victoria I cannot see, nor how it bears on the question. I myself do not think that she would have approved of the new departure. I have had to sign the objectionable paper". Meanwhile, Minto supported Lord Morley in a letter to the King and said that the Secretary of State should not be debarred from submitting the name of an individual only because it was that of a Hindu. The days of racial disability had passed Minto said. To this, King replied that he would accept the suggestion, but with reservations. King said, "At the same time I hold very strong and possibly old-fashioned views on the subject, which my son who has so recently been in India, entirely shares. During the unrest in India at the present time and the intrigues of the Natives it would, I think, be fraught with the greatest danger to the Indian Empire if a Native were to take part in the Councils of the Viceroy, as so many subjects would be likely to be discussed in which it would not be desirable that a Native could take part. Besides, if you have a Hindu why not a Mohammedan also? The latter would strongly claim it. The Indian Princes, who are ready to be governed by the Viceroy and his Council, would greatly object to a Native, who would be very inferior in caste to themselves, taking part in the Government of the country. However clever the Native may be, you never could be certain that he might not prove to be a very dangerous element in your Councils and impart information to his countrymen which it would be very undesirable should it go further than your Council Chamber."[15]

'The Times' had reservations about the appointment of an Indian on the Viceroy's Council. On March 24 it said, "Lord Morley has doubtless had satisfied himself that the qualifications of his nominee in this respect will not discredit the experiment on which he ventured. A member of the Viceroy's Executive Council is much more than a departmental chief. He is, in a truer sense than the Ministers of the most European States, a ruler of men, and he should have the intellect and the moral training of a ruler. The largest and the weightiest problems in all branches of Government come before him, and the decisions which he and his colleagues reach not only affect the lives of the 300,000,000 inhabitants of India, but often exercise the powerful influence upon the policy and fortunes of the Empire. Breadth of political knowledge and of judgement, insight into men and things, a sure sense and grasp of realities, coolness, courage and rapid decision in emergencies, absolute impartiality between races, creeds and classes, and an instinctive devotion to England, to her traditions and to her ideals, are amongst the qualities which have been deemed the best recommendations for so immense a trust. Mr. Sinha may possess them all, but they are rare amongst the men of any race, and some of them are notoriously uncommon amongst Orientals. Mr. Sinha will have native successors, who in turn may have Mohammedan colleagues. We have no assurance, and but few grounds for hope, that either would be endowed with the capacities and virtues, which have hitherto made Viceroy's Council what it has been". Lord Morley had assured that he had consultations with the Viceroy and had his consent. But 'The Times' wanted to know whether he had consulted ex-viceroys and governors. It was doubtful whether the Muslims and the Princes would welcome Mr. Sinha's appointment. However, Minto informed Morley that both Hindus and Muslims had welcomed the appointment and there was to be a joint meeting of felicitation. Morley then conveyed to the viceroy, "'The Times' which in 'India matters' is almost the only journal that really counts, shakes its head a little solemnly, but without scare. They shed towards the fact that Sinha has not some of the rarest political virtues in any world—courage, patience, tact, foresight, penetration, breadth of view, habit of authority and heaven knows what else—just as if all these noble qualities were inherent in any lawyer that I could have fished".[16] Both Morley and Minto agreed that with the nomination of an Indian member on the councils of the governors and the viceroy, the government would be able to know what was going on in the minds of the Indians. Appointment of an Indian on the Viceroy's Council was the long-standing demand of the Indian National Congress. Gokhale strove hard to get this demand accepted by the government. So when Sinha's nomination was announced, Gokhale and Indian leaders had the satisfaction that one of their demands was accepted. But Sinha, who had a lucrative legal practice, was not so happy. He continued in the office for about one and half year. Srinivas Sastri informed Krishnaswami Iyer that after relinquishing the office, Sinha started his legal practice, and in one year his income was rupees seventy thousand, and of that, rupees twenty-five thousand was from a government brief.

The new Legislative Assemblies and Council were to function under the new Act in 1909. Gokhale speaking on the budget of 1909 in the Central Legislative Council discussed budget proposals and then alluded to the political reforms, which were to be implemented. He said that the country was witnessing disorder and violence, but the political reforms brought in by the viceroy and the Secretary of State were generous and eased the tension. He said there was appreciation of the importance of order which was the basis of progress and there were indications of closer cooperation henceforth. Gokhale, however, pointed out that there were some other instances which had created bad feelings. He cited the deportation of nine Bengalis under 1818 Act. Among them were Ashvini Kumar Dutt and Krishna Kumar Mitra. Gokhale said that he knew them both. "They are undoubtedly persons of high character and deep piety, and it is incredible that either of them could have been most remotely connected with crime." Gokhale then asked for their restoration to their home. He referred to the Mohammedan representation under the new Act. "I think that the most reasonable plan is to throw open a substantial minimum of seats to election on a territorial basis in which all qualified to vote should take part without distinction of race or creed. And then supplementary elections should be held for minorities which numerically or otherwise are important enough to need special representation, and these should be confined to members of the minorities only. The great advantage of this plan is that it provides for composite action by all communities up to a certain point, and then it prevents injustice, in practical operation, to minorities by giving them special supplementary electorates of their own. The idea of two water-tight compartments for Hindus and Mohammedans separately will not promote the best interests of the country, and moreover it is not feasible".

It was the Government of India, which upheld the plea of separate electorates for the Muslims, as the Muslim leaders opposed the territorial basis for electoral colleges. Though the Act itself was not amended to accommodate the Muslim leaders, rules and regulations under the Act were so framed by the Government of India that they in effect created separate electorates. So the Muslim leaders called off the protest movement and welcomed the regulations. Minto held that as the partition of Bengal had brought Muslims to the government, so also the separate electorates. But the partition and then the separate electorates increased the tension between Hindus and Muslims and more so in Bengal, Kerala and some other provinces. Bureaucrats like Risley and others used their skill to so draft the regulations under the new Act that Muslims, landlords and the Princes would remain the allies of the government. They defeated an intellectual like Morley by, so to say, stealth.

Moderates in the Congress, though divided on the issue of separate electorates, were not inclined to throw away the Reforms, and the Radicals were outside the Congress and not organized. Lokmanya Tilak was in jail and Bipin Chandra Pal was in London living the life of a miserable man. R.P. Karandikar, who was in London, met Pal and learnt that Shamji Krishna Verma went back on his promise to give fellowship to Pal, as latter was not demanding the end of the British Rule in India. Pal was then asked to apply for another fellowship. Khaparde had also confirmed Karandikar's account and noted in his diary that he had advanced some amount to Pal. Arvindbabu, before renouncing the political life had criticized the Reform Proposals. He said that the mountain had given birth to a proverbial mouse, but it was no less ridiculous. Indians were not less intelligent than the people of China, Turkey or Iran, but they had self-rule or they were on its way, unlike Indians. People have not got anything in the field of elections, executive or the powers of the legislatures. So the Reforms Proposals would not change anything, affirmed Arvindbabu.

While Gokhale was in England discussing the Reforms scheme, the cult of Bomb had reached before him. Madan Lal Dhingra shot Sir Curzon Wyllie in a London meeting and Dr. Lalkaka who rushed to his rescue was also shot dead. Madan Lal was tried in a London court and was given a death sentence which was executed on August 17, 1909. In his statement to the court Madan Lal justified his act, as he said that the British had looted and exploited India and were responsible for the deaths of so many Indians. He asked for a death sentence so that his countrymen would take revenge. When Madan Lal's trial was going on in the court, Lord Morley wrote to Lord Minto on July 29: "(Madan Lal's) execution may lead to retaliation and blood-feud not only against us at the India office, but against lonely Europeans in remote places in India itself. But be that as it may, we hang a murderer when we are lucky enough to catch one, and so we shall hang Dhingra. I am not in love with Indian affairs, all the same. Are you"? After Dhingra was hanged, King Edward told Lord Minto on August 17: "Serious steps should be taken to prevent these young men coming over to England with no fixed occupation, and falling into bad hands which they invariably do. They only learn sedition and treason, which they infuse into the minds of their countrymen both in England and India. What can one, however, expect if such a scoundrel as Keir Hardie, who is also a Member of the House of Commons, foments sedition in India and at home against our mode of Government? The harm he has done is incalculable—makes one's blood boil".[17]

Minto expressed his shock and indignation in his letter to Lord Morley. He said that at the time he was sad and at the same time felt relieved as the people of England would realize how dangerous it was to let loose those who hatch assassination plots. Murder made no impact in India, but England was disturbed and Shamji Krishna Verma might be enthused. His 'India Sociologist' and Hyndman's 'Justice' would go on their own way as usual." Minto regretted that Englishmen had crossed their limit in worshiping freedom and had lost sense of reality. Minto hoped that the lesson learnt after the assassination of Wyllie would not be forgotten soon. Wilfrid Blunt viewed this assassination differently. He wrote: "It is the just shock needed to convince the selfish rulers that selfishness has its limits of imprudence. It is like that other fiction that England never yields to threats. My experience is that when England has her face slapped, she apologizes, not before".[18]

The political climate, thus, had changed radically and it was not very congenial to Gokhale who strove hard to bring in political reforms and firmly believed in the constitutional politics.

REFERENCES

1. Martin Gilbert, *Servant of India*, Longmans, London, 1966, p. 131.
2. Nirad Chaudhari, *An Autobiography of an Unknown Indian*, Uni. of California Press, Berkeley, 1968, pp. 221-231.
3. John Morley, *Recollections*, Vol. II, The Macmillan, NY, 1917, pp. 259-260.
4. Stanley Wolpert, *Morley and India, 1906-1910*, Uni. of California Press, Berkeley, 1967, p. 115.
5. Stanley Wolpert, *Morley and India, 1906-1910*, Uni. of California Press, Berkeley, 1967, pp. 66-67.
6. Gokhale Papers.
7. Gokhale Papers.
8. Gokhale Papers.
9. R.P. Karandikar, *Letters From England :1908*, Vithal Raghunath Karandikar, Poona, 1935, p. 346.
10. John Morley, *Recollections*, Vol. II, The Macmillan, NY, 1917, pp. 272-273.
11. Gokhale Papers.
12. Wilfrid Blunt, *My Diaries*, Single Volume Edition, Markin Secker, London, 1932, p. 220.
13.. P. Hardy, *The Muslims of British India*, CUP., London, 1972, p. 162.

14. Ed. Martin Gilbert, *Servant of India*, Longmans, London, 1966, p. 185.
15. Sir Sidney Lee, *King Edward 7, a Biography*, 2 Vols., Macmillan, NY, 1927, pp. 386-387.
16. John Morley, *Recollections*, Vol. II, The Macmillan, NY, 1917, p. 303.
17. Martin Gilbert, *Servant of India*, Longmans, London, 1966, p. 195.
18. Adams W.S., *Edwardian Portraits*, Secker and Warburg, London, 1957, p. 95.

Chapter Fifteen

FAR-REACHING CHANGES

Moderates controlled the Congress after the Surat split but their base in the country did not widen or strengthen. Gokhale was optimistic that with the political reforms, the tension in the country would be considerably eased and the Moderates would improve their position. But gains of both the Moderates and the Congress were marginal. Roots of the malady lay in the organization itself and also the quality of leadership. Lala Lajpat Rai had lost all faith in most of the leaders years ago. With the honourable exceptions of some leaders like Gokhale, he thought that most of them did not want to sacrifice for the country. Moderate leadership on the lower level had no direction. The Radicals or Nationalists, even though out of the Congress organisation, were active on the lower and middle levels.

Srinivas Sastri, who was sent to Assam and East Bengal by Gokhale in 1907 after the Calcutta session of the Congress, in his detailed accounts to Gokhale had clearly stated that Nationalists had the backing of the people. Sastri, writing from Mymensingh on January 27, 1907 said, "The extreme boycott of Mr. Pal finds adherents chiefly among the younger generation". Sastri did not find national schools in good condition and felt sorry for the same. "However, there is one thing on which I looked upon with unmixed satisfaction—the triumph of swadeshi among the Hindus. Zamindars and tenants, extremists and Moderates, Vakils and schoolmasters, all are firm adherents of Swadeshi, and use their influence in spreading it. I wish it were possible to say half as much of other parts of India. I cannot argue it out, but I believe in sound economics and true patriotism. East Bengal is doing its duty bravely and may well be proud". In Chittgaong area Sastri found his hosts had contempt for those from Bombay, Punjab and Madras who had not taken to Swadeshi. In Jorhat, Sastri met Moderates who were nowhere in the picture except among the Mussalmans.[1] So the credit for the spread of swadeshi naturally went to the Radicals while Moderates were relegated to the background in East Bengal. Before the Madras session of the Congress, Gokhale, at the request of the local leaders, sent Srinivas Sastri to help in the arrangements of the session. In a letter to Krishnaswami Iyer, Sastri told him that he did not get any assistance from the Moderates but to his surprise, the Nationalists came forward to help him, as they felt that Congress session must be held. Sastri then observed that Moderates might have been wealthy and might have prestige, but no grit and backbone.

Gokhale's speech in the Madras Congress emphasized the positive aspects of the Reform Proposals. He appealed to the delegates to create an atmosphere for cooperation and implement the reforms, which the majority of delegates accepted with reservations. But after the regulations under the new Act were published, Gokhale himself was disheartened. In a letter to his friend, Wedderburn, Gokhale opened his heart and expressed his anguish. He informed Wedderburn that except for the Muslim block, regulations under the Reform Act had generated dissatisfaction all over the country. Representation to the Muslims in the Viceroy's Executive Council, according to Gokhale, was extremely unjustified. From Bombay province, out of the four representatives to be sent on the Council, three would be Muslims, even though they were one fifth of the population. A man like Ferozeshah was also disgusted with the whole affair, and told Gokhale that he was thinking of withdrawing from politics. Gokhale further explained that "Punjab was given three seats in the Central Legislature and at least for initial period all were to go to Muslims. Afterwards Hindus would get one seat and sometimes not even one. But in Punjab, Hindus were fifty per cent and in education, property and public service they were far ahead of the Muslims in the province". Gokhale had no objection to giving some weightage to the Muslims; but he said it should not be so disproportionate. He also objected to the discrimination with regard to the voting rights, and pointed out that in Bombay the Muslims, who had an annual income of 135 pounds were eligible for vote, but however rich a Hindu might be, he was to get the voting rights only if he were a member of at least three societies out of four, which were approved by the Government. Gokhale told Wedderburn that 'this discrimination was annoying and harmful'. Gokhale's friend Krishnaswami Iyer, who was to the far right, frowned upon the provision of the separate electorate and conveyed his feelings to Gokhale through Srinivas Sastri that he (Gokhale) placed too much faith in Morley. Krishnaswami also wrote to Wacha to call a special conference of the Congress, which was rejected by the latter.

Motilal Nehru strongly disapproved the separate electorates to Muslims. Ramesh Chandra Dutt said in a statement, when the history of the Hindu-Muslim division would be written, a note would be taken of those who tried to widen it and who accepted it. He said it was unfortunate that Muslims sang to the tune dictated to them and were under an illusion that they would carry weight and influence by keeping away from their own countrymen. Dutt blamed the

Tory papers in England and the Anglo-Indian Press for misleading the Muslims. He contrasted the behaviour of the Muslims to the Americans. He said 'The Times' had tried hard to impress on the Americans that those from the North and the South differed from each other, but they did not fall prey to that propaganda campaign. To 'Hindustan Samachar' (September 1907) it appeared that the separate electorates were given to the Muslims with a view to suppress the voice of members like Gokhale by the Muslims and landlords. But it warned that such tactics would spell disaster and spread despondency. The journal pointed out that while in the existing legislature there were five independent members out of twenty-five, under the new Act, the independent members would be seven or ten in the total of fifty. That would not only be harmful to Hindus but also to the Muslims; and the bureaucracy would be more powerful. 'Hindustan Samachar' regretted that the voice of the independent Muslims would be submerged in the cacophony of the majority from the community. It was indignant about the Reform Act for widening the cleavage between the two communities.

Lala Lajpat Rai's two letters in the 'Punjabi' were indicative of the mood of the people in general and Congressmen in particular. Lalaji paid high tributes to Pherozeshah and Gokhale, but he differed on the question of the unity of the Congress. He then said: "One may honestly doubt the wisdom of the policy that has been persistently followed since the unfortunate split in 1907". Lala Lajpat Rai affirmed that, left to himself, Tilak was not eager to precipitate the crisis. Twice on his requests, Tilak was prepared to withdraw his opposition to the election of Dr. Rash Bihari Ghose. But, unfortunately, according to Lalaji, Tilak, instead of leading, allowed himself to be led by some of his colleagues. "While it is true that Tilak's party was directly responsible for the scenes, can one deny that the leaders of the other side were also anxious to bring about the split? I am of opinion that the party called 'Moderate' should retain the actual control and management of the Congress, but that the other party should remain inside the Congress, and should exercise its influence in the way in which all strong minorities do. To a man of my humble understanding—the moderate 'nationalists' are committing an error of tactics in making the split a 'settled fact.' I am emphatically of opinion that the extinction of the extreme left wing of the Indian National Party is a grave menace to the Congress itself. However, taking the situation as it is, the split reduces the position of the Congress to an organization run by a section of the educated Hindus in the name of the united nation. The bulk of the Mohammedans are opposed to it. A strong section of the Hindus disown its politics, being disposed to a policy of reaction. The majority have, since the split, become indifferent. The minority that still stand for propaganda of Self-Government are divided. Under the circumstances it is futile to pretend that the Congress stands condemned by the mouth of its own leaders who have given an unqualified support to the dispatch of the Government of India, embodying the principle of separate denominational representation and an excessive representation to a minority on the ground of their 'political importance.'"[2]

Thus, the Congress was in disarray, and Reforms Act further weakened it. Morley could have restrained the Government of India and modified the reform proposals; but he was least interested in finding out a long-term solution and fashion his policy accordingly. Morley, like other English statesmen, had declared that the aim of the self-government for India was a remote one, but he or for that matter the British government had no well thought-out plan to achieve that goal. It might be that British statesmen might have agreed with Morley that it would be at least a century or so before a self-government would be given to India, and therefore, they had given no thought to a long-term plan. Morley had made it clear to Minto that their task was limited to making Indians worthy of self-government. Gokhale and Pherozeshah could not have agreed with such a proposition, nevertheless they did not criticize Morley for holding this view. However, their other Moderate colleagues did not follow them. In the process both Pherozeshah and Gokhale had lost ground and saw further weakening of the Congress. In fact, Morley had forgotten his own thesis in his book on Mill, where he said that a small and temporary measure of reforms is harmful when it does not lead to a permanent one.

By the middle of 1909, Gokhale lost hope of Moderates in the Congress becoming strong and influencing the political life of the country. He wrote to Wedderburn on September 24, 1909: "I fear one of our numerous disintegrations has overtaken us again—this time it is the national movement that appears to be going to pieces, throwing back on Provincialism, and one grieves to find that there is no influence available anywhere in the country, capable of staying the process. The organization evolved by Mr. Hume out of the material prepared by a succession of workers in different parts of the country is crumbling to pieces, and the efforts of the nation's heart and mind that brought us together in that organization seem to have almost exhausted themselves. The split at Surat, followed by the vigour with which the Government came down on the Extremists everywhere, has turned the whole Extremist party into active enemies of the national constitutional movement. And 'Moderates' placed between the officials and the Extremists have not the necessary public spirit and energy of character to hold together effectively for long, though they are numerically strong in the country. In addition to the incessant attacks by the Extremists, the conduct of the Bengal Moderates is hastening the disintegration of the national movement. Bengal really has no leader on our side. Surendranath Banerjea is an orator, but he has no great courage or backbone, and he cannot keep in hand the unruly pack, whom he professes to lead. Moreover, there is no doubt that the position of the constitutional party has been rendered practically impossible by the Government's refusal to reconsider partition (of Bengal) and the continued incarcerations of the deportees".[3] The situation was aggravated by the regulations under the Reform Act which gave Muslims undue weightage, depriving the Hindus and other minorities their just share. So the moderates could not claim victory in passing the Reform Act. In fact, division in their ranks came to the fore. That was why the Moderates from Bengal were opposed to the nomination of Pherozeshah as president of the Congress session at Lahore. Pherozeshah had to withdraw, and Madan Mohan Malviya was nominated as president at Lahore.

Lahore Congress was a failure. Attendance was poor; Bengal, even with Pherozeshah's withdrawal, did not respond, and very few delegates from the province were present. There was a strong desire for uniting all the different groups in the Congress organization but the Constitution proved to be a stumbling block. Naturally, those who sponsored the Constitution came under criticism. Those included Gokhale, who was aware of his unpopularity in the organization. Thus, within two years of the split, the Moderates including Gokhale had lost ground. Moreover, as Gokhale wrote to Wedderburn: "a feeling in the Hindu community has been spreading since last year that Congress has done no good to it, that it bore the brunt of the struggle all these years, the Mohammedans have walked away with the greater part of the spoils, and that it was necessary for Hindus now, first and foremost, to look after their own interests, as distinguished from those of the Mohammedans." Gokhale in an earlier letter to his friend in England had squarely blamed the bureaucrats scuttling and distorting the reform scheme and widening the cleavages between the two major communities.[4] As Morley had a copy of this letter, he sent it to Lord Minto, who vented his anger in reply to Morley. Minto said on October 19, 1910: "It is very important as showing his (Gokhale's) hand, I am sorry to say. I can only call it mischievous, and written with an intention to mislead. Our repressive measures are certainly not severe. Then the suggestion that the official world is opposed to reform is quite untrue. There has been an extraordinary change in that direction. But the wrong symptom in what Gokhale writes is that he apparently does not mean to accept the reforms with the goodwill, which is so important for their success. After all Gokhale represents a very small minority in India, but it is a dangerous minority in that undue weight is attached to its views".[5] Though Minto had defended his officials and assured Morley that there was a perceptible change in their attitude towards the reform, the reality was quite otherwise. Among the officials who played a key role in diluting the reforms and bringing in the communal element, Dunlop-Smith and Risley were most active and enthusiastic.

Discontent and agitation had not abated in India. Correspondent of 'The Times' had described the situation in its issue of June 28, 1909 in great detail and discussed 'Britain's Future In India'. He said that the notion that Lord Curzon was responsible for the discontent in India, and with his departure the things would be normal, had been proven wrong. "The first statement which it is necessary to make is that the reforms recently instituted in India have left almost entirely unaffected those essential conditions which chiefly concern us. On the contrary, it would not be difficult to demonstrate that their ultimate and inevitable effect must be to accentuate it. We are face to face with the antagonism, open or veiled, of a very large proportion of the Indian peoples. Our rule is disliked, not because it is bad, but because it is alien. It may be freely admitted that reforms were necessary; but there was no need to lavish concessions which were unsought". The correspondent characterised the Congress as an organisation run irresponsibly by half a dozen or some would say by one or two men. He said that Congress represented mostly Hindus dominated by Brahmins; and was opposed by Muslims and the princely states.

As the split in the Congress and the political reforms did not help the Moderates and did not strengthen their position, so also the separate electorates did not make the Muslim League strong. League was not satisfied even with the Reform Act; but when it found that regulations under the Act could give three additional seats, they stopped criticising it. However, those who were elected to the Legislatures were not beholden to the League. They got in on their own. What was the aftermath of this? Francis Robinson explains, "In the making of the Morley-Minto reforms, which translated the English view of Indian society into formal constitutional arrangements, they prevailed, their pervasiveness helping to turn Muslim League protest into Muslim seats. In establishing the Muslims as a separate and special interest in the Indian constitution, the Muslim League was important, but government's assumption about Indian Muslims in general, and its politics towards them were crucially important. Muslim demands for the extension of separate representation to municipal and district boards gained new force; a great campaign for a Muslim University at Alighar was actually launched. The most important effect of the new position of the Muslims, however, was that government began to treat them less circumspectly. The Muslims have had a large slice of cake, the feeling went, now it is the turn of others. This change in the government's attitude divided the UP Muslims into two main groups".[6] A new spirit was manifest in the Muslim society, especially the educated youths. A movement for a Muslim University at Aligarh might have been an educational movement for some leaders, but the educated youths regarded it as a political move. Historian Robinson has quoted some extracts from a communication from the District Collector to the Governor. This official wrote that even though the movement had started as defensive one, shortly it would turn aggressive. "The Muslims are not thinking of education in itself at all, but more candidates for government employment, more lawyers to fill seats in Councils, and more political power generally". Muslims also began taking more anti-Congress posture. This resulted into more tension and division between the two communities.

Moderates in the Congress were divided on the question of separate electorates to the Muslims and their differences came in the open when Madan Mohan Malviya criticised this provision. Gokhale, on the other hand, said that though the provision was wrong in principle, it had to be accepted in the given situation. He reminded the members of the Legislative Council that the Muslim fear of inadequate representation was genuine, but after a while they would realize that it was not the real solution to their problems. In the changed circumstances separate electorates would disappear. Gokhale supposed that the separate electorates would come into force after the elections to the Legislatures. But Morley in his speech announced that they would be ushered in the coming elections. So Gokhale had to face the opposition from his own party colleagues. In the Lahore Congress in December 1909, President Madan Mohan Malviya declared that he had no objection to giving adequate representation to the Muslims but they should fight the election in the joint electorates, and if they could not get the prescribed seats, then they should get them by nomination. Malviya complained that in U.P., Muslim candidates fought from the separate as well as general constituencies and the result was that they got disproportionate seats in the municipalities and District Boards, compared to their population. He pointed out that though Muslim population in U.P. was six percent, they had eight seats in an assembly of twenty-six. Malviya asked why the Hindus in Punjab and Bengal should not get same protection, as they were in the minority. Lahore Congress then passed a resolution condemning the separate electorates and the regulations enforced under the Act. This was done in the presence of Gokhale, who could not change the mood of the delegates. The resolution was moved by Surendranath Banerjea, who complimented Morley and Minto for the political reforms, but denounced the provision of separate electorates and regulations. The resolution expressed the displeasure about excessive representation to Muslims, thereby creating animosity between Muslims and other communities. Banerjea took strong exceptions to the provisions, which unnecessarily took away the rights of eligible Hindus to vote.

Surendranath was in London before the Lahore Congress. He pleaded with Morley to release Aswini Kumar Dutt. However, according to him, he failed because of the assassination of Curzon Wyllie. But his optimism was misplaced. Whatever might have been the inclination of Morley, he was reluctant to go against the wishes of Minto in such delicate matters. And Minto was not moved by Gokhale's appeal to release Dutt. In fact, he was annoyed with Gokhale. He wrote to Morley that though Gokhale might be honest, he did not have adequate information, which the government had gathered from various sources. Minto, therefore, did not want to accept Gokhale's views about deportation.

Writing about the Lahore Congress, 'The Times' commended Pherozeshah and Gokhale, but disapproved of the speeches by Malviya and Surendranath. It did not accept that Hindus were given a raw deal under the Reform Act and the regulations. 'The Times' reminded the critics that the regulations were prepared by the Law Ministry headed by S.N. Sinha, and asked the elected members to discharge their responsibility properly. Morley was equally displeased with the Indian critics. He explained to journalist Nevinson in what difficult situation he brought the reform measure. Morley, therefore, dismissed the objections as unreasonable. But a decade later, when the Montagu-Chelmsford Committee gave its report, it found that Morley-Minto reform scheme had several shortcomings. It said Morley and Minto had to find out a balance between an autocratic rule of the Moguls and the Constitutional government under the British. They also had to see that the government majority should not be jeopardized. According to the report, Morley-Minto reforms failed to create a sense of responsibility in the Legislative Council members. As the Members had no responsibility, their questions were, at many times, trivial. If the members had the confidence that one day they had to run the administration, they would have been more responsible. Ultimately, reforms did not retain the best of the old and the new methods of administration, according to Montagu and Chelmsford.

The year 1910 saw more oppressive measures by the government. It was, of course, true that the cult of bomb had spread widely. But it was equally true that this cult was strengthened because the government was not prepared to abolish or modify the partition of Bengal. This had infuriated the people, and the young men joined the revolutionary groups in increasing numbers. The number of secret societies had increased considerably. The government then brought two bills; one for restricting the press freedom and the other to ban the explosives. Gokhale was in two minds about these bills. The government had made its position clear in the preamble. It said that violence had considerably increased and some newspapers by their provocative writings were stoking the fires. The Penal Code was ineffective to restrain such newspapers; hence, stringent measures were unavoidable. Gokhale did not discount the gravity of the situation, and admitted that violence had increased. He also conceded that at times some newspapers indulged in intemperate and provocative writing. Gokhale's basic faith was in the British rule and he was opposed to those, who were bent on destroying it by any means. His apprehension was that the powers under the bill might be misused by the officials. Gokhale also drew the attention of the government to some Anglo-Indian papers indulging in scurrilous writings against the Indians. Kasturi Ranga Iyengar, editor of 'The Hindu' criticised both the Press Bill and the bill about the explosives. He said that the bills were brought in hurry and that was why few members were present in the House. To him this Press Bill was much more restrictive than that under Lord Lytton. Iyengar said that the Indian newspapers might not be ideal or perfect, but most of them were law-abiding. The government should not have taken 'Yugantar' as representative example of the Indian Press. He said that the language of the bill was vague, giving more powers to the officials; but even under the Penal Code, the government had wide powers to restrict the provocative writing.

Some members of the House of Commons came down heavily on the government for justifying the unjust measures of the Government of India. On April 28, 1910, Ramsay MacDonald remarked that the government's justification was amazing. He asked what Arvindbabu wrote. He wrote that the British were exploiting India; and brought famines. These were his opinions and there was nothing seditious about them. He expected the officials in India not to regard themselves as Akbar, but devote their energies to redress the grievances of the people. On July 26 Ramsay MacDonald warned in his speech in the Commons that intellectual anarchy in India was much more dangerous than the economic one. He said, the educated class was small, but very much disturbed and discontented. Oriental mind had come under the influence of the Western thoughts, which would not give you any solace or peace. J.C. Wedgwood, participating in the same debate in the Commons, said that if England had been under the Indian rule, all members of the House would have been engaged in the same activities as the Indians were. He suggested that if there were to be another Durbar, which was being contemplated, then all political detainees including Tilak should be released. Keir Hardie criticized the policy of the Government of India of compelling the government officials to do intelligence work. This criticism was not unfounded, as the Government of India had issued a directive to the ICS officers to help in every possible way to thwart seditious activities, and educational officers were asked to keep an eye on the answer papers of the students. They were also told that the textbooks should not carry anything derogatory of the British rule. The government suspected that under the garb of religious education, seditious ideas were preached and officers were to look out for such activities. When Gokhale came to know of the government directive to the ICS officers, he made inquiries with Lord Minto, who helped to tone it down.

The special powers, which the Government of India had assumed, were justified by 'The Times' as well as other periodicals. 'The Edinburgh Review' in its issue of October 1910 discounted the two sets of criticism against Minto's regime. It said the regime came under criticism by some for being timid and by the others for disowning the principles of justice and freedom. The periodical said that the situation in some parts of India was grave and the government had no other option than to assume special powers to curb the seditious activities. 'The Edinburgh Review' quoted Mill, who had said: "People must be considered unfit for more than limited and qualified freedom, who will not cooperate freely with the law and the public authorities in the repression of evildoers. A people who are more disposed to shelter a criminal than to apprehend him; who, like the Hindoos, will perjure themselves to screen the man who has robbed them rather than take trouble or expose themselves to vindictiveness by giving evidence against him; people who are revolted by an execution but not shocked at an assassination—require that the public authorities should be armed with much sterner powers of repression than elsewhere. A people so disposed, cannot be governed with so little power exercised over them as a people whose sympathies are on the side of the law and who are willing to give active assistance in its enforcement".

Gerald Barrier has given the statistical details about the implementation of the Press Law. According to him, between 1909 January and 1910 December, there were 57 cases against the newspapers. From 1910 to 1913, the government asked 272 printing presses and 168 newspapers' proprietors to pay deposits. Some provincial governments had banned 200 books and booklets. The provincial governments had the option to take action, which they deemed appropriate. Hence, there was no uniformity in the action. It was strange that instead of Bengal, Bombay was ahead in taking preventive action against the newspapers and publications and took action against 204, compared to 119 in Bengal. But the number of cases registered against newspapers in Bengal was forty-three, while in Bombay it was thirty-two. In confiscation of the deposit amounts, Madras was far ahead than Bombay or Bengal. The Punjab government restricted itself in demanding deposits and issuing warnings. Even Burma was not free from such actions.[7]

'The Times' had taken serious note of the situation in India and sent Valentine Chirol to tour the country and write newsletters. First such letter appeared on July 16, 1910. At the conclusion of his tour, Chirol collected them in a book under the title, *Unrest in India.* Chirol had the felicity of pen, but had a closed mind and rigid outlook. Even Dunlop-Smith held the same view about him. Chirol's criticism of the Congressmen and especially Radicals was very trenchant. He was an admirer of Lord Curzon, and called Lord Minto 'timid'. Minto called him to explain his position. The burden of the newsletters of Chirol was that only a handful of educated Indians criticized the government and the masses at large were not dissatisfied. Educated people, and specially the Radicals, indulged in spreading discontent and most of the Radicals were Brahmins. Chirol alleged that the Brahmins did not want others to share power and wanted to secure their dominance. He justified the partition of Bengal and separate electorates for Muslims. Chirol said that because of these measures several newspapers were busy in spreading seditious ideas in India. Chirol then quoted some extracts from newspaper writings. These newsletters were much discussed both in India and England. Chirol, who got carried away by his prejudices and preconceived notions, was off the mark, and made several glaring mistakes. Among the trio, Lal, Bal and Pal, who were supposed to be heading the radical faction, only Bal Gangadhar Tilak was a Brahmin. Arvindbabu, who sometime stood for armed struggle, was not a Brahmin. Besides, Gokhale, who was opposed to the Radical politics, was a Brahmin and that too from Poona. Chirol was a severe critic of Lokmanya Tilak, who, after his release, sued him for libel in a London court. Morley, however, was very much pleased with the writings of Chirol. Writing in February 1911 issue of the 'Nineteenth Century and After' he said, that it was done with an objectivity of a scientist and had also shown that Chirol was conscious of his responsibility. "The scientific explorer goes hand in hand with the critic of the occasions of the hour. Not composed in the air, it has attraction of wide experience and long observation. Above all, we are conscious of being in the hands of a man animated by that peculiar sense of practical responsibility, the lack of which makes so much political discussion". By this Morley betrayed that veneer of his liberalism was, indeed, very thin.

Whatever limited powers were given by the new Act, Gokhale did his best to make use of them to the maximum. In 1910 he moved a resolution in the Central Legislature to enforce compulsory and free primary education throughout India. It was a very important resolution, and if accepted, would have been a revolutionary step with far-reaching consequences beneficial to India. Though the government, accepted it in principle, it was disposed to oppose it on the point of unbearable expenditure. As the government made its intention clear, Gokhale had no other option than to withdraw the resolution. However, next year Gokhale brought a proper Bill on the same subject. The Bill, which Gokhale introduced, was limited in scope, as he was aware of the monetary constraints. But the idea itself was new and revolutionary. It was called Elementary Education Bill, which sought to direct the local bodies, municipalities and District Boards, which felt ready for such innovation to adopt compulsion in their jurisdiction. Bill gave an option to these bodies and did not intend to make it compulsory. Besides, the compulsion was to be used in case of boys, as the female education was in a very primitive stage; though Gokhale would have readily accepted the compulsion for girls as well. But the government declined to send the Bill to the Select Committee. Gokhale made an eloquent speech and cited the literacy figures of various countries, and compared them with India. Gokhale said, unless the foundation was strong, broad higher education alone would not solve the main problems of the country. He said, "Even if the advantages of elementary education be put no higher than a capacity to read and write, its universal diffusion is a matter of prime importance, for literacy is better than no literacy any day, and the banishment of whole people's illiteracy is no mean achievement. But elementary education for the mass of the people means something more than a mere capacity to read and write. It means for them a keener enjoyment of life and a more refined standard of living". Gokhale sought this opportunity to propagate his Bill and asked his colleagues in the Servants of India Society to visit many places and explain the provisions of the Bill. Accordingly, Srinivas Sastri and others addressed several meetings in different parts of the country. As the government refused to send the Bill to the Select Committee, it was the end of the matter. But Gokhale received support from some officials. Srinivas Sastri later told that though two officials supported the Bill, they did not want it to be adopted. They said that one day the government would act on its own. It did not want the impression to go round that they were afraid of the public opinion, or Gokhale or his Servants of India Society.[8]

B.R. Nanda has cited some correspondence between the then education minister, Harcourt Butler and Viceroy Lord Hardinge. Butler had estimated that the compulsory elementary education on all India level would entail an expenditure of rupees five million. In May 1911 Butler drew the attention of the viceroy to the fact that this demand was quite widespread and both Hindus and Muslims had made it a part of their platform. "It is advocated in Legislative Councils, at public meetings and in the press by landowners no less than by lawyers, and by philanthropists; and politicians are starting free institutions, night schools and the like. True, Gokhale's Bill contemplates the payment of fees by parents whose income exceeds Rs. 10 per mensem, but the public prefers the abolition of the fees to the contingent introduction of the compulsory principle, and that was Mr. Gokhale's own attitude in the Imperial Legislative Council a year ago. Personally I regard the provision of free elementary education is a matter of real urgency and vital consequence not only because I foresee that we shall be forced to concede it within a year or two, nor because I think that more than any other measure it will remove the deep-rooted belief in India and outside it, that we are afraid of education and put difficulties in its path, but mainly because the economic and political conditions of the country require it. I am convinced that unless we move in harmony with popular opinion in this matter we shall find control slipping through our fingers". The viceroy was also impressed and told the Secretary of State that his government would take some steps in the matter.

Gokhale then went to England and met the new Secretary of State, Lord Crew. He told the Secretary how the free and compulsory elementary education was necessary. Lord Crew agreed with Gokhale. However, the responsibility to implement the scheme was that of the provincial governments and no such government was enthusiastic about the scheme. Punjab and U.P. governments conveyed their opposition and warned of the dissatisfaction of the people. Sir George Clarke warned the viceroy, "The agitation for education (so far as Primary education is concerned) is of quite recent origin, and comes from the people who are anxious to make our Rule impossible. They well realise that their power to stir up discontent would be immensely increased if every cultivator could read. We cannot teach the great mass of people to read and write; but we can and we shall do much to promote general discontent. In that part of their calculations Gokhale's are perfectly right".[9]

In the Central legislature, Nawab Abdul Majjid and Sir Gangadhar Chitnawis also opposed Gokhale's Bill. Both of them were reactionary and were alienated from the people about whom they had contempt. Gokhale, speaking on his Bill, told the Council that there were some in England who had no confidence in the people, and the two members of the Central Legislature were no exceptions. Gokhale also reminded Chitnawis that his Nagpur municipality and the district board had passed resolutions demanding free and compulsory elementary education. Because of the opposition by the provincial governments, Lord Hardinge's enthusiasm also waned. However, Gokhale's Bill evoked wide response in the Indian Press, and his meetings drew large crowds. In 1910 and 1911 Gokhale made important speeches in the Council on the duty on cloth and sugar, and the financial condition of the railways.

By 1910 the textile industry was in recession and Dadabhai, a representative of the Mill owners, had demanded various concessions. Gokhale could not support him. He took the interests of the consumers and the industry proper into consideration. He pointed out that though the textile industry was going through a recessionary period, mill-owners had gained huge profits a year ago, and so should not protest too much. Gokhale urged the government to give protection to the textile and other industries and impose thirty per cent duty on the import on the cotton of fine count. Gokhale said that protection would be beneficial to the consumers. He also wanted duty on the imported sugar.

The Servants of India Society completed five years of its existence in 1910. As a first member and the chairman, Gokhale reviewed the work done in the period. He said, "When this Society was started, it was a novel experiment; in the country there was no institution conducted on the lines which we have adopted. During these five years greater part of our energy was devoted to the work of the organisation. The building and the library had to be developed; confidence had to be established among friends. Members had to be trained". Gokhale expressed satisfaction with the progress made so far. The governor, Sir George Clarke, paid a visit to the Society and commended its work. The Society's branch was opened in Madras in 1910, in Nagpur in 1911 and in Allahabad in 1913. It was receiving encouraging response from all over India, which helped to strengthen its finances. The Society had sent two representatives to U.P. when the province was in the grip of famine. In later years the Society remained in the forefront in famine relief work in Maharashtra and other provinces. However, all was not well with the Society. In 1914 when Gokhale had gone to England, the Society's annual meeting had to be held in his absence, in which some subjects on the agenda became controversial. Mavalankar, who was a member of the Society, was a businessman, who decided to start an agency in London. Gokhale had promised him monetary help from the Society. But some members conveyed to Gokhale that Mavalankar's business was in jeopardy and the Society should not get involved in his financial affairs. A couple of other members were opposed to collecting money and lending to some business enterprise. According to them it was against the aims and objectives of the institution. The other controversial subject was objections raised to some sections of the constitution of the Society and its functioning. Some of the members felt that they were left out and the Society was in the hands of an inner circle. They demanded more give and take among the members and the necessity of taking the 'outer circle' into confidence.

Gokhale was later appraised of the discussion in the annual meeting, which made him sad and dejected. He wrote back to admit that Mavalankar had made some mistakes, but as he was in trouble, he should be helped. Gokhale laid down the rules as to how much amount was to be given to Mavalankar and what should be the mode of payment. It was characteristic of him that he acted in this affair as a guarantor with the obligation to pay the amount in case Mavalankar failed to pay. In the Society's meeting, a demand was made to amend the constitution. Gokhale then asked the members to write down the amendments or write a totally new constitution. Some members sent their suggestions, which had no support from others. He felt the whole discussion, in a way, showed a lack of confidence in him. But Dr. Dev and others convinced him that it was not the case.

Lord Minto had completed his term as viceroy. Lord Morley also tendered his resignation as the Secretary of State. 'The Times' in two articles on October 17 and November 21, 1910 reviewed the regime of Lord Minto and also that of Lord Morley. 'The Times' said Lord Minto played a great role in the fulfilment of the promise to bring in political reforms. "How far the reforms are responsible for the improvement at present visible in the condition of India is a more debatable question. We should prefer to say that, if India is now outwardly at peace, it is rather because sedition has been visited with swift punishment, conspirators have been laid by the heels, and political malefactors have been taught that they cannot pursue their nefarious courses with impunity". 'The Times' gave credit to Minto for taking a firm stand about doing justice to Muslims. It expressed satisfaction that "Lord Morley had to face agitation in India, but he brought in political reforms". It said that "even though a liberal, Lord Morley had clear and sound conceptions about the responsibilities of Britain in India". Morley tendered his resignation as the Secretary of State for India in November 1910. However, it was not that he did not want to continue in the ministry. J.A. Spender, a journalist, had close relationship with Morley as well as with Prime Minister Asquith. When Spender met Asquith, he was told by Asquith that he had with him several resignation letters from Morley before, and thought that it was the last, and so accepted it. But after meeting Spender, Asquith realised that Morley wanted only a change in the portfolio, and so he was appointed as the chairman of the Council of the Ministers.

Much was written about Morley in office and out of it. There was unanimity about his intellectual eminence and his elegant style of writing. As an editor of 'Fortnightly Review' and 'Pall Mall Gazette', he brought prestige to both publications. His books on Burke and Gladstone were regarded as the best political biographies. Morley's book *On Compromise,* brought him admirers in England and abroad. Though a liberal he was averse to taking any extreme progressive step, as his priority was order, and not liberty. To him, British Empire was important, and the place of India, vital in the empire. He believed that India should be governed with sympathy along with firmness. Because of such disposition, Morley not only invited criticism from the Radicals in India but even the Moderates were not happy with him. While writing about Burke, Morley deplored that Burke could not understand or sympathise with the emotional outbreak of the general mass of people at the time of the French revolution. Morley was no different. He could not understand, nor sympathise with the emotional outbreak at the time of the partition of Bengal. Analysing the character and the ideological positions taken by Morley, Beatrice Webb said: "A charming person for a talk on literature; but a most depressing spectacle as a liberal leader. In sympathy with no single one of the progressive ideas, he clings to his old shibboleths of non-intervention and non-expansion abroad, and Church disestablishment and a sort of theoretical 'home rule,' at home. When I suggested that, if I had supreme power, I would hesitate before I disestablished the Church, he seemed aghast. And yet he dare not pronounce in favour of his own convictions; he feels instinctively the country is against him. To do nothing, and to say nothing, to sit and wait for the tide to ebb from this Government is the long and short of his policy. Naturally enough he is pessimistic; thinks that all things are going to the bad and country has lost its intellect and its character".[10]

Lord Hardinge replaced Lord Minto. Lord Kitchener, who aspired to this position and did his best to fulfil his desire, had the support of many Tories. King Edward also suggested that Kitchener should be appointed as viceroy. But both prime minister Asquith and Lord Morley were opposed to send a retired Army chief as viceroy to India, and postponed the decision. Meanwhile, King Edward died and Lord Hardinge's appointment was announced. After taking the office he reviewed the situation in India and decided to move in some direction. Before Lord Hardinge's appointment 'The Times' had said on May 1910 that the situation in India had improved and the agitation against the partition of Bengal had died down. In such circumstances no thought should be given to any revision of the partition. If the position of the Bengal was restored, then again an unwieldy and unmanageable province would be created, warned

'The Times'. Lord Hardinge and the new Secretary of State, Lord Crew, were not impressed by such arguments. Both decided to explore whether there would be some scope to amend the partition scheme. Lord Hardinge wrote to Lord Crew on June 17, 1911 that his chief of the Home Department had prepared a note, which said that the capital of India should be shifted to Delhi from Calcutta for the security of the country. Hardinge himself felt that such a shift would be statesmanlike and might give a new turn to the history of India. The viceroy also suggested that the province of Bengal should be restructured after annulling the partition. According to him, King George V should make this announcement at the time of the Durbar in Delhi.

In fact, Lord Hardinge was in two minds about the annulling of the partition, as he feared that the Muslims would be agitated by such a decision. But when he saw that the Secretary of State was favourable, he prepared a confidential memorandum. In his reminiscences Lord Hardinge says that within two months of his arrival in India, Lord Crew sent him a letter suggesting a modification of the partition scheme. He wanted to appoint a governor for Bengal instead of a lieutenant-governor, and move the capital of the province to Dacca or elsewhere to form an imperial enclave of Calcutta directly under the viceroy. King was in favour of this, informed Lord Crew. After consulting several high officials, Lord Hardinge conveyed to the Secretary that the scheme he had suggested was impractical for various reasons. However, later in the year, Viceroy was appraised by his officials that something had to be done to remove the feeling of injustice. He also found that the lieutenant-governor always looked to the Viceroy for advice and did nothing to administer the province. The Legislative Assembly sitting in Calcutta was unduly influenced by Bengalis, which was detrimental to the Legislative impartiality. It was a note by Sir John Jenkins, Home Member, on June 17, 1911 that set the ball rolling and materialised the Viceroy's views into a definite policy. Sir John was very keen to transfer the capital to Delhi and revise the policy of the partition of Bengal. Hardinge wrote: "After long discussion with Sir John Jenkins, with whose views I was quickly in general agreement, I drew up a very secret memorandum which I submitted to my council. The principal points were: (1) The transfer of capital from Calcutta to Delhi, (2) The creation of United Bengal into a presidency with a Governor in Council appointed from England, (3) The creation of Bihar and Orissa into a Lieutenant-Governorship with a Legislative Council and a capital at Patna, and (4) the restoration of the Chief Commissionership of Assam. All the members of my council agreed in principle".[11] On July 19, Lord Hardinge sent his proposals to the Secretary of State, placing before him all the advantages of the scheme and the objections that might be raised. He received a satisfactory reply on August 7.

Extreme secrecy was observed about the new scheme and when, at the end of December 1911, Durbar was held at Delhi, King George V announced it in the open Durbar. British Parliament had an established tradition not to oppose the proclamation by the King or the Queen. However, this time when the bill making necessary legal changes came before the Parliament, some members expressed their displeasure. Lord Curzon complained that even though there were four to five retired viceroys in the House of Lords, the government did not find it appropriate to consult them about the new scheme. He also said that it was not proper to make this a Royal Proclamation. He made it clear that he did not want to criticize the sovereign, but those who advised him. Curzon said it was unprecedented to make the announcement in India, bypassing the Parliament. Henceforth, if the policy failed, the King would come under criticism. Curzon opposed the idea of transfering the capital to Delhi, which would harm not only Calcutta, but the government. Curzon did not think that annulment of partition was necessary in view of the receding tide of agitation. He warned that Muslims would be disappointed. Lord Minto said that discontent and violence in India were under the surface, but Lord Curzon brought them on the surface by his scheme of partition of Bengal. Though agitation against the partition was on the wane, disproportionate importance was attached to the speeches of the leaders from Bengal. The agitation was never nationwide. Lord Minto disapproved of the secrecy with which the whole new scheme was prepared and executed. To Lord McDonnell, original scheme of partition of Bengal was wrong in view of the animosity between Hindus and Muslims. He observed that the Muslims of Bengal were not the descendents of Timur, Chengiz Khan or Mohammad Ghori; they were originally Bengali Hindus converted to Islam after the invasion.

Lord Morley took exception to the criticism against the secrecy and said it was futile to discuss the scheme with the governor and the lieutenant-governor about the historical facts, as the question was not of history, but of the present. Curzon had said, if the government wanted the annulment of the partition, the proper time was when he returned from India, as the partition scheme had not come into force. Morley's explanation was that he had assumed the office of the Secretary of State few days before Lord Curzon returned, and so, it was not possible to reverse the decision. The Secretary of State, Lord Crew declared that the new scheme was decided upon after due consultations with the Government of India and would be implemented after full deliberation. He said that the partition scheme was an administrative decision. Therefore, for its reversal, Parliamentary consent was not necessary. House of Lords then approved the new scheme on June 17, 1912.

When the Central Legislature discussed the transfer of the capital to Delhi, Gokhale, like Lord Curzon, raised the question of expenditure for the construction of the new capital. Of course, Gokhale did not oppose the transfer, but suggested that instead of using the budget surplus, the government should raise public loans. He feared that if the surplus were used, it would adversely affect the outlay on education and public health. The government's decision evoked conflicting reactions in India. Muslims were angry, while newspapers like 'Bengali', 'Amrit Bazar Patrika' welcomed the announcement. Moderates from Bengal, in a statement, welcomed the decision and said, as it was connected with the transfer of the capital, it should not be criticised. They also said that as Delhi was the historical capital, nation's prestige would enhance by the transfer of the capital. Leonard Gordon has quoted from the *Life of Lord Carmichael* by W.A.J. Archibald, the first governor of the united Bengal. It said, "The Europeans of Calcutta felt that they were sacrificed, and the Indian landowners were fearful that value of their property would suffer. As a witty Indian told his fellow-Bengalis: "You have been crying for the moon, and they have given it to you, they have at the same time taken away the sun." Mohammed Ali, a non-Bengali and editor of a weekly from Calcutta, wrote: "Except in Bengal, where it touches certain vested interests too closely, the transfer of the Government seat to Delhi has been received with considerable satisfaction in every other part of the country. Calcutta had made it possible for the Bengali to loom beyond all proportions in Indian affairs, and it is no fault of the Indian Government it viewed public questions affecting the whole of the country sometimes in a false perspective and consequently blundered. The Anglo-Indian press in Calcutta is up in arms against the change. The non-official community in this city is as a class very powerful and the Anglo-Indian press is ever ready to dance to its tunes".[12]

'The Statesman' had opposed the partition of Bengal, but the new editor found the abrogation of partition wrong. In an editorial the paper criticised the decision taken by few officials without full consultation with the people of the country. 'The Times' on December 13, expressed its dismay and disapproval about the government decision. It said: "There are, no doubt, some who will regret that, just when the agitation against the Partition of Bengal was flickering out, it should have been deemed necessary to upset the new *regime* in both Bengals before it had really had time to mature. If these changes stood alone, one might question the wisdom of subjecting once more the whole machinery of administration to the strain of such radical alterations. Next to the administrative efficiency, the Partition was designed to secure fair play for the Mohammedan community; and in the new Province of Bengal the numerical equality, if not, indeed, the superiority of the Mohammedan population will be such as to preclude altogether any revival of the old Bengali ascendancy". 'The Times' welcomed the transfer of the capital to Delhi and advised that, as the decision was announced by the King, the opponents of the decision should take appropriate notice.

After the Durbar in Delhi, King George V visited Calcutta, and at the reception met, among others, Gokhale. Both the King and the Queen were impressed by their conversation with him. The Durbar was memorable because of the Royal announcement to annul the partition of Bengal, but it was also notable because of another incident, which was the subject of much discussion and controversy. All the princes came with their entourage wearing their finest jewellery. But Sayajirao, the Maharaja of Baroda, had the minimum of jewellery on him. 'The Times' correspondent on January 2, alleged that Baroda Maharaja was discourteous to the King and the Queen, as he did not stand when the Royal couple entered the pandal; he did not bow much as others, and showed his back while resuming his seat. 'The Times' later criticised Sayajirao and alleged that he was giving asylum to the seditious persons in his state. Sayajirao had refuted the charge of being discourteous. Keir Hardie in a letter to 'The Pioneer' said that the high officials and others would not be remembered long but no one would forget the behaviour of Sayajirao, which was correct and not insulting or discourteous. In view of the continuous controversy, Sayajirao tendered an apology, but 'The Times' was not satisfied. The Baroda Maharaja then found no other option than to see the Viceroy and apologise. The storm then subsided.

REFERENCES

1. Gokhale Papers.
2. V.C. Joshi (Ed.). *Lala Lajpat Rai's writings and Speeches, Vol. I 1888-1919*, Uni. Publishers, Delhi, 1966, pp. 180-182.
3. Gokhale Papers.
4. Gokhale Papers.
5. V.S. Srinivas Sastri, *My Master Gokhale*, Model Publications, Madras, 1946, pp. 174-175.
6. Francis Robinson, *Separation Among Indian Muslims*, CUP, Cambridge, 1974, pp. 173-175.
7. Gerald Barrier, *Banned Controversial Literature and Political Control in British India 1907-1947*, Uni. of Missouri Press, Columbia, 1974, pp. 54-57.
8. V. S. Srinivas Sastri, *My Master Gokhale*, Model Publications, Madras, 1946, p. 239.
9. B.R. Nanda, *Gokhale, the Indian Moderates and the British Raj*, OUP, Delhi, 1977, pp. 391-392.
10. Beatrice Webb, *Our Partnership*, Cambridge University Press, Cambridge, 1975, pp. 143-144.
11. Lord Hardinge of Penhurst, *My Indian Years, 1910-1916*, John Murray, London, 1948, p. 38.
12. Leonard Gordon, *Bengal, The Nationalist Movement, 1876-1940*. Columbia Uni.Press, NY, 1974, p. 98.

Chapter Sixteen

LAST PHASE

The Commission appointed by the Government of India to go into the question of de-centralisation was proceeding in a leisurely way and came under criticism. It was then decided to appoint Gokhale on the Commission and to ask it to expedite the work. The objective of the Commission was to find out the ways and means to involve more Indians in the administration. It was the finance member of the Viceroy's Executive Council, Sir Fleetwood Wilson, who initiated the move to appoint Gokhale on the Commission with full knowledge that both the Viceroy Hardinge and the Governor of Bombay, Sir George Clarke, held opposite view. But they yielded when the Secretary of State, Lord Crew, insisted that Gokhale should be a member of the Commission. Then bureaucracy played its hand and objected to Gokhale's membership of the Commission, as he was a member of the Legislative Council. It was pointed out that Gokhale would draw salary and so would not be eligible to be a member of the Legislative Council, as a Council member could not hold office of profit under the law. Gokhale countered this by giving up the salary due to a Commission member. But then the problem about the allowance was raised. The allowance, which Gokhale was to get, was to be less than the European members, which Gokhale objected to as being discriminatory and below the dignity of a member of the Commission. Meanwhile, the Law department gave the opinion that the allowance was not a salary, and so Gokhale could receive the allowance and continue to be a member of the Legislative Council. Among the other members of the Commission were Ramsey MacDonald and Valentine Chirol.

Gokhale had other responsibilities besides that of a member of the Commission, and hence, more burden to carry than other members. Besides Calcutta the Commission went round to Bombay, Madras, Lucknow, Lahore, Nagpur etc. and interviewed many officials and non-officials. After the work of the Commission was over, Gokhale used to make extensive notes of the depositions and prepare himself for the next day. He was thus extremely busy and was exerting himself beyond his capacity. He had diabetes and was also suffering from chest pain, as he had had an accident during a railway journey in England. But unmindful of personal discomfort, Gokhale plunged himself wholeheartedly in the work. He would come to the rescue of the Indians in case they were not so well prepared to stand the scrutiny by the European members. Chirol had a grudge against the chairman of the Commission, Lord Islington, as he thought that Lord Islington was under the influence of Gokhale. Viceroy Hardinge feared that the Commission's recommendations would reduce the number of Europeans from the government's service. He, therefore, wrote to Lord Islington that no European should lose his job, as protecting their percentage was imperative to the security and wellbeing of the empire. He was prepared to accept more Indians in the provincial service. In the circumstances it was inevitable that the Commission members were divided. Gokhale was disillusioned with Ramsay MacDonald, as he started opposing the demands of the Indians. Commission had its final meetings in London. When he had some respite, Gokhale went to a spa in France to have hot water treatment that relieved his pain for a while.

Gokhale decided to visit South Africa and meet officials and Indians to find out whether any solution could be found for the grievances of the Indians. Gandhi, who was valiantly fighting for the humane treatment of the Indians settled in several colonies in South Africa, wanted Gokhale to visit these colonies, Transvaal, Natal etc., which had taken Indian indentured labour for decades. Many settled there, after their contract ended. But the governments of the colonies imposed various stringent conditions and restrictions on them, which were resented by the Indians. It was Gandhi, who organised them and even started mass satyagraha. It might appear strange but a conservative and an imperialist like Lord Curzon supported the cause of the Indians and even went so far as to defend Gandhi's passive resistance movement. Lord Curzon used to ask, how one could justify the inhuman and unjust treatment to Indians, when South Africa was a part of the British empire. 'The Times' also lent support to the demands of the Indians in South Africa. Gandhi came to India in 1896 and met Pherozeshah, Tilak and Gokhale. After meeting these leaders Gandhi thought Pherozeshah was like the Himalayas and Tilak an ocean, while Gokhale was like Ganges. So chemistry of both Gokhale and Gandhi matched, and Gandhi started keeping Gokhale informed about the latest developments in South Africa. When Gandhi wanted to address a public meeting in Poona, both Tilak and Gokhale advised him that he should request Dr. Bhandarkar, a respected Sanskrit scholar, to preside over the meeting in view of the group politics in the city. Accordingly, a meeting was held. Thereby, both Tilak and Gokhale came on the common platform to hear Gandhi and also to lend support to his movement. In 1901, Gandhi came again to India and was present at the Calcutta session of the

Congress. Pherozeshah wanted the draft of a resolution by Gandhi to be passed without any discussion, but Gokhale intervened and arranged for Gandhi to place the resolution before the session. However, it could not be said that the session had taken any serious note of the problems in South Africa. After returning to Natal, Gandhi was greeted with a shower of stones and bricks by the European settlers. Gokhale condemned this in an article in the 'India', a Congress periodical from London. He asked whether Indians were to be treated as slaves in the British Empire.

Gandhi was in regular correspondence with Gokhale, who received issues of the 'Indian Opinion', edited and published by Gandhi. Gokhale used to help Gandhi by collecting funds. One letter by Gandhi reveals that he had received a generous donation from Sir Ratan Tata at the behest of Gokhale. Gandhi was running an ashram in Phoenix in South Africa. He regularly sent the balance sheets to Gokhale, which showed how the ashram was run with very little cost. The Natal government had detained many Indians, who were participating in the passive resistance movement; and Gandhi kept Gokhale abreast of these developments. In 1904 Gandhi had sent a copy of an official report to Gokhale, and in an accompanying letter invited his attention to a sentence from the memorandum of the British Indian Association, which said that if more Indians were permitted to immigrate, then they would outnumber the Europeans, therefore, some restrictions on Indian immigration would be in order. Gokhale followed this up and entered into a compromise with the South African government. But Pherozeshah and others criticised the agreement. Gandhi wanted, in exchange of these restrictions, a right to property for the Indians in Transvaal, which the government of the colony did not accept. Wives and children of the indentured labour and also the Indians in general were taxed, which was unbearable and unjust. Gandhi had conveyed to Gokhale that Hindus, Muslims, Parsis unanimously opposed the unjust laws and regarded themselves as Indians first. Armed with such information, Gokhale made a few speeches in the Legislative Council. On February 25, 1910 Gokhale explained the travails of the Indians in South Africa. He said that in the united states of Cape, Transvaal and Natal there were hundred and fifty thousand Indians. Natal had the largest number, i.e., hundred thousand. From 1860 Indians were being sent as indentured labour to work on railways and other construction works. It was not that they went on their own. The government of Natal requested the Government of India to send Indian labourers, who were not sent as slaves or bonded labour. After the contract was over, several returned to India, but many stayed back, as they were not sure of employment in India and also feared that they might be treated as outcastes, as they had travelled overseas. These Indians had to pay a tax of three pounds per head, which was a burden. It had been found that the suicide rate was very high among the indentured labourers. Gokhale cited an observation by Sir John Hewett, who later became the prime minister of Natal, which was a rundown colony, but the whole picture changed after the arrival of the indentured labour from India and the colony became prosperous. In March 1912 Gokhale moved a resolution demanding a ban on the indentured labour for South Africa.

This problem of the indentured labour for South Africa became a burning one by 1911; and in India as well as in England this policy came under fire. Like Curzon, Lord Minto also voiced his concern for the Indians in the African colonies, and wrote some letters to the British government. In 1911, one Satyananda Basu suggested that Gandhi should be nominated as president of the Congress session in Calcutta. Gokhale wrote to Basu that he would be glad if his friend received such an honour; but it was doubtful if Gandhi could spare time and also whether he would agree with the objectives of the Congress. In the end Henry Cotton was nominated as president. In the Calcutta session Gokhale announced that he would visit South Africa and would try to find whether any compromise could be reached. The government welcomed this announcement.

Gokhale decided to travel on August 5, 1912 to Cape Town from London by the Union Castle Mail steamer. He booked his passage well in advance and asked for reservation in a first class cabin. The Company accordingly made reservations, but in a few days intimated that as European passengers did not want to share cabin with an Indian, Gokhale should travel by a lower class or pay for the two berths and have a cabin for himself alone. To this Gokhale replied on July 29: "My position is this: I want no favour of any kind for myself. I only want bare justice and that for me as an Indian I feel it is grossly unjust that I should be penalised and compelled to pay more than my fare because some Europeans have a prejudice against travelling with Indians. I think that the Company should give me one berth and then leave to those who come after me to take the second or not as they like. The position of the Company that I must pay ten extra Guineas whether I want a whole cabin or not, simply because some Europeans have a prejudice against travelling with Indians, is to my mind most unjust and it involves a principle against which I deem it my duty to enter an emphatic protest".[1] Ultimately, the Company agreed to charge Gokhale only for a single berth, and as no European wanted to share a cabin with him, Gokhale had the whole cabin to himself.

Gokhale reached Cape Town on October 22, 1912 and he left South Africa on November 18. Henry Polak, who was working with Gandhi in South Africa, compiled the reports of Gokhale's programmes, his speeches, receptions etc. The booklet makes it clear that Gokhale was cordially received by the government and the Indians everywhere. The government had made special arrangement for his travel and at some places he was received by European Mayor and other

European officials. Europeans also held reception for him. Gandhi accompanied him everywhere and Gokhale paid a handsome tribute to Gandhi for his work. He impressed upon his audiences that India was a part of the British Empire, and every nation in the Empire must be treated equally. He emphasised that with the lifting of the restrictions, it was wrong to assume that there would be a great influx of Indians, as they were not the people who migrate to distant lands. Gokhale said that even if there were no Indians in South Africa, it was unjust to pass laws based on racial discrimination. It was wrong in principle. He admitted that if the demand was to stop further immigration of Indians, that was understandable. But he demanded a humane treatment to those who had established themselves in South Africa. He held discussions with the Indian and European leaders.

It should not be assumed that Gokhale was welcomed everywhere and by everybody. Some European and especially Dutch newspapers published articles, editorials, and letters contending that it was impossible to treat Indians with equality. Many of them asserted that South Africa must remain 'White' and Indians should return to their country. Some of them objected to being lectured by the Europeans, who were criticising South Africa's policy of racial discrimination. They said that as the European countries did not face the problem of Asian immigration, they should not give sermons. Several were opposed to even limited immigration, as they feared that the population of Indians would appreciably increase.

Gokhale, being aware of such extreme attitude, decided to have some compromise. He suggested that Europeans should give humane treatment to Indians in South Africa and Indians should accept the ban on future immigration. Polak summarised the outcome of Gokhale's visit in his booklet. He wrote: "He did not set out to stop or restore the system of indentured Indian immigration, as has been erroneously supposed by some. He had succeeded in ending it before his arrival, and he, last of all, would have countenanced its restoration, believing it to be servile in its nature. He did not come here to put an end to free Indian immigration. For all practical purposes, such immigration had already been rigorously restricted, thanks to the reasonableness and statesmanship of the local Indian leaders. It is generally admitted that the grievances of the Indian community are of the most serious importance, and a genuine desire has been evinced to secure the removal of at least some of them. The repeal of the 3 Pound tax is practically assured in the near future, but other disabilities would disappear only with time and better mutual understanding. Mr. Gokhale's visit has made it clear that local Indian leaders are not so intransigent as they are popularly supposed to be".[2]

At the conclusion of his visit Gokhale assured the Indians that whenever they start a struggle for principle and for just causes, India would support them.

What exactly was assured by the South African government to Gokhale became a matter of controversy at the end of his visit. Gokhale maintained that the government had assured him to remove the tax on Indians. Gandhi was sceptical. He believed that Government would not abide by its assurances. The government, on the other hand declared that it only promised to consider the demands put forward by Gokhale and no definite commitment was made. Gandhi did not hesitate to express his scepticism and told Gokhale that he was not sure whether he would be able to return to India in an year as suggested by Gokhale. Gandhi had no doubt that Indians would have to offer resistance for getting the three pound tax revoked. He was proved right and had to lead a movement against the South African government and court arrest which Lord Curzon, among others, condemned. However, when Gokhale again went to England in 1914, he called Gandhi to visit him in London and discuss the South African situation. After his return Gokhale had long discussions with Viceroy Lord Hardinge, and even though gravely ill, acted as a mediator between the Viceroy and Gandhi and persuaded the latter to appear before the Commission and afterwards come back to India, which he did in 1915.

In 1912, London branch of the Muslim League had submitted a memorandum to the British government asking it to see that the Muslims' interests should not be lost sight of while delegating more powers to the provinces. The Government of India, while suggesting the transfer of capital to Delhi, had emphasised the advisability of co-opting more and more Indians in the administration of provinces without jeopardising the efficiency and overall control of the Central Government. League's memorandum followed this suggestion of the Government of India. 'The Times' on April 10 referred to the government dispatch which was not endorsed by Lord Crew in his speech in the Lords. The Secretary of State had denied that there was any intention to introduce a federal system in India. The paper had no doubt that some powers would have to be transferred to the provinces so that they would not have to look to the Central Government for trivial matters. But 'The Times' warned that a precaution had to be taken not to grant large measure of provincial autonomy. It said that India's past history did not warrant such innovation, which might endanger the security of the country. According to the 'The Times', India, China and Persia could be held together only by a strong Central Government.

'The Edinburgh Review' differed from 'The Times'. In its July 1912 issue it said: "Thus the departure from Calcutta is not a mere change of residence—it is an outward and visible sign of an inward and overpowering tendency. Decentralisation is a necessity, and decentralisation was impossible as long as the capital of the Viceroy was located in the capital of one of the Provinces. The whole position is admirably summed up in Lord Crewe's dispatch, which he has in substance re-affirmed in the House of Lords… It is certain in the course of time the just demands of Indians for a larger share in the Government of the country will have to be satisfied, and the question will be how this devolution of power can be conceded without impairing the supreme authority of the Governor-General in Council. The only possible solution of the difficulty would appear to be gradually to give the provinces a larger measure of self-government, until at last India would consist of number of administrations, autonomous in all provincial affairs, with the Government of India above them all, but ordinarily restricting their functions to matters of 'Imperial concern'. But our argument is that the machinery is too complicated for the new race of men who have been trying to manipulate it with unskilled and hesitant hands. 'Supreme authority' flitted over the sea to Whitehall some years ago. The Government of India has become the mere mouthpiece of the Secretary of State, and its functions must therefore be strictly limited. It was difficult enough to supervise from Calcutta or from Simla the detailed government of the whole of India. Lord Morley's transference of the centre of authority to London involved either a revolutionary change of system or the breakdown of the British connection. The revolution, which is now on the way to accomplishment, is the creation of a number of centres of real authority in place of the one centre which had already been shifted from Calcutta to London."

There was a perceptible change in the political atmosphere of Europe, and the appointment of the Decentralisation Commission had helped to change the mood in England. Some British statesmen began thinking of changes in the policy towards India. In a dispatch to the British government the Government of India conveyed that the aspiration of the Indians to have more share in the administration of the country was legitimate and would have to be conceded in the days to come. The real question according to the dispatch was how to do this without impairing the authority of the governor-general and his Council. The dispatch suggested devolution of power to the provinces, and though the Government of India would have overriding powers, its main concern would be to look after the wider interests of India. Though the Secretary of State categorically denied that the Government was thinking of bringing federal system in India, the Deputy Secretary of State, Montagu's speech on February 28, 1912 in Cambridge became a subject of much discussion. Montagu said, the British Empire was built on the principles of freedom and free institutions. He criticised Lord Curzon whom he described as a mere administrator without any policy. He compared Lord Curzon to a motor mechanic who knew how to repair various parts but did not know how to drive and where to take it. Montagu also made it clear that the policy of the British government was to implement the suggestions in the dispatch of the Government of India with due deliberation and without any haste. He said that a new generation had come up in India with the education which the English had imparted, and it was asking what England intended to do with regard to its demands.

Radicals in India had declared that their objective was Dominion Status, while the Moderates wanted the British to clarify their objective. Gokhale wrote to Montagu on July 30, 1912, complimenting him for having a broader view and sympathy for the Indian aspirations. Srinivas Sastri had discussed the implications of the dispatch of the Government of India and the discussion in the British Parliament. Writing in the August issue of the 'Indian Review', Sastri expressed his disappointment at the announcement by Lord Crewe. He said that Lord Crewe was expecting the Indians to declare that they themselves as well as the future generation of Indians were unfit for the Dominion status, and thus endorsing the views of the Tories like Salisbury and Curzon.

The abolition of partition of Bengal and transfer of capital to Delhi had not helped in controlling the violence in the country. When Lord and Lady Hardinge made ceremonious entry into Delhi, a bomb was thrown on their carriage, which hurt Lady Hardinge while the viceroy escaped unhurt. At the same time the government had confiscated a large amount of arms in Bengal, and the political future of India again became the topic of discussion. The 'Nineteenth Century and After' in its issue of August 1913 carried an article by Geoffrey Cookson, who asked why there was disloyalty in India? And then went on to explain that before the advent of the British rule, others who ruled India were Asians. British might have built roads, railways and brought many reforms and improvements, but as the Indians were not participants, they had no affinity for Englishmen. The White man had created impersonal administrative machine. "The astonishing thing is not that there is unrest in India, but that we have enjoyed so long a period of tranquillity. Our ideas of liberty have given India the semblance of freedom, while our love of power has withheld the substance of it".

'The Times' was inclined for introspection. On December 20, 1913 it wrote: "Agitation in all forms is spreading throughout the land, and is producing the inevitable effects. A large section of the Indian Press devotes itself to a relentless campaign designed to undermine the authority of Government and to promote acute racial antagonisms. Indian writers, educated in our schools and universities, have reduced to a science the methods of saying what their readers perfectly understand while keeping within the four corners of laws which—in India—are mildly administered.—Secret societies grow in membership and range from little groups of decadent youths to large organised bodies of which the full ramification is unknown. Within a few years attempts have been made on the lives of two successive Viceroys, and in neither case did the offer of a large reward produce evidence from the many persons who were cognizant of the plots or spectators of their execution. In Bengal, dacoity, whether for private gain or for replenishing the coffers of the agitators, has become the diversion of educated youths; and victims and law-abiding people are unwilling or afraid to assist the ends of justice. In Punjab where 12 million acres are now under irrigation, where new towns are springing up and the wealth of the cultivators has marvellously advanced, the increase of serious crime has reached alarming proportions".

By the end of 1912 war clouds were gathering over Europe. Turkey had allied herself with Germany, which had created a rift between her and England. Muslim leaders in India had no love for Germany, as they had for Turkey. The new alliance of Germany and Turkey had set them thinking on different lines. This was seen by a demand for autonomy for India voiced in the Muslim League session in 1912. This had provoked two issues of a quarterly, 'The Round Table', to warn the British government not to sit tight and avoid taking measures which would satisfy the Indians. On the other hand there were some who feared a revolt in India in the event of hostilities breaking in Europe. British always believed that so long as Hindus and Muslims were divided, their interests were safe. But when Muslims started demanding Dominion Status like the Hindus, the British government was alarmed. It was no wonder that Indian Muslims had shown great affinity with Turkey. P. Hardy, in his book on Indian Muslims, had given extracts from various books by Muslims praising the regimes of the first four Khalifas, which they deemed as ideal. Britain was drifting from the Turks even before the last decade of the nineteenth century. In the battle between Greeks and Turks, Britain stood on the side-lines, which shocked the Indian Muslims. So when the Sultan of Turkey made a deal with Germany, he received support from some Muslim leaders in India. The Government of India feared that Nizam and the Amir of Afghanistan might create trouble. A moulvi of Lucknow openly commended the Sultan of Turkey and Amir of Afghanistan, when they gave a call in the name of Islam. He was then prosecuted and imprisoned. Several British officials had reported how the Sultan of Turkey was enjoying the prestige among Indian Muslims.

In these circumstances in 1912, some Western countries brought under their control some parts of Turkey, thus dismembering it. Sir Edward Grey, British foreign secretary, was convinced of the aggressive designs of Germany and was trying to make peace with Russia to check Germany and Turkey, her ally. But this alienated Muslims in India. Aga Khan, meanwhile, in a speech in London emphasised that both Hindus and Muslims gave religion a priority and that Indian Muslims expected Britain to have good relations with Turkey. *The Times* taking exception to this speech said that some radical Indian Muslims should not try to dictate how Britain should conduct her foreign policy. The paper was alarmed by the growing Pan-Islamic trends in India. Aga Khan also said that the dismemberment of Turkey posed danger to India. 'The Times' told him that Britain was the best judge of her own interests. 'The Times' followed this by a newsletter, which described how some radical Muslims were indulging in incendiary speeches and spreading false stories about the desecration of Muslim holy places by Christians. After trenchant criticism by 'The Times', Aga Khan changed his tune and tone. He said, in an article in the January 1914 issue of 'The Edinburgh Review', that it was worthwhile taking note of the fact that many Indian Muslim youths were enrolled in the British universities, which had made radical changes in their thinking. Aga Khan also suggested that it was high time for Hindus and Muslims not to think in terms of their respective religions; and the moderates from both communities must come together.

In the changed atmosphere, Government of India was not enthusiastic about the Alighar University project. At the same time communal riot broke out in Canpore. All these incidents made the position of the traditional leadership of the Muslim League tenuous. Some radical Muslim youths believed that time had come to take a bold stand against the government and be ready for confrontation. Their politics was not so rabid anti-Hindu as that of the traditional leadership. Mohammad Ali was one of their leaders. At the outbreak of war between Germany and England, he issued a statement saying that if England were fighting for justice, she should end her dominance over Egypt, but at the same time he declared that as war had been declared, it was better to end all disputes with Britain.

At this time Gokhale was giving serious thought to finding out some solution to Hindu-Muslim problem and bringing some understanding between the two major communities. 1913 session of the Congress was presided over by Nawab Syed Mohammed and there was no mention of the controversial subject of the separate electorates for Muslims. A young Secretary of the Muslim League, Mr. Vazir Hussain, and some of his colleagues from Lucknow took the initiative in having some cooperation with the Congress. However, Malviya and Bhagwandas were opposed to such a move, as they feared that it would lead to the acceptance of some more unjust Muslim demands. Gokhale had no doubt about the compulsion and importance of cooperation between Hindus and Muslims. In a speech in Poona on July 4, 1909 he had made his position clear even when the controversy about the separate electorates had not become so serious. This speech in Marathi admitted that the animosity between the two communities had a historical background. But he impressed upon the audience that it was imperative to forget this history and come together. Gokhale suggested territorial electorates. He said that Muslims should fight the elections in joint electorates and if their quota of seats was not filled, then it could be done by nomination. He appealed to Muslims to give up the demand for separate electorates, and Hindus to consider sympathetically the apprehensions of the Muslims and be ready to give them adequate representation. By 1913 young Muslims had relegated the traditional Muslim leaders to the background. Thus, moderates from both Hindus and Muslims had fallen on bad times and so, Aga Khan revised his position and appealed for some joint efforts by the moderates from both communities. Gokhale, who had been to England, returned by November of 1914. He thought that after the war there were bound to be some far-reaching constitutional changes, and if Hindus and Muslims made joint efforts, these changes would be much more substantial. Some British officials were also anticipating constitutional changes, and the Governor of Bombay, Lord Willingdon, suggested to Gokhale that he should prepare a note on such reforms. Gokhale wanted to have a meeting with both Pherozeshah and Aga Khan and discuss the outline of the political reforms. As it was not possible for various reasons, Gokhale prepared a note on his own.

Sastri narrates that Gokhale was seriously ill but he summoned whatever strength he had, and two days before he died, made a pencil draft. Three copies were made. One was sent to Lord Willingdon and one each to Pherozeshah and Aga Khan. Because of Gokhale's death, nobody thought of publishing his draft. However, Lord Willingdon transmitted it to London. Gokhale's document saw the light of the day in 1917 at the time of Montagu declaration. It was published by Aga Khan in London and by Srinivas Sastri in India. It was called 'Gokhale's Political Will and Testament'. Gokhale wanted the recommendations to be announced by the British government voluntarily and at once. At the outset of his note he said that the British Government seemed to be thinking of giving provincial autonomy to India, which meant that governors would have Executive Councils on which Indians would be appointed. Gokhale suggested that the number of members of the Legislative Council should be between seventy-five and hundred, out of which four fifth should be elected. They should be elected by various interests, and some communities must have reserve seats. Muslims should have separate electorates. Legislative Council should meet often; members must have the right to express their opinion about the administration and the budget should not be passed without the approval of the Legislative Assembly. However, the governor must have a veto power in respect of the budget. Relations between the Central and Provincial Governments would have to be recast and the Provincial Governments would have more powers, which would be controlled by the Legislatures. The scheme of the Provincial Autonomy would not be complete unless municipalities and District Boards were developed; therefore, adequate steps should be taken in that direction. It would be in order to increase the number of members of the Central Legislative Council and give them more powers. Official majority and the special powers of the viceroy would have to be retained. Though Gokhale envisaged full provincial autonomy, the scheme that the British government adopted, fell short of it and it took another twenty years for provincial autonomy to come to India.

Sastri had appealed to consider the background on which the draft was prepared. In those days India was under Morley-Minto Reforms, which granted extremely limited rights to the Indians. That was why Gokhale could not anticipate very radical reforms, as they would not have been acceptable to the government. Sastri says, "The idea of the people's elected representatives passing a resolution or a bill or making a demand and getting it accepted or put on the statute book, was almost unthinkable. He (Gokhale) did not contemplate anything like real responsibility". In the light of the Montagu reforms and subsequent happenings, Gokhale's suggestion would appear too modest. But as Sastri had said, one has to consider the historical background. Importance of Gokhale's Testament lay in his solution of the communal impasse. He had accepted separate electorates to the Muslims, as they had come to stay under the Morley-Minto Reforms. It was not that Gokhale alone had accepted separate electorates. In 1916 an agreement was signed between Hindu and Muslim leaders in Lucknow with Tilak taking a lead, which followed the main points in Gokhale's draft and decided on the number of seats to be divided between the two major communities. This was what became known as the Lucknow Pact.

Srinivas Sastri, speaking in 1923 on the eighth death anniversary of Gokhale, in Poona, gave the background of the Pact and narrated how Gokhale's influence was felt even after his demise. Of course, later it was realised that the separate electorates under the Morley-Minto Reforms and the weightage to the Muslims under the Lucknow Pact did not satiate the demands of the Muslims and could not solve the Hindu-Muslim problem. Sastri said, in the year when Gokhale died and in the following year, an attempt was made to unite all the political parties in the country and make a strong united endeavour to present demands for more political powers to the Indians. Sastri himself played his part in bringing about this unity. He not only helped in bringing those who had to go out of the Congress in 1907, but also in bringing Hindu and Muslim leaders to sign what was later known as Lucknow Pact. Because the parties led by Gokhale and Tilak came together, an understanding was reached between the Hindu and Muslim leaders. Sastri believed that Gokhale would not have acted otherwise and would have taken initiative in bringing about an understanding between Congress and the Muslim League.

War broke out in Europe in August 1914 and Gokhale returned to Poona in November. By that time Lokmanya Tilak was released after six years imprisonment at Mandalay. Several politicians and commentators in England were apprehensive that taking advantage of the war, Indians would revolt, and Muslims who were disturbed by England's policy with regard to Turkey would join hands with Hindus. They feared that such a revolt would be far more fierce and widespread. If that happened, Britain would have to fight on two fronts; one in Europe and other in India, which would stretch her resources to a breaking point. Chirol was one of those who raised this bogey. But he and others of his persuasion were proved totally wrong. To the surprise of the British politicians and commentators, Indian leaders spontaneously rose to help the government. So the Government of India did not ask for more British troops from home, but wanted to know how many troops the British government was expecting from

India. Indian leaders expressed their loyalty to the British government and the Emperor. The War Fund had excellent response from the people and the Princes. By the winter of 1914 some Indian troops were fighting on the European front and then onwards several were sent to different theatres of war. At the end of 1914 the Congress session at Madras unanimously passed a resolution of full cooperation with government in the prosecution of war. 'The Times' said that England was overwhelmed by the spontaneous support by the Indians.

The government feared that Lokamanya Tilak and Bipin Chandra Pal would organize a revolt, taking advantage of the hostilities. But both supported the war and appealed for help to the government. Tilak in a statement on August 27, 1914 denied that he was ever spreading discontent in the country. He then declared that though the Morley-Minto Reforms were not satisfactory, they were a step in right direction. He believed that the reforms also indicated that the government was inclined to go further. Tilak then said, "India was much benefited by the British rule, as it brought several castes and communities together, which was bound to result in creating a united Indian nation. British being freedom-loving people, had permitted such trends to take roots which any other foreign rule could not have done. German emperor, breaking the promises, committed an aggression against a small nation, which compelled England to take up arms against Germany. In the circumstances it is the duty of every Indian, high and low, poor or rich to extend help to England". Tilak then appealed to call a public meeting in support of the war. However, Governor Willingdon did not change his attitude towards Tilak and did not allow him to speak in a citizens' meeting in the Town Hall, which was resented by people like Jinnah and Horniman, who staged a walkout. Bipin Chandra Pal in 1913 appealed to the people not to oppose the transfer of capital from Calcutta to Delhi. He said the provincial autonomy was on the cards and the transfer of the capital should be seen as a part of the larger scheme. In 1914 Pal went even further and said in an article that compared to the bureaucracy, armed revolutionaries were a greater menace to the Indian nationalism. He saw a danger in the combined revolt by the Chinese and the supporters of Pan-Islam. Pal, therefore, called for the unity of British and the Indian nationalism. Lokamanya Tilak did not go so far, but as he supported the war and called for the help to the war efforts, there was no cause for Radicals and the Moderates in the Congress to be at loggerheads. In this changed situation some Congressmen in Madras and Bengal thought it wise to make necessary changes in the constitution and make it easy for people like Tilak and others to pave the way to return to the Congress fold. Annie Besant took the lead and went to Calcutta to discuss the matter with the leaders of Bengal. Then she went to Poona to hold discussion with Gokhale. After his release from the long incarceration Tilak might have concluded that it was difficult to build a new party. Besides, war had changed the situation radically.

After Surat, Congress was considerably weakened. Sydney and Beatrice Webb were present at the Bankipur session of the Congress in 1912 and noted in their diary: "The Indian National Congress which we had come to attend—proved rather a 'frost'. There were only four to five hundred delegates, instead of twice or thrice that number; the great 'pandal' or temporary Congress hall—a vast tent—constructed for six thousand spectators, was seldom more than half full, and there was an element of listlessness and unreality about the eloquent speeches. Our impression is unless something is done to revive and reorganise the Congress, it will 'peter out'".[3] Congress was continuously losing its élan, and the number of delegates as well as spectators was on the decline. Webbs noted that four to five hundred delegates attended the Bankipur session, but the official Congress records show that the number was merely 207, which was the lowest. At Lahore in 1909 it was 243. It rose significantly in 1916 and 1917.

Gokhale was aware of and was pained by the dwindling strength of the Congress. In the changed atmosphere, though he did not initiate any move to unite the Congress, he was not opposed to it like Pherozeshah. Unlike Pherozeshah he did not want to take an extreme position and oppose those who were doing their best to bring the estranged Congress factions together. His conversation with Gordon Milburn in London is characteristic of his attitude with regard to the Radicals. Milburn was a teacher in Calcutta and had good relations with Indian and British leaders. Gokhale, who knew Milburn, met him in London. Milburn told Gokhale that the British would be able to work with some Indians but not with all. "Gokhale (much moved): I know what you mean—you want us to repudiate the Extremists. But that is a thing, which we could never do, and it is an insult to demand it of us. How would you like us to demand that you should never dine with such and such Anglo-Indian civilians? It is well known that our political opinions are different from theirs. If we were to repudiate the Extremists, political life would become a hell. They would retaliate, and Europeans would simply stand by and watch us fight. We do fight, as it is now. If you read the vernacular Press you would know how bitterly they attack us. But we do not repudiate them, and you have no right to demand that we should repudiate a brother Indian. We would not accept European cooperation upon such terms. Unity is necessary for the future. Both sides are struggling to win the rising generation. Neither I nor Mr. Surendranath Banerjea is immortal. We do not want to leave India divided and in disunion".[4]

Gokhale thus, could not discourage Annie Besant from making efforts to bring unity. His correspondence with Mrs. Besant reveals his mind. From London he wrote to Mrs. Besant, who was to proceed to England, that she could continue her efforts for unity. "I am not without hope that if I am so fortunate as to be well enough to go to Madras next December, we may succeed in devising some scheme which will bring together the more earnest spirits in the country in active cooperation in the service of our motherland". After his return from England, Gokhale wrote to Annie Besant on November 18, 1914 that he had her letter and the clippings, which she had sent. He informed her that he was trying to personally meet Tilak and his lieutenant N.C. Kelkar and then reply to her: "On one point I may state my position at once. It is that every effort must now be made to close the unfortunate divisions of 1907. And I am convinced that with some tact and with real goodwill this can be achieved without encountering serious difficulties". On November 21, Gokhale informed Mrs. Besant that he had two meetings with Kelkar. "There is no doubt that considerable importance is attached by many of our 'extremist' friends to the provision that public meetings should have the right to elect delegates to the Congress. This was the practice more or less all over the country up to 1907. Those were the days when there was no written constitution for the Congress. I have the personal responsibility for laying down the rules that the election of delegates should be confined to Congress Committees or to the public bodies affiliated to the Congress. It became quite obvious that the scheme of the Constitution, as a means of pushing the Congress organisation throughout the country had totally failed and that its only utility, real at the beginning, doubtful later on, was to keep those who had seceded from the Congress in 1907 out of that body".

Gokhale then narrates that at the Congress session in 1910, when he was assisting Sir William Wedderburn who presided, many Congressmen from especially Berar and other places from Deccan were keen to rejoin the Congress, but their self-respect prevented them from asking their opponents to enroll them as members of the Congress. He also admitted that those people had fairly good case to revive the old practice of electing the delegates in the public meetings. But Surendranath Banerjea and Bhupendranath opposed the change. However, proposal was revived in 1911 session of the Congress at Calcutta, which was supported by Malviya and was carried. But both Bhupendranath and Wacha threatened to leave the organization, and so the proposal was put off to avoid another split. A compromise solution was also adopted by the Subjects Committee at Calcutta; and Kelkar according to Gokhale could see the reasonableness of this solution. "But even if Mr. Tilak in the end accepts this solution—and knowing him as I do, I feel almost certain that he will accept it—it will be necessary to secure assent of the Bombay Party, represented by Sir Pherozeshah Mehta and Mr. Wacha, to the change".[5] Srinivas Sastri in one of his lectures on Pherozeshah Mehta said that Bhupendranath Basu who presided over the Madras Session of the Congress had an ambition to see the Congress united again. When Gokhale had nearly concluded his talks with Tilak, Pherozeshah and Wacha expressed their strong disapproval. Gokhale was shaken by this attitude.

Then it was Tilak's turn to take a rigid position, and it shows a lack of tact. When he met Subba Rao, a congress leader from Madras, Tilak told him that he would join the Congress and capture it. Subba Rao conveyed this to Gokhale. On December 14 Gokhale wrote to Bhupendranath: "Mr. Tilak has told Mr. Subba Rao frankly and in unequivocal terms that though he accepts the position laid down in what is known as Congress creed—he does not believe in the present methods of the Congress, which rests on association with Government where possible and opposition to it where necessary. In place of these he wants to substitute the method of opposition to Government pure and simple within constitutional limits". Gokhale, therefore, was not hopeful that there would be any understanding with Tilak. He feared that Tilak with such predisposition might join the Congress and again create trouble. But Gokhale wanted other Congressmen to join the organisation.

Tilak, after reading an editorial in the 'Amrit Bazar Patrika', alleged in a letter to Gokhale that it was Gokhale who had written to Madras Congressmen that Tilak would pursue Irish methods after joining the Congress. The letter was harsh in tone and seemed to intend to give a notice to Gokhale, who denied the charge. This controversy spilled over the columns of the newspapers; hot words were exchanged and the efforts of reconciliation between the Moderates and the Radicals came to an end, at least temporarily. On his deathbed Gokhale told Setlur, his friend, that his last wish was to see the Congress united again.[6]

Gokhale's health was deteriorating. His diabetes had worsened, his heart was weak and he had difficulty breathing. He realized that this end was near. On his last day he was calm. He smiled and said, "I have had enjoyment in this world, now let me go and have it in another world." In the evening he bade farewell to his two daughters and friends. Two hours passed and he died peacefully at 10:25 p.m. on February 19, 1915. Thus ended the life of the one, who was a true and distinguished disciple of Justice Ranade, a great liberal and a scholar. Dr. B.R. Ambedkar had said about Ranade that he might not have stood by the victorious side, but unlike some of his opponents he did not stand by the wrong side. The same holds true for Gokhale. The Liberals like Dadabhai, Ranade and Gokhale had an abiding faith in the benevolence of the British rule in India. However, by a searching analysis of various laws enacted and the policies adopted by the British Government, they helped in undermining the moral basis of the imperial rule.

When Gokhale died, Tilak paid glowing tributes. In an editorial in 'Kesari', Tilak said that Gokhale was endowed with many natural gifts and cultivated them with zeal and dedication. With this, he could have led a comfortable life, but he chose the path of service in the cause of nation and that distinguished him from many other gifted persons. Tributes poured in from Indians and Englishmen, men in power and those in several different fields. Central Legislative Council had special tributes for Gokhale. A letter was released by Dadabhai Naoroji, which said: "Gokhale is dead; I heard these words from a friend and said, 'what great calamity and what loss to India'! What more could I say? What hopes of mine, for much good at Mr. Gokhale's hands, have been broken up! But I feel some consolation. The Universal grief and loss and appreciation of Gokhale's work and worth by all India shows that India knows and appreciates what Gokhale intended to do and that patriotic youths will follow Gokhale's example and do what Gokhale wished to accomplish. Yet I cannot help mourning deeply at the loss of what he would have done had he lived but only the ordinary expectation of three score and ten". In the House of Lords, Lord Curzon and the Secretary of State Lord Crewe remembered many facets of Gokhale's life. Lord Crewe said that Gokhale was a man of wide vision and he benefited by his meetings with Gokhale. Lord Curzon said Gokhale was in a way a leader of the opposition in the Parliamentary sense. Curzon also said that though he was the target of Gokhale's criticism, Gokhale was the model of parliamentary leadership. He would have made his mark in any Parliament including British Parliament by his ability and capacity.

It would be appropriate to wind up these tributes with those paid by Mahatma Gandhi, who regarded Gokhale as his political Guru. In fact, a collection of all his writings and speeches about Gokhale under the title *Gokhale My Political Guru* was published some decades ago.

At some places we see Gandhi addressing Gokhale as Mahatma. When Gokhale visited South Africa, Gandhi was proud to function as his secretary. Gandhi reminded his audience in a meeting that Gokhale always acted with full dedication and would not claim any credit to himself; whatever he did, he surrendered at the feet of mother India. Gandhi observed that Gokhale had devoted his life to knowledge and he was an example of the ancient Hindu ideal of plain living, high thinking and high doing.

Gandhi emphasised that Gokhale did not discriminate between the upper cast Hindus and the so called untouchables. Gokhale used to say that "we are not polluted by touching our brother, the untouchable, but by falling a prey to the wicked feeling that we should not touch him."

As regards Hindu-Muslim tension, Gandhi quite unequivocally cited an incident when a Hindu monk came in order to prevail upon Gokhale to grant an inferior status to the Muslims and secure an advantage for the Hindus. Gokhale would not listen to him. The monk complained that the great leader did not take pride in Hinduism. Gokhale frowned and told the monk that if Hinduism meant what the monk described, then Gokhale was not a Hindu; and he would request the monk to leave. The so called monk left the man who was a real Sannyasi.

Gandhi had quoted Gokhale's last words to his followers who were gathered around his deathbed. Gokhale told them, 'Don't waste your time in writing a biography or setting up a statue, but pour your whole soul into the service of India. Then only shall you be counted among her true and faithful servants.'

Like his master, Justice Ranade, Gokhale was a firm believer in constitutional politics. Independent India has adopted parliamentary democracy. This was the logical and inevitable outcome or culmination of the process, which was going on for about half a century. Now after more than half a century of Parliamentary democracy, its future in this country is still being discussed because the parliamentary mentality is not firm and has not formed deep roots. Democracy cannot be devoid of emotions, but when politics is reduced to emotions and not restrained by reason, it turns into demagogy which in turn relies more on extra parliamentary activities; and streets, not the Parliament or Legislatures, become the focal point. Though extra-parliamentary politics is unavoidable even in parliamentary politics, it should strengthen the parliamentary process and not weaken it. In England, the Chartist movement was the biggest extra Parliamentary movement, which did not destroy or weaken the British Parliament but strengthened it. Gokhale's life was a shining example of devotion to the rule of law and to the Parliamentary politics, and of the aptitude which sustains them.

REFERENCES

1. Gokhale Papers.
2. H.S.L. Polak, *Gokhale's Visit to South Africa*, (This is a collection of articles, which were published in various newspapers during Gokhale's visit to South Africa. Compiled by Polak in 1912. This collection is not published.) p. 2.
3. Ed. Nirja Gopal Jayal, *Sydney and Beatrice Webb, Indian Diary*, Oxford Uni. Press, Delhi, 1987, pp. 5-7.
4. Gordon Milburn, *England And India*, George Allen and Unwin, London, 1918, pp. 20-21.
5. Gokhale Papers.
6. T.V. Parvate, *Gopal Krishna Gokhale*, Navajivan Publishing House, Ahmedabad, 1959, p. 388.

BIBLIOGRAPHY
(ENGLISH)

English Books

Abbasi Muhammad Yusuf, *London Muslim League (1908-1928) a Historical Study*, National Institute of Historical and Cultural Research, Islamabad, 1988

Aberigh-Mackay George R., *Twenty one Days in India*, W. Thacker and Co., London, 1910

Adams W.S., *Edwardian Portraits*, Secker and Warburg, London, 1957

Admas W.S., *Edwardian Heritage: A. Study in British History 1901-1906*, Frederick Muller, NY, 1971

Ahmed Syed Sir, *The Present State of Indian Politics: Speeches and Letters*, Sang-e-Meel Publication, Lahore, 1969

Aiyar B.V. Kamesvara, *Sir A. Sashiah Sastri An Indian Statesman*, Srinivasa Vardachari and Co., Madras, 1902

Ambedkar B.R., *Ranade, Gandhi and Jinnah*, Bheem Patrika Publications, Jullunder City, 1964

Ambedkar B.R., *Pakistan or Partition of India*, Thacker and Co., Bombay, 1946

Argov Daniel, *Moderates and Extremists in the Indian Nationalist Movement 1883-1920*, Asia Publishing House, NY, 1967

Arnold David, *Police Power and Colonial Rule Madras 1859-1947*, OUP, NY, 1986

Aurobindo Sri (Aurobindo Ghose), *Bankim-Tilak-Dayananda*, Arya Publishing House, Calcutta, 1947

Aziz K.K., *Britain and Muslim India*, Heinemann, London, 1963

Balfour Betty Lady, *The History of Lord Lytton's Indian Administration 1876 to 1880 complied from letters and Official Papers*, Longmans, London, 1899

Balfour Lady Betty ed. *Personal and Literary Letters of Robert First Earl of Lytton*, 2 Vols., Longmans, London, 1906

Ballhatchet Kenneth, *Social Policy and Social Change in Western India, 1817-1830*, OUP, London, 1957

Banerjea Surendranath Sir, *A Nation in Making*, OUP, Bombay, 1963

Barrier N. Gerald, *Banned Controversial Literature and Political Control in British India 1907-1947*, Uni. of Missouri Press, Columbia, 1974

Bassett Tilney, *The Life of the Rt. Hon. John Edward Ellis*, Macmillan, London, 1914

Beloff Max, *Imperial Sunset Vol. I, Britain's Liberal Empire 1897-1921*, Methuen and Co., London, 1969

Besant Annie, *How India Wrought for Freedom*, Today and Tomorrow's Printers and Publishers, New Delhi, 1974

Bevan Edwyn, *Indian Nationalism*, Macmillan, London, 1914

Bhatia B.M., *Famines in India: a Study in Some Aspects of the Economic History of India*, Asia Publishing House, London, 1963

Blunt Wilfrid S., *My Diaries*, Single Volume Edition, Markin Secker, London, 1932

Blunt Wilfrid S., *India Under Ripon*, T. Fisher Unwin, London, 1909

Bose Bipin Krishna Sir, *Stray Thoughts of Some Incidents in My Life*, G.A. Natesan and Co., Madras, 1923

Braybrooke Patrick, *Lord Morley: Writer and Thinker*, Drane's, London, 1924

Briggs Asa, *Victorian People, a reassessment of persons and themes 1851-67*, Uni. of Chicago Press, Chicago, 1955,

Brown Judith M., *Modern India: the Origins of an Asian Democracy*, 2nd ed., OUP, NY, 1994

Buckle George Earl, *The Life of Benjamin Disraeli*, 6 Vols., Macmillan, London, 1920

Buckle George Earle ed., *The Letters of Queen Victoria*, 3 Vols., Longmans, NY, 1928

Butler Harcourt Sir, *India Insistent*, William Heinemann, London, 1931

Carr Edward Hallett, *Nationalism and After*, Macmillan, London, 1967

Cecil Alegernon, *Six Oxford Thinkers*, John Murray, London, 1909

Chailley Joseph, *Administrative Problems of British India*, Macmillan, London, 1910

Chandra Bipan, *Ranade's Economic Writings*, Gian Publishing House, New Delhi, 1990

Charlesworth Neil, *British Rule and the Indian Economy 1800-1914*, Macmillan, London, 1982

Chatterjee Santimay and Sen Amitabha eds., *Acharya Prafulla Chandra Ray: Some Aspects of His Life and Work*, Indian Science News Association, Calcutta, 1986

Chaturvedi Benarsidas and Marjorie Sykes, *Charles Freer Andrews: a Narrative*, George Allen & Unwin, NY, 1950

Chaudhari Nirad C., *The Autobiography of an Unknown Indian*, Uni. of California Press, Berkeley, 1968

Chintamani C.Y., *Indian Politics Since the Mutiny*, George Alllen and Unwin, London, 1940

Chirol Valentine, *India Old and New*, Macmillan, London, 1921

Chirol Valentine, *Indian Unrest*, Macmillan, London, 1910

Choksey R.D., ed., *Twilight of the Maratha Raj 1818*, Choksey, Poona, 1976

Choksey R.D., *The Last Phase (1815-1818)*, Phoenix, Bombay, 1948

Choksey R.D., *A History of British Diplomacy at the Court of the Peshwas (1786-1818)*, R.D. Choksey, Poona, 1951

Choksey R.D., *Mountstuart, Elphinstone The Indian Years 1796-1827*, Popular Prakashan, Bombay, 1971

Churchill Winston, *Great Contemporaries*, Uni. of Chicago Press, Chicago, 1973

Clark Grover, *The Balance Sheets of Imperialism Facts and Figures on Colonies*, Columbia Uni. Press, New York, 1936

Cohn Bernard S., *The Development and Impact of British Administration in India*, Indian Institute of Public Administration, New Delhi, 1960

Colebrooke T.E. Sir, *Life of the Hon. Mountstuart Elphinstone*, 2 Vols., J Murray, London, 1884

Cook Edward Sir, *The Life of Florence Nightingale*, 2 Vols., St. Martin's Press, London, 1914

Cotton Henry Sir, *Indian and Home Memories*, T. Fisher Unwin, London, 1911

Cotton, Henry Sir, *New India or India in Transition*, Kegan Paul, London, 1907

Cotton J.S., *Mountstaurt Elphinstone and the Making of South-Western India*, Clarendon Press, Oxford, 1896

Coupland R., *The Indian Problem*, OUP, London, 1944

Coupland Reginald Sir, *India: a Re-Statement*, OUP, London, 1945

Courtney W.L., *The Making of an Editor*, Macmillan, London, 1930

Crawford Arthur, *Our Troubles in Poona and the Deccan*, Archibald Constable and Co., London, 1897

Creagh O'Moore General Sir, *Indian Studies*, Hutchinson and Co., London, 1924

Cromer Earl, *Political and Literary Essays*, 3 Vols. Macmillan, London, 1913-1916

Cross Cecil Merne Putnam, *The Development of Self-Government in India 1858-1914*, Greenwood Press, NY. 1922

Cross Colin, *The Liberals in Power 1905-1914*, Barrie and Rockliff, London, 1963

Cunningham H.S., *British India and its Rulers*, Daya Publishing House, London, 1986

Curzon Nathanial, *Viceroy and Governor General of India 1899-1905*, British Govt. in India 2 Vols., Cassell, London, 1925

Curzon, Nathanial, *Speeches by Lord Curzon of Kedlestone Viceroy and Governor General of India*, Vol. II and III, 1900-1904 Office of the Superintendent of Govt. printing India, Calcutta, 1904

Das M.N., India *Under Morley and Minto*, George Allen and Unwin Ltd., London, 1964

Dasgupta Hemendra Nath, *The Indian National Congress*, Vol. I, J.K. Das Gupta, Calcutta, 1946

Davis Mike, *Late Victorian Holocausts*, Verso, London, 2002

Davitt Michael, *The Fall of Feudalism in Ireland*, Harper, London, 1904

Desai, A.R. ed. *Peasant Struggles in India*, OUP, Bombay, 1979

Digby William, *The Famine Campaign in Southern India*, 2 Vols., Longmans, London, 1878

Dilke Charles Wentworth, *Greater Britain: A Record of Travel in English Speaking Countries During 1866-67*, J.B. Lippincott and Co., NY. 1869

Dilke Charles Wenworth, *Problems of Greater Britain*, Macmillan and Co., London, 1890

Dilks David, *Curzon in India*, 2 Vols., Taplinger Publishing Co., NY., 1969

Dobbin Christine, *Urban Leadership in Western India: Politics and Communities in Bombay City 1840-1885*, OUP, London, 1972

Dodwell H.H. ed., *The Cambridge History of the British Empire, Vol. IV, British India 1497-1858*, CUP, Cambridge, 1929

Drewitt F. Dawtrey, *Bombay in the Days of George IV Memoirs of Sir Edward West*, Longmans, London, 1907

Dufferin Marquis of Duffrin and Ava, *Speeches Delivered in India 1884-1888*, J. Murray, London, 1890

Dugdale Blanch E.C., *Arthur James Balfour: First Earl of Balfour*, 2 Vols. G.P. Putnams' Sons, NY, 1937

Dugdale Edgar ed., *Chapters of Autobiography by Arthur James Balfour*, Cassell and Co., London, 1930

Durand Mortimer Sir, *Life of the Right Hon. Sir Alfred Comyn Lyall*, William Blackwood and Sons, Edinburg, 1913

Dutt Paramananda, *Memoirs of Moti Lal Ghose*, Amrita Bazar Patrika Office, Calcutta, 1935

Ebenstein William, *Great Political Thinkers: Plato to the Present*, Harcourt Brace College Publishers, Fort Worth, 1991

Edwardes Michael, *Glorious Sahibs, The Romantic as Empire-Builder 1799-1838*, Taplinger Publishing Co., NY, 1968

Edwardes S.M., *The Rise of Bombay: a Retrospect*, Times of India Press, Bombay, 1902

Elphinstone Mountstuart, *An Account of the Kingdom of Caubul*, 2 Vols., OUP, Karachi, 1972

Elphinstone Mountstuart, *History of India*, 2 Vols., J. Murray, London, 1841

Elphinstone Mountstuart, *Territories Conquered from the Paishwa*, Oriental Publishers, Delhi, 1973

Embree Ainslie Thomas, *India's Search For National Identity*, Alfred A. Knopf, NY. 1972

Erikson Erik H., *Gandhi's Truth*, W.W. Norton, NY, 1969

Fawcett Henry, *Indian Finance: Three Essays*, Macmillan, London, 1880

Fawcett Henry, *Speeches on Some Current Political Questions*, Macmillan, London, 1873

Fowler Edith Hentrietta, *The Life of Henry Hartley Fowler: First Viscount Wolverhampton*, Hutchinson and Co., London, 1912

Fraser Lovat, *India Under Curzon and After*, Sagar Publications, London, 1911

Freeland Chrystia, *Sale of the Century: the Inside Story of the Second Russian Revolution*, Little Brown and Co., London, 2000

Friedberg Aaron L., *The Weary Titan: Britain and the Experience of Relative Decline 1895-1905*, Princeton Uni. Press, Princeton, 1988

Fuller Bampfylde Sir, *India: the Land and its People*, Harman Publishing House, New Delhi, 1988

Furniss Harry, *Some Victorian Men*, John Lane the Bodley Head Ltd., London, 1924

Gadgil, D.R., *The Industrial Evolution of India in Recent Times, 1860-1939*, OUP, Bombay, 1971

Gandhi, M.K., *An Autobiography or the Story of My Experiments with Truth*, Beacon Press, Boston, 1962

Gandhi M.K., *Gokhale: My Political Guru*, Navajivan Publishing House, Ahmedabad, 1958

Gardiner A.G., *The Life of Sir William Harcourt 1886-1904*, Vol. 1 and 2, Constable, London, 1923

Ghose Sankar, *The Western Impact on Indian Politics, 1885-1919*, Allied Publishers, Bombay, 1967

Gidumal Dayaram, *Life and Life-Work of Behramji M. Malabari*, Education Society's Press, Bombay, 1888

Gilbert Martin, *Servant of India*, Longmans, London, 1966

Gladstone William E., *After Thirty Years*, Macmillan, London, 1928

Gokhale Gopal Krishna, *Speeches*, G. A. Natesan, Madras, 1930

Goldman Charles Sydney, *The Empire and the Century*, Routledge, London, 1998

Gooch G.P., *Under Six Reigns*, Longmans, London, 1958

Gopal Ram, *British Rule in India*, Asia Publishing House, Bombay, 1963

Gopal Ram, *Lokmanya Tilak*, Asia Publishing House, London, 1966

Gopal S., *The Viceroyalty of Lord Ripon 1880-1884*, OUP, London, 1953

Gopalkrishnan, P.K., *Development of Economic Ideas in India 1880-1914*, People's Publication House, New Delhi, 1959

Gordon Leonard A., *Bengal: the Nationalist Movement 1876-1940*, Columbia Uni. Press, NY, 1974

Goyal O.P., *Political Thought of Gokhale*, Kitab Mahal Pvt Ltd., Allahabad, 1965

Grant Duff Mountstuart E., *Notes from a Diary kept Chiefly in Southern India 1881-1886*, 2 Vols., J Murray, London, 1899

Gupta J.N., *Life and Works of Romesh Chunder Dutt*, J.M. Dent, London, 1911

Gwynn Stephen ed., *Letters and Friendships of Sir Cecil Spring Rice*, 2 Vols., Houghton Mifflin Co., Boston, 1929

Gwynn Stephen, *The Life of the Rt. Hon. Sir Charles W. Dilke*, 2 vols., J. Murray, London, 1917

Haldane Richard Burton, *An Autobiography*, Hodder and Stoughton, Garden City, 1929

Hamilton George Lord, *Parliamentary Reminiscences and Reflections 1868-1885*, John Murray, London, 1917

Hamilton George Lord, *Parliamentary Reminiscences and Reflections 1886-1906*, John Murray, London, 1922

Hamilton Mary Agnes, *Sidney and Beatrice Webb*, Houghton Mifflin and Co., Boston, 1933

Hardie Keir J., *India: Impressions and Suggestions*, B.W. Huebsch, NY., 1909

Hardinge Lord of Penhurst, *My Indian Years 1910-1916*, John Murray, London, 1948

Hardy P., *The Muslims of British India*, CUP, London, 1972

Harrison Frederic, *Autobiographic Memories*, 2 Vols., Macmillan, London, 1911

Hayes Carlton J.H., *The Historical Evolution of Modern Nationalism*, Russell and Russell, NY, 1968

Heimsath Charles H., *Indian Nationalism and Hindu Social Reform*, Princeton Uni. Press, Princeton, 1964

Hirschmann Edwin, *White Mutiny: the Ilbert Bill Crisis in India*, South Asia Books, Columbia, 1980

Hirst F.W., *Early Life and Letters of John Morley*, 2 Vols., Macmillan and Co., London, 1927

Hobhouse, L.T., *Democracy and Reaction*, T. Fisher Unwin, London, 1904

Hobsbawm E.J., *Industry and Empire*, Penguin, Harmondsworth, 1999

Hobsbawm E.J., *The Age of Capital 1848-1875*, Weidenfeld and Nicolson, London, 1975

Hobsbawm E.J., *The Age of Empire 1875-1914*, Pantheon Books, London, 1987

Hobsbawn E.J., *The Age of Revolution 1789-1848*, A Mentor Books, NY, 1962

Hobson J.A., *Imperialism*, George Allen Unwin, London, 1948

Houghton Bernard, *Bureaucratic Government: a Study in Indian Polity*, P.S. King and Son, London, 1913

Hoyland John, S., *Gopal Krishna Gokhale: His Life and Speeches*, YMCA Publishing House, Calcutta, 1933

Hunter W.W., *The Indian Musalmans*, Indological Book House, Delhi, 1969

Hunter William Wilson Sir, *Annals of Rural Bengal*, Smith Elder, London, 1897

Hunter William Wilson Sir, *Life of Sir William Wilson Hunter*, Longmans, London, 1901

Hunter William Wilson Sir, *The Earl of Mayo*, Clarendon Press, Oxford, 1892

Huttenback Robert A., *Gandhi in South Africa, British Imperialism and the India*

Question, 1860-1914, Cornell Uni., Press, NY, 1971

Indian National Congress, *The Surat Congress and Conferences: a Collection of Presidential and Inaugural Speeches*, G.A. Natesan, Madras, 1908

Jagadisan T.N. ed., *Letters of the Rt. Hon. V.S. Srinivas Sastri*, Asia Publishing House, Bombay, 1963

Jagirdar P.J., *Mahadeo Govind Ranade*, Govt. of India Publications Division, New Delhi, 1971

Jagirdar, P.J., *Studies in the Social Thought of M.G. Ranade*, Asia Publishing House, Bombay, 1963

Jayakar M.R., *The Story of My Life*, Vol. II, 1922-1925, Asia Publishing House, Bombay, 1959

Jayal Niraja Gopal, ed., *Sydney and Beatrice Webb, Indian Diary*, Oxford Uni. Press, Delhi, 1987

Jeejeebhoy J.R.B., *Some Unpublished and Later Speeches and Writings of the Hon. Sir Pherozeshah Mehta*, The Commercial Press, Bombay, 1918

Jenkins Roy, *Gladstone*, Macmillan, London, 1995

Johnson Gordon, *Provincial Politics and Indian Nationalism*, CUP, Cambridge, 1973

Joshi G.V., *Writings and Speeches*, Arya Bhushan Press, Poona, 1912

Joshi Vijaya Chandra, *Lajpat Rai: Autobiographical Writings*, Uni. Publishers, New Delhi, 1965

Joshi Vijaya Chandra, *Lala Lajpat Rai: Writing and Speeches, Vol. I, 1888-1919*, Uni. Publishers, Delhi, 1966

Kabir Humayun, *Muslim Politics 1906-1947 and Other Essays*, Firma K.L. Mukhopadhyay, Calcutta, 1969

Karandikar S.L., *Lokmanya Bal Gangadhar Tilak*, S.L. Karandikar, Poona, 1957

Karandikar R.P., *Letters From England: 1908*, Vithal Raghunath Karandikar, Poona, 1935

Karve D.D., *The New Brahmans*, Uni. of California Press, Berkeley, 1963

Karve D.G., *Ranade: the Prophet of Liberated India*, Aryabhushan Press, Poona, 1942

Kaushik Harish P., *Indian National Congress in England*, Friends Publications, Delhi, 1991

Kaye J.W. Sir, *Lives of Indian Officers*, 2 Vols., W.H. Allen and Co., London, 1889

Kelkar N.C., *Full and Authentic Report of the Tilak Trial*, N.C. Kelkar, Bombay, 1908

Kellock James, *Mahadev Govind Ranade, Patriot and Social Servant*, Association Press, Calcutta, 1926

Kennedy Paul, *Realities Behind Diplomacy: Background Influences on British External Policy 1865-1980*, Fontana, London, 1985

Kent Roylance C.B., *The English Radicals*, Burt Franklin, NY, 1971

Ker James Campbell, *Political Trouble in India 1907-1917*, Oriental Publishers, Delhi, 1917

Khan Aga, *The Memoirs of Aga Khan*, Simon and Schuster, NY, 1954

Khan Mohammad Shabbir, *Tilak and Gokhale*, Ashish Publishing House, New Delhi, 1992

Khan Syed Sirdar Ali, *The Life of Lord Morley*, Sir Isaac Pitman and Sons, London, 1923

Kilbracken Lord, *Reminiscences of Lord Kilbracken*, Macmillan, London, 1931

Knaplund Paul, *The British Empire 1815-1939*, Howard Fertig, NY, 1969

Knickerbocker Frances Wentworth, *Free Minds, John Morley and his Friends*, Harvard Uni. Press, Cambridge, 1943

Kopf David, *British Orientalism and the Bengal Renaissance, the Dynamics of Indian Modernization 1773-1835*, Uni. of California Press, Berkeley, 1969

Koss Stephen E., *John Morley at the India Office 1905-1910*, Yale Uni. Press, New Haven, 1969

Kumar Ravinder, *Western India in the Nineteenth Century*, Routledge and Kegan Paul, London, 1968

Kunzru H.N., *Gopal Krishna Devadhar*, Servants of India Society, Poona, 1939

Langer William L., *The Diplomacy of Imperialism 1890-1902*, 2 Vols., Alfred Knopf, NY, 1951

Latthe Anna Babaji, *Memoirs of His Highness Shri Shahu Chhatrapati Maharaja of Kolhapur*, 2 Vols., Times of India Press, Bombay, 1924

Lee Francis, *Fabianism and Colonialism: the Life and Political Thought of Lord Sydney Oliver*, Defiant Books, London, 1988

Lee Sidney Sir, *King Edward VII, a Biography*, 2 Vols., Macmillan, NY, 1927

Limaye P.M., *The History of the Deccan Education Society*, Deccan Education Society, Poona, 1935

Lippincott, Benjamin Evans, *Victorian Critics of Democracy*, Uni. of Minnesota, Minneapolis, 1938

Lipski Alexander, *Bengal, East and West*, Asian Studies Center, Michigan State Uni., East Lansing, 1969

Lovett Verney Sir, *A History of the Indian Nationalist Movement*, J Murray, London, 1921

Low D.A. ed., *Soundings in Modern South Asian History*, Uni. of California Press, Berkeley, 1968

Low Sydney, *Vision of India*, E.P. Dutton and Co., NY, 1907

Lowe C.J., *The Reluctant Imperialists, British Foreign Policy 1878-1902*, 2 Vols., Routledge and Kegan Paul, London, 1967

Lucy Henry W., *A Diary of the Home Rule Parliament 1892-1895*, Cassell, London, 1896

Lucy Henry W., *Memories of Eight Parliaments*, Heinmann, London, 1908

Lyall Alfred Sir, *The Life of the Marquis of Dufferin and Ava*, 2 Vols., J. Murray,

London, 1905

Lyall Alfred Sir, *The Rise and Expansion of the British Dominion in India*, Howard Fertig, NY, 1968

Maharashtra Information Center, *Gopal Krishna Gokhale: a Centenary Tribute*, Maharashtra Information Center, New Delhi, 1966

Mainkar T.G., ed., *Writings and Speeches of Dr. Bhau Daji*, Uni. of Bombay, Bombay, 1974

Major E., *Viscount Morley and Indian Reform*, James Nisbet and Co., London, 1910

Majumdar J.K. ed., *Indian Speeches and Documents on British Rule 1821-1918*, Kanti Publications, Delhi, 1987

Majumdar R.C. ed., *The History and Culture of the Indian People: Struggle for the Freedom Part 2*, Vol. 11, Bharatiya Vidya Bhavan, Bombay, 1969

Majumdar R.C. ed., *The History and Culture of the Indian People: British Paramountcy and Indian Renaissance*, Part I, Bharatiya Vidya Bhavan, Bombay, 1963

Majumdar R.C., *History of the Freedom Movement in India*, Vol. 2, Firma K.L. Mukhopadhyay, Calcutta, 1963

Majumdar R.C., *The Sepoy Mutiny and the Revolt of 1857*, Firma K.L. Mukhopadhyay, Calcutta, 1963

Malik Hafeez, *Sir Sayyid Ahmad Khan and Muslim Modernization in India and Pakistan*, Columbia Uni., Press, NY, 1980

Mandlik Narayan Vishvanath ed., *Writings Speeches of the Late Hon., V.N. Mandlik*, Native Indian Press, Bombay, 1896

Mankar G.A. Rao Bahadur, *A Sketch of the Life and Works of the Late Mr. Justice M.G. Ranade*, 2 Vols., Caxton, Bombay, 1902

Mansergh Nicholas, *The Commonwealth Experience*, Weidenfeld and Nicolson, London, 1969

Martin Briton, *New India 1885*, Uni. of California Press, Berkeley, 1969

Martineau John, *The Life and Correspondence of Sir Bartle Frere*, 2 Vols., J. Murray, London, 1895

Masani, R.P., *Dadabhai Naoroji the Grand Old Man of India*, George Allen and Unwin, London, 1968

Mathias Peter, *The First Industrial Nation: an Economic History of Britain 1700-1914*, Methuen, London, 1969

Mathur D.B., *Gokhale, a Political Biography*, Manaktalas, Bombay, 1966

Mazumdar Amvika Charan, *The Indian National Evolution*, Michiko and Panjathan, New Delhi, 1974

McAlpin Michelle Burge, *Subject to Famine: Food Crisis and Economic Change in Western India 1860-1920*, Princeton Uni. Press, Princeton, 1983

McCarthy Justin, *British Political Portraits*, Books for Libraries Press, Freeport, 1968

McCully Bruce Tiebout, *English Education and the Origins of Indian Nationalism*, Columbia Uni. Press, NY, 1940

McDowell R.B., *British Conservatism 1832-1914*, Faber and Faber, London, 1959

McLane John R., *Indian Nationalism and the Early Congress*, Princeton Uni. Press, Princeton, 1977

Mehrotra S.R., *The Emergence of the Indian National Congress*, Barnes and Noble, NY, 1971

Mehrotra S.R., *India and the Commonwealth 1885-1929*, Frederick Praeger, NY, 1965

Midleton Earl, *Records and Reactions 1856-1939*, John Murray, London, 1939

Milburn R. Gordon, *England and India*, George Allen and Unwin, London, 1918

Mill John Stuart, *Autobiography*, Columbia Uni. Press, NY, 1924

Mill John Stuart, *On Liberty and Other Essays*, Macmillan, NY, 1926

Minayeef I.P., *Travels in and Diaries of India and Burma*, Debi Prasad Mukhopadhyay, Calcutta, 1956

Minto Earl of, *Speeches by the Earl of Minto*, Superintendent Govt. Printing Calcutta, 1950

Minto Mary, *Minto and Morley 1905-1910*, Macmillan and Co., London, 1934

Mittal S.C., *India Distorted: a Study of British Historians on India*, M.D. Publications, New Delhi, 1995

Mody Homi, *Sir Pherozshah Mehta*, Asia Publishing House, NY, 1963

Moore R.J., *Liberalism and Indian Politics 1872-1922*, Edward Arnold, London, 1966

Moore R.J., *Sir Charles Wood's Indian Policy 1853-66*, Manchester Uni., Press, Manchester, 1966

Morley John, *Burke*, Macmillan, London, 1923

Morley John, *Indian Speeches 1907-1909*, Macmillan, London, 1909

Morley John, *Recollections*, Vols. I and II, The Macmillan, NY, 1917

Morley John, *The Life of William Ewart Gladstone*, 2 Vols., Macmillan, 1911

Morris D. Morris and Matsui Toru, *Indian Economy in the Nineteenth Century: a Symposium*, Indian Economic and Social History Association, Delhi, 1969

Moulton Edward C., *Lord Northbrook's Indian Administration 1872-1876*, Asia Publishing House, Bombay, 1968

Mukharjee Haridas and Uma, *The Growth of Nationalism in India 1857-1905*, Presidency Library, Calcutta, 1957

Muller Friedrich Max, *The Life and Letters of Friedrich Max Muller*, 2 Vols., Longmans, London, 1902

Naik V.N., *Indian Liberalism*, Padma Publications, Bombay, 1945

Nanda B.R., *Gokhale, the Indian Moderates and the British Raj*, OUP, Delhi, 1977

Narasimhan V.K., *Kasturi Ranga Iyengar*, Govt. of India, Delhi, 1963

Nash Vaughan, *The Great Famine and its Causes*, Longmans, London, 1900

Natarajan S., *A Century of Social Reform in India*, Asia Publishing House, Bombay,

1959

Natesan G.A., *The Hon. Mr. G.K. Gokhale: His Life and Career*, G.A. Natesan, Madras, 1914

Nevinson Henry W., *More Changes, More Chances*, Nisbet and Co., London, 1925

Nevinson Henry W., *The New Spirit in India*, Metropolitan Book. Co., Delhi, 1975

Newton Lord, *Lord Landsdowne, a Biography*, Macmillan, London, 1929

Nicolson Harold, *King George the Fifth*, Constable and Co., London, 1952

O'Donnell C.J., *The Failure of Lord Curzon: a Study in Imperialism*, Shree Publishing House, Delhi, 1982

O'Donnell F. Hugh, *A History of the Irish Parliamentary Party*, 2 Vols., Longmans, NY, 1910

O'Donnell G.J., *The Causes of Present Discontents in India*, T. Fisher Unwin, London, 1908

O'Malley L.S.S. ed., *Modern India and the West*, OUP, London, 1968

Pal Bipin Chandra C., *Indian Nationalism: its Principles*, S.R. Murthy and Co., Madras, 1918

Pal Bipin Chandra, *Memories of My Life and Times*, Bipin Chandra Pal Institute, Calcutta, 1973

Pal Bipinchandra, *Writings and Speeches, Bipinchandra Pal*, Vol. I, Part one, Yugayatri Prakashan, Calcutta, 1954

Pal Dharm, *Administration of Sir John Lawrence in India 1864-1869*, Minerva Book Shop, Simla, 1952

Palande M.R., *Source Material for the History of Freedom Movement in India Vol. I, 1818-1885*, Govt. of India, Bombay, 1957

Palande M.R., *Source Material for History of the Freedom Movement in India, Collected from the Bombay Govt., Records, 1885-1920*, Govt. of Bombay Vol. II, Bombay, 1968

Parameswaran Pillai Govind, *Representative Men of Southern India*, Price Current Press, Madras, 1896

Paranjpye R.P., *Gopal Krishna Gokhale*, The Aryabhushan Press, Poona, 1916

Parry Jonathan, *The Rise and Fall of Liberal Government in Victorian Britain*, Yale Uni. Press, New Haven, 1993

Parvate T.V., *Mahadev Govind Ranade*, Asia Publishing House, NY., 1963

Parvate T.V., *Bal Gangadhar Tilak*, Navajivan Publishing House, Ahmedabad, 1958

Parvate T.V., *Gopal Krishna Gokhale*, Navajivan Publishing House, Ahmedabad, 1959

Patwardhan R.P., *Dadabhai Naoroji Correspondence*, Vol. II, Part I and II, Allied Publishers, Bombay, 1977

Pawar A.G., Convener, *Maratha History Seminar*, May 28-31, 1970, Papers, Shivaji Uni., Kolhapur, 1971

Pearsall Ronald, *Edwardian Life and Leisure*, David and Charles Newton, NY, 1973

Philips C.H. ed., *The Partition of India*, The MIT Press, Cambridge, 1970

Philips C.H., *The Evolution of India and Pakistan 1858-1947*, OUP, London, 1962

Polak, H.S.L., *Gokhale's visit to South Africa, A compilation of articles*, (unpublished)

Pope-Hennessy, James, *Lord Crewe 1858-1945: the Likeness of a Liberal*, Constable and Co., London, 1955

Porter Bernard, *The Lion's Share: a Short History of British Imperialism 1850-1970*, Longman, London, 1975

Pradhan G.P., *Lokamanya Tilak*, National Book Trust India, New Delhi, 1994

Prasad Rajendra, *Autobiography*, Asia Publishing House, Bombay, 1957

Radcliffe Cyril John, *Mountstuart Elphinstone*, Clarendon Press, Oxford, 1962

Rai Lajpat, *Young India*, Howard Fertig, NY, 1968

Ranade Mr. Justice M.G., *The Miscellaneous Writings with Introduction by D.E. Wacha, Address by V.S. Srinivas Sastri*, Sahitya Akademi, New Delhi, 1992

Ranade, M.G., *Essays on Indian Economics: a Collection of Essays and Speeches*, Govt. of India, New Delhi, 1982

Rao P. Kodanda, *The Rt. Hon., V.S. Srinivas Sastri: a Political Biography*, Asia Publishing House, NY, 1963

Ratcliffe S.K., *Sir William Wedderburn and the Indian Reform Movement*, George Allen and Unwin, London, 1923

Ray Satischandra, *An Essay on the Economic Causes of Famines in India and Suggestions to Prevent their Frequent Recurrence*, Uni. of Calcutta, Calcutta, 1909

Rickards Robert, *India or Facts*, Smith Elder and Co., 2 Vols. London, 1829-32

Ripon The Marquis, *Speeches of the Marquis of Ripon, 1883-4*, Office of Superintendent of Govt. Printing India, Calcutta, 1884

Robinson Francis, *Separatism Among Indian Muslims*, CUP, Cambridge, 1974

Robinson Henry, *Memories: Wise and Otherwise*, Cassell and Co., London, 1924

Robinson Ronald and Gallagher John, *Africa and the Victorians*, St. Martins Press, NY, 1961

Rogers James E. Thorold ed., *Speeches on Questions of Public Policy by John Bright*, Vol. I, Macmillan, London, 1868

Ronaldshay Earl, *The Life of Lord Curzon*, Vols. I and II, Ernest Benn Ltd., NY, 1928

Rothermund Dietmar, *The Phases of Indian Nationalism and other Essays*, Nachiketa Publications Ltd., Bombay, 1970

Sardesai G.S. ed., *Poona Affairs (Elphinstone's Embassy)*, Part 1 and 2 Popular Press, Bombay, 1950

Sarkar Benoy Kumar, *The Political Philosophies Since 1905*, B.G. Paul and Co.,

Madras 1928
Sarkar Hem Chandra, *A Life of Ananda Mohan Bose*, Ram Mohan Roy Publication Society, Calcutta, 1929
Sarkar Sumit, *Modern India 1885-1947*, St. Martin's Press, NY, 1983
Sarkar Sumit, *The Swadeshi Movement in Bengal 1903-1908*, People's Publishing House, New Delhi, 1973
Sastri, V.S. Srinivas, V. S. *Srinivas Sastri, Centenary Souvenir*, Servants of India Society, Madras, 1969
Sastri V.S. Srinivas, *Life and Times of Sir Pherozeshah Mehta*, Bharatiya Vidya Bhavan, Bombay 1975
Sastri V.S. Srinivas, *Life of Gopal Krishna Gokhale*, Bangalore Printing and Publishing Co., Bangalore, 1937
Sastri V.S. Srinivas, *My Master Gokhale*, Model Publications, Madras, 1946
Sastri V.S. Srinivas, *Speeches and Writings of Rt. Hon. V.S. Srinivas Sastri*, 2 Vols., South Indian National Association, Srinivas Sastri Endowment Fund, Madras, 1969
Sastri V.S. Srinivas, *The Rights and Duties of the Indian Citizen*, Uni. of Calcutta, Calcutta, 1935
Schneer Jonathan, *London 1900*, Yale Uni. Press, New Haven, 1999
Schuster George Sir and Wint Guy, *India and the Democracy*, Macmillan, London, 1941
Seal Anil, *The Emergence of the Indian Nationalism*, Cambridge Uni. Press, London, 1968
Seeley J.R., *The Expansion of England*, Uni. of Chicago Press, Chicago, 1971
Sen Priyaranjan ed., *Florence Nightingale's Indian Letters*, Mihir Kumar Sen, Calcutta, 1937
Seton Malcolm C.C. Sir, *The India Office*, G.P. Putnam's Sons, London, 1925
Shah A.B. and Aiyar S.P. eds., *Gokhale and Modern India*, Manaktalas, Bombay, 1966
Shahani T.K., *Gopal Krishna Gokhale*, R.K. Mody, Bombay, 1929
Shannon Richard, *The Crisis of Imperialism 1865-1915*, Hart-Davis, London, 1974
Sharan Parmatma, *The Imperial Legislative Council of India From 1861-1920*, S Chand & Co., Delhi, 1961
Shaw Bernard ed., *Fabianism and the Empire: a Manifesto by the Fabian Society*, Grant Richards, London, 1900
Singh Hira Lal, *Problems and Policies of the British in India 1885-1898*, Asia Publishing House, NY., 1963
Sitaramayya Pattabhi B., *History of the Indian National Congress*, Vol. I & II, S. Chand & Co., Delhi, 1969
Sleeman W.H. Sir Major-General, *Rambles and Recollections of an Indian Official*, OUP, Karachi, 1844

Smith William Roy, *Nationalism and Reform in India*, Yale Uni., Press, New haven, 1988,

Somervell D.C., *English Thought in the Nineteenth Century*, Longmans, NY, 1929

Spender J.A., *The Life of the Rt. Hon. Sir Henry Campbell Bannerman*, Hodder and Stoughton, 2 Vols., London, 1923

Spender John A., *Life, Journalism and Politics*, Vol. II, Frederick A. Stokes Co., NY, 1988

Sastri, Srinivas, *Srinivas Sastri V.S., Centenary Souvenir*, Servants of India Society, Madras, 1969

Stephen James Fitzjames, *Liberty, Equality, Fraternity*, Cambridge Uni. Press, London, 1967

Stephen Leslie, *Life of Henry Fawcett*, Smith Elder and Co., London, 1885

Stephen Leslie, *The Life of Sir James Fitzjames Stephen*, G.P. Putnam's, NY., 1895

Stokes Eric, *The English Utilitarians and India*, OUP, Oxford, 1982

Stokes Eric, *The Peasant and the Raj*, Cambridge Uni., Press, Cambridge, 1978

Stokes Eric, *The Political Ideas of English Imperialism*, OUP, Oxford, 1960

Stokes Whitley, *Sir Henry Maine: a Brief Memoir of His Life by Rt. Hon. Sir M.E. Grant Duff*, Henry Holt, NY., 1892

Strachey John, *India: its Administration and Progress*, Macmillan, London, 1911

Strachey Lytton, *Characters and Commentaries*, Harcourt Brace and Co., NY., 1933

Sunthankar B.R., *Maharashtra 1858-1920*, 2 Vols., Popular Book Depot, Bombay, 1933

Sunthankar B.R., *Nineteenth Century History of Maharashtra*, 2 Vols., Shubhada-Sarswat Prakashan, Pune, 1988

Suntharalingam R., *Politics and Nationalist Awakening in South India 1852-1891*, Uni., of Arizona Press, Tucson, 1974

Sydenham of Combe Lord, *My Working Life*, John Murray, London, 1927

Temple Richard Sir, *India in 1880*, John Murray, London, 1880

Temple Richard Sir, *Men and Events*, John Murray, London, 1882

The Indian National Congress, *Congress Presidential Addresses*, G.A. Natesan, Madras, 1917

The Swadeshi Movement: a Symposium, View of Representative Indians and Anglo-Indians, G.A. Natesan, Madras, 1917

Thomson David, *England in the Nineteenth Century 1815-1914*, Penguin, Harmondsworth, 1963

Thornton A.P., *The Imperial Idea and Its Enemies*, Macmillan, London, 1959

Trevelyan George Sir, *The Competition Wallah*, Harper Collins, NY, 1991

Tucker Richard, *Ranade and the Roots of Indian Nationalism*, Uni. of Chicago Press, Chicago, 1976

Tyabji Husain B., *Badruddin Tyabji*, Thacker and Co., Bombay, 1952

Varma Sushma Dr., *Mountstuart Elphinstone in Maharashtra 1801-1827*, K.P. Bagchi & Co., Calcutta, 1981

Varma Vishwanath Prasad, *The Political Philosophy of Sir Aurobindo*, Asia Publishing House, NY, 1960

Vidwans M.D. ed., *Letters of Lokamanya Tilak*, Kesari Prakashan, Pune, 1966

Wacha D.E., *Reminiscences of the Late Hon. Mr. G.K. Gokhale*, D.E. Wacha, Bombay, 1915

Wacha D.E., *Rise and Growth of Bombay Municipal Government*, G.A, Natesan, Madras, 1913

Wacha D.E., *Speeches and Writings*, G.A. Natesan and Co., Madras, 1920

Wacha D.E., *A Financial Chapter in the History of Bombay City*, A.J., Cambridge & Co., Bombay, 1910

Wacha D.E., Sir, *Shells From The Sands of Bombay, Being My reflections and Reminiscences 1860-1875*, K.T. Anklesaria, Bombay, 1920

Wallbank Walter T., *India in the New Era*, Scott Foresman and Co., Chicago, 1951

Walling R.A.J., ed., *The Diaries of John Bright*, William Morrow, NY, 1931

Walpole Spencer Sir, *History of England From the Conclusion of the Great War in 1815*, Vols. 4 and 5, Longmans, London, 1912

Washbrook D.A., *The Emergence of Provincial Politics: the Madras Presidency 1870-1920*, CUP, Cambridge, 1976

Wasti Syed Razi, *Lord Minto and the Indian Nationalist Movement, 1905-1910*, Clarendon Press, Oxford, 1964

Webb Beatrice, *Our Partnership*, Cambridge University Press, Cambridge, 1975

Wedderburn William, *Allan Octavian Hume*, Pegasus, New Delhi, 1974

Wells H.G., *The New Machiavelli*, Duffield, NY., 1919

Wilson Guy Fleetwood Sir, *Letters to Nobody 1908-1913*, John Murray, London, 1921

Wolf Lucien, *Life of the First Marquess of Rippon*, 2 Vols., John Murray, London, 1921

Wolpert Stanley A., *Morley and India 1906-1910*, Uni. of California Press, Berkeley, 1967

Wolpert Stanley A., *Tilak and Gokhale*, OUP, Delhi, 1989

Young G.M., *Victorian England, Portrait of an Age*, OUP., London, 1964

Zacharias H.C.E., *Renascent India From Rammohan Rai to Mohandas Gandhi*, George Allen and Unwin, London, 1933

Zaidi A.M., *Evolution of Muslim Political Thought in India: Vol. I From Syed to the Emergence of Jinnah*, Indian Institute of Applied Political Research, Michico and Panjathan, Delhi, 1975

Zaidi A. Moin (ed.), *The Grand little Man of India: Dadabhai Naoroji Speeches and Writings*, 2 Vols., S. Chand, Delhi, 1984

Zaidi A.M., *The Story of Congress Pilgrimage 1885-1915*, 2 Vols., Indian Institute of Applied Political Research, 1990

Zetland Marquess of, *Lord Cromer*, Hodder and Stoughton, Delhi, 1932

Documents

Dadabhai Naoroji Papers
Gokhale Papers

Weeklies, Monthlies, Newspapers and Journals

American Review of Reviews
Asian Review
Asian Survey
Cambridge Historical Review
The Economist
Edinburgh Review
English Historical Review
Fortnightly Review
Hindu
Hindustan Review (Kayasth Samachar)
Indian Economic and Social History Review
Journal of the Poona Sarvajanik Sabha (Quarterly)
Macmillan Magazine
Modern Asian Studies
New York Times
Nineteenth Century
Quarterly Review
Round Table
Statesman
The Times (London)
Times of India
Voice of India
Westminster Review

BIBLIOGRAPHY (MARATHI)

Aatre Trimbak Narayan, *Gaongada*, Varada Books, Pune, 1989

Apte Hari Narayan, *Madhali Sthiti*, Ramyakatha Prakashan, Pune, 1973

Bapat Kishor Shankar, *Guru Shishya Yanchya Athavani Va Charitra*, Anath Vidyarthi Gruha Prakashan, Pune, 1965

Bendre Va. Si., ed., *Maharashtretihasachi Sadhane*, 2 Khanda, Mumbai Marathi Grantha Sangrahalaya, Mumbai, 1966

Dadoba Panduranga, *Atma Charitra*, Anubhava Publication, Mumbai, 1993

Ghate Vi. Da, *Diwas Ase Hote*, Mouj, Mumbai, 1998

Jambhekar Bal Gangadharshastri, *Bal Gangadharshastri Yanche Jeevanvrutta Va Lekhasangraha*, 4 Khanda, Jambhekar, Pune, 1950

Javdekar Shankar Dattatraya, *Adhunik Bharat*, Raghunath Ganesh Joshi, Pune, 1953

Joshi Vaman Malhar, *Vichar Lahari*, Deshmukh ani Company, Pune, 1943

Keer Dhananjay, and Malshe, Ed., *Mahatma Phule Vangmaya*, Maharashtra Rajya Sahitya ani Sanskruti Mandal, Mumbai, 1984-86

Kelkar, Na. Chi., *Lokmanya Tilak Yanche Charitra*, Khanda 3, Second Edition, Varada, Pune, 1988

Kelkar, Na. Chi. *Gatagoshti, Arthat Mazhi Jeevan Yatra*, Ya. Na. Kelkar, Pune, 1939

Kelkar Na. Chi. *Marathe va Ingraj*, Modern Book Depot, Pune, 1963

Kulkarni Puroshottam Balkrishna, *Na. Nana Shankar Sheth Yanche Charitra*, Chintaman, Dwarkanath Deshmukh, Mumbai, 1959

Khaparde Balkrishna Ganesh, *Sri Dadasaheb Khaparde Yanche Charitra*, Ya Go, Joshi, Prasad Prakashan, Pune, 1962

Natu Ma. Ga., Deshpande Di. Gha, Sampadak, *Agarkar Vangmaya*, 3 Khanda, Maharashtra Rajya Sahitya Sanskruti Mandal, Mumbai, 1984-86

Oak Pramod, *Elphinstone: Mumbaicha Governor Mount Stuart Elphinstone Yanche Charitra*, Rajhansa Prakashan, Pune, 1990

Phatak Raghunath Narahar, *Dnyayamurti Mahadeo Govind Ranade Yanche Charitra*, Neelkantha Prakashan, Pune, 1966

Phatak Raghunath Narahar, *Narahar Adarsha Bharat Sevak*, Gopal Krishna Gokhale Yanche Charitra, Mouj, Mumbai, 1967

Phatak Raghunath Narahar, *Lokmanya*, Mouj, Mumbai, 1972

Phatak Raghunath Narahar, *Arvachin Maharashtratil Saha Thor Purush*, Mumbai Marathi Grantha Sangrahalaya, Mumbai, 1967

Priyolkar A. Ka., *Raobahdur Dadoba Panduranga*, Dhavale Prakashan, Mumbai, 1947

Priyolkar A. Ka, Dr. Bhau Daji, Marathi Sahitya Sangha, Mumbai, 1971

Rajvade, V. K., *Marathyanchya Itihasachi Sadhane*, Vol. 6, Rajvade Sanshodhak Mandal, Dhule, 2002

Ranade Mahadev Govind, *Marathi Sattecha Utkarsha*, Varada Books, Pune, 1995

Ranade Mahadev Govind, *Marathi Vangmayachi Abhuvruddhi*, Di. Mahadeo, Mumbai, 1913

Ranade Mahadev Govind, *Dharmapar Vyakhyane*, Dwarkanath Govind Vaidya, Mumbai, 1940

Ranade Ramabai, *Amachya Aushyatil Kahi Athavani*, Anubhava Publication, Mumbai, 1993

Saradar Gangadhar Balakrishna, *Ranadepranit Samajik Sudharnechi Tatvamimansa*, Pune Vidyapith, Pune, 1973

Saradar Gangadhar Balakrishna *Maharashtra Jeevan, Parampara, Pragati ani Samasya*, 2 Khanda, Joshi ani Lokhande Prakashan, Pune, 1960,

Saradar Gangadhar Balakrishna, *Maharashtrache Upekshit Mankari*, Sunanda Prakashan, Pune, 1951

Sardesai Sakharam Govind, *Marathi Riyasat, Dhavle*, Mumbai, 1985

Shejwalkar Tryambak Shankar, *Nivadak Lekha Sangraha*, Mote, Mumbai, 1977

Shinde Vithal Ramji, *Mazhya Athavani Va Anubhav*, 3 Khanda, Lekhan Vachan Bhandar, Pune, 1958

Sovani Ni. Vi., Sampadak, *Dnyaya. Ma. Go. Ranade Yanni Dileli Vyaparasambandhi Vyakhyane (1872-1873)*, Gokhale Arthashastra Sanstha, Pune, 1963

Talwalkar Govind, *Virat Dnyani ; Nyayamurti Mahadeo Govind Ranade*, Prestige Prakashan, Pune, 1990

Talwalkar Govind, *Naoroji Te Nehru*, Majestic Prakashan, Bombay, 1989

Tilak Lokmanya, *Samgra Lokmanya Tilak*, Kesari Prakashan, Pune, 1969

Tilak Lokamanya, *Lokmanya Tilakanche Kesaritil Lekh*, Kesari Maratha Sanstha, Pune, 1922

Tilak Lokmanya, *Lokmanya Tilak Lekha Sangraha*, Sahitya Academy, New Delhi, 1969

Vidwans Ma. Dhon, *Lokmanya Tilak Yanchi Vyakhyane*, Kesari Maratha Prashan, Pune, 1938

INDEX